Leadership and Authority

Bula Matari and Life-Community Ecclesiology in Congo

Series Preface

Regnum Studies in Mission are born from the lived experience of Christians and Christian communities in mission, especially but not solely in the fast growing churches among the poor of the world. These churches have more to tell than stories of growth. They are making significant impacts on their cultures in the cause of Christ. They are producing 'cultural products' which express the reality of Christian faith, hope and love in their societies.

Regnum Studies in Mission are the fruit often of rigorous research to the highest international standards and always of authentic Christian engagement in the transformation of people and societies. And these are for the world. The formation of Christian theology, missiology and practice in the twenty-first century will depend to a great extent on the active participation of growing churches contributing biblical and culturally appropriate expressions of Christian practice to inform World Christianity.

Series Editors

Julie C. Ma	Oxford Centre for Mission Studies, Oxford, UK
Wonsuk Ma	Oxford Centre for Mission Studies, Oxford, UK
Doug Petersen	Vanguard University, Costa Mesa, CA, USA
Terence Ranger	University of Oxford, Oxford, UK
C.B. Samuel	Emmanuel Hospital Association, Delhi, India
Chris Sugden	Anglican Mainstream, Oxford, UK

A full listing of titles in this series
appears at the end of this book

REGNUM STUDIES IN MISSION

Leadership and Authority

Bula Matari and Life-Community Ecclesiology in Congo

Titre Ande Georges

Foreword by John Parratt

First published 2010 by Regnum Books International

in partnership with

Church Mission Society,
Watlington Rd,
Oxford, OX4 6BZ, UK

Regnum is an imprint of the Oxford Centre for Mission Studies
St. Philip and St. James Church
Woodstock Road
Oxford, OX2 6HR, UK
www.ocms.ac.uk/regnum

09 08 07 06 05 04 03   8 7 6 5 4 3 2 1

British Library Cataloguing in Publication Data
A catalogue record for this book is available from the British Library

ISBN 978-1-870345-72-9

Typeset by Regnum Books International
Printed and bound in Great Britain
for Regnum Books International
by Nottingham AlphaGraphics

I dedicate this book to African church leaders.

Contents

FOREWORD

This book is the very opposite of armchair theology. It comes out of intimate and painful experience of the repression, corruption, violence and brutality of the recent history of Congo-Zaire. Indeed the author had twice during the period of his doctoral study in Birmingham to return to his home country to ensure the safety of his family. What he has to say therefore - on power and authority in traditional societies, on the nature of the church, on the relative roles of bishops, priests and laity, and on Christian theology in Africa - gains immeasurably from having been refined in the crucible of living as a Christian leader in one of the most exploited and disturbed regions of Africa.

Bishop Ande Titre seeks to discover a post-colonial liberation theology for his church. He naturally deals with the brutality of colonialism in Congo. But (contrary to so much post-colonial posturing) he also fully recognises the responsibilities of post-colonial political and ecclesiastical leaders for the present situation. He points out that leadership in much of traditional Africa was far more consensual and democratic than is commonly thought. To that extent Africa's manic dictators like Mobutu (and Mugabe), however much they may claim to uphold traditional values, are cultural aberrations. At the same time Dr Ande presents a trenchant critique of the role of church leaders in their failure to challenge adequately the excesses of political absolutism. His assessment of the episcopy, for too often preferring privilege and the open exercise of power instead of humble service, has a much wider relevance than simply to the Anglican Church of Congo. The author's examination of African theology is in every way as sharp as his political and social analysis, especially in his argument that its use of theological concepts and biblical language may mask underlying assumptions as to ideology and power structures. Bishop Ande's own theological reconstruction for self-understanding and authority within the Anglican Church of Congo is christological, or rather trinitarian. The people of God, for him, is a Christ centred life community, inspired by the Spirit of God. Leadership in such a community is a function, not a status, and 'apostolic succession' belongs to all the people of God including the laity.

Dr Ande Titre has produced a most valuable work which deserves to be read not only by those with an interest in the future of the Christian faith in Africa, but also by anyone concerned with the debate over authority within the church.

John Parratt
Formerly Professor of Third World Theologies,
University of Birmingham

ACKNOWLEDGEMENTS

Producing books is a collective venture. I have received generous help from a great many people in preparing this book. It is risky to mention some and leave out others when acknowledging contributions to a work such as this. I will mention some, with apologies to those who are left out.

I am most grateful to Professor John Parratt, who supervised the research first as PhD thesis, for his encouragement and guidance, which maintained my vision and determination throughout the project.

My heartfelt and profound gratitude is due to the staff of CMS/UK for granting me financial assistance, without which this research would not have been possible. I owe special thanks to Dr Cathy Ross for her commitment to get this book published. On her invitation, my time at Crowther Centre as Missiologist in Residence allowed me to work on this book. May Berdine Van Den Toren find my appreciation for her assistance. I am indebted to CMS and Regnum for publishing this book.

I would like to offer my very sincere appreciation and thanks to Judy and Tim Rous who have offered me and my wife delightful hospitality and a loving family while I was working on this book in Oxford.

My gratitude goes to my wife Maturu Anyaako for her accompanying me to England. I am indebted to all those who gave so willingly of their time for interviews and gatherings of archives.

My modest prayer is that what I have written about leadership and authority may make some small contribution to a wider discussion on the issue of authority in the Church.

Titre Ande Georges
January 2010

Abbreviations

ABAKO:	Alliance des Bakongo
ADEC:	L'Apostolat des Dirigeants, Entrepreneurs et Cadres Catholiques
AIC:	African Independent Churches
AMECEA:	The Association of Member Episcopal Conferences of Eastern Africa
CAC:	Anglican Church of Congo
CMS:	Church Mission Society
CPC:	Protestant Council of Congo
CVR:	Corps des Volontaires de la République
D.R. Congo:	Democratic Republic of Congo
EAC:	Anglican Church of Congo
ECC:	Church of Christ in Congo
EJCSK:	Eglise de Jésus-Christ sur Terre par le Prophète Simon Kimbangu
JMPR:	Jeunesse du Mouvement Populaire de la Révolution
MLC:	Mouvement de Libération du Congo
MPR:	Mouvement Populaire de la Révolution
RCD:	Rassemblement Congolais pour la Démocratie
SCC:	Small Christian Community

Glossary

Anioto:	leopard-men
Baba:	father in Swahili
Bacwezi:	royal ancestors considered as divinities
Bula Matari:	he who breaks rocks, a name applied to colonial officials
Engabu:	shield
Katikiro:	the Kabaka's Prime Minister(s)
Kikale:	Mukama's compound
Lukiko:	council
Muchungaji:	shepherd
Mukama:	chief in Lunyoro
Mutumishi:	servant
Mzee:	elder
Opi:	chief
Salongo:	free work for the government
Tata:	father in Lingala
Typoy:	traditional chair used for traditional chiefs
Ujamaa:	family
Umukama:	kingdom
Waalimu:	teachers in swahili
Wahokohoko:	men disguised as leopards

Introduction

Can Africa still be referred to as 'the paradise on earth'? When African countries began to gain independence from colonial rule in the 1960s, the nationalists who won freedom for their respective countries were hailed as heroes. Aware of Africa's wealth, they promised a paradise for her. The first black president of Ghana, Kwame Nkrumah, even declared, 'we shall not rest content until we demolish these miserable colonial structures and erect in their place a veritable paradise.'[1] In many African countries, the 'paradise' promised soon turned out to be and remains a nightmare. For Africa, the annual passage of time seems to reduce the dreams and expectations of a people who have known little peace. Corruption, dishonesty, diseases, wars, mismanagement and illiteracy are still rife. Many African countries are experiencing extreme economic, political and environmental stress because of the erosion or even disappearance of central state authority. The flimsy state structures established after independence are simply unable to cope with the demands of housing and feeding their growing populations with the meagre resources at hand. In such circumstances Africans often lose all confidence in the state's ability to meet their basic needs and turn to churches for help.

For instance, Kenya has been regarded until now as a relatively peaceful nation with the biggest economy in East Africa. But the current government, that five years ago promised to end police brutality, harassment, corruption, nepotism and the widening gap between the rich and the poor, is deeply engaged in the same practices that they were preaching against. Kenya recently held national elections which were chaotic, very violent and with more allegations of cheating. As a result, hundreds of people have perished.

Another example of despair is Zimbabwe, which was Africa's former golden child, now fallen into severely hard times. There has been much preoccupation with its escalating failures leading to violence, suffering and hopelessness in Zimbabweans. While Zimbabwe is struggling with its presidential election, Botswana has just inaugurated its fourth president in a smooth transition. The Libyan president Muammar al-Gaddafi, during the Afro-Arab Festival in

---

[1] Kwame Nkrumah, *Ghana: An Autobiography* (London: Nelson, 1957), 54.

Uganda in March 2008 even said that Mugabe does not have to be bothered with elections because he should just rule until he dies.

In Congo, in 1960 Belgium hastily granted independence to an ill-prepared people, which led to five years of violence, anarchy and secessionist strife. A military coup in 1965 brought Mobutu Sese Seko to national leadership. He soon began to create a new authentic Congolese society. To do this, Congolese society had to create 'new' traditions, structures and principles of behaviour for the citizens. Yet this new order had to be imposed by the army.

The national policy of integration provided the churches with a juridical framework where all religious institutions, small and large, national and international, Christian and Islamic, would henceforth function according to the secular state. Any lack of respect for this law of 'Mobutism' led to conflict with the regime's ideology. It is in the context of this new order that the Anglican Church of Congo (EAC) developed its ideas of authority.

How did the invention of the contemporary Congolese society affect authority in the Church?

Life is the key concept of the African worldview. It is believed to be holistic and is understood as the totality of the dimension which constitutes the human being as a person. But tyrannical regimes have misused their power to reduce the lives of people to meaninglessness by cynically manipulating the concept of authority in traditional society. The misuse of traditional authority has been evident within the Congolese church. I realised that within the *Eglise Anglicane du Congo* (EAC), the centralisation of the leadership has harmed local congregational life and initiatives, strongly stimulated hierarchical structures and power seeking so that pride of position led to neglect of the church's prophetic role.

Two main tendencies can be perceived within African Theology. One of them emphasizes the African cultural heritage in order to incarnate the Christian message in African cultures. Though the Gospel is universal, the 'habits of authority' are surely different in different cultures. Local churches are always in dialogue with local culture. In Congo, however, the intertwining relations between cultural theology and Cultural Revolution actually helped the political leaders to gain support for their nationalism and has made African categories for authority exclusive and violent. But our approach in this book is that of postcolonial liberation theology, which recognises the value of the local culture but adopts a critical attitude towards modern society. It takes into account the contemporary context confronting the post-colonial era and analyses the factors that are responsible for the tragic situation of violence, poverty and hopelessness that the people of Congo are facing.

Over the last decade, the post-colonial history of Africa has tended to be analysed from two different perspectives. On the one hand, there are people like Patrick Chabal who argue that the political institutions adopted by African States after independence were more or less imposed by the former colonizers, who continue to play an active and direct role in African political processes, the complexities of which often mask external efforts to maintain or increase the political and economic hegemony of these same neo-colonialists.[2] However, this perspective does not give an important place to the African leaders' responsibility for the African post-colonial crisis.

On the other hand, the approach popularised by Jean François Bayart argues that the social and political dynamics of African societies today perpetuate their ancestral history in a modern form. So, in order to understand the functioning of African states, we must focus on the internal dynamics of African societies.[3] They have thus proposed that it is the cultural and historical experiences of African people that can help us to understand phenomena such as patrimonialism, predatory states and tension between state and 'civil society'. However, they recognise the 'small' role played by external factors in the occurrence of African modern phenomena.

Our approach, which has an alternative perspective, argues that capitalism did not completely destroy the specificity of African cultures, but that those values have been misused by African 'independent' leaders who inherited the colonial machinery of government. This approach is slightly different from the radical view of Axelle Kabou of Cameron, 'I do not believe in a western plot against Africa, I do believe in bad management of African states.'[4] Therefore, in its attempt to incarnate the gospel of Christ into local cultures, theology in Africa must primarily unmask those African values manipulated by politicians for the sake of power, that have served as a pitfall for African cultural theology.

This book proposes that Christian theology in Africa can make a significant development if a critical understanding of the socio-political situation in contemporary Africa is taken seriously. Specifically, we argue that authority in the Anglican Church of Congo (EAC) is based on the post-colonial model of power in order to fit into the new socio-political context. This book sets out to provide a critical analysis of the theology and exercise of authority in the EAC, which has been significantly influenced by its development within a barbarous socio-political context. The postcolonial theories of authority and power, and the use of them as the basis of a wider critique of both the local situation of the Anglican Church and the wider project of recent African theologies, has led us to propose a Life-Community ecclesiology which can provide the church with liberating authority for the fullness of life. It can also provide theology in Africa with a critical assessment of cultural theological categories which do not speak prophetically to the multi-cultural violent state and of the cultural models which no longer function in many contemporary situations.

---

[2] Patrick Chabal quoted by Francois Ngolet, 'Democratization and Interventionism in Francophone Sub-Saharan Africa', in Cheryl B. Mwaria, Silvia Federici and Joseph McLaren (eds), *African Visions* (London: Greenwood Press, 2000), 85.

[3] Jean Francois Bayart quoted by Ngolet, 'Democratization', 85.

[4] *Jeune Afrique*, no 1651 du 8 au 15 Août 1998, 14.

The field of ecclesiology is not a new one. In the Anglican Communion, Anglican theologians have demonstrated through publications that ecclesiology assumes greater urgency as they tackle issues of authority, leadership, government and discipline in the Church of England and in the Anglican Communion, mostly for ecumenical discussion. [5] The aim was to assist Anglicans to root their ecclesiological thinking more deeply in Anglican tradition in order to offer the ecumenical reader a picture of that tradition and history. Furthermore, many African theologians have proposed models for contemporary African Christian churches.[6] We shall question those models as they can easily lead to the abuse of power, violence and exclusivism. The questions which will be discussed through this book are: Should the style of 'exercising' authority within the Church resemble contemporary political government in its shape and methods of administration? What is the relationship between the ministry of the whole people of God and the ministry of the 'officers' in the Church?

We shall begin with a critical review of the socio-political and religious situation in post-colonial Congo. We shall then examine the understanding and exercise of authority in the Anglican Church of Congo. The book will end by exploring the potential of Life-Community ecclesiology for liberating authority in the Church.

---

[5] Some of these publications are: Paul Avis, *The Anglican Understanding of the Church: An Introduction* (London: SPCK, 2000); Stephen Sykes, *Unashamed Anglicanism* (London: Darton, Longman and Todd, 1995); G.R. Evans, *Authority in the Church: A Challenge for Anglicans* (Norwich: The Canterbury Press, 1990); R. Hannaford (ed), *A Church for the 21st Century, Agenda for the Church of England*, 1998; R. Jeffery (ed), *By What Authority?: The Open Synod Group Report on Authority in the Church of England* (Oxford: Mowbray, 1987).

[6] See essays on African ecclesiology in J.N.K. Mugambi and Laurenti Magesa (eds), *The Church in African Christianity: Innovative Essays in Ecclesiology* (Nairobi: Initiative, 1990).

Chapter One

Bula Matari Model of Authority in Congolese Society

Africa is a continent with a tremendous diversity of culture, religions, political and social experiences and orientations. The people of Congo come from several major African ethnic groups, and Congo has one of the most complex ethnic structures in Africa. There are more than two hundred ethnic groups, of which the majority are Bantu, and the rest are Sudanese and Nilotics.

It is in the context of this ethnic and social *melange* that the Anglican Church, the subject of our study case, was planted in Congo amongst people who already had their own history, their own social and political organisations, and a variety of concepts on the issue of authority. The words 'authority' and 'power' need explanation, as they have not always been clearly distinguished. Sometimes both are used with the same meaning. A discussion of power lies outside the scope of this book. However, it is referred to in order to make the concept of authority clearer. For Thomas E. Cronin, power has a negative meaning but authority, a positive: 'Power is the strength or raw force to exercise control of or coerce someone to do something, while authority is power that is accepted as legitimate by subordinates.'[1] However, others regard power as the motivation of authority. For them, power is not a negative concept but rather a neutral one. For instance, Marion J. Levy understands power as the ability to exercise authority and control over the actions of others.[2] Authority is thus the expected and legitimate possession of power. In this book, power will be considered as a neutral concept, but different from authority, as stated by John Pobee, 'Power is the ability of an

---

[1] Thomas E. Cronin, 'Reflections on Leadership', in William E. Rosenbach and Robert L. Taylor (eds), *Contemporary Issues in Leadership* (Third Edition. Oxford: Westview Press, 1993), 7-25, 13.

[2] Marion J. Levy, *The Structure of Society* (Princeton: Princeton University Press, 1952), 333.

individual or group to carry out its wishes or policies, and to control, manipulate, or influence the behaviour of others, whether they wish to co-operate or not ... Authority is power that is legitimised and institutionalised in a society or other social system.'[3]

This first chapter analyses the characteristics of authority and power in traditional Congolese society and then explores how these characteristics were exploited by the colonisers and misused by Congo's own leaders in the post-colonial period. Traditional Congolese society refers to the pre-colonial era, with particular consideration of the aspects of tradition that have persisted up to contemporary times This chapter thus sets out the socio-political context which has influenced the development of the theology and exercise of authority in the Anglican Church of Congo.

Authority in Traditional Congolese Societies

Life as 'dynamic existence' is fundamental to the African conception of authority. It is hierarchically ordered and determines the source of authority.

This hierarchy belongs to both the invisible and the visible world, which are coterminous: the visible world in which human beings live is inconceivable without the infiltrating power of the invisible (spiritual) world. There is thus a vital union between the physical and spiritual worlds, which constitutes the universe.[4] In the invisible world the primordial source of life is God and he occupies the highest place. Then come the founding fathers' clans, who participate fully in the life of God, followed by the ancestors, the nature spirits and the malevolent spirits. In the visible world, the rank flows from 'man-in-community' to animals and plants: 'man-in-community' meaning the king, the heads of clans, the heads of families and the members of families.[5]

The function of leaders, at every level of society, is to transmit life, which embraces the whole of human existence; life is understood as the totality of the dimensions which constitute the human as a person. The unity of life is thus a communion, with consideration for individuals who have physical and spiritual qualities: 'I am because we are, but also we are because I am.'[6] The reality and the destiny of the individual are not lost in this unity of life. The moral character of a person then depends on how he or she treats other people and things. By virtue of his/her wisdom he/she becomes a moral agent, capable of causing

---

[3] John S. Pobee, 'Take Thou Authority: An African Perspective', in Stephen Sykes (ed), *Authority in the Anglican Communion* (Canada: Anglican Book Centre, 1987), 189-190.
[4] Placide Tempels, *Bantu Philosophy* (Paris: Présence Africaine, 1959), 32.
[5] Deusdedit R.K. Nkurunziza, *Bantu Philosophy of Life in the Light of the Christian Message: A basis for an African vitalistic theology* (Frankfurt am Main: Peter Lang, 1989), 53.
[6] John Mbiti, *African Religions and Philosophy* (London: Heinemann, 1969), 108-109.

happiness or misery to others. Consequently, God, who is the source of life and of every structure, is also the source of all authority. The hierarchical ordering of life determines where the authority lies. Hence one who is nearer to the source of life has authority over all descendants.

The authority in many traditional societies was people-centred although it was thought to be laid down in the 'sacred structure'. God is obviously the source of every authority, and authority is God's gift to the people for their welfare. Authority was thus charisma and service. It was dynamic and belonged to the community through the structure left by ancestors. This authority is credible and real because it derives from the sociological fact that the chief as priest symbolizes the whole society. Though hierarchically ordered, the authority is legitimate because the people choose the chief. Among the Hema in Congo this people-centred authority is emphasized when the new *Mukama* (chief) is installed. It is striking that the advice given by the elders to prevent corruption and abuse of power is similar to what was used in Ghana among the Asanti:

> Do not go after women. Do not become a drunkard. When we give you advice, listen to it. Do not gamble. We do not want you to disclose the origin of your subjects. We do not want one who disregards advice; we do not want you to regard us as fools; we do not want autocratic ways; we do not want bullying; we do not like beating. Take the stool. We bless the stool and give it to you.[7]

Further, the chief derives the right to authority from the sanctity of customs which are located in the family to which he belongs and which entitle him to authority.[8] Therefore, authority belongs to an office or a role in society and only the person in that office or role has right to use it.

In the case of the Hema, the *Mukama* is selected from a particular lineage of Baboro, reinforced by consensus of those to whom custom assigns the right. The latter are members of *Engabu* (shield), which is the name given to the council of wise men, chosen from different clans that make up the *Ubukama*. It is important to underline that all Hema are members of *Engabu*, although only a few are representatives on the council. In this sense, *Engabu* is not an organ of the elite, but an organ which represents the citizens and has to listen to them. Each Hema has the right to express his ideas and challenge the *Engabu*. The *Mukama* is also a member, but he is not the president of *Engabu*. The members of *Engabu* are counsellors of the *Mukama* in traditional matters. They also oversee the behaviour of leaders at all levels: chiefs, the heads of clan and the heads of lineage. In contemporary Hema society, they sometimes challenge the church leaders' behaviour. They safeguard the customs and transmit them to the next generation. They watch over the *Mukama* and promote peace and justice.

---

[7] George B.N. Ayittey, *Africa in Chaos* (London: Macmillan Press, 1999), 89.
[8] John S. Pobee, 'Take Thou Authority: An African Perspective', in Stephen Sykes (ed), *Authority in Anglican Communion,* 198.

Engabu thus has two functions: to advise and assist the *Mukama* in administration, and to prevent the chief from abusing his power by voicing dissatisfaction, criticizing the chief, and keeping him under necessary control.

The personal word of the chief was not law, although an especially opinionated chief might try to impose his will upon the council. He had to obey laws of custom and taboos. Rational discussion as an avenue to consensus among adults was made one of the most crucial qualifications for high office. It is the case that, as Julius Nyerere said, 'The elders sit under the big trees, and talk until they agree.'[9] Here Nyerere, although pleading for one political party, clearly emphasizes the importance of consensus in decision-making in traditional Africa. It is believed that there is no problem of human relations within society that cannot be resolved by dialogue.

The role of chief was to weigh all viewpoints, not to impose his decision on the council; doing so would defeat the purpose of the council's debates. Therefore the official word derived from the chief was the consensus of his council, and it is only in this capacity that it can be law. The consensus of the council was the result of a deliberate effort to go beyond decision-making arrived at by majority opinion, because majority opinion is not in itself a good enough basis for decision making. It deprives the minority of the right to have their will reflected in the given decision.

If the council could not reach unanimity on a contested issue, the chief would call a village assembly to put the issue before the people for debate. Freedom of expression was an important element of these village assemblies, and no-one was arrested or detained for disagreeing with the chief. Thus the people served as the ultimate judge or final authority on disputed issues. Nande of Congo express this people-centred authority by *Omwami ni valume* (a good chief is his subjects). The concept of an absolute chief therefore appeared inadequate in many African societies.

In the Bantu world, the leaders were members of the association that fought the hidden forces of evil. The evil one in society was the enemy of life and society. This evil one may have been conceived of as a spiritual power, but in some circumstances it was a living person, a man or a woman engaged in witchcraft. Such a person, for example a sorcerer, was considered as evil incarnate. It was believed that they manipulated the dynamic vital force in the organic universe to cause harm to society, for they had knowledge and ability to tap, control and use this force.[10] For this reason the leaders needed to be surrounded by 'wise persons'. Wisdom is conceived here as the knowledge of

---

[9] Julius Nyerere quoted by Kwasi Wiredu, 'Democracy and Consensus in African Traditional Politics: A Plead for Non-Party Polity', in Emmanuel Chukwudi Eze (ed), *Postcolonial African Philosophy: A Critical Reader* (Oxford: Blackwell Publishers, 1997), 303.

[10] Nkurunziza, *Bantu Philosophy of Life in the Light of the Christian Message*, 55.

things in terms of forces and their effects. It is attributed first to God, the Sage par excellence, for he knows every being and he comprehends the nature and the quality of the energy of each. The knowledge man has of these forces therefore is derived from God.

In the light of the fact that wisdom is the knowledge of forces and their effects, a deeper knowledge of the interaction of forces than the ordinary one possessed by every human is needed. A wise person in this case, as D.A. Masolo said, 'is one who is able to explain and interpret events in terms of their deeper and metaphysical causes.'[11] Hence the great significance of 'magicians' and 'diviners', who were the specialists. They were able to gain access to the solutions of the problems of life. Everyone in the community depended on such a person as one who held the means to happiness. Such knowledge was admired and desired by all.

However, even if knowledge was admired and desired, it was also feared at the same time. Those who possessed it not only had to bear much responsibility for the welfare of their communities, they were also constant objects of fear and suspicion in cases of misfortune. Those in power regarded them, openly or secretly, as challengers of their positions. D.A. Masolo believes that, even in contemporary society, African intellectuals, as repositories of knowledge, have continued to live under this ambiguity of status:

> For many African leaders, knowledge has a paradoxical and magical value, and is consequently paradoxically treated. Although its constructive value is widely acknowledged, its power is feared or even hated; its authority is frequently, easily, and conveniently misinterpreted; although it is good to have it, it is more convenient and stabilising to stifle it. This certainly is one of Africa's greatest persistent and historically consistent contradictions. Africans hate most what they need most.[12]

Knowledge was fundamental for development and socio-political stability among Africans in general.

Finally, authority provided security, which is the fundamental concern of the Africans. In Congo, the links between tribes are loose, often with an extremely bitter rivalry between them. A person's security depends on the power and the importance of his clan and ethnic group as these groups often fight each other. The use of weapons is the means of resolving conflicts with others, whilst dialogue is reserved for resolving conflicts within the same society. Therefore in societies with a system of hierarchical authority, military organisation becomes confused with social organisation. When enemies attack the clan or tribe,

---

[11] D.A. Masolo, *African Philosophy in Search of Identity* (Bloomington: Indiana University Press, 1994), 50.

[12] Masolo, *African Philosophy in Search of Identity*, 50.

everybody must take weapons and fight for the sake of his people. The chief is thus the commander-in-chief, providing security for his people.

In conclusion, the study of authority in African traditional societies, especially among the Congolese, has shown that authority was sacred and manifested the power of God's authority in action. It was God's gift to his people for their welfare within a holistic view of life. Authority maintained the unity of life for a harmonious ordering of society, providing abundant life and a happy environment. Authority was thus people-centred with a consensual and participatory democracy, subject to the control of the people as expressed through their representatives. However, authority was ethnocentric and exclusive, providing security to individuals and to the community within the same clan or tribe, where authority was made up of charisma and service. Unfortunately, these cultural values of authority built on a theo-centric concept of life were depreciated by the colonial power and misused by the post-colonial regimes. This will be the concern of the following sections.

Bula Matari Leadership in the Colonial Regime

The fundamental principle of the colonial regime was explicitly expressed by the Belgian proconsul, Pierre Ryckmans: '*Dominer pour servir.*'[13] The aim of this section is to examine how this principle helped to build the Leopoldian system of authority, which laid the foundation for the postcolonial abuse of power.

Creation of the Congo

The Democratic Republic of Congo, currently known as a state, did not exist before Leopold II's conquests in central Africa. Congo is a 'creation' of Leopold II, the King of the Belgians and the constitutional monarch of a small European state, who felt too confined in his little kingdom. Long before he reached the throne he became interested in Belgium's economic expansion abroad, and thus in acquiring a colony as an outlet for Belgian manufactured goods. His insistence was almost entirely upon the commercial advantages which the possession of a colony would bring to the Metropolis. Although in 1876 he summoned an international conference to Brussels to discuss the question of a colony for Belgium, the senate was not enthusiastic, as 'the Belgians had no desire to colonise.'[14] Leopold II therefore had to win a colony without the co-operation of his people on his own personal initiative and responsibility.

When the exciting news that Stanley had successfully travelled the whole course of the Congo river came in autumn 1877, Leopold did not wish to miss the opportunity, although Stanley's hope was that Great Britain would interest

---

[13] Pierre Ryckmans, *Dominer pour servir* (Brussels: Edition Universelle, 1948), 5.

[14] Ryckmans, *Dominer pour servir*, 37.

herself in opening up the Congo basin. At the end of 1878, Leopold II called together representatives of important financial interests from England, France, Germany, Holland and Belgium and formed a *Comité d'Etudes du Haut-Congo* to study trading prospects in the Congo and the possibility of building a railway to round the cataracts on the lower river and thus link the coast with Stanley Pool.

In 1882, the *Comité d'Etudes* was replaced by the *Association Internationale du Congo*, which was not international at all, but an instrument of Leopold II. As a master of clever propaganda, he persuaded Europe that the *Association Internationale du Congo* was a small, philanthropic and non-political organisation which aimed at suppressing the slave-trade and introducing legitimate commerce into the Congo basin, while strongly supporting the principles of free trade. The Berlin conference trusted Leopold's promise of a free trade regime and approved of his avowed intention of suppressing the slave trade. This gave him an advantage over Portugal and France which were rivals of Leopold in their desire to rule Congo. The conference ended with the General Act of Berlin, signed on 26 February 1885, under which the powers agreed that the Congo should be governed by certain principles: 'freedom of trade and navigation, neutrality in the event of war, suppression of slave traffic, and *improvement of the condition of the indigenous people.*'[15] Then in July 1885 at Boma, De Winton, who had replaced Stanley as the King's representative in the Congo, proclaimed the King of the Belgians the Sovereign of the Congo Independent State. The Belgian Parliament had given permission to assume the sovereignty of Congo Independent State, but insisted that there was no link whatever between Belgium and the new state save in the person of the king. Leopold II acted in a purely personal capacity.

Congolese were thus submitted to the authority, not of an elected European Parliament, but of a single European monarch. At home Leopold II was a constitutional ruler, but in the Congo he was an absolute sovereign. The question which opens our following discussion is whether Leopold II in his regime known as *Bula Matari* used his despotic powers wisely in pursuit of his avowed objective of bringing legitimate commerce and western civilisation in order to improve the condition of the Congolese.

Civilising Mission

The colonial state was widely known by this profoundly revealing metaphor *Bula Matari* which means *he who breaks rocks*, and it signifies terror for Bakongo. It was first applied to Leopold's agent Henry Stanley, reflecting the impression created by his feat of moving a large caravan bearing dismantled steamers around the rapids of the lower Congo River, over a new and tortuous

---

[15] F. Scott Bobb, *Historical Dictionary of Democratic Republic of the Congo (Zaire)* (Lanham, Maryland, and London: The Scarecrow Press, 1999), 61.

route from Vivi to Kinshasa in 1879-1880.[16] After that it became the image of a force which crushes all resistance, or of European representatives as impersonal agents of domination. Even colonial officials found the image of *Bula Matari* irresistible. It was widely used in colonial literature as an informal designation for the state. It also served for instruction: *Bula Matari* wants to see you. *Bula Matari* was never applied to an African chief. It was alien, outside society but irresistibly imposed upon it. *Bula Matari* has thus become a common term for the Leopoldian system of 'authority'.

    The ideology of the *mission civilisatrice* based on the principle *dominer pour servir* was at the heart of Belgian administration and policy in the Congo. The topic of colonialism remains controversial. F. Scott Bobb expressed it in this way:

> Most Africans view colonialism as a period of occupation of their soil by a foreign power, a period of humiliation and of repressed rights and freedoms. Many *colons*, however, saw it as a well-intentioned attempt, perhaps flawed, to administer a vast, ungovernable land by dedicated pioneers who helped create Africa's independent states, albeit 20 to 50 years too early. According to many historians, the *colons* considered the African to be a child, superstitious and generally in need of supervision. The role of the colonizer, they felt, was paternal, to educate and prepare their charges for their eventual independence by teaching them merits of hard work, productivity and responsibility.[17]

In reality, the civilizing mission doctrine in Congo worked from the premise that local cultures were without redeeming value and the Congolese were cruel, lazy, ignorant, untruthful and, as one of the agents of the independent state wrote:

> In entering into contact with [the Bantu peoples] the Belgians have found them in a state of extreme barbarity and corruption. Nothing which these disinherited peoples remember, nothing in their traditions, their social life, nor the material objects which surround them, give any indication of a better period in the past, of a time when they possessed a more advanced civilisation ... The intelligence of the black, although quite lively, only seems to exercise itself in evil.[18]

The same demeaning and humiliating concept existed even among missionaries. A Catholic missionary, a Holy Ghost Father, could even write:

> The black race is certainly the race of Ham, the race cursed of God ... These black pagans are lazy, greedy, thieves, liars and given over to all kinds of vice. The picture is not a flattering one, but it does not express the whole truth, and the scanty

---

[16] Crawford Young and Thomas Turner, *The Rise and Decline of the Zairian State* (Madison, Wisconsin: The University of Wisconsin Press, 1985), 31.
[17] Bobb, *Historical Dictionary of Democratic Republic of the Congo (Zaire)*, 89.
[18] Ruth Slade, *King Leopold's Congo* (London: Oxford University Press, 1962), 64.

clothes which these unfortunates wear make them even more savage and worthy of pity.[19]

Protestant missionaries gave the same picture of blacks, 'fiendish cruelty and heartlessness have made their home in these dark places until one wonders that the race has not been exterminated.'[20] The English missionary Bentley even declared, 'The people of Congo, as we found them, were practically without religion, there is no worship, no idolatry in fetishism, only a dark agnosticism, full of fear, helpless and hopeless.'[21]

Of course religion was affected by what had happened to society in general. When the political system was destroyed, traditional religion lost its social character. Disease and illness, the high mortality rate, the extreme insecurity, violence and oppression, led to a situation in which fetishism became more of a traditional medicine than a religion. Consequently, we argue that this focussing on magic at the expense of more religious aspects was an effect of colonization, not a traditional feature, because it was shaped by events that occurred at the time. Also when people felt incapable of solving their problems on their own, they tended to seek help from the supernatural world. For instance, witches were fundamental agents of resistance, preaching an immediate liberation from colonialism relying on their supernatural power. It is in this sense that in the Ituri region, 'the "syncretistic movements" of witches spread all over the region among different ethnic groups and set people against the Belgians.'[22]

However, even though discouraged, there was some hope, as shown by Mrs Guinness, 'But they are teachable, for they are of a childlike nature. Curiosity, wonder, sympathy, docility, all are there, and the missionary finds faculties to which he can appeal.'[23] Others ironically showed their compassion for these unfortunate 'children' of God, 'to this awful depth have these children of the Heavenly Father fallen, until they have indeed become children of the devil! Shall we let these "innocent heathen" go on in their simple way, or shall we "trouble" them with the Gospel?',[24] stated Holman Bentley.

However, critical though Europeans might be of Congolese society as they found it, some of them were moderate and convinced that they were in contact with a race whose evolution had been retarded, but which was, nevertheless

---

[19] Slade, *King Leopold's Congo,* 32.

[20] Slade, *King Leopold's Congo,* 32.

[21] K. Ekholm Friedman, *Catastrophe and Creation: The transformation of African culture* (Chur, Switzerland: Harwood Academic Publishers, 1991), 139.

[22] Samba Kaputo, *Phénomène d'Ethnicité et Conflits Ethno-politiques en Afrique Post-coloniale* (Kinshasa: Presses Universitaires du Zaïre, 1982), 237.

[23] Kaputo, *Phénomène d'Ethnicité et Conflits Ethno-politiques en Afrique Post-colonial,* 33.

[24] Slade, *King Leopold's Congo,* 65.

essentially perfectible, for their own ancestors had once been in a like state. Albert Thys expressed it well:

> It is true that the Negro does not think enough about drawing profit from the richness of his soil that he is somewhat lazy, that he scarcely ever thinks of the morrow, but it was the same for us, if we will take a look at history. For how long have famines ceased to be prevalent in Europe? Remember what terrible ravages they made in the fertile plains of Provence! In Caesar's time was not our beautiful Flanders fallow, and our fertile plains of Hesbaye uncultivated?[25]

So the situation of the Congolese peoples was not without hope, since the colonial powers themselves had had to pass through a period during which they had been introduced to civilisation. Now they conceived it to be their duty to give a similar initiation to the Congolese. The geologist Edouard Dupont, Director of the Belgian Royal Museum of Natural History in 1887, described the European mission after he had spent a few months of study in the Congo:

> Africa has entered into a decisive and definitive stage of development ... Under a kindly and enlightened direction (the Africans) will be able to make an effort to draw fertility and riches out of their devastated and unproductive soil, their habits will become gentler, and they will abandon the customs which decimate their population even now and are evil almost comparable with that of the slave trade itself. At last Europe has taken up her true role - that of bringing civilisation to the world - in central Africa.[26]

So the role of *Mission Civilisatrice* was to create a 'new people' who could fit in the new *Bula Matari* model. And this noble mission of civilization was offered to Christian missions, on which, until the 1950s, much of the cultural policy and welfare of the state also devolved. Therefore the Church became an active participator and tool of the state's power. Before we describe the role played by the church, we shall examine how the Leopoldian system worked.

Structural Unity

The Belgian colonizers first seemed to have ambitious aims of structural unity rather than the unity of people. It took many decades for them to gather all the ethnic groups under their power. The Belgians first begun to free the 'new country' from Arab occupation, having introduced guns that helped centralised societies to become more powerful and to raid the tribal groupings or village organisations. The aim of that pacification was also to get rid of Arabs, who were seen as an alien rival power. Belgians then moved to the stage of subordinating

---

[25] Slade, *King Leopold's Congo,* 68.
[26] E. Dupont, *Lettres sur le Congo* (Paris: Reinwald, 1889), 707.

all groups under Leopold II's control. In doing so, they succeeded in subordinating the structured societies, while it was difficult to handle the small groupings. They decided to gain the powerful societies first and then use them to subordinate others. For instance, in the territory of Aru, the colonial administration used Logo to administrate the Lugbara, Kakwa, Logo, Ndo, while the Hema subordinated the Lendu.[27] This method still plays a major role as a background in ongoing clashes between the Hema and the Lendu that have taken thousands of innocent lives.

Indeed it was very difficult for the Belgians to create a sense of unity among clans and ethnic groups and to bring all the people together as one nation. It was due to the colonial dilemma of creating a national state while keeping the principle of 'divide and rule'. The Belgians thus developed ethnic consciousness among the Congolese. For example, when filling in a form, Congolese were not allowed to mention the clan or the family, but only the name of their ethnic group as a form of identity, even on identity cards and for elections. Territories in the same district were set up in the names of their main ethnic groups: territories of Walendu-Sud, Walendu-Nord, Logo, Lugbara, Wanande-Nord, and so on. The idea was to undermine the importance of families and clans in order to assemble people in ethnic groups that could easily be controlled and manipulated. Therefore, even if the Belgians succeeded in gathering all the Congolese ethnic groups under their authority, the challenge in their mind was how to civilize or to make them 'human'.

Leopoldian System

As already pointed out, the Leopoldian system, known by Congolese as *Bula Matari,* was built on the principle *Dominer pour servir*. The Belgians claimed to bring good governance to Congo through a paternalistic office; they created a beneficent framework within which the long-term interests of the subjects would find fulfilment. Domination would thus lead to the welfare of the Congolese. This explains why the colonial regime was essentially elitist, centrist and absolutist. The metropolis was the 'centre' leading the 'periphery' (the colony) toward enlightenment and progress, and by definition, subjects were not qualified to evaluate this process. There was an absence of constitutionally based rule of law for local development efforts.

Authority in colonial *Bula Matari* was marked by paternalism. It consisted of the tendency to treat the Congolese as childlike creatures and the firm commitment to political control and compulsion. Authority, until the eve of independence, remained almost exclusively in the hands of Belgians, who

---

[27] Kaputo, *Phénomène d'Ethnicité et Conflits Ethno-politiques en Afrique Post-colonial,* 68.

included 10,000 civil servants, 1000 military officers, 6000 Catholic missionaries and several thousand managers of colonial corporations.[28]

In this Leopoldian system, all legislative and executive power in the Congo was concentrated in the hands of Leopold II. Legally speaking, all authority belonged exclusively to him, as the Belgian lawyer Felicien Cattier wrote at the end of the century, 'The Sovereignty [of the Congo] is invested in the person of the Sovereign ... His will can be resisted by no juridical obstacle whatsoever. Leopold II could say, with more justification than Louis XIV did, "*L'Etat, c'est moi.*"'[29]

He delegated very little real authority to his subordinates. As Ruth Slade explained,[30] the central government of the Congo independent state was in Brussels, where the king could supervise its day-to-day work; it consisted of a Secretary of State, three Secretaries-General and a Treasurer-General. The local administration in the Congo was in the hands of a Governor-General, who could issue temporary laws in urgent circumstances. He was assisted by a vice-Governor-General, four Directors in charge of Government matters, and by the Commander-in-Chief of the *Force Publique*. All decisions were to be referred to a higher authority, and finally to Leopold II himself. The system consisted of a huge amount of correspondence and paralysed effective action. It was not until 1906 that there was a serious attempt to invest the hereditary chiefs with authority, and to inaugurate some form of indirect rule. But by this time almost all Congolese political organisation had disintegrated, for which both the Arab slave trade and also the earlier administrative policy were responsible.

Authority in colonial *Bula Matari* was also affected by the thirst for the wealth. The Congo State had deliberately deprived the Congolese of their traditional rights in the land and its products, and had compelled them to work either for the state itself or for concessionary companies in which the state was interested. State and company agents were at the same time administrators and traders; 'their basic salaries were low, but they received large bonuses scaled according to the amount of rubber and other products which they were able to collect.'[31] There were thus no incentives to check the methods employed by their Congolese subordinates, whose instructions encouraged them to force the local populations to furnish considerable quantities of these products.

The army became the tool of power for wealth and submission. Everything was organised on a military basis and everyone had to please his superiors by increasing output (rubber). This certainly led to a varying intensity of abuses including the cutting-off of ears and other forms of mutilation. Alfred Parminter,

---

[28] Young and Turner, *The Rise and Decline of the Zairian State*, 31.
[29] Felicien Cattier, *Droit et Administration de l'Etat Indépendent du Congo* (Brussels, n.p., 1898), 134.
[30] Slade, *King Leopold's Congo*, 171.
[31] Slade, *King Leopold's Congo*, 171.

an Englishman who worked in the Congo, told Reuters in an interview, on one occasion, at Bopoto, '… I was smoking with him on the back. It was late in the evening when suddenly a force of his troops returned from an expedition on which he had sent them in the morning. The sergeant held up triumphantly a number of ears fastened together on a string … The soldiers were praised for their success, and ordered to return next day and capture the chief.'[32]

'Lootocracy' also was one of the methods used: in 1899 a state official told a British consular officer his method of rubber collection in the Ubangi region:

> The soldiers were landed in a village, and commenced looting, taking all the chickens, grain, etc., out of the houses; after this they attacked the natives until they were able to seize their women, these women were kept as hostages until the chief of the district brought in the required number of kilograms of rubber. The rubber having been brought, the women were sold back to their owners for a couple of goats a piece, and so soldiers continued from village to village until the requested amount of rubber had been collected.[33]

The Belgian parliament wanted the system to be changed when it became responsible for administering the Congo, but it could not be done overnight. According to the reform decreed in July 1912, employees of commercial companies were no longer agents of the administration, the salaries of state officials were raised, some check on abuse of power had been made more possible by the reorganisation of the judicial system, and the labour tax imposed on the Congolese had been reduced. However, this was the result of international pressure, particularly from Britain and the United States, which forced Leopold II to hand Congo to the Belgian government. But the change of master did not mean a total change of the government system.

However, *Bula Matari* colonial regime had its achievements that some people still remember, although their memory may be influenced by a comparison with the harsh situation they are currently facing. For instance, when I asked those who lived in the colonial period about their lives, some striking answers were given: 'We used to eat well', 'Justice in the colonial period was excellent'; 'We had a real national army with great discipline.' Even Gerard Buakasa, although very critical of the colonialists, recognises that flourishing companies of the colonial period, a source of envy at that time, have now collapsed.[34] But the foundations laid by the colonial state for these achievements were not solid enough to survive in post-colonial Congo.

---

[32] Roger Anstey, *King Leopold's Legacy: The Congo Under Belgian Rule 1908-1960* (London: Oxford University Press, 1966), 6.

[33] Anstey, *King Leopold's Legacy*, 6.

[34] Gerard Buakasa, *Réinventer l'Afrique de la Tradition à la Modernité* (Paris: L'Harmattan, 1996), 108.

The Churches' Role in Trinité Coloniale

The Colonial administration, trade and the Roman Catholic Church made the *Trinité Coloniale* (Colonial Trinity). The colonial state diffused a certain paternal imagery which became a deliberate aspect of colonial policy. The aim was total control: political, physical, intellectual, ideological and cultural. As said by the Minister of the colonies:

> The maintenance of the authority of the government must, before everything, be the constant object of our functionaries. The population can be developed and the colony progress only under the aegis of a solidly established authority ... The native must be convinced that the authority intends to make itself obeyed and that all serious disobedience, as soon as known, will be punished without an excess of severity, but also without weakness.[35]

According to article 6 of the General Act of the Conference of Berlin of February 1885, mission activity is supposed to contribute to 'instructing the natives and bringing home to them the blessings of civilization.'[36] Hence an instrumental value is ascribed to Christian missions in relation to the colonial state. In Congo, it was the Roman Catholic Church and its missionaries, as part of *Trinité Coloniale*, who were offered a monopoly over education, and then acted as the colonial state's ideological apparatus. The Catholic Church encouraged compliance to state authority. Louis Frank, one of the major colonial ministers explained why the Catholic Church had been granted such a privilege. 'Only the Catholic Christian religion, based on authority, is capable of changing the native mentality, giving our blacks a clear and intimate awareness of their duty, inspiring in them respect for authority and a spirit of loyalty towards Belgium.'[37]

Education was offered selectively to men who would pass on the principles of respect and duty towards the Belgians. This was another aspect of 'divide and rule' and a means of keeping the ordinary man under control. Women were excluded from education. At the earlier stage, the metaphor of fatherhood within the Catholic hierarchy at first reinforced filial tendencies among Congolese converts. Then the repercussions of this went beyond the members of the church, and reinforced the dependency complex in society as a whole.

---

[35] Michel G. Schatzberg, *The Dialects of Oppression in Zaire* (Bloomington and Indianapolis: Indiana University Press, 1988), 85.

[36] Holger Bernt Hansen, 'The Colonial State's Policy Towards Foreign Missions in Uganda', in Holger Bernt Hansen and Michael Twaddle (eds), *Christian Missionaries and the State in the Third World* (Oxford: James Currey; Athens: Ohio University Press, 2002), 158.

[37] L. Frank quoted by J. Greenland, 'Western Education in Burundi 1916-1973: The Consequences of Instrumentalism', in *Cahiers du CEDAF*, nos. 2-3, 1980, 37.

The Belgians preferred, as an educational method, recitation, dogmatic methods and an appeal to the ultimate religious authority. Unfortunately this method did not develop the students' ability to reason. As parents exercise authority in the family, the teacher exercised absolute authority over the pupils. The teaching consisted of 'all authority comes from God who delegates it to legitimate superiors. These superiors pass it on to the teacher, whom the pupils are obliged to obey as God.'[38] This background helps to show how theology served politicians instead of tackling issues raised by colonialism. It also helps us to understand why colonial schools did not have a critical political view at that time.

The above discussion reveals the two objectives the Catholic Church had: first was religious through teaching the Catholic faith to the Congolese. There was also a patriotic interest in helping the Belgian state to exploit the Congo and achieve economic development in a short period. Protestant churches, however, were accused of serving British and American interests for possible territorial and economic conquest. It was not only the Belgian colonial state which hated the Protestant churches, but also industrial companies. For instance the *Directeur-Général* de *Kilo Moto* (goldmining) was strongly against the establishment of Protestant churches in the area because 'they are led by Americans and British and so they do not have sympathy with Belgium and its colonial administration.'[39] They were also accused of the uncontrolled spread of the Bible and it was said that neither the content nor the form of their religion was relevant to the Congolese.

Another means of attracting 'recruits' was the creation of *Chrétientés* (Christian villages). Catholic missionaries worked on groups – often those normally marginalized such as slaves, abandoned children and orphans – with the aim of building up a Christian community in the midst of a pagan society to create a new 'sacred family'. These new communities were given material wealth in order that they could live in greater comfort than their Congolese neighbours.

Protestants for their part did not intentionally gather large crowds of Africans together into the same kind of *Chrétientés*, but Christian villages grew up by the side of each of their mission stations. Freed slave children, or Christians who suffered from a good deal of persecution in pagan villages, were sometimes driven to seek protection around the mission. The village headman was appointed by the missionary, disputes were settled at the mission, and the village became a model that the missionary hoped would be copied by other Congolese villages in the neighbourhood. The colour of his skin, apart from his technical

---

[38] Frère Bernardin, *L'Ecole Congolaise: Eléments d'Organisation Scolaires* (Bondo: Frères de St Gabriel, 1958), 4.

[39] Kaputo, *Phénomène d'Ethnicité et Conflits Ethno-politiques en Afrique Post-coloniale,* 20.

knowledge, gave the missionary an authority that rivalled that of a chief. He was often given the task of arbiter in case of quarrels and disagreements; he thus became powerful and won a recognised position in Congolese society. G.J.M. Pearce may be right when he suggested that the term 'missionary' described one vocation and many occupations.[40] So missionaries had to spend, and often to waste, energies in doing work for which they had no aptitude and no training. Fortunately, doctors, teachers, builders came later to help and missionaries were required to engage in specialized activities.

However, missionaries have contributed much in challenging *Bula Matari*'s authority. They have played a prominent role in the education of many leaders and in drawing world attention to human rights abuses in Congo: first with the campaign against slavery during the 1800s, later with the campaign against abusive labour practices in the Congo Free State and the Belgian Congo.[41] For instance, in the Equateur district in the 1890s, the conflict concerning the manner in which the state exercised its power and authority in the Congo involved missionary societies and the colonial regime and finally European public opinion. In the nearly unanimous opinion of the state officials and army officers, it was no business of the missionaries how this power was exercised, so long as no missionaries' lives were lost and no mission property was damaged in the process.[42] Although some missionaries were influenced by this approach, others insisted on their right and duty to plead the cause of the Africans and try to free the people from a system of coercion that they considered inhumane. Sometimes difficulties arose between the civil authorities and the missions out of competition for carriers. For instance, in 1889, the Governor-General had forbidden the missionaries to recruit porters from Babwende country. This was a strongly felt injustice because it was the missionaries and the traders who had trained the lower Congo peoples to act as carriers, and who had been forced to pay heavily for licences to employ them and were finally forbidden to make use of them at all.

But here the conflict was mostly due to the missionaries' reaction to the suffering of the Congolese, as David Lagergren wrote:

> In general, the treatment meted out to the African population was often harsh and humiliating: for a number of State agents it seemed natural to treat them like dogs which get a kick at every corner and which, for the slightest offence, must crawl to

---

[40] G. J. M. Pearce, *Congo Background* (London: The Carey Kingsgate Press, 1954), 79.

[41] Bobb, *Historical Dictionary of Democratic Republic of the Congo (Zaire)*, 283.

[42] David Lagergren, *Mission and State in the Congo: A study of the relations between Protestant missions and the Congo Independent State authorities with special reference to the Equator District 1885-1903* (Uppsala: Gleerup, 1970), 76.

their masters feet to be whipped. The most usual punishment administered was a flogging with a 'chicote', a whip made from hippopotamus hide.[43]

The Protestant missionaries aimed at gradually transferring authority from the Europeans missionaries to the African leaders of the local churches. But as Slade said, 'It was impossible to hand over the authority in this way, however, until the Government had accorded the right of association to Africans, for an African church, independent of the European mission organisation, could not legally exist.'[44] In the 1950s the Protestant missionaries, like the Catholics, were becoming convinced that the paternalism of the past was finished and the Congo churches must be given responsibility for their own future, aided, but not directed, by the European missionaries. However, this was already during the Congolese *prise de conscience* (awareness) for self-determination.

Bula Matari imposed structural unity through paternalism. Congolese were trained to mistreat their own people and sell them as slaves in the interest of foreigners, and the system also aimed to sustain colonial power. Because of the lack of political and personal freedoms, which had prevented the evolution of political or administrative experience among the Congolese, colonialism ended much earlier than most Belgians expected. This happened because of the revolt by the Congolese, who preferred to develop their own version of the modern state. The question is how different the modern state was from the *Bula Matari* model of authority.

Political Power in the Mobutu Years

Mobutu Sese Seko, who boasted that he might ultimately become known as the late president, but never as the former president, took power in conditions created by the deterioration of the precarious constitution of the first republic after independence in 1960. It is known that Mobutu, who was not in the front rank of the pre-independence figures, seized power with the help of the United States of America.[45] He justified his action by saying that it was his will to establish unity and to reinstate cultural authenticity and work for economic independence. This section aims to examine the main characteristics of authority used by Mobutu's regime in reinventing contemporary Congolese society.

---

[43] Slade, *The Belgian Congo: Some Recent Changes,* 118.

[44] Slade, *The Belgian Congo: Some Recent Changes,* 36.

[45] *Jeune Afrique*, Hebdomadaire International Independent, no 1614, 4 au 10 Décembre, 1991.

Proprietary Authority

According to A. Sawyer, 'proprietary authority is the emergence of authority relations based on principles that apply to the control of a private or personal domain. In such orders, authority is exercised as if it were a personal acquisition.'[46] Whether justified by a revolutionary ideology or by a perception of divine ordination, authority is personalized and exercised through a patron-client network. Most frequently, repressive measures and unequal exchange replace reciprocity in the maintenance of authority relationships. Rules become synonymous with the desires of the proprietor. It is the patrimonialism in which constantly reaffirmed personal fidelity and services are indispensable. Any suspicion of lack of loyalty is ground for instant removal. The ruler depends upon the office-holder to demonstrate an ability to secure compliance with presidential orders, and to cope with the management of his particular sphere of authority, the first priority being the maintenance of political control. The following are some characteristics of Mobutu's proprietary authority.

Authority in Mobutu's regime, as in the *Bula Matari* regime, was marked by paternalism. In 1965, after Mobutu had seized power, he appropriated full legislative authority, and claimed extra-constitutional legislative powers for a five-year period. Political parties were banned soon afterwards. Mobutu described 'the social, economic, and financial situation of the country as catastrophic'. He designated the 'chaos' created by his predecessors by a degrading word 'Congolisation'. In order to redress this situation, he decided to return to the state tradition of *Bula Matari*. Engulu Baanga Mpongo articulated this revived state doctrine in a 1974 speech to soldiers in training at Makanda Kabobi:

> The administrative organisation of the colony, the hierarchical military type, was a heritage of the structure established by Leopold II for the occupation of Zaire. It was founded on the principle of unity of command, which means that, for whatever action, an official receives his orders only from one chief. Wishing to create and maintain in the administration, as among the people, a unity of views and action, Belgium entrusted complete responsibility for the colonial enterprise to a single cadre: the territorial service. The real motivation for concentration of function in the territorial cadre was political. It was necessary to indicate to the population that authority was one and indivisible.[47]

Mobutu copied from the colonial regime its centralisation of power for the unit of command in the administration. To keep authority 'one' became the key principle of the regime. Mobutu formalised a new institutional order. He first

---

[46] Amos Sawyer, 'Proprietary Authority and Local Administration in Liberia', in James S. Wunsch and Dele Olowu (eds), *The Failure of the Centralized State: Institutions and Self-Governance in Africa* (Oxford: Westview Press, 1990), 149.
[47] Sawyer, 'Proprietary Authority and Local Administration in Liberia', 111.

re-introduced the one party system by creating the *Mouvement Populaire pour la Révolution* (MPR) as an instrument of political monopoly. The president of the MPR was automatically the president of the republic, and it was from him that the legitimacy of the state authority derived, not from the people. The MPR became the Party-State. As Longandjo Okitakekumba expressed it:

> As in all countries, the State Authority is in principle divided between the three acknowledged branches: the Executive, the Legislative and the Judiciary. In Zaire, this separation of powers is purely academic. In practice, under the MPR Party-State regime all these powers are personified and wielded by the president of the Republic. Whatever power the other branches enjoy they derive from the president. In sum, all branches of power are agencies of the MPR Party-State headed by the president of the Republic.[48]

Apart from the president as the state authority, there was the Political Directorate, which was an important wheel in the machinery of absolute presidential power, even though it had no formal institutional status. As Okitakekumba said, 'It wields real power, but more than that, it exercises enormous influence within the political elite. Essentially, it comprises the President's close kin, but it includes a sprinkling of hangers-on brought in for the sake of appearances, that is to say, to demonstrate the observance of regional quotas and the balanced distribution of national power.'[49]

The political Directorate was ceaselessly reshuffled by the State Authority, the sole source of power and legitimacy. It served as a formidable instrument used by the MPR whenever it felt a need to marginalize targeted individuals or groups. It blocked the emergence of revolutionary nationalist movements at local level.

The constitution drafted confirmed the re-centralisation of state power and its concentration in the hands of the president. Even the constitution of 1988 still reaffirmed his authority to nominate and remove the leaders at different levels.[50] Mobutu identified himself as the incarnation of the Congolese people and thus claimed an automatic and unquestioning obedience, personal fidelity and services.

Personalisation and centralisation of power made Mobutu 'omnipresent'. Nothing could be done without his approbation. His picture was hung on public walls, monuments, government and church offices, schools and hospitals, even in private homes. An office without the president's picture was suspected of plotting against him. His portrait also embellished coins and paper currency;

---

[48] Longandjo Okitakekumba, 'State Power under MPR Control: An Interpretive Essay', in Kankwenda Mbaya, (ed), *Zaire: What Destiny?* (Chippenham, England: Codesria, 1993), 86.

[49] Okitakekumba, 'State Power under MPR Control', 87.

[50] *Constitution de la République du Zaïre mise en jour le 27 Juin 1988*, art. 42, 17.

schools, hospitals and avenues were named after him. He became a 'strongman' as described by Richard Sandbrook:

> The strongman, usually the president, occupies the centre of political life. Front and centre stage, he is the centrifugal force around which all else revolves. Not only the ceremonial head of state, the president is also the chief political, military and cultural figure: head of government, commander-in-chief of the armed forces, and head of the governing party. His aim is typically to identify his person with the 'nation.'[51]

Mobutu's strategy clearly was to use his power and the institution he controlled not only to promote his own individual interest, but also to manipulate and undermine the rights and freedoms of the rest of society. Personalised power and patronage consequently led to an obligatory personality cult. He was the Guide of the Zairian revolution, Peacemaker, Liberator, Unifying and Founding President. Political songs were sung in his honour. He frequently travelled through the country, immersing himself in the crowds, who were not merely attracted by his presidential visit, but because it was compulsory for them to attend.

Furthermore, authority was marked by paternalism. Mobutu was the Father of the Nation. In official speeches and songs, he was known as *Tata* (father) Mobutu. The comparison between family and administration or political party is striking, as expressed by Bakonga Ekonga, 'The basis of Zairian cultural policy is Mobutism, the doctrine of the People's Revolutionary Movement, that vast family which brings all the citizens of Zaire together under one roof.'[52] Thus the MPR and the Zairian nation were seen as one large family, unified under the leadership of its father.

This symbol of *Tata* was used by Mobutu to totally control all resources and be the ultimate distributor. 'These are gifts from the father to his children'. All flowed from Mobutu, the ultimate source of bounty, and citizens had to show frequent gratitude to their national father. For instance, in 1990 Mobutu offered a very small satellite dish which covered 40 square km to the town of Bunia and he deliberately sent Tibasima Mbogemu Ateny to explain to the population that it was a gift from the Father who continued to love his children even when the situation was tough. Immediately, without any critical thought, a march for support was held to express gratitude to *Tata* Mobutu, while people were experiencing inexpressible suffering. In fact, as we shall see later, the father-children relationship in Congolese families creates everlasting dependence, total and blind obedience.

---

[51] Richard Sandbrook, *The Politics of Africa's Stagnation* (New York: Cambridge University Press, 1993), 90.

[52] B. Ekanga, *Cultural Policy in the Republic of Zaïre* (Paris: UNESCO, 1976), 45.

Within this paternalism violence is seen as a sign of the father's love in rebuking a guilty child. Fear and intimidation are adopted as means to consolidate power. In May 1966 Mobutu hanged, before 50,000 spectators, four former ministers accused of conspiracy. When asked about it, he justified it by saying, 'One has to strike by a spectacular example, and create the conditions for a disciplined regime. When a chief takes a decision, he decides, full stop.'[53] The violation of human rights was thus the state's way of controlling social groups and individuals, including religious institutions and their followers.

It is in this climate of fear and intimidation that what is known as *Mal Zairois* (Zairian evil) took place: dictatorship, armed conflicts, rebellions, clan wars and widespread violation of human rights, such as arbitrary arrests, illegal detention, torture, harassment, irregular places of detention, sexual abuse and so on. This led to the terrible suffering and hopelessness of a great number of internally displaced people.

Incarnational Character of Authority

Mobutu as state authority preferred to legitimise his power by the use of selected traditional symbols of authority. He identified himself as the 'incarnation' of the Leopard, which occupies a central place in Congolese armorial banners. He related an incident, which he explained as the genesis of his fearlessness:

> One day, [Mobutu, his grandfather, and his great-uncle] found themselves nose to nose with a leopard perched in the lower branch of a tree. Joseph-Desiré [Mobutu] had never been so near such a large beast, and threw himself into his grandfather's arms. 'You are not a man', the old one hissed. Joseph-Desiré, wounded to the quick, regained his composure. Swift as lightning, his spear struck the head of the leopard. The beast was not dead, and fled into the bush. The grandfather forced his grandson to pursue it and to recover his weapon. 'Since that day', Mobutu explains, 'I have feared nothing.'[54]

The story of 'Leopard-men' is well known in Africa. Many violent secret societies existed on the continent. There were 'Leopard-men' in Cameroon, Liberia, Ivory Coast and Nigeria. In Congo there were *Anioto* (Leopard-men) in Bafwasende, 'Crocodile-men' in Walengola, 'Lion-men' in Marungu and 'Leopard-men' in Equateur, Mobutu's region. The question is whether there is a link between Mobutu's myth and the story of 'Leopard-men' in his region. Among the Nande they were called *Wahokohoko*, men disguised as leopards, wearing leopard skin all over the body and shoes made of wild rubber; and walking like leopards. They had knives made of iron in the form of claws. They

---

[53] Kamitatu, *La Grande Mystification* (Paris: Maspero, 1971), 176.
[54] Young and Turner, *The Rise and Decline of the Zairian State,* 173.

would catch their victims and eat them.[55] They thus committed inexpressible crimes and atrocities in their societies.

The leopard skin is still a symbol of authority among many traditional societies. For instance the *Mukama* of the Hema possesses the skins of leopards in his traditional house. 'He is leopard, nothing else in leopard's skin,'[56] as expressed by Balinda Kabarole. This shows the fearsome character of the *Mukama* as a warrior defending his people. But, in Mobutu's case, it meant that, as the Father at the peak of the pyramid, he feared nobody and nothing. He created the *Ordre de Léopard*, one of the highest distinctions, which places the recipient above the law, for he enjoys the personal protection of the president. It was only offered to leaders, including Church leaders. The Anglican bishops of Congo applied for the *Ordre de Léopard,* but did not get it.

Thus the identification of authority with fierce wild animals demonstrates effectively the fierce and wild character of Congolese regimes. Even Kabila identified himself with the Lion, an image that was reproduced by the Congolese army. As the incarnation of wild and fierce animals, the soldiers systematically and enthusiastically pillaged towns and villages. Indeed, the Congolese military is viewed by the populace as the main cause of criminality and violence in the country. They are synonymous with extortion, looting, murder, rape and utter disregard for the protection of lives and property. Businessmen are obliged to 'donate' goods or money to soldiers, often at gunpoint. They extorted illegal fines from unlucky citizens who fell into their hands. Sezabo Batiana related his sad story, 'I was once arrested by three soldiers. First they asked me to show my Identity card which I did, then my service card, then my driving licence; finally I was found guilty and fined because I did not have my Christian baptism card.'[57] Many citizens sympathized with the plight of the soldiers who, like themselves, are rarely paid and tended to blame their behaviour on the government and the political paralysis caused by bickering politicians.

Can this violence of a brutal military regime be explained by Africa's warrior tradition, as many scholars suggest? Traditionally, many tribes did not have standing armies. In most states, the people were the army and the monarchs had no independent full-time forces of their own. Warrior tribes did exist, but warriors were there to defend the village and the tribe against rival tribes or slave raiders. This brutality of the Congolese soldiers might have come from the *Bula Matari* state which used the Congolese to commit atrocities on their fellow

---

[55] Mbonzo M'banzwa Mathe, 'Evolution des Problèmes Politiques Administratives entre les Batangi-Mbau et Mbabuba de la Collectivité de Beni' (ISP/Bunia, dissertation, 1990), 36.

[56] Balinda Bin Kabarole, 'Etude Socio-Politique du Pouvoir Traditionnel chez les Bahema de la Zone d'Irumu' (Mémoire de Licence, Campus de Lubumbashi, Juillet 1976), 68.

[57] Sezabo Batiani, interviewed in Bunia, 12/11/2001.

citizens. But also this behaviour is the result of their training philosophy, as written on the front of the building of the Kota Koli training centre, 'A Society without Logic.'[58] Even Mobutu himself recognized the failure of his army when he said, 'But the truth is simply that all these cadres seem to have lost the rigour of military life and discipline in favour of all sort of commodities: commerce, beautiful cars, beautiful villas, bourgeois life.'[59] So the army became the tool of sustaining the proprietary power. It is the same colonial policy of 'lootocracy' but with new postcolonial actors.

Ethnonationalism

Postcolonial authority is much marked by the ethnic dynamic which was there even before political independence. In 1956, the political party *Alliance des Bakongo* (ABAKO) openly declared that it was pure utopianism to rally all the Congolese behind a single opinion. It proposed that groups which are historically, ethnically and linguistically united or linked, should organize themselves to form political parties.[60] The attempt was to reunify, in a revived Kongo state, the Bakongo people who had been divided by the colonial partition of Africa between the French Congo, the Belgian Congo and Angola.

In fact, many political parties, on the eve of independence, were organised on an ethnic basis. Even in the First Republic after independence, the political deadlock was due to the uprising of different ethnic groups, which led to bloody rebellions. There was an ethnic based secession of Katanga and the creation of 48 parties and 24 provinces, all on an ethnic basis. After coming to power, Mobutu was careful to suppress all institutions that could mobilize ethnic loyalties. He opposed ethnicity as a basis for political alignment. He weakened traditional rulers and in 1972 he transferred chiefs to other areas, but abandoned this policy because of public protests. Officials were posted to areas other than their own. Even admission to the University was based on regional quotas providing access to all ethnic groups. Nevertheless, as dissatisfaction increased, ethnic tensions surfaced again. For instance, in 1975, after the Shaba invasion, army purges involved mainly the Tetela, Luba and Lunda. Even Mobutu himself, seen as essentially a man from the province of Equateur, relied more and more on people from that region. After 1978 the core group around him, who controlled the key posts, were nearly all from Equateur.

Furthermore, in 1993 the Mobutu regime knowingly encouraged ethnic hatred and violence in both Kivu and Shaba. There was 'ethnic cleansing' in Shaba

---

[58] Nganka Edrungi, Army Chaplain, personal communication in Bunia, 30/10/2000.
[59] *Salongo*, 5 February 1980, 6.
[60] Young and Turner, *The Rise and Decline of the Zairian State*, 4.

against Kasaians, and in Kivu against those of ethnic Rwandan origin.[61] 'Ethnocentrism' has continued even after Mobutu. Kabila certainly denounced the ethnic tendency of Mobutu's rule, but then fell himself into what is called the *Katangaisation* of power in Congo. It means that the core group around him are from his ethnic group in Katanga. As noticed in *Jeune Afrique*, 'the car was broken down. Instead of changing the engine, we have got a new driver.'[62]

The most devastating inter-ethnic war has occurred recently in the Ituri area between the Hema and Lendu. There have always been tensions between them. They have lived together for years, they speak the same language and they have often intermarried. But a few wealthy extremist Hema were able to hire soldiers to kill innocent civilians, sparking off terrible revenge killings by both sides. It confirms the principle of ethnocentricism; as previously said, in traditional society a person's security depends on the power and the importance of his clan and ethnic group.[63]

Thus we see ethnic consciousness persisting from the precolonial era to the contemporary period. Those who fought against it finally committed the same error. Even extreme nationalism did not succeed in banning ethnonationalism. On the contrary, ethnic groups tended to protect their identities against full nationalism. However, ethnicity has served as a tool for politicians to impose their power and to commit various atrocities. It was the 'divide and rule' principle applied to weaken the Congolese when nationalism was needed for the unity of command. A workable pan-ethnic vision that is inclusive rather than exclusive is needed in Congo in order to make authority helpful for every Congolese person.

Wealth and Power

In post-colonial Congo, as in many African countries, politics and economic enterprise are intertwined. As Chabal has observed, 'In Africa it is expected that politics will lead to personal enrichment, just as it is expected that wealth will have a direct influence on political matters. Rich men are powerful. Powerful men are rich.'[64] Effectively, in Congo political and economic systems are the same, for those who hold the political power are the same people who make decisions regarding the allocation of resources.

---

[61] Michel G. Schatzeberg, 'Highjacking Change: Zaire's Transition in Comparative Perspective', in M. Ottaway (ed), *Democracy in Africa: The Hard Road Ahead* (London: Lynne Rienner Publishers, 1997), 121.

[62] *Jeune Afrique* no 1980-1981 du 22 Dec 1998 au 4 Janv 1999, 39 année.

[63] Oxfam report 2110. http://www.globalissues.org/Geo-politics/Africa/DRC.asp. Already in 1999, the fighting between Hema and Lendu led to 7,000 deaths.

[64] Patric Chabal and Jean-Pascal Daloz, *Africa Works: Disorder as Political Instrument* (Bloomington: Indiana University Press, 1999), 52.

Mobutu became fabulously rich by using the resources of the state as his own. Although the true extent is unknown, his wealth is almost the same as the debt of Congo, around US$14 billion, whereas his people were starving. There is no clear evidence that this money will be returned to the Congolese government, despite the claim of Kabila's government. The situation is as described by George B. N.Ayittey, 'The African state has been reduced to a mafia-like bazaar, where anyone with an official designation can pillage at will. In effect, it is a 'state' that has been hijacked by gangsters.'[65] At each level of administration, power is used as a means to gain wealth, which becomes a gauge of authority in the society. Officials who administered state controls have been discovered to have used them for selfish ends and to advance their own supporters. Also, civil servants exploited their position in government to supplement their meagre salaries. Endless new rules were added to government regulations to gain self-aggrandizement.

If power was used to gain wealth, in return wealth was used as a tool to sustain power through corruption. In 1990, after Mobutu had 'authorized' the multiparty system, several of the more important of the new parties made an attempt at unity through an umbrella front called the Sacred Union, which, in July 1991, counted 115 members. Nonetheless, Mobutu was able to sow the seeds of discord among the opposition by using his wealth. This fact irritated Thomas Kanza, who lamented,

> Are we manipulated and remote-controlled by money? Certainly. It seems to me that it is money which leads the political dance in [Congo]. Ideological oppositions are almost non-existent. The political oppositions are only theoretical. Everything, or almost everything, is a function of money.[66]

In 1991, moreover, every university professor received a Mitsubishi Gallant from the president. He was able to manipulate the elite by offerings gifts instead of paying them their salaries. The elite thus became silent instead of being the 'voice' of the population. Thus wealth controlled political life and the democratic process during Mobutu's regime.

Bula Matari's Democracy

The attempt of democratisation of power in the post-colonial regime was not a sincere will for change, but another evil strategy of *Bula Matari*'s model of authority to sustain its power. During his regime (1965-1995), Mobutu repeatedly explained that democracy is not suitable for Africa because there is

---

[65] Ayyitey, *Africa in Chaos,* 151.
[66] Thomas Kanza, 'Le Zairois serait-il maudit, inconscient?', in *Elima* (Kinshasa, September 19, 1991), 8.

only one African chief and he rules for life. He based his rejection of a
multi-party system on the colonial period when the authorisation of 44 political
parties ended in tribalism and rebellion. He found that a one-party system was
needed for national unity and he boasted about the 'achievement' and the
'democratic' character of his movement.

However, despite the fear and intimidation used by Mobutu to sustain his
ascendancy, his authority and legitimacy saw a visible decline because of the
Mal Zairois (Zairian evil) which was taking place in society. For instance, in
1980, thirteen parliamentarians challenged his authority when they published a
fifty-one-page open letter accusing him of being the incarnation of the *Mal
Zairois*:

> For fifteen years now we have obeyed you. What have we done, during this time, to
> be useful and agreeable to you? We have sung, danced, in short, we have been
> subjected to all sorts of humiliations; and forms of subjugation which even foreign
> colonisation never made us suffer ... After fifteen years of the power you have
> exercised alone, we find ourselves divided into two absolutely distinct camps. On
> one side, a few scandalously rich persons; on the other, the mass of the people
> suffering the darkest misery.[67]

By the end of three decades of Mobutu's rule, government structures had
collapsed and the infrastructure had crumbled. However, Mobutu had allowed
the infrastructure to crumble for political reasons, because he knew that with
impassable roads and non-existing communications, it was impossible for
political opponents to organize themselves against him. Thus the state almost
totally neglected its responsibility to seek the welfare of its citizens. On April 24,
1990, Mobutu announced the end of the single-party state and declared the Third
Republic. This tactical and clever change of method was the result of internal and
external factors which had a great impact on political development in this period.

External factors began with the end of the Cold War, and this meant that the
West's (French, Belgian and USA's) major reason for supporting the Mobutu
regime had disappeared because of the downfall of several long-ruling
communist leaders. Second, beginning in Benin in 1990, the concept of the
'Sovereign National Conference' swept across francophone Africa. Students,
workers, long-suppressed opposition groups and politicians demanded political
change. In this moment of enthusiasm, 'the United States, France and Belgium
formed a united front to insist that Mobutu participate in the wave of
democratisation.'[68]

As to internal factors, there was a deterioration of the economic and political
situation. The state's ability to provide its citizens with even the most

---

[67] Jean-Claude Willame, *L'Automne d'un Despotisme: Pouvoir, Argent et Obéissance
dans le Zaire des Années Quatre-Vinght* (Paris: Karthala, 1992), 132-3.
[68] Young and Turner, *The Rise and Decline of the Zairian State*, 123.

rudimentary social services declined, and it stopped paying salaries to the army and civil servants. In August 1991, the Sovereign National Conference was convened with the aim of removing Mobutu from office, but it failed when Mobutu suspended it. In fact this was not the only reason for the failure of the National Conference. In a democracy supreme power belongs to the citizens, so it was for the Congolese to elect their delegates to the National Conference; but it was the leaders who nominated them. In this case, as P. Massina stated, the National Conference could not claim itself to be sovereign, for its members were not chosen by the people. [69] Also, Mobutu succeeded in corrupting other members; and much of the opposition was composed of those who were seriously implicated in the excesses of the Second Republic. Finally, the transitional period did not bring about a democratisation process because Mobutu manipulated the system rather than allow a genuine democratisation process to go forward. In these ways he controlled events until Kabila's armed victory in Kinshasa finally caused his downfall.

The New Wave of Democratisation

Laurent Kabila was sworn in on 22 May 1997 as the new president of the Congo. He soon gained international recognition and was received all over the country as a 'liberator'. Re-traditionalisation was one of the key features of Kabila's government. He first gained support from traditional chiefs and introduced a police force to protect civilians and their possessions. He called himself *Mzee* (elder) in order to legitimise his authority by holding a position recognised in the traditional hierarchy.

This re-traditionalisation of power also aimed to provide legitimacy on political grounds. Kabila became popularly known as a true nationalist who followed Lumumba's path. He fought against corruption, even jailing his own ministers accused of embezzlement. However, he issued a decree banning all political parties and public demonstrations. On 28 May 1997, Kabila issued a constitutional decree, to remain in force until the adoption of a new constitution. The international community expressed concern that the decree allowed the president to wield near-absolute power, since it accorded him legislative and executive power as well as control over the armed forces and the treasury.

Kabila was in a corner. He had no experienced army and was under threat from both his political opponents and the international community on the issue of 'refugees and human rights abuses'. He was assassinated on 16 January 2001, leaving the country in chaos. From 1998 to 2003, Congo was then divided into five groups: the government and rebel factions with which violence in Congo has reached its apex. The example of Bunia in northeast Congo is relevant.

---

[69] P. Massina, 'De la Souveraineté des Conférences Nationales africaines', in *Révue Burkinabé de Droit*, 24, Décembre, 234.

Luc-Roger Mbala in his article *Bunia: The Hell in the Heart of Africa*, related a horrific scene, 'Witnesses affirm having seen scenes of cannibalism between the Hema and Lendu militiamen, and having killed, tearing off the head and removing their victim's heart, which they ate, they say to obtain supernatural force.'[70] Atrocities as bad as cannibalism are not only committed by ethnic militias. Already in February 2003, a rebel operation called 'Erasing the Picture' was reported. The operation's objective was, starting from the city of Beni, to destroy everything and not leave any person living. It is the systematic and organised character of the operation that shocked the world, the massacres, tortures and displacement of populations,[71] as Sergio de Vieira's report says.

The *Bula Matari* model of leadership led Congo to forge a path through hard rock. The absence of mechanisms for the peaceful transfer of political power and for the peaceful resolution of conflicts was a sign of a real crisis of authority in Congo. Was there then a suitable way for the country to get out of the chaos? The UN has sent troops to help in Congo, as it did after independence to rescue the country from the hands of mercenaries and police from Katanga. The poem written by the Senegalese Lamine Diakhate to express the anguish he felt at the endless Congolese crises straight after independence still remains relevant:

> Leopoldville (now Kinshasa),
> Have you become the Capital of the distressed,
> The great wounded of the century?
> Aeroplanes discharge multitudes of men
> On your heart
> On your shoulders.[72]

The current president, Joseph Kabila, succeeded in holding a national dialogue and bringing about a transitional government. It also succeeded in holding the 'first' democratic elections in Congo in 2006. The current wave of democracy in Congo is undoubtedly a welcome development as it derives from a constitutional structure which guarantees fundamental freedoms and rights, and serves as the only basis of governance in a state which wants to be of law. But the challenge to democracy in Congo, as elsewhere, is mainly in the practice of equating freedom not only with better human treatment but also with better life.

---

[70] Luc-Roger Mbala Bemba, 'Topicality: Bunia: The Hell in the heart of Africa: Police officers, priests infants massacred with the machete,' http://www.digitalcongo.net/fullstory.php?id=24133, Kinshasa, 23/05/2003.
[71] F.K.L. 'IFHR complaint and Sergio de Vieira's report before the UN Security Council', http://www.digitalcongo.net/fullstory.php?id=20727, Kinshasa, 15/02/2003. In Vieira de Melo's report to the Security Council, 220 arbitrary executions are reported, 95 cases of rape are listed, and 102 people disappeared, 30 cases of torture and 15 cases of cannibalism preceded by mutilations listed.
[72] 'Primordiale du Sixième jour', in *Présence Africaine*, 1963, 41.

Conclusion

Congo is an artificial entity encompassing a diversity of indigenous ethnic groups with different languages, origins and socio-political organisations. The study of the traditional view of authority has shown that it was built on a theo-centric concept of life, hierarchically ordered. Authority was also people-centred with a consensual and participatory democracy. Though ethnocentric, authority included charisma and service. But during the colonial period, Belgium formed a 'national state', managed on the principle of *Dominer pour servir* explicitly expressed by 'divide and rule'. It soon gained the name *Bula Matari* because of its cruelty, terror, greed and the personalisation of power. Using missionaries to serve its cause, the *Mission Civilisatrice* introduced the concept of a 'new sacralisation' of power and society, which became a threat to the 'old sacralisation' offered by traditional cultural values. The colonial authority thus worked to prepare the path of post independence politics towards a depreciation of the value of the indigenous and decentralised social infrastructure and towards reliance on centralised, hierarchical mechanisms to order human relationships. Post-colonial authority therefore is built on the *Bula Matari* model, marked by paternalism and ethnonationalism. Even so, two very important ideologies of the Congo post-colonial era developed in the context of cultural revolution were the philosophies of *authenticité* and of nationalism. Our next chapter will deal with these two ideologies and find out how they contributed to shaping the theology and exercise of authority in the Congolese Churches.

Chapter Two

Church – State Relations in Post-Colonial Congo

Postcolonialism in Congo has been profoundly marked by cultural revolution, which consists of restoring Congolese identity and building authority and power on 'traditional' principles. It has involved both politics and theology. In this chapter, we want to analyse the dynamics and causes of such cultural revolution and its impact both on the society and the Church.

Cultural Revolution

In order to understand the cultural revolution in post-colonial Congo, we shall mainly examine nationalism and *authenticité*, considering the use of traditional symbols of authority and political legitimacy.

Postcolonial Nationalism

Nationalism, rooted in Pan-Africanism, underwent fluctuations not merely in its nature and forms, but also in its functions. In fact, the history of Pan-Africanism begins with Henry Sylvester Williams, a West Indian barrister who established relations with West Africans in Britain, and later acted as legal adviser to several African chiefs who visited the United Kingdom on political missions to the colonial office. He took the initiative in 'convening a Pan-African Conference in London in 1900 in order to combat the aggressive policies of British imperialists. Thus the idea of Pan-Africanism first arose as a manifestation of fraternal solidarity among Africans and peoples of African descent.

Dr William E.B. Du Bois, usually cast as the 'Father' of Pan-Africanism, was then the first to systematize pan-Africanist ideas with the exclusion of its racist aspects. He considered Pan-Africanism as 'a dynamic political philosophy and guide to action for Africans in Africa who were laying the foundations of national liberation organisations.' Therefore national self-determination, individual liberty and democratic socialism constituted the essential elements of DuBois' Pan-Africanism. This Pan-Africanism, as a stimulant to anti-colonialism, had a more permanent effect on African political awakening. Thus, Pan-Africanism was not primarily a credo for the domination, but an ideology for the emancipation of African peoples.

Then, after the Second World War, the focus shifted from Pan-Africanism to African nationalism. In this early stage, nationalism in the Congo was conceived in terms of ethnonationalism, which, as an anticolonial movement, aimed to restore the old order with a political programme based on pre-colonial traditions. This resulted in the creation of political parties marked by ethnic consciousness. Even the immediate independence claimed by *Alliance des Bakongo* (ABAKO) was a pitfall for secession rather than a means of creating unity. Therefore, by using the past for promoting their new ideas of independence, the elite succeeded in creating internal dynamics of resistance, mainly in rural areas. This type of nationalism was extremely backward looking.

But the opening up of Africa to the world as result of the Second World War brought a new wave of resistance to colonialism, principally among town-dwellers. The African soldiers who had fought in Europe brought a new vision of the world, and started to question their passive role towards independence. The meaningful awareness of nationalism, which went beyond ethnonationalism, was effectively due to this broader sense rather than merely to unite against colonizers, as preached by Pan-Africanism. The encounter of Lumumba with other African nationalists such as Kwame Nkrumah helped to shape Congolese nationalism, uniting orientations of nationalism and leading to independence. However, this nationalism did not go deep enough in search of unity, as communities did not have natural ties or affinities to form a basis for nationhood.

Nationalism in post-colonial Congo began to emerge as a theme in 1966 when Mobutu declared Lumumba a National Hero. This was simply strategic. He then created a personal political instrument, first known as the *Corps des Volontaires de la République* (CVR) which was intended to fight resolutely and firmly against the forces which destroy national consciousness and a sense of responsibility, to assure the education and the supervision of the people in order to build a truly free Congo, to get rid of the fear of imperialism, the exploitation of man by man and obscurantism, and which would be oriented towards the progress of the popular masses.[1]

The CVR believed that a single strong organization of the masses must be begun in order to inculcate a consciousness of their national and international responsibilities. More specifically, they thought that the birth of one or two political parties must be favoured, unburdened by tribalist ideologies that were contrary to the interests of the Congolese people.

As published in the *Manifeste de la N'Sele* on 19 May 1967, nationalism became the doctrinal touchstone of the newly created political party, *Mouvement Populaire de la Révolution* (MPR). It revolved around the affirmation of the independence of the country, for which restoration of the authority of the state

---

[1] Institut Makanda Kabobi, *Histoire du MPR* (Kinshasa Institut Makanda Kabobi, 1975), 109.

was an absolute prerequisite. Party hegemony was imposed upon social groupings and all citizens. Mobutu fused the state and the party structures and the basic slogan was *olinga olinga te ozali na kati na MPR* (willing or not, you are a member of the MPR). Even church leaders were first of all citizens of the country and militants of the MPR. 'This submission cannot be a matter of faith, nor a benevolent engagement, it is a constitutional duty,' insisted Mobutu.[2]

Mobutu's revolutionary movement was 'neither left nor right', and it could not have been derived from alien ideologies. It meant that for the Congolese the pathway to modernity was to be unique, conceived within a national perspective, without reference to foreign thinkers. As Mobutu said:

> The Congolese revolution has nothing to do with that of Peking, of Moscow, or of Cuba. It is not based upon prefabricated theories, or borrowed doctrines. It is revolutionary in its will to base itself upon the population, and [in] its goal, is to change the former state of affairs. But it is a truly national revolution, essentially pragmatic ... It repudiates both capitalism and communism, for both these systems, which dispute the hegemony of the world, have divided countries and peoples into opposed camps.[3]

So, beyond simply restoring the country to order and stability, the regime would carry out a societal transformation without a blueprint. This national revolution had to subdue any authority under the regime's power.

Authenticité

In the *N'Sele Manifesto*, Mobutu emphasized the importance to the Congolese of discovering their own personality by seeking out in the depths of the past, the rich heritage bequeathed by their ancestors. Mobutu clearly expressed it in his speech at the United Nations:

> Authenticity is a 'prise de conscience' by the Zairian nation to return to its own sources, to research the values that belonged to their ancestors, in order to be able to appreciate those which will contribute to its harmonious and natural development. It represents the refusal by the Zairian people blindly to adopt imported ideologies. It is the affirmation of Zairian man, or quite simply of man, just where he is and as he is, with his own mental and social structures.[4]

---

[2] Tshikala K. Biaya, 'Postcolonial State Strategies, Sacralization of Power and Popular Proselytization in Congo-Zaire, 1960-1995', in Abdullahi Ahmed An-Na'im (ed), *Proselytization and Communal Self-Determination in Africa* (Maryknoll, New York: Orbis Books, 1999), 151.

[3] Mobutu Sese Seko quoted by Young and Turner, *The Rise and Decline of the Zairian State*, 210.

[4] Mobutu Sese Seko, *Discours à l'ONU*, 1973.

Mobutu consequently changed all place-names that evoked memories of the colonial past such as Leopoldville and Stanleyville. For him, the renaming of localities and streets, the replacement of Christian forenames with African postnames and the renaming of the country, the currency and the river were all gestures of genealogical dignity, for 'the name and postnames have a deep meaning. They evoke the clan epics, tribal history, the character and personality of the ancestor to be honoured. The restoration of names thus introduces Congolese into the line of their ancestors.' However, regime critics pointed out that 'Zaïre' was in reality a Portuguese deformation of a Kikongo word *nzadi* meaning vast river. Mobutu even went so far as to say that *authenticité* was a tool for evangelism. He stated, 'The Congolese bishops were the first to introduce this great movement of *authenticité* into the Church. The introduction of 'Congolese rites' in Church services was well adapted to our culture, and they make the service to be lively and catchy. We feel closer to God.'[5]

However the concept of *authenticité* encountered a number of critics. The first criticism was about the undue glorification of the past. The Catholic hierarchy detected in *authenticité* an antichurch position in the celebration of the wisdom of the ancestors.

Another troubling intellectual problem lay in defining what cultural heritage served as a point of reference for *authenticité*. For critics such as Tutashinda and Nzongola, *authenticité* was simply irrelevant or worse, for it masked the subordination of the country to external imperialist interests and to the hegemony of the politico-commercial class. They maintained that the portrayal of Congo's problem as primarily cultural deflected attention from the more basic issues of class and dependency.[6] It meant, for those critics, the real problem for Congo was economic rather than cultural. So, Mobutu's emphasis on Cultural Revolution was a deflection of people's attention from the economic issues that they were facing. Indeed, *authenticité* was not a genuine ideology to improve the life of the Congolese, but a cynical use of ideology for power. Mobutu was not sincere in launching *authenticité*, he simply wanted to use the ideology as a manipulating tool to sustain and legitimise his power. Therefore *authenticité* was a complex dialectical power game drawn from Mobutu's own philosophy with supposed precolonial metaphors.

Dialectics of Power

Philip DeBoeck argued that the neologistic cultural doctrine of the '*retour à authenticité*' (return to authenticity) was partly structured around a whole reality of more deeply rooted ideological and symbolical references that drew from a

---

[5] Albin Michel, *Mobutu, Dignité pour l'Afrique* (Paris: Albin Michel, 1989), 114.
[6] Nzongola Ntalaja, 'The Continuing Struggle for National Liberation in Zaire', in *Journal of Modern African Studies* 17, no 4, (December 1979), 595-614, 595.

pool of colonial metaphors and images pertaining to the office of the traditional sovereign paramount.[7] It means that many of the traditional symbols and values related to sovereign rulers have been selectively manipulated to manifest Mobutu's right to power as an ancestral right.

One of the cultural heritages Mobutu discerned was monistic leadership. He reinterpreted and adapted it in his new context, as clearly expressed below:

> In our African tradition, there are never two chiefs; there is sometimes a natural heir of the chief, but can anyone tell me that he has ever known a village which has two chiefs? ... Among us, in the Congo, a chief must seek counsel and inform himself, he must decide and resolve the issue alone, in full cognisance of the problem. For it belongs to the chief to live with his own decision, to evaluate it, and to accept its consequences. It is on this sole condition – because he will have weighed in advance the consequences and accepted alone all the risks of his option – that his decision will be honest, and therefore good for the people and, finally, authentically democratic.[8]

This statement seems to be in contradiction to what he affirmed in *Mobutu, Dignité pour l'Afrique*, 'Democracy has always existed in our villages. It is a union around a chief, seeking the consensus.'[9] However, in both statements, he shows the desire of grouping the energies of the citizens under a single national party. Furthermore, his claim to be the heir of traditional chiefs is a manipulating device since the position of chief was traditionally inherited.

Indeed, Mobutu's interpretation of a chief's authority is different from the traditional view of authority as shown in the previous chapter. Although the chieftaincy was not the same for the whole of the Congo, authority in general was people-centred, controlled by the council of elders. Mobutu was not ignorant of his culture, but his desire was to seek a symbol for proprietary authority which requires personal loyalty instead of an observance of the law, and dependency and submission instead of social autonomy.

The other cultural concept used by political leaders is the father and family image. In almost all Congolese cultures, the role of father was certainly serious and important. The father's position at the head of the nuclear family made him the first concrete representation of authority. Even in matrilineal peoples such as Bakongo, this initial presence of paternal authority is important because the maternal uncle comes to play a dominant role in the child's life and fortunes. The father remains the principal authority in the family because he is the one who 'gives life' and procures the necessary material benefits for the children. He is the provider. In the political area, as expressed by Schatzberg, this imagery is

---

[7] Richard Werbner and Terence Ranger (eds), Postcolonial *Identities in Africa* (London: Zed Books, 1996), 80.

[8] Mobutu quoted by Young and Turner, *The Rise and Decline of the Zairian State,* 211.

[9] Michel, *Mobutu, Dignité pour l'Afrique*, 86.

attractive for it speaks to a psychological need for assurance of security. It creates an intimacy between rulers and ruled, and thus succeeds in representing complex political realities in a simplified form. Furthermore, such symbols and imagery mask an exploitatively unequal flow of resources with authoritarian overtones, paternal 'generosity' and the resultant 'debt'.[10]

If all the president does is for the benefit of the corporate family, sacrifices are necessary for the good of the national family and a vital part of nation building. In this sense, gifts and other manifestations of presidential largesse may be portrayed merely as the father taking care of his children. These metaphors also enabled Mobutu and those in power to portray political repression as firm 'parental' discipline for prodigal 'children' in need of a political spanking for their own good. Speaking before an audience composed of chiefs from Kasai Oriental, the home of many of the dissident parliamentarians, President Mobutu declared, 'I am the chief of state, [and] as such I cannot be vindictive toward those fellow citizens who insult me. In effect, even among my own children there are those who are docile and others stubborn. One must not therefore believe that Tshisekedi, Makanda, Ngalula and their associates are my enemies.'[11] Then he added, 'I am the father of the large Zairian family and if I know how to love, I must equally know how to punish.'[12] It is obvious here that Mobutu manipulated this imagery for his own political purposes.

These images of Mobutu as father and of the state as family were reinforced not merely through the mass media, but also in schools, as in *Bula Matari's* state. Teachers used the regime-approved civic text to teach that the president is chief of the large Congolese family and the father of the Nation, and respect for the public authority is a civic obligation. Of course, such imagery strikes a responsive chord that legitimates governance based on the idea that government stands in the same relationship to its citizens as a father does to his children. But leaders have ignored the cultural norms and understandings they imply.

Re-traditionalisation

Patrick Chabal has profoundly discussed the issue of 're-traditionalisation'. He starts from the observation that much of what is happening in contemporary Africa seems to reinforce the notion that the continent is moving 'backwards', that it is in some ways 're-traditionalizing'.[13] What he means is that what is seen in Africa confounds expectations of modernization. Both the ways in which Africans appear to define themselves and the manner in which they behave fail to

---

[10] Michael Schatzberg, *The Dialectics of Oppression in Zaire* (Blooming: Indiana University Press, 1988), 90.
[11] Schatzberg, *The Dialectics of Oppression in Zaire,* 96.
[12] Schatzberg, *The Dialectics of Oppression in Zaire,* 96.
[13] Chabal and Daloz, *Africa Works,* 45.

conform to what social scientists expect of societies which are modernizing.[14]

He finds there are two aspects of this question. The first is the extent to which individuals in Africa increasingly are, or are perceived to be, behaving according to norms, criteria, values and so on, more associated with those their former colonial masters thought they had constructed. The second is the degree to which politics are supposed to have been.[15] Of course his understanding that a group of people could be regressing is one which rests on an assumption about the linearity of 'progress', and this assumption is held most comfortably by those who see themselves as being at the leading edge of such a process. However, he sees that most of the Africans are today no nearer to being similar to North Americans than they were in the 1960s, and wonders if this is because they have failed to 'develop' or, more realistically, because they are modernizing differently.[16] What Chabal ignores is the fact that all do not have to be like North Americans. That is to impose not only a particular view of progress, but also their human values and destiny on all human beings.

Chabal has discovered that the indicator of such 're-traditionalisation' is not only the apparent resurgence of ethnicity and its attendant 'tribal' politics and violence, but also the importance of African religions, the continued significance of witchcraft, the expansion of criminal activities and the increasing resort to extreme and, often, ritualised violence in situations of civil disorder. Concerning particularly the significance of witchcraft, what Chabal has found interesting is the extent to which it has managed to modernize, to respond to the demands of the contemporary world and to adapt to the needs of Africans in the post-colonial societies in which they live.[17]

Apart from the healing process and the role of binding communities together, Chabal has noticed that witchcraft is used to seek political support, and, in an age of party political competition, multi-party electoral systems could seriously increase the role of witchcraft in modern African societies. This of course is true also in one party states where opponents are 'demonised' and security services play the role of witch finders.

Patrick Chabal's view of re-traditionalisation is obviously radical and negative. It is the theory of 'backwardness'. This aspect of denigration is clearly seen when he says, 'To read about African life today is almost to be transported back a hundred years, when the newly established colonial powers "revealed" to the world how backward Africa was, how much it needed to be civilized. Today, like yesterday, our perception is that Africans continue to be singularly superstitious.'[18]

---

[14] Chabal and Daloz, *Africa Works,* 45.
[15] Werbner and Ranger (eds), *Postcolonial Identities in Africa,* 32.
[16] Chabal and Daloz, *Africa Works,* 46.
[17] Chabal and Daloz, *Africa Works,* 73.
[18] Chabal and Daloz, *Africa Works,* 63.

However, the theory of 're-traditionalisation' also seems partly to express what is happening in Africa. For instance, when Mobutu first launched *retour à l'authenticité* (return to authenticity), its aim was to revive and reinvent traditions, not to seek the base of 'modernity' in precolonial Africa, but to legitimate power and prevent external criticism. But even if Mobutu soon changed *retour à l'authenticité* to *recours à l'authenticité* (recourse to authenticity), the meaning remained the same, because the change was simply a way out of the criticism made by the Catholic hierarchy. Thus *authenticité* was an illegitimate use of tradition to support his own ambitions.

In fact, the secularisation of power by Mobutu was to escape from religious control as an aspect of African holistic life, even though, he rooted his power in the supernatural world. He was a member of a 'secret religion' known as 'Prima Curia', seeking the supernatural protection of the regime. 'He was the "High Priest" offering human sacrifice, and his assistants were untouchable ministers called *Carus frater*, and those ministering for the life of the "High Priest" were called *"frater-2-palmes."*'[19]

When his son Kongolo and his brother successively died in 1996, the Congolese said, 'You (Mobutu) have used *gri-gri* and witchcraft so much that you pay back with the death of your own children. Stop this black magic and this witchcraft because when you use it, you have to pay it back in your own flesh with something dear to you.'[20] Furthermore, Laurent Kabila took power with the help of 'Mai-Mai' (water-water). The name, which is in the Congolese dialect of Swahili, comes from a belief that bullets can be turned to water as a result of the *dawa* (medicine) that is poured over the body to prevent weapons from killing and maiming. Mai-Mai have a strong faith in magic; they do not wash with soap and are forbidden to have sex with women. Many fighters dressed with leaves. Since 27 February 2002, they have been officially recognized as a political force within the country and they therefore have representatives in the Congolese government.

In conclusion, the cultural revolution launched by Mobutu was another way of alienating the people by a blind return to the past when what was needed was an intelligent use of the past in modern times. Therefore the peak of the cultural revolution was the cult of personality, as strongly stipulated by Engulu:

> In our religion, we have our own theologians. In all religions, and at all times, there are prophets. Why not today? God has sent a great prophet, our prestigious Guide Mobutu – this prophet is our liberator, our Messiah. Our Church is the MPR. Its

---

[19] 'Potentiel de Janvier 1991' quoted by E. Gbabendu and N. Efolo, *Volonté de Changement au Zaïre: De l'Acte de la Souveraineté en Acte* (Paris: L'Harmattan, 1991), 209.

[20] Video tape recorded from BBC Two, Storyville, 'Mobutu', 1997.

Chief is Mobutu; we respect him like one respects a Pope. Our gospel is Mobutism. This is why the crucifixes must be replaced by the image of our Messiah.[21]

Therefore, the cultural revolution, built on the philosophy of *authenticité* clearly became a religion, with transference of Christian symbols into that of the state. What, in fact, was the Christian response to the cultural revolution? Was the church in the process of cultural theology affected by the parody of *authenticité*? The following section intends to deal with these questions.

Roman Catholic Church

Theology and political power in post-colonial Congo had the common issue of Africanisation on their agenda for cultural and political freedom. Our aim is to find out how theology intertwined with political power in reinventing traditions of authority for Congolese contemporary society. We will take into account only three main churches recognised by the state.

The Catholic Church is by far the most important religious organisation in Congo. The church owns and controls a vast infrastructure of hospitals, clinics, and social programmes. It educates 60% of the nation's primary school students and more than 40 percent of its secondary students. The Catholic Church was certainly the state's premier ideological apparatus, and helped to ensure the long-term efficacy of the entire colonial system.

The Catholic Church was part of the *'Trinité Coloniale'* (colonial trinity), and it worked hand in hand with the colonial power. But, after political independence, Cardinal Joseph Malula perceived the problems which would result from a unity the church and state shared, and realized this association would cause the church grave problems after independence:

> At the beginning of the evangelisation, church and state walked together. From their collaboration came this abundant harvest ... There also resulted from it a disastrous confusion between the two powers. For our people, the church was the state, and the state was the church. They considered religion as a matter for the Whites ... The two powers are indistinctly accused of colonialism, of wanting to perpetuate their paternalism to maintain Blacks under their dependence. It is time to break these ties.[22]

The aim of breaking these ties was to promote an internal autonomy of the Congolese Catholic Church and it was a reaction against an 'imported Christianity' which fails to distinguish between that which is divine and that which is simply Western. This was a path towards African theology. The idea

---

[21] Quoted in Kabongo Mbaya, *L'Eglise du Christ au Zaïre: Formation et Adaptation d'un Protestantisme en situation de dictature* (Paris: Karthala, 1992), 321.

[22] Malula quoted by Schatzberg, *The Dialects of Oppression in Zaire*, 117.

might have emerged in the publication in 1957 of *Des Prêtres Noirs S'interrogent* (Blacks priests ask themselves questions), which for contributors meant that 'evangelisation should take people's way of life seriously (and that) Christianity was to espouse the forms of local culture'.[23] African nationalism was surely behind this publication, as Mulago noticed that it was not they (students) who pushed to publish their articles, it was Alioune Diop who chose the title *Des Prêtres Noirs S'interrogent.*[24]

Malula thought real efforts at adaptation should be made, for 'the African soul remains untouched'. Although a fervent supporter of Congolese independence, Malula, by 1960, condemned Patrice Lumumba's nationalist government, for in it he perceived both the threat of tyranny and the menace of international communism. However, Malula welcomed the Second Republic and promised Mobutu the Church's full support,

> It is a comfort to us that our government associates itself with us to bend its knees with us before God. Man is big only when on his knees. It is God who distributes authority. Mr president, the church recognizes your authority, for authority comes from God. We will loyally apply the laws that you establish. You can count on us in your work of restoring the peace toward which all so ardently aspire.[25]

Malula believed that it was possible to collaborate with the new regime. It is in this sense that he launched the idea of the objective insertion of the church within the nationalist project of the new regime. At that time, the Archbishop of Kinshasa was extolling the project of the 'Congolese catholic church in the Congolese nation.'[26] In fact Malula wanted to promote a certain internal autonomy of Congolese Catholicism from Rome, the Belgian Catholic church and different Western missionary organisations.

However, Malula became progressively critical of the regime. In September 1971, the state nationalized and unified the three universities, including Lovanium University in Kinshasa. They became *Université Nationale du Congo* (UNAZA). This nationalization of the Catholic university was the beginning of tense relations between the Catholic Church and the regime. When a delegation from the Catholic episcopate met Mobutu on 22 August 1971, seeking to clarify the place of the Catholic Church within the new structure, Mobutu saw their

---

[23] Patrick Kalilombe quoted by John Parratt, *Reinventing Christianity: African Theology Today* (Cambridge: William B. Eerdmans Publishing Company, 1995), 28.

[24] Gordon Molyneux, *African Christian Theology: The Quest for Selfhood* (San Francisco: Mellen Research University Press, 1993), 132.

[25] Schatzberg, *The Dialects of Oppression in Zaire*, 115.

[26] Kabongo Mbaya, *L'Eglise du Christ au Zaire: Formation et adaptation d'un Protestantisme en situation de dictature* (Paris: Karthala, 1992), 303.

intervention as a threat and simply said that, 'There will come a day when the nation will be led by a non Catholic.'[27]

More serious was the state's attempt to implant a section of the *Jeunesse du Movement Populaire de la Révolution* (JMPR) in the Catholic seminaries. The church objected strongly, but then allowed them in minor seminaries. Before that, on 12 June 1969, the political authorities decided that *Manifeste de la N'Sele*, which contains the doctrines of Mobutu, must be taught compulsorily in schools and universities. This politicisation of the education system was a means of reaching the youth. On 30 July 1969, after a demonstration of the students of the University of Lovanium (Catholic), the political office of MPR banned all youth organisations throughout the country in favour of JMPR, the youth movement of the one party. The Catholic Church lost all of its hundred youth organisations.

The situation deteriorated further during the campaign for *authenticité*. The daily Catholic newspaper *Afrique chrétienne* published an article judged to be critical towards the campaign of *authenticité*:

> Are we going to recall an 'original African philosophy' which, if it existed, was merely the expression of a situation and social life continually out-dated … It is not for us today to gain ephemeral satisfaction by insisting loudly on our right to be ourselves and trying to destroy our past as colonised people … We must take action and impose our dignity as Africans through different achievements. The question is not to brandish slogans about our originality, our values, but to practise, in front of the world, that originality and those values.[28]

Consequently 31 journals and periodicals, most of them catholic, were banned by the regime.

As part of the campaign for authenticity, all Congolese had to drop their Christian baptismal names in favour of authentic Congolese ones. Cardinal Malula protested this decision and instructed his bishops to ignore it. In retaliation, the regime seized the Cardinal's residence in Kinshasa and converted it into JMPR headquarters, stripped him of his national honours, and forced him into exile in the Vatican.

By late 1974 and 1975, the state as a 'secular state beyond religion' decided Christmas would no longer be a Congolese holiday and schools could no longer teach courses in Religion. Religious instruction gave way to courses in Mobutism and Engulu, the political Commissioner, likened the president to a new Messiah, a comparison not calculated to please the clergy. He ordered the removal of crucifixes, pictures, or photos other than those of the president, from all public buildings, except private dwellings and places of worship. Mobutu then saw the Catholic Church as a threat to his regime and said:

---

[27] Mbaya, *L'Eglise du Christ au Zaire,* 299.

[28] Mbaya, *L'Eglise du Christ au Zaire,* 302.

The human institution, I say human, which is called the church, which exists at the Vatican, has nothing to do with Zaire, with Mobutu ... We will no longer accept political, economic, religious, or spiritual domination imposed from the outside. Before independence, three authorities were acknowledged: Administration, Business firms, and the Church. The first two have given way; there is no reason why the church should not do the same. I have never had any trouble from the Protestants, nor from the Kimbanguists, because they do not receive their orders from overseas. But the Zairian Bishops do ... They are nothing more than agents working for foreign powers.[29]

In fact, Mobutu wanted to integrate the Catholic Church in his new socio-ideological era of nationalism (with Mobutism). The Catholic Church should receive orders from inside for it used to work with colonizers as part of the 'Colonial Trinity'. As they had left, it was for the Catholic Church to reform its structure to work with the current local 'colonizers'.

The Catholics understood the problem as a clash between two powers, and they pointed out that it was not an ideological or religious conflict; it was rather that:

The Catholic Church (and to a lesser extent other Christian bodies) is the only solidly implanted institution in Zaire which still dares to pass judgement or give directives independently from the political party ... The regime feels it is being observed, scrutinized, and even condemned by the international character of the Catholic Church.[30]

During the 1974 synod in Rome, Cardinal Malula used language very close to Mobutu's ideologies. He showed that he understood the movement of authenticity as applied in Congo, and strongly emphasized the Africanization of Christianity. Was he flattering Mobutu to allow him to come back home from exile? Perhaps. however, it is better to take this in the context of the problem of African Theology, because Congolese Catholic theologians were involved in this problem before Mobutu took power. Another factor is that Catholic leaders were not much interested in Mobutu's authenticity. For instance, his reassertion of traditional Congolese culture does not find a sympathetic echo in the publications of the Faculty, and their articles on the issue of authenticity concentrate mostly on steps towards inculturation advocated by the post-Vatican II Catholic Church.

Mobutu's authenticity did not completely distract leaders' attention from the abuses and violence that were going on. The letter of the Archbishop of Kananga to his parishioners in 1976 was highly critical:

---

[29] *Le Soir* quoted by Molyneux, *African Christian Theology,* 108.
[30] Ngindu Mushete, 'Le propos du recours à l'authenticité et le Christianisme au Zaïre', in *CRA* Vol. 8, no 16, 1974, 10.

At the present hour, we are witnessing an internal colonialism: a class of rich people is in the process of developing whose wealth rests on the misery of millions of citizens; for there exists a large group of those who find themselves rejected on the margins of society and who do not have what they need to live.[31]

In 1976, the Archbishop of Lubumbashi published a pastoral letter denouncing the regime's injustice and corruption. He predicted the revolt of the poor. Effectively, there were soon strikes all over the country, which happened for the first time since Mobutu took power. However, despite tension and hostility, the Catholic Church's position was ambiguous in some ways. Of course it was monolithic and possessed a single voice, but this was in the main ideas of church-state interaction. There were serious differences of opinion within the upper reaches of the Catholic hierarchy, as well as between the bishops and many parish priests.

In the 1970s, Mobutu expressed the view that the crisis between himself and Malula was personal and private, and the state and Catholic Church were not concerned. This was to create more division within the Catholic Church. Mobutu turned to moderate bishops, seeking their support, mainly those who did not have a good relationship with Malula. Even when Mobutu introduced *Jeunesse du Mouvement Populaire de la Révolution* (JMPR) in seminaries, some bishops remained reserved and cautious. Another point is that the hierarchy was certainly aware of the risks more overt political activity could bring. Even Malula himself, although he had periodically criticized the regime, instructed his clergy to avoid situations likely to result in public confrontation with the state.[32] However, some priests organized and led popular protest demonstrations. Ultimately the conflict between the Catholic Church and the Congolese state was about power. Internationally backed, the Church is the only institution with the strength, will and independence to question and criticize the regime openly. People have more confidence in the church than in the state. As Schatzberg has noticed, 'the Church's independent existence as an important focus of social, educational, economic and ideological power makes the Congolese state feel insecure.'[33]

Therefore, Mobutu was interested in ecclesiastical reforms aiming to incorporate the churches in his 'revolution'. Considering the sociological dimension, he wanted the Catholic Church to play the same role as it did during '*Trinité Coloniale*', ignoring its universal institutional reality, and to integrate it at the national level. It was to be the integration of the church in a new socio-ideological era to make it 'an authentically Congolese Catholic Church', which would mean a particular church that was sovereign, and did not receive orders from overseas. Symbolically, it was an attempt of the political power to

---

[31] Mbaya, *L'Eglise du Christ au Zaire*, 306.
[32] Schatzberg, *The Dialects of Oppression in Zaire*, 121.
[33] Schatzberg, *The Dialects of Oppression in Zaire*, 123.

'create' the church with a new ecclesiology. The Catholic Church resisted this attempt, but Protestants and Kimbanguists accepted being churches in this new socio-political environment.

Protestant Churches

The Church of Christ in Congo

We want to consider only the Protestant churches gathered into the Church of Christ in Congo (ECC). The ECC started in 1923, first as the Protestant Council of Congo (CPC) with the aim of representing the Protestant churches and consolidating their efforts to fight the pro-Catholic tendency of the colonial government. But CPC was mainly composed of missionaries. Congolese participation took place for the first time in the CPC meeting which occurred in 1956.[34] CPC became ECC in March 1970, after a long battle with missionaries who did not want to have a 'united church'. ECC professes unity in diversity, and freedom for each denomination to organise its administration, liturgy and doctrine. It consists of 64 denominations, the Anglican Church included. Contrary to the Catholic Church view, for Protestant missionaries in general church hierarchy was not a priority in the process of building local churches. The ecclesiastical model was built on the strong consciousness of the 'scripture-centred' character of the church.

ECC came into existence in a socio-political context particularly hostile to Protestants not only from the government, but also from other churches such as Catholic and Kimbanguists. But despite this hostility, it played a great part in the life of Congolese society. It is running a considerable number of schools, colleges and universities. The schools have a good reputation for moral behaviour, although their overemphasis on the moral aspect initially undermined the drive for academic excellence. It has well equipped hospitals and a considerable number of projects for the welfare of the whole society. In the political area, it has managed to develop a good relationship with the regime, thus having opportunities to advise the political leaders in some matters. Recently, it succeeded in bringing together government groups with their political rivals and rebel leaders enabling them to have a dialogue.

ECC's Support of the Regime

The position of the ECC was at first ambiguous when Mobutu took power. Nothing was noted about his coup either in their official review or in their sermons. This does not mean they were against Mobutu. It was a matter of prudence to be neutral. However, this silence did not last long. Soon the ECC clearly took a position to support the regime when Rev Bokeleale became

---

[34] Mbaya, *L'Eglise du Christ au Zaire,* 198.

president of the CPC. This support resulted in the appropriation of the regime's system.

First the ECC wanted to gain the regime's favour, its protection and thus security. In 1972, the ECC Executive Committee declared, 'We, members of the National Executive Committee of the Church of Christ in Congo, sit in extraordinary session in Kinshasa … officially declare our support to the Founder-President of the national Party, MPR … We support with relief the battle for authenticity.'[35] This was a strong statement for it came from church leaders of different denominations. The ECC leaders considered authenticity as a new start for a successful and honest evangelism of the Congo. This orientation had to be not merely Congolese, but also pan-African to make authentic its aim to revalue the African personality with all its ancestral history. Therefore, the National Executive Committee on 22 April 1972 'recommended all leaders of theological colleges and theological faculties to adapt themselves to this new national option.'[36] The ECC provided Mobutism with a biblical and theological justification of the regime's ideologies. During the 12th anniversary of national independence in 1972, Bokeleale, in his official statement, raised Mobutu to the rank of Noah, Abraham, Joseph, Moses, David and Jesus Christ, Martin Luther King and John XXIII. He implicitly recognized the messianity of Mobutu when he affirmed, 'God needs men to solve the problems in the world … After five years, as our musicians sang, God has given us a man. It is General Mobutu Sese Seko, with a clear mission: give peace in Congo and save our country.'[37] Another statement broadcasted was:

> A powerful political movement characterised by recourse to authenticity seized and raised the national consciousness of the Congolese people. A deep and general change is occurring in the Congolese nation, which gets rid of alienation and colonisation to create its own identity. Attached to the creative Word of God, we recognise in this movement of our epoch a new order of the Lord of the Church. This Lord came to the world for liberation, and thus to liberate Congolese people who, created in the image of God like other peoples, were neglected and exploited. We say a grateful YES to this turning point in history … It is God who gave it to us as our daily bread to nourish the Congolese and for the liberation of the oppressed. Praise the Lord and may he provide this movement and his Guide with wisdom, peace and his love.[38]

It is striking that during the second national synod, Bokeleale insisted that the Christian life and ecclesial realities must conform to values and reforms extolled by the political authorities.

---

[35] Makanzu Mavumilisa, *L'Eglise et l'Authenticité Zairoise,* (Brochure published by Cedi, Kinshasa, 1973), 6.

[36] Mbaya, *L'Eglise du Christ au Zaire,* 311.

[37] Mavumilisa, *L'Eglise et l'Authenticité Zairoise,* 7-9.

[38] Mbaya, *L'Eglise du Christ au Zaire,* 312-313.

In 1974, when Mobutu was lifted up as Messiah, or prophet of the political religion, Mobutism, the Catholic Church reacted by confessing its Christian faith. But ECC leaders reaffirmed Mobutu's mission as sent by God. It is well stated in Jean Makanzu's discussion:

> God was both pastor and Caesar. From Adam to Saul, God was the head of the state, supreme spiritual chief, Chief of the army and general captain. The real Head of state was invisible, but he has his representatives on the earth ... When you are against your king, God will not listen to you (Sam 8,18). Notice that this verse gives a strong position to a human king.[39]

He went on to insist on the collaboration between the church and the state: He has raised us from the animal 'ape' to man created in the image of God. Mobutu gave us another valuable thing: the dignity of black people with which to praise Mobutu. If nobody wants to praise Mobutu, I will do it, for he is the answer to my prayers. I do not pray to the president instead of God, but I pray to the God who gave this chief to the Congolese people. Therefore, as long as the president reigns with the rights given to him by God, any separation between church and state is useless.

He even underlines that the government was inspired by the values and references of Christianity, 'Some missionaries are accusing us of bringing the church as ... a department of the state. It is true, for our government is using biblical language, and it is educating the Congolese according to biblical principles. Some of our president's discourses are simply biblical sermons.'[40]

It becomes clear that, apart from seeking state protection and security, the ECC has offered its support also for material interest:

> When Zaire was a Belgian colony, the separation between the church and the state was necessary. But now that Zaire has become independent, that separation is no longer necessary, for if we want the separation, we must refuse whatever the state offers: tax exemptions for our pastors, grants for our schools, dispensaries and hospitals, plots for the churches ...[41]

The important issue is how authority is understood in the ECC and how it relates to political authority. For Bokeleale, the president of the ECC, respect for authority is biblical. He thus explains, 'For us Protestants, respect for authority is a biblical recommendation: as we respected foreign authorities during the colonial period according to missionary teaching, we must keep the same

---

[39] Makanzu Mavumilisa, *L'Eglise du Christ au Zaïre, son passé, son présent et son avenir* (ECZ, Kinshasa, 1975), 1-3.

[40] Mbaya, *L'Eglise du Christ au Zaire,* 317.

[41] Mavumilisa, *L'Eglise du Christ au Zaïre, son passé, son présent et son avenir,* 5.

attitude. We must love and respect our authorities.'[42] He went on to provide a biblical basis for the respect for state leaders:

> We remember how we used to pray for the dynasty and the King of Belgium. Despite the sufferings caused by colonisation, we never said anything against the King or the Queen, because our missionaries explained to us well that they (kings and queens) were sacred persons, God's anointed … Has the Bible changed? The Word remains the same, yesterday, now and forever. So we owe to our authorities not only respect, but also love.[43]

In fact, the justification is not biblical, but it is built on what missionaries did in the past. What Bokeleale means is that if people respected foreigners, they must respect also indigenous leaders. Doing so is to show obedience to the church's colonial tradition. Bokeleale went on to confirm that respect for authority is expected even when violence is practised, 'We, Congolese Christians, must be serious and accept the lashes that God gives us through the state.'[44] For Makanzu, 'The Congolese have authority in their blood, not as a virus can be in the blood, but as part of the being'.[45] What he means is that the Congolese are naturally predisposed to submission, and they voluntarily accept any manifestation of power. As in the Cultural Revolution, Makanzu misused the reading of the past to serve as the basis for what he wanted to see in the contemporary Protestant church. This is clear in the following quotation:

> Before the arrival of missionaries, each tribe had a traditional chief, who had all the power to maintain order in his tribe. He had authority to protect each member of the tribe, he made the decisions, he showed the path to follow for the welfare of all, he had the last word. Each member feared and obeyed him. When the chief wanted to move, he was carried on a *typoy*. When he wanted to spit the people held out their hands to catch the spittle. He was the intermediary between the living and the ancestors of the tribe … [But also] when missionaries wanted to move, the Congolese used to carry them on *typoy*, as they did for the traditional chiefs. These chiefs lost their power in favour of the missionaries.[46]

What interests Makanzu is the genealogy of the power. He went on to say, 'Because of the power of missionaries, there was peace and order in the denominations. There was no proliferation of sects … We thank our missionaries

[42] Eglise du Christ au Congo, 'Le recours à la Bible pour un christianisme authentique', in Eglise du Christ au Congo, *Procès Verbal*, 1973, 104-105.
[43] Eglise du Christ au Congo, 'Le recours à la Bible pour un christianisme authentique', 105
[44] Quoted in Mavumilisa, *L'Eglise du Christ au Zaïre, son passé, son présent et son avenir*, 19.
[45] Mbaya, *L'Eglise du Christ au Zaire*, 351.
[46] Mbaya, *L'Eglise du Christ au Zaire*, 348.

for their authority. But after independence, they lost their authority, and denominations fell into anarchy and chaos, and the Congolese filled the country with sects that are against authority and missionary doctrines.'[47]

For him, the loss of authority is a sign of social destabilisation. However, Makanzu and Bokeleale are pleading not only for political leaders to be respected, but also for them to be respected as church leaders. They are not on the side of those called to obey, but on the side of the Institution and the political authorities. As leaders of the church at national level, they wish to justify what they want their subjects to do for them. This is clear when they later plead for a centralised, hierarchical and personalised model of institution for the Church of Christ in the Congo, where they are leaders. The issue of authority was seriously discussed during the 1989 synod, as the report states:

> As the Word of God and Bantu tradition teach us to respect authority (parents, socio-political and religious authorities), as according to the Bible every authority comes from God and considering the lack of authority now in our church, the national synod calls all Christians to respect authorities established according to Christian ethical and biblical teaching. The synod also asks all denominations to offer solid Christian teaching on the issue of authority in the family, society and parishes. The synod finally recommends evangelists, pastors and Protestant schoolteachers to encourage respect for authorities in the church, in their campaign of evangelism, their sermons, and their religious and ethical teachings.[48]

However, some Protestant leaders were afraid of the declarations of the ECC national office through its president and evangelist, especially about Mobutu as the (political) Messiah. Probably afraid of what happened to Malula, a great majority of leaders opted for neutrality, and a sort of ideological abstention in a socio-political context, which has hidden its real face from the church.[49] But a small group wanted the ECC to be prudent and to subject all official declarations to all the interested denominations. In fact, the fear was still of having a centralised church structure. The national office was not under the real authority of the synod, and this left the church dependent on the regime. It proves how a minority of the elite can exercise social influence (on power) over a very large majority of a social group.

The Bible and Political Ideologies

Let us see how the ECC offered biblical support to political ideologies, and built its own life on these ideologies. In the 1970s, Mobutu launched the 'Septionat Social' and 'Objectif 80', and the slogan was 'Salongo alingi mosala' (Free

---

[47] Mbaya, *L'Eglise du Christ au Zaire*, 349.

[48] Eglise du Christ au Zaire, *Procès Verbal du Synode National*, 1989, 26.

[49] Mbaya, *L'Eglise du Christ au Zaire*, 323.

service). Everybody had to offer a weekly time for free service to help the government to achieve its goals for remarkable development and social change by the end of 1980. Mobutu dreamt of a paradise for the Congo by the end of 1980 realisable only if the Congolese committed themselves to hard work. The ECC responded to that by taking as its theme for the 1971 national synod, 'Abundant life and the work' (Jn. 10.10). In a telegram sent by the synod to Mobutu, it says, 'Our synod that opened with the theme "Abundant life in Jesus Christ" examines and deepens within the ECC the realisation of our effective contribution to the decade you have declared the 'decade of economy in the service of the Congolese.'[50] In his discourse during the opening session, Bokeleale explained:

> Of course, the Lord, our God, wants an abundant life through work, and here we find biblical explanation for the expression *'Salongo, Congo alingi mosala'* (*Salongo*, Congo needs the work) of the President Mobutu. All Christians, as all citizens, are called to work in order and peace, for it is a sacred and divine order. 'By the sweat of your brow you will eat your food, says the Bible. Sweat is health, for the one who works has health.[51]

> Then the governor of Equateur in the same synod asked members of the ECC to transmit to the Congolese elite a religion which relates to Congolese philosophy, because the religious ideas and realities constitute an important contribution to the harmonious development of the nation, particularly for liberation.[52]

The same theme of free service for the nation appeared again in the synod of 1979, exhorting people to work instead of considering it as a punishment.

Another theme was 'Recourse to the Bible for an authentic Christianity'. The synod in the telegram sent to president Mobutu underlined that this theme shows the 'concern of our church to adapt Christian values to the national context. The ECC welcomed with conviction the spirit of *Salongo* which suits Christian and biblical values. This policy will help our people to live according to the Holy Scriptures, a full and abundant life.'[53]

The synod also asked theologians to do research on Bantu spiritual values so that with the help of 'recourse to authenticity' they could assist the ECC with reference to preaching the gospel. The 1975 synod went so far as to support the change of Christian names to African names imposed by Mobutu. The synod recognised that 'the names which do not have a biblical basis and are not rooted in an African cultural context do not ensure the implantation of Christianity in

---

[50] Eglise du Christ au Congo, *Synode National de l'ECC: La vie en abondance en Christ*, *Procès Verbal*, 1971, 7.
[51] Eglise du Christ au Congo, *Synode National de l'ECC*, 54.
[52] Eglise du Christ au Congo, *Synode National de l'ECC*, 60.
[53] Eglise du Christ au Congo, *Procès Verbal du Synode*, 1973, 23.

the Congo for the future generation. The policy of recourse to authenticity offers the ECC an opportunity for self-criticism, the re-examination of its methodology for evangelism, and Christianity in its current form.'[54]

Also in response to the *septennat du social*, the 1985 synod explored the theme 'The mission of the church today.' The aim was to show that the church must serve people where they are. Of course, to serve the world is the mission of the church. But the question is why ECC leaders have considered the regime's ideologies and the Cultural Revolution as the cornerstone of the church. Could the regime's ideologies constitute a 'dogma' for the church where its only task is to provide them with a biblical and theological basis? Why would the ECC national synods draw their themes from Mobutu's slogans?

It is also striking to see that all general assemblies or synods, not only in the ECC but also in other protestant denominations are opened and closed by a state official. And each national synod of the ECC since 1970 has sent a telegram to the president to praise him for the peace, unity and freedom in the country that help the church to fulfil its mission in society. All that has been said above proves the hidden agenda of the regime as echoed by the political regional commissioner, Djowo Tayeta, during the opening session of the national synod of the ECC in Bukavu on 18 August 1981. He said, 'I am personally pleased that our church is the loyal and faithful auxiliary of the Popular Movement of the Revolution ... I believe that is the church's duty, and in doing so, our church satisfies the aspirations of its followers.'[55]

This 'loyalty' of the church to the state is still impressive in Protestant circles in the Congo. Since the beginning of the war in the Congo in 1996, the ECC has been very supportive, first to the dying regime of Mobutu, then to the Kabila and hereditary regimes. Of course, the war has brought Christian churches and Islam together working to reconcile Kabila's regime with the rebels for the sake of peace. However, the position of the ECC has not yet challenged the regime. For instance, on 16th January 2003, during the remembrance service for Laurent Kabila, assassinated in January 2002, Bishop Marini Bodho, the current President of the ECC, preached from the book of the prophet Zechariah comparing the death of Christ, Messiah, King, Liberator of the human race, to the extreme sacrifice of the life of Laurent Kabila seen as the prince and liberator of the Congolese people. Marini himself has been appointed as the president of the Senate. In his interview with the Catholic agency *Dia,* he underlined that he wanted to give more theological connotation to the work of theologians, and he was in favour of politics with a capital 'P', based on justice, love and reconciliation. We hope the theological connotation Marini is talking about is not

[54] Eglise du Christ au Zaïre, *Procès Verbal du Synode,* 1975, 104.
[55] Eglise du Christ au Zaïre, Synode National, *Un commandement nouveau: Aimez-vous les uns les autres, Procès Verbal,* 1981, 63.

simply the theological politics as before. Many ECC leaders have now joined the government as members of the national assembly and senate.

If the Roman Catholic position was ambiguous vis-à-vis the regimes of the Congo, then protestant churches, including the Anglican Church, showed themselves to be 'loyal' supporters of the regime. But the Kimbanguists' position was even clearer than that of the Protestant churches.

Kimbanguist Church

The Kimbanguist church, or *Eglise de Jésus-Christ sur Terre par le Prophète Simon Kimbangu* (EJCSK) emerged from the prophetic actions and charisma of Simon Kimbangu. Born at Nkamba on 12 September 1887[56] in Bas Congo, not far from Kinshasa, Simon Kimbangu, which means the one who reveals the hidden things, lost his father at an early age. He was introduced as a youth to the Baptist Missionary Society, where he learned to read and to write, and became versed in the Bible. Kimbangu was then appointed as catechist for the area of Akamba.[57]

Concerning the origin of Kimbanguism, Asch explained that Kimbangu's call came from the fact that the lower Belgian Congo, shaken by international turmoil during the First World War, was being ravaged by epidemics of sleeping sickness and, immediately after the war, Spanish influenza, typhoid fever, smallpox and drought. Thus Kimbangu's vision and call came at this time of apparent powerlessness of European medicine on the one hand and the weakening of the Belgian administration as a result of the war on the other.[58]

But, according to Diangenda, Kimbangu's call came from Christ in 1892 while he was praying and received the words: 'Simon Kimbangu, my people are unfaithful. I have chosen you to be my witness and to lead them on the path of truth and salvation. Your mission will be difficult, but do not fear, for I will always be at your side.'[59] On 6 April 1921, Kimbangu healed the woman Nkiantondo. Consequently thousands of people from all over the province and the capital made their way to Nkamba to see what was happening. He not only healed, he also preached. In fact his preaching and healing ministry was only very brief. He preached that fetishes should be cast aside and trust should be placed in God alone. He was concerned with faith in Christ and repentance. He warned his followers not to take part in the dances of the non-Christians and he emphasized purity of morals and monogamy.

---

[56] Diangenda Kuntima, *L'Histoire du Kimbanguisme* (Kinshasa: Editions Kimbanguistes, 1984), 17.

[57] Kuntima, *L'Histoire du Kimbanguisme*, 18

[58] Susan Asch, *L'Eglise du Prophète Kimbangu: de ses origines à son role actuel au Zaïre* (Paris: Karthala, 1983), 9.

[59] Kuntima, *L'Histoire du Kimbanguisme*, 22.

Does Simon Kimbangu and the movement he called forth represent Christian African reaction against colonization and missionary work? This does not seem to be the initial purpose of Kimbangu, for the movement had not been expected. Indeed, with his ministry, Africans were experiencing Christ in a tangible way as he shared their troubles and lived with them. However, his prophecy, 'Whites will change to Blacks and Blacks will become Whites' might have been a reaction against colonization. While interrogated by De Rossi, Judge-President of the military court which condemned Kimbangu to death, Kimbangu replied, 'The meaning of the prophecy will be revealed by God when the time is here.'[60] Thus, Kimbanguists seem to consider the political independence of the Congo as the fulfilment of Kimbangu's prophecy.

From 1946 the Congolese began to proclaim the slogan 'Congo for the Congolese', with a demand for social, economic and political reforms. As previously said, the first cultural and social organisation, which became a political party in 1955, was ABAKO (Alliance des Bakongo). It aimed at the reunification of all the ethnic groups which belonged to the *Bakongo*, separated by the European powers in 1885. Since Kimbangu was a *Mukongo*, there were those who saw in the president Kasavubu, a Mukongo, the emissary or incarnation of Kimbangu and related Kimbaguism to ABAKO, though, as argued by Louise Martin, this was completely contrary to the intentions of the leaders of the Kimbanguist Church.[61] However, even before independence, Joseph Diangenda made clear that the Kimbanguist Church would not interfere in politics and that it left to each individual the decision to join the party which seemed best to him.[62]

However, as Schatzberg has observed, in recent years the Kimbanguist church, although technically apolitical, has fervently supported the Mobutist state and actively uses its religious authority to diffuse the regimes ideological watchwords.[63] Of course EJCSK's political conservatism towards Mobutu's State has enabled it to procure the status of third religious power among the official national institutions. In 1971 the State passed a law recognizing the three major religions: Catholicism, Protestantism, Kimbanguism.

In fact, the Kimbanguist Church has benefited both from its status as an authentically Congolese religion and from the regime's desire to establish friendly relations with another religion to counterbalance its conflict with the Catholics. But the aim of the state to praise EJCSK as being the authentically Congolese religion was to reach the population of Bas Congo where Kimbanguists were based. In 1973, the spiritual leader Diangenda asked

---

[60] Kuntima, *L'Histoire du Kimbanguisme,* 98.
[61] Marie-Louise Martin, *Kimbangu: An African Prophet and his Church* (Oxford: Basil Blackwell, 1975), 118.
[62] Martin, *Kimbangu,* 124.
[63] Schatzberg, *The Dialects of Oppression in Zaire,* 124.

Kimbanguists to take part in, and to submit themselves to the philosophy of authenticity. He also asked them to baptize with African names. But Asch stated Diangenda's important declaration:

> As one of the objectives of the Kimbanguist church is to ensure the symbiosis, harmony of secular and spiritual values of man for his total blossoming and for the redemption of his soul; considering the saving action of the new regime in favour of the cultural and religious values, authentically Congolese, denied by foreign civilian and religious power; the Kimbanguist church expresses to the Father of the Nation its sincere gratitude for the kindness, and, particularly, for the cultural and religious revolution, authentically Congolese.[64]

It can be noticed that the Kimbanguist church did not intend to offer a theological legitimacy to the regime's ideologies. But the fact that EJCSK's main objective was to ensure the symbiosis and harmony of secular and religious values prove their desire to be the national or official church in the Congo.

The Kimbanguist church went far in adopting the state as a normative organizational model. The church members wear shirts and dresses with the leaders' picture on them, the church leader is referred to as the 'Guide'; members must carry their church cards as citizens do for the state, and church officials rotate outside their regions of origin to depoliticise ethnicity and centralize power. As in the political sector, the Kimbanguist leader requires absolute obedience, does not tolerate doctrinal disputes, and insists on all communicants being 'militant' participants in the life of the church.[65] Therefore, the Kimbanguist church has fully supported the post-colonial regimes. Consequently, it has adopted the state as a normative organisational model.

Conclusion

Pre-independence Congolese nationalism, as in other African countries, was an anticolonial movement that intended to restore the old political order based on precolonial principles. But in post-colonial Congo, the Cultural Revolution based on nationalism and the philosophy of authenticity became an alienating tool, using the past to introduce new elements for domination and exploitation.

The Roman Catholic Church, although ambiguous in its position, was able to challenge the post-colonial regimes. This was not only because of its international institutional structure, but also because of its socio-cultural hegemony in the Congo. But for the Protestant churches weakened by internal denominational divisions, and Kimbanguists suffering from persecution, political independence meant not merely the restoration of socio-religious equality, but also it was an era for new alliances. For them it was time to take

---

[64] Asch, *L'Eglise du Prophète Kimbangut*, 133-134.
[65] Schatzberg, *The Dialects of Oppression in Zaire*, 124.

over the authority the Catholic Church had enjoyed in the past. It was a competition for a new dynamic of social integration, for the 'Church' was the one institutionalised and legitimised by the state. Therefore these churches became the 'branches' of the political party, and they have opted to clone the state's authority as a normative organisational model. In the following chapters, we shall examine the process of 'cloned authority' in the Anglican Church of Congo (CAC) and its theological impact on the self-understanding and exercise of authority in the life of the church and society.

Chapter Three

Authority in the Earlier Anglican Church of Congo

Historical Background from Uganda

The Anglican Church of Congo was founded by Ugandan Evangelists and functioned under the Church of Uganda from 1896 to 1972, when it was given its first diocese. So the study of the early Anglican Church in Uganda sheds light on the historical facts which have partly contributed in shaping the understanding and the exercise of authority in the contemporary Anglican Church of Congo.

Earlier Christianity in Buganda

Buganda, one of the main tribes in south Uganda, was a prosperous, well-organised, and militant kingdom, dominated by its king, *Kabaka* Mutesa, and it was expansive and receptive to new ideas. The political history of Buganda in the second half of the nineteenth century is intertwined with the introduction of foreign religions. Arab traders initially came to Uganda during the first quarter of the nineteenth century. The first known Arab to come to Uganda and remain to teach the principles of Islam was Ahmed bin Ibrahim in 1844. *Kabaka* Mutesa became a Muslim during the early 1870's and many of the Baganda followed him into Islam.[1] At that time East Africa was experiencing the disruptive effects of the growing slave trade by Arabs. Burning with indignation at the suffering and oppression borne by Africans, David Livingstone (1813-1873) travelled extensively throughout East Africa and he was convinced that an end to suffering

---

[1] G. Van Rheenen, *Church Planting in Uganda: A Comparative Study* (California: William Carey Library, 1976), 15.

would only come through the radical reordering of society: 'I go back to Africa to make an open path for commerce and Christianity.'[2]

In 1875 Henry Morton Stanley visited Buganda when *Kabaka* Mutesa had two major concerns. The first was fear of the possible resurgence of the neighbouring rival kingdom of Bunyoro. Furthermore, Mutesa feared the steady advance of Egyptians with well-armed troops, aimed at domination of the entire Nile basin and the lake. Buganda lay between the lake and the approaching Egyptians forces. The second threat was his physical body infected with gonorrhoea.

Stanley advised *Kabaka* that he could counter the Egyptian threat by acquiring his own European-Christian missionaries who 'would do better than the potentially suspect Muslim traders from the coast, who were anyway merely middlemen in the vital importation of guns, bullets and powder; those who actually manufactured the arms were Christian Europeans.'[3] Stanley, presenting Christian Missionaries as 'superpower' appealed for missionaries to come to Buganda and not to fear for the expenses. In his letter to the Daily Telegraph of 15 November 1875, Stanley wrote:

> It is not the mere teacher that is wanted … He must be tied to no Church or sect, but profess God and live a blameless Christian life. He must belong to no nation in particular, but the entire white race. Such a man Mutesa invites to report to him … You need not fear to spend money upon such a mission as Mutesa is sole ruler, and will repay its cost tenfold with ivory, coffee, otter skins of a very fine quality, or even in cattle, for the wealth of this country in all these products is immense.[4]

Indeed Stanley's description of Buganda was not simply an ill populated and poverty-stricken land, but a welcoming and rich country. However, the way he presented Mutesa as the sole ruler who was able to pay back the missionaries' expenses is again to identify the ruler with the wealth of his country.

As a response to Stanley's letter, the first Anglican missionaries from the CMS arrived in Uganda in 1877, followed by the first Catholics, the White Fathers in 1879. King Mutesa was glad to have at least two groups of Europeans in his country to add to Arabs already there. He made absolutely sure that they should never leave his court. According to Adrian Hastings, these Arabs and Europeans were to be Mutesa's mentors about the world, its politics and religion, pleasant conversationalists, or just playthings.[5] We argue that recognition of the

---

[2] Adrian Hastings, (ed), *A World History of Christianity* (London: Cassell, 1999), 213.

[3] John Rowe, 'Mutesa and the Missionaries: Church and State in Pre-Colonial Buganda', in Holger Bernt Hansen and Michael Twaddle (eds), *Christian Missionaries and the State in the Third World* (Oxford: James Currey, 2002), 52.

[4] Rheenen, *Church Planting in Uganda*, 16.

[5] Adrian Hastings, *The Church in Africa 1450-1950* (New York: Oxford University Press, 1994), 374.

potential material gains was the reason behind Mutesa's tolerance of foreign influences. Of course, by the time the Europeans came to Buganda, Mutesa was a mature ruler and his control over his kingdom was complete. Strangers were not allowed to wander over the kingdom for whatever purpose and any transactions they wished to carry out in Buganda were closely supervised by the *Kabaka* or by his chiefs. So for Mutesa, each group of foreigners represented something which Buganda could utilize to its advantage. As Richard Reid emphasized, 'The coastal traders were agents of the vital international trade system, connected to Zanzibar, carried to Buganda cloth and guns among other commodities. The European missionaries were similarly ambassadors of powerful technological culture whose presence in Buganda could only lead to the Kingdom's advancement.'[6] But when the *Kabaka* soon found that Christianity was likely to prove just as subversive as Islam, some one hundred Christian converts were burnt to death, many at Namugongo execution site. The aim was not to systematically eliminate the Christian community, but to intimidate, to get rid of rivals, to make clear that the *Kabaka* should be obeyed, not foreign missionaries. This resulted in a coalition of Muslims, Catholics and Protestants, who overthrew *Kabaka* and seized power in 1888. But this coalition did not last long. They were soon involved in a struggle which was only solved by colonial force and the emergence of Protestant factions as political victors, but under British overrule. It must be underlined that the Protestants had a considerable position, as Kevin Ward stated, 'It (The Native Anglican Church) had a quasi-established position in colonial Uganda. The Bishop of Uganda was third in precedence in the colonial state after the Governor and the *Kabaka* ... In Bishop Tucker's time (1890-1911), the Church had often seemed the dominant partner in this alliance.'[7]

However, at this earlier stage, if the missionaries found themselves Africanised, a whole Ganda ruling class became Christianised and, within a remarkably short period of time, initiated a thoroughgoing Christianisation of the society. Islam survived as an important minority; but the Christian Church, in both its Protestant and Catholic versions, became integral to Ganda society. However, 'the NAC was closely identified with the group of Baganda Protestant chiefs who had consolidated their power in 1900. It was they who dominated the lay representation on the Diocesan Synod, a body which covered the whole diocese of Uganda.'[8] They then felt that it was their responsibility to spread the

---

[6] Richard J. Reid, *Political Power in Pre-Colonial Buganda: Economy, Society and Warfare in the Nineteenth Century* (Oxford: James Currey, 2002), 6.

[7] Kevin Ward, 'The Church of Uganda and the Exile of Kabaka Mutesa II, 1953-55', in *Journal of Religion in Africa* (Volume XXVIII, Leiden, The Netherlands: Koninklijke Brill NV, 1998), 411-449, 4.

[8] Ward, 'The Church of Uganda and the Exile of Kabaka Mutesa II', 416.

Gospel to other parts of the country. But this had to be done through different Ugandan social systems.

A whole Ganda ruling class became Christianised and, within a remarkably short period of time, initiated a thoroughgoing Christianisation of the society. The Ganda evangelical movement swept almost at once beyond the borders of Buganda in all directions, and Christian Baganda were appointed as chiefs over non-Baganda in spite of social system differences. This happened when the tiny British administration was battling to establish its control over the peoples around.

In the Bantu kingdoms of Bunyoro, Toro and Ankole, Protestant Ganda success here too was closely related to political factors. The rulers adopted Christianity as British power became incontestable; the model of Christian, and especially Anglican, chieftainship became dominant in Buganda, the principal state in the area. Kasagama of Toro was baptized in 1896, Kitehimbwa of Bunyoro in 1899 and Kahaya of Ankole in 1902.[9] It is only after these chiefs with their subchiefs had adopted Christianity that they became patrons of Ganda catechists. When tensions arose, these local chiefs were now empowered to ask Baganda catechists to be driven out, and they could make demands for the Bible and Prayer Book to be translated in local languages.

Therefore, it is true that Baganda were looking for a sort of paramountcy over its neighbours and wanted to use both British rule and Christianity to extend the size of the country. Also the spread of the movement out across the countryside depended largely upon the favour of the chiefs. However, the spread of Christianity would have been unthinkable without the Baganda evangelists, who were to be found by 1910 throughout most of what is today Uganda and beyond. If in some cases they were cultural sub-imperialists, arrogant and unwilling to use language other than their own, in others they proved to be the most committed and unbiased of missionaries.

Ugando-Anglican Hybridisation of Authority

It was part of Anglican tradition to have a lay element in the government of the Church. From an earlier stage CMS was aware of the special advantages in the Uganda setting of creating a platform for political leaders within the framework of the Church. And the Protestant structure was built as a mechanism for using its domination within the African political system. This approach allowed the Protestant church to exploit its advantages over the Catholics in the political sphere, and it served to institutionalise the linkages between the two systems. In fact the *Kabakaship* was the subject of the battle in the 1890s between the Protestant and the Roman Catholic missions.

---

[9] Hasting, *The Church in Africa 1450 – 1950,* 469.

The CMS interest in the *Kabakaship*, as Holger B. Hansen noticed, 'was not only prompted by the strategic consideration that building on the *Kabaka*'s inherited authority would facilitate access to Buganda society, but also by the assumption that a Protestant *Kabaka* would give the impression that Protestantism was the established religion of Buganda.'[10] Moreover, it was not enough that there was a Christian King on the throne of Buganda, he must also be a Protestant King. This is why, when the *Kabaka* Daudi Chwa was approaching the age of five in 1901, CMS insisted that his education should be based upon Christian principles. Then the CMS mission was pleased when J.C.R. Sturrock, a young member of the colonial administration, was appointed to look after *Kabaka*'s education, for he was both Anglican and an English gentleman, and had the full confidence of the mission.[11]

Therefore *Kabaka* became the pillar of the religious as well as of the political system. *Kabaka* was considered as a symbol of church's authority and power to act in the society. The christianisation of the traditional centre of power can clearly be seen during the investiture of *Kabaka* in 1914. For Protestant Baganda leaders, the Bishop's presence was necessary for the 'coronation of a Christian *Kabaka*', although the colonial administration was not happy with Protestant supremacy. During the coronation, Bishop Tucker 'drew implicit parallels to European monarchies by speaking of the *Kabaka*'s 'responsibilities as a Christian prince'.[12] Thus the coronation was carried out in accordance with Anglican prescriptions. However a number of traditional elements were included to underline its legitimacy, mainly the fact that the ceremony was held at the traditional site, the sacred Budo Hill. Hastings' argument for the use of this traditional site is that the *Kabaka* ruled not only by God's grace, but also with the blessing of his ancestors, it acknowledges the continued strength of the old gods.[13] However, neither Anglicans nor traditional Baganda separated the King's authority from the priest's authority. The priest was like 'the prophet' in the King's court. The source of their authority was from God. Ancestors from the African view were only channels of authority from God himself.

The 1900 agreement of Buganda gave chieftainships to the predominating religion in each *saza* (county). This gave Anglicans control of most of Buganda and Anglicanism gained a foothold within the political system of Uganda. Therefore, Christianity and politics remained inseparable within the framework of colonial history as F.B. Welbourne said, 'To be Christian was inseparable from being a citizen. Religion and politics were part and parcel of the same

---

[10] Holger Bernt Hansen, *Mission, Church and State in a Colonial Setting: Uganda 1890-1925* (London: Heinemann, 1984), 318.

[11] Hansen, *Mission, Church and State in a Colonial Setting,* 318.

[12] Hansen, *Mission, Church and State in a Colonial Setting,* 321.

[13] Hansen, *Mission, Church and State in a Colonial Setting,* 321.

complex relationship to God and the king ... There was no easy distinction between "political" and "religious" considerations.'[14]

The 'hybridisation' of Christian authority with traditional authority was not confined to Buganda, but also took place in the neighbouring Kingdoms. For instance in Toro, the *Omukama* Daudi Kasagama stated that the time had come for a revival of the *Empango*, an ancient coronation ceremony, and decided that the celebration should have taken place on the anniversary of his baptism, on which occasion a special service had been held every year.[15] As 'the Christian King wanted a Christian priest to place the crown upon his head, the missionary delegated to Toro was called in to officiate'. It is remarkable here that this was happening on the initiative of the *Omukama* himself. It confirmed that African political leaders were fully aware of the possibility of using the mission and the church for their own purposes.

In Bunyoro in 1908, the time was considered ripe to perform the ancient coronation ceremony as in Toro. 'At the insistence of the *Omukama* the dedication of the new Anglican Church was combined with the coronation. The missionary in charge of Bunyoro, the Rev A.B. Fisher, crowned the *Omukama* with the full approval and active participation of the government.'[16] A Church event and a state event had been combined. According to the Sub-Commissioner, this symbolized the progress of Bunyoro and marked the common aim towards which the mission and the government were working: 'the welfare of the country and the happiness of the people'.[17] Events were influenced by the mission's automatic application of an Anglican-monarchic model in its dealings with the institution of kingship in Uganda.

However, in the 1900s the government felt that its authority was now threatened because of the alliance between the Protestant chiefs and the CMS mission. The government found that the time had come to teach them a lesson, 'I think the time has come to make the principle that the *Katikiro* and the CMS are not the governors, pastors and masters of the *Kabaka*, and that there is an exterior power to which they must bow.'[18] In fact Protestant dominance raised two problems for the Government: it had to strengthen the position of the Catholic leader in the *Lukiko*; and it had to curtail the power of the *katikiro* and instil in him more respect for the colonial authorities. The concern of the government was how much importance should be granted to religious factors in arriving at political decisions. They had also to decide whose authority in native affairs was paramount. Surprisingly, although the government secured certain minority

---

[14] Frederick Burkewood Welbourne, *East African Rebels* (London: Oxford University Press, 1961), 2-3.

[15] Hansen, *Mission, Church and State in a Colonial Setting*, 322.

[16] Hansen, *Mission, Church and State in a Colonial Setting*, 323.

[17] Hansen, *Mission, Church and State in a Colonial Setting*, 323.

[18] Hansen, *Mission, Church and State in a Colonial Setting*, 319.

rights for the Catholic faction, the Protestant hegemony at the centre of power represented by the *Kabakaship* was untouched. As Hastings remarked, 'In this case the government worked within a framework formed by a high degree of religious involvement in politics and Protestant political dominance.'[19] The government had not succeeded in neutralizing the religious element in political decision-making, but accepted its existence as a necessary basis for action. Nor did it succeed in reducing the importance of the Protestant establishment. Therefore the relationship between traditional authority and missionary authority resulted in a new 'hybrid authority', used as a mission model of authority to implant Christianity in other new areas, such as the Democratic Republic of Congo.

Implantation of Anglicanism in Congo

The Anglican Church in Congo developed as a result of the immigration of several groups of people. The first group of evangelists entered Congo through Boga from Toro in Uganda. They influenced the southern part of the present dioceses of Boga, Kisangani, Bukavu (excepting the archdeaconry of Goma) and Kindu. The second migration was of Anglicans from Zambia, who in the early 1950s laid the foundations of the church in Shaba. The other wave was the influx of refugees from Gisenyi in Rwanda who planted the Anglican Church in the border zone between Congo and Rwanda before 1970, preceding the arrival of Canon Mukasa and Rev. Sebicirare. This last area forms part of the present archdeaconry of Goma. The Ugandan refugees who took refuge in the zones of Aru and Mahagi about 1980 constitute the last group. In this work, we will mostly consider the waves of immigration from Uganda as they cover the area of our study, and also because they were first indigenous missionaries to spread Anglicanism in new areas.

Ugandan Missionaries in Congo

The Ugandan missionaries first entered Boga, a territory west of the Semliki river which was included within the British 'sphere of influence', the boundary between Belgian and British territory being marked by the supposed position of the 30 meridian of longitude east of Greenwich.[20] The people of Boga, originally pastoral Bahuma, moved from Bunyoro, possibly in the latter half of the seventeenth century. Boga sub-dynasty was originally established by the chief

---

[19] Hastings, *The Church in Africa 1450-1950*, 320.
[20] Anne Luck, *African Saint: The Story of Apolo Kivebulaya* (London: SCM Press, 1963), 68.

Isingoma of the Muboro clan, who got into trouble with the royal house of Bunyoro and fled to the high grassland west of the Semliki river.[21]

In 1894 the *Mukama* Tabaro, the seventeenth incumbent of this sub-dynasty, crossed the Semliki to visit the newly installed Christian chief Kasagama in Toro, and asked that his territory might also come under British protection. There Tabaro heard about the new 'reading', and Kasagama told him that it was good, as everyone in Buganda was reading. Considering the fact that Christianity was the major requisite to enter the 'new order' of the missionary and colonial 'world', Tabaro therefore asked for Baganda teachers, and soon Petro and Sedulaka were sent to join Tabaro in Boga. Indeed, they succeeded in building a small church near the *kikale, Mukama*'s compound. However, they were soon forced to return to Toro because, as Yakobo Tibenderena stated, 'They were somewhat arrogant, and also they refused to join in beer-parties, which were a constant feature of the *Mukama*'s establishment. As a result, Tabaro forbade the people to feed the teachers.'[22]

In August 1896 when A.B. Fisher and A.B. Lloyd visited Boga, they found that people were enthusiastic for further teaching, although the *Mukama* was not keen. They decided to send a reliable teacher, and Apolo Kivebulaya volunteered to go with another Sedulaka. Apolo, formerly known in the name of Waswa, the converted drunkard and opium smoker, had been a Moslem, forced to join their army and participated in their cruel raids against Christians. For instance one day Apolo and his group raided the country and performed deeds of sickening cruelty, setting huts on fire after having tied the men, women, and children to the surrounding banana trees, so that in the heat of the burning huts they begun to burst like dried maize being roasted.[23] Apolo later stated, 'I could see no love in the Moslem religion and so I resolved to run away, and then joined the Protestant Christians. It was then that I really began to be friends with the readers.'[24] Once at Boga, Apolo, having taken with him his hoe handles, was warmly welcomed by the *Mukama* Tabaro who beat the drum to call the people and asked his subjects to feed Apolo until his garden produced. They also helped Apolo to build the teachers' house, which was square with openwork reed walls, unlike the local round grass huts. In fact it was the Bagandan style of buildings. This already showed the 'external' character of Christianity in Boga. However, there was no warm response to Christian teaching, partly because the first teachers had been so easily driven away. It is therefore in this political background of bringing Boga under British control that the first Ugandan Anglican missionaries came to Congo.

[21] Luck, *African Saint*, 68.
[22] Eglise Anglicane du Zaïre, *Kwa Imani Apolo: Maisha ya Apolo Kivebulaya* (printed in Great Britain, filmset by Northumberland Press, Gateshead, Tyne and Wear, 1986), 4.
[23] Luck, *African Saint*, 45.
[24] Luck, *African Saint*, 45.

Methodology of Evangelism

From his arrival, Apolo's priority was to equip young people for Christian ministry by starting literacy lessons, biblical teaching and catechism. The same concern encouraged him to send certain young people to study in Uganda. Such was the case of Nassani Kabarole and Yusufu Lumenya. In fact, Christian missions were the first to bring education to Congo and still most schools are controlled by the churches. In Boga, education was brought by the Ugandan missionaries who followed the same model used in their country. As Frederick B. Welbourne found in East Africa, in Congo also there was no distinction between the concepts of 'to read' and 'to go to church'. Both are expressed as *kusoma* (literally, 'to read'),[25] and the same word is still used. The same building used to serve both as place for prayers and as a classroom for school. Thus, the school functioning in the church building was considered as a sort of initiation into the local Christian community.

Furthermore, education served as a tool for separating Christian youths from their pagan environment so that they might be 'thoroughly converted'. In Boga, Apolo had a house with several rooms. Young boys and girls were sent to live with him, and they worked as servants when there was no school. Widows and women who had been deserted occupied a house in the compound. They would do the cooking for the household and cultivate his garden. It was believed that this household cluster of women and young people followed the traditional social pattern, but the difference was that in Apolo's home it appears to have been purified. As Erisaniya said, 'Apolo's house was a holy house; you would feel that you must not do anything wrong in that place.'[26] The tension between the 'old sacralisation' as lived in traditional society, and the 'new sacralisation' as brought by Christianity is evident. Therefore, education was not only the key to enter the 'new civilization', but also meant to enter the 'new sacralisation' of the 'new world'.

Moreover, Apolo's method, as that of other missionaries of his time, was of approaching the ruler and sub-chiefs first. This policy suited Tabaro who was looking for powerful allies to tackle Lega's and the Belgian invasions. In this sense, it is important to notice that the request for *waalimu* (teachers) was primarily politically motivated, although the missionaries tended to think that the development represented a change of attitude of rulers towards their work. Like *Kabaka* in Buganda, Tabaro was interested in political survival rather than religious 'conversion'. Furthermore, Tabaro knew that *waalimu* would be useful to help him understand the new world that was invading the traditional world. That is why he agreed to feed them and help them to build their houses nearby his *ekikali*. Therefore the realization that the missions were a channel to new sources

---

[25] Welbourne, *East African Rebels,* 188.
[26] Quoted in Luck, *African Saint,* 45.

of power, influence and security made it possible for the local people to participate in spreading Christianity.

Hema Missionaries

Hema played a remarkable role in spreading Christianity in Congo, mainly in the Anglican Church. Indeed, the church remained for nearly a decade without any expansion out of Boga. But Apolo, with the help of Baganda missionaries, trained Hema to take the gospel to other places. They succeeded in planting churches in the villages of Buley, Kyabanganzi, Bukima, Bundingiri, Kainama and Bulega. The two last were among Nande and Lendu. In 1924, they had already planted seventeen new churches. It is interesting that women took part in evangelism right at the beginning of the Anglican Church in Congo, as Apolo's report shows:

> On 23 February 1924, I set out on a visit to the churches, Bukima, Tchabi, Bundingiri ... We took some women teachers, Meri and Yunia. At Tchabi we gathered about 20 Bahuku. We got to the house of Selemani at Kainama, we found the teachers Edward Byakisaki and Efrahimu here. We prayed with about 40 people. We built there a church and a house for the teacher.[27]

Women's involvement in evangelism at this earlier stage seemed to be accepted by the people in Boga for there were women priests in their traditional religion. Indeed, Hema were courageous to spread Christianity. However, like Baganda, they used to despise other tribes, as was noticed by Pygmies: 'Apolo had great patience with Pygmies and their ways and customs. They knew he loved them and therefore he could manage them, but they knew the teachers did not care for them, the Banyamboga despised them.'[28]

Again the Anglican Church remained stagnated in the rural zones of Boga and the northwest part of Beni. There are three probable reasons for this. First, the church could not go beyond the mission field attributed to CMS by the Edinburgh Conference of 1910. The region given to CMS was situated more in the British colonies than in French-speaking countries. Secondly, the Belgian colonials did not encourage the missionary work of churches other than the Roman Catholic Church, which followed the political aspirations of the Belgians. However, it is worth noticing here that in all the years Apolo was in the Congo he was helped and respected by the Belgian administration. The last reason is the ethnic appropriation of the Gospel at Boga and its environs. The church was thought to be an ethnic religion. It is only in the 1970s that Anglican

---

[27] Quoted in Luck, *African Saint*, 128.
[28] Quoted in Luck, *African Saint*, 131.

Church reached other regions apart from Lubumbashi, but again through Hema missionaries, or those associated with them.

In fact, during its late geographical growth, the Anglican Church suffered from the doctrinal problems arising from a hasty acceptance of members of fringe churches. For instance, in 1972 when the government decreed that all Protestant churches should belong to one of the Church of Christ (ECC) member communities, many independent churches which were not able to obtain the civil authorization asked to join the Anglican Community. Most of them were African initiated churches. In Maniema, The Free Protestant Church of Congo joined the Anglican diocese of Bukavu, while in Kisangani The Independent Church of Central Congo and others from the Baptist Missionary Society joined the Anglican diocese. Similarly in Shaba, the small independent churches asked to join the Anglican churches. Indeed it was a numerical boom, but it brought many practical and doctrinal problems. Several groups took time to adapt to the Anglican way of doing things. It is not clear why these independent churches chose to integrate with Anglican Church. However, the 'openness' and the interest in numerical and geographical expansion by the Anglican Church might be among the reasons. As Isingoma Kahwa said, 'Anglican Church in Congo is more inclusive than exclusive like other churches are.'[29] The question is how authority functions in this 'inclusivity'.

Authority in the Earlier Anglicanism in Congo

This section intends to analyse the impact of CMS missionaries and the Church of Uganda in decision-making in Congo and the tension between authority in traditional society and the authority in the Anglican Church.

The Englishness of Authority

Waswa was baptized on 27 January 1895, and took the name Apollos (Apolo in Luganda), having in mind the passage, 'and being fervent in the spirit, he spoke and taught diligently the things of the Lord' (Acts 18.25). As name is an important element in African culture, he wanted to acquire a biblical name which would give him authority to carry out the ministry. He then acquired another name, 'Kivebulaya', meaning literally 'the thing from England'. This name was given him on account of his clothes, because he wore a scarlet military jacket over a white *kanzu.* Did Apolo get it when he served in Lugard's small police patrol in 1891? A.T. Schofield, missionary doctor in Toro, suggests it was a guardsman's red dress tunic, which had been given him by an English officer, probably Major Roddy Owen.[30] The issue is that Apolo would never be parted

---

[29] Isingoma Kawha, interview in Bunia, 17 October 2001.
[30] Schofield quoted by Luck, *African Saint,* 62.

from his jacket, and as Ruth Fisher, wife of the Rev. A.B. Fisher, the pioneer missionary to Toro, confirmed, 'When he (Apolo) was to be ordained a deacon in 1900 it was with great difficulty that he was persuaded to take off his favourite red jacket.'[31] To keep this red jacket on the white *kanzu* now worn by all men of substance, stood in Apolo's mind as a symbol of the origin of his new identity and in consequence the symbol of his authority. This became clear when he first went with the good news in his heart to Toro; he looked upon himself as 'the messenger of the good tidings from England.'[32]

Consequently, the belief in 'Englishness of authority' led Apolo and other Ugandan missionaries to rely on British missionaries' authority. For instance, when in 1897 Elizabete Ruhubya came to see Apolo and asked him to enrol her to 'read' for baptism, her husband came with spear and throwing stick, and threatened to spear Apolo if his wife was to be baptized. Apolo's response showed he was simply acting on behalf of Englishmen, 'I shall not baptize her, the Englishmen will, I shall just write her name down and she will come to be instructed.'[33] But when the British missionary Lloyd came to visit Boga, he got the matter settled. Elizabete's husband had to join the 'reading' and *Mukama* Tabaro agreed to allow people to read for baptism. Even when Apolo built a church for the pygmies, he named it the J.J. Willis church. This name was a reminder of missionary authority among pygmies. Missionaries were seen as a blessing for local people as evidenced in their response. Anne Luck relates how enthusiastic people pleased them when they visited Boga, 'They came in upon us in great crowds, embracing and shaking hands with us again and again, and thanking us for coming to them. It was most touching to see their simple trust in us, and the fixed conviction in their minds that we were in some way to be a means of blessing to them ...'[34]

People transferred the symbols of traditional authority to the new masters. Missionaries were also carried on *typoy*, traditional chairs occasionally used for traditional chiefs. For instance, in 1934 when Rev Lloyd visited different churches, he travelled in his carrying-chair, carried by eight persons, and he used others as bodyguards with spears. Lloyd himself narrated the tour:

> On and on I went over the hills. On every hillside I was met by crowds of children as well as men and women. Sometimes the young Christians were so delighted to see me that in order to show their joy, they asked my carriers to give place to them and allow them to carry me. Often the results were not quite satisfactory, for their

---

[31] Ruth Fisher quoted by Luck, *African Saint,* 62-63
[32] Luck, *African Saint,* 63.
[33] Luck, *African Saint,* 71.
[34] Luck, *African Saint,* 71.

inexperience of the ways of a carrying-chair, and their excess of enthusiasm, made my seat uncomfortable and indeed precarious.[35]

The Englishness of authority in the Church was also due to the name 'Anglican' given to the Church. The 'Anglican Church *in* Congo' was seen as an English church transplanted in Congo. Therefore it was worthwhile and vital to remain linked to the 'Mother church' in England through British missionaries. This needed obedience from local people. This is why appointments as catechists to work with missionaries were based on 'good behaviour' rather than on educational criteria. But Ugandan missionaries played a great role in this transference of the symbols of the local traditional authority to the missionaries' authority.

The Ugandanness of Authority

The *Ugandanness* of authority also played a remarkable role in the growing Anglican Church of Congo, which functioned under the complete control and administration of the Church of Uganda over a long period from 1896 to 1972. Dirokpa Balufuga attests that the synods which used to decide on the future of the Anglican Church of Congo were held in Uganda without the involvement of any Congolese.[36] Therefore the decision-making authority was held in Uganda and the destiny of the Anglican Church of Congo was decided in Uganda. Moreover, to train Congolese people for the ministry was not a priority of the Church of Uganda. Luck reported, 'The catechists sent over from Toro (Uganda) as teachers were ill equipped for their immensely important work of preaching, teaching, evangelising the heathen, and shepherding the faithful.'[37]

Cultural elements such as clothing were also part of *Ugandanness*. The *Kanzus* were long robes for men in Buganda. It was brought by Muslims, and then became traditional Buganda clothing. In Buganda, all Christians had to wear white *Kanzus*, which was also a symbol of 'holiness'. Apolo introduced the same in the church of Congo and all readers and catechists wore *Kanzu*, as Tomasi explained, 'The *Kanzus* had to be carefully made and decorated with the red stitch as they are in Uganda!'[38]

Therefore, the *Anglo-Ugandanness* of authority provokes two challenges: first, the creation of a 'puppet church' in Congo completely dependent on the outsiders without involvement of the Congolese people on the doctrinal,

---

[35] A.B. Lloyd, *Apolo the Pathfinder: Who follows* (London: CMS, 1934), 18.
[36] Dirokpa Balufuga, 'Liturgie Anglicane et inculturation, hier, aujourd'hui et demain: regard sur la célébration eucharistique en République Démocratique du Congo' (PhD Thesis, Université Laval, Quebec, Avril 2001), 36.
[37] Luck, *African Saint*, 110.
[38] Quoted in Luck, *African Saint*, 115.

liturgical and moral issues. Second, the traditional authority was undermined and this caused local people to oscillate between the traditional authority and the new authority.

Enigmatic Authority

In 1899 Boga and its neighbouring villages were victims of the tension between two foreign political powers. The Belgians were contesting the right of the British to administer territory west of Semliki river, and Belgian government officers were already exacting tribute from the chiefs in the Boga area. The Rev T.B. Johnson described their methods as harsh, 'The main duty laid upon a government officer was to secure so much revenue, and his reputation for ability depended upon his success in getting it brought in, therefore there could be little scope for good for the individual administrator ... At Mboga the soldiers employed by the Belgians were kidnapping women and children and the situation was very unsettled.'[39] The CMS, in these conditions of tension, saw fit to withdraw its teachers from Boga temporarily. The *Mukama* Tabaro accompanied Apolo and Sedulaka back to Toro, and he took up residence there for a while. Once back in Boga, Tabaro found that Sulemani Karamesa had been made *Mukama* by the Belgians.

Boga was officially handed to Belgians in 1911. This placed handicaps on missionary work from British Uganda. Belgians restructured the administration; they subjected Sulemani to Bomera, whom they made senior chief of the whole area between Irumu and the Semliki river. The warlike Lendu rose in rebellion because they resented the transfer of their territory to Belgium and the imposition of Bomera's authority, him being a Hema. As a result, Boga was dramatically sacked and Bomera killed by the Lendu. This political struggle overshadowed the church in Boga, mainly as Sulemani, who reverted to his 'traditional' ways, had strongly opposed what remained of the small Christian community, who were now without a teacher, as the Belgians would allow no entry of persons from Uganda.[40] This period therefore led to confusion about the reliability of the various authorities.

Indeed, traditional authority symbolized in the *Mukama* was important for the Church in Boga. Nothing could be done without *Mukama*'s agreement. The first three to be baptized were Yakobo Tibenderana, Daudi Ndagamberaha, and Petro Kamihanda, all from Tabaro's family sent by him to the teachers' household, to work for them and learn at the same time. But he could also forbid church activities. In 1897, a body of 4,000 Maniema armed with guns had mutinied from the Belgian expedition led by Baron Dhanis against the Mahdists in the upper

---

[39] Luck, *African Saint*, 83.
[40] Eglise Anglicane du Zaïre, *Kwa Imani Apolo*, 26.

reaches of the Nile.[41] They attacked Boga villages, carrying off women, children and property. Then after this one of the *Mukama*'s children died. The priests and diviners attributed all these misfortunes of Boga to the presence of the catechists. Consequently, Tabaro published a decree saying, 'There is no God; let them bring back the charms and incantations.'[42] Tabaro saw Apolo as his rival with his Hema followers; he accused him of plotting to usurp his kingdom, because those who 'read' were popular with the British. 'Tabaro abused and slandered these people and commanded their books to be destroyed. Some of those who had believed on Jesus went back, for fear for the *Mukama*.'[43] Yet Tabaro feared reprisals from the British if he openly murdered the Christian teachers, but he was eager to get rid of them. He ordered that no church was to be built in his area, Christians were not allowed to visit each other; anyone found visiting would be beaten, and nobody was allowed to feed the teachers, but should let them die of hunger or drive them away.[44]

In fact it was a tension between the 'new world' and the 'old world'. The new life presented by the gospel was a revelation to these people. But as Luck said, they found it difficult to relate it to their own lives.[45] Of course during persecution they had withstood in the enthusiasm of their new love and their loyalty to Apolo. But most of them unthinkingly made a response to the new faith. They were subject to the powers of the unseen world, of magic and spirit possession, as well as the more visible powers of chiefs and clan and ethnic customs. In 1916 Apolo lamented, 'When I reached Boga, I found some of the Christians possessed by an evil spirit. Some were practicing witchcraft. Some had three wives, some two, and there was too much drinking of beer. I was much worried by these evil practices amongst the Christians at Mboga.'[46] However Tabaro feared the growing authority of Apolo and thought it to be a political move from Buganda to get rid of the *Mukama*.

It is worth noticing here that Tabaro finally recognised and submitted his traditional authority to the new sacred and powerful authority represented by Apolo. The first attempt to neutralize the traditional authority to the 'new' was when Apolo asked Tabaro for the sacred drum Rubango to be used in church for calling the people to services. This drum was a symbol to the people of the tribal spirit; it was kept in a sacred enclosure and cared for by a woman guardian, it was revered and worshipped like a god, with its own shrine, offerings and priest, and

---

[41] *Uganda Journal*, vol. 17, 1953, 19-20.
[42] Eglise Anglicane du Zaire, *Kwa Imani Apolo*, 7.
[43] Luck, *African Saint*, 73.
[44] Luck, *African Saint*, 74.
[45] Luck, *African Saint*, 109.
[46] Luck, *African Saint*, 113.

it was carried before the *Mukama* on ceremonial occasions, but if it was used for other purposes it lost its power.[47]

Apolo did not fear chiefs and openly censured their behaviour. For instance, one Sunday in church, Apolo rebuked the *Mukama* Sulemani and he prayed with all Christians saying,

> O God looks down upon us miserable creatures, without a good ruler in this country of the Congo. May you take away this bad chief from us and make haste to help us'. And another day they prayed saying, 'O God, the Father, Son and Holy Spirit, we put forth to you this person, so that you may do to him whatever you wish, whether to take him away or to let him live and convert him, for if you do not interfere, he is going to lead many astray and kill them.[48]

Then Sulemani died the same year. This is an important point which needs to be underlined. Apolo cared for the population and did not fear the chief. His prayer was clear that God should remove the bad chief. This fearless challenge to *Mukama*'s behaviour may partly be due to the awareness of the fact that Apolo was backed by British missionaries. The same thing happened with the next Chief. While Apolo was in Toro in June 1918 to meet the Bishop, a conflict broke out between the *Mukama* Enoke and the Christian community. Isaka Aliguma who found Enoke with his brother's wife rashly gave him a beating. Enoke arrested Isaka and accused him of being rebellious and not paying Belgian taxes. Isaka was beaten by Belgians. When Apolo came back, he sent the following message to Enoke, 'Your father first began to fight against the church. He lifted his arm to strike it down. You are a child of the church, and you have done the same thing. In raising your arm against the Church, you will leave your kingdom, and you will take hold of a hoe, and with your hands you will dig potatoes.'[49] Apolo was pleased to see him in prison at Irumu two years later after he had assaulted a Belgian official in a state of drunkenness.

The mystification of Apolo's authority was also proved through his diverse healings. It was believed that Apolo had a gift of healing that he did not use in a general way, but as a special need arose. He had the faith to trust God and act as God directed him. We will illustrate this only by two instances. Bezaleri, a two year old boy who later became the first Bishop of Congo, was in a semi-conscious state. He was clammy and his teeth were clenched. Tomasi, his father, called to Apolo who came quickly, took the child to his own room and laid him on his own bed. Apolo was alone with the child because he forbade the wailing people to follow him. Tomasi was also not allowed to enter the room. Tomasi commented after the event:

---

[47] Titre Ande, 'Le Christianisme face au Système d'Héritage chez les Bahema de Boga' (Memoire de Licence, Bunia, 1994), 32-35.

[48] Luck, *African Saint, Quoted* from Apolo's diary.

[49] Luck, *African Saint,* 117.

Apolo spent time in prayer with him there alone and said to Tomasi, 'God has helped the child, cheer up, he will be better.' Bezaleri sneezed and showed signs of recovery, so Tomasi called the mother and the child opened his eyes and they were very, very surprised. All this took about three hours but the boy was getting well and talking a little. Apolo showed a remarkable confidence all through and had no doubt whatsoever on these occasions.[50]

The second concerns Tomasi's wife who had been suffering from the issue of blood, like the woman in the gospel. Apolo asked Tomasi to let him go with his wife into the forest. Luck described the event as followed:

She went with him and eventually they came to a river. Apolo sent the teachers on ahead, he then told the woman to get right into the water. She obeyed him, going right in, and sat there for about an hour. Apolo then told her to get up and come out, and from that time on she was perfectly cured. She continued with him during the two weeks' tour of the forest and came back well.[51]

Of course, in Hema society there were *Wafumu* (witches), who were consulted and trusted for their ability for healing. But their healing was more commercial and damaging for the society, for one of the family members must be held 'responsible'. Apolo's outstanding healing was believed to come from God through prayers, using different material means such as water, coffee and so on. However, its 'secret' character made it not only mysterious to people, but also suspicious.

The enigmatic aspect of Apolo's authority is also clearly expressed in the story of pigs. Rev Tomasi Ndahura related, 'One strange example of his (Apolo's) power – his garden was not eaten by wild pigs. People were surprised to see their tracks, but none of the food was touched'. Peradarsi Kahwa even said that they used to say to Apolo, 'You come and stand in our garden and then the pigs won't come!'[52] Apolo could demonstrate the power of the 'new world' over the traditional one through 'miracles'. Nasani Kabarole stated that 'Apolo showed no fear of witchcraft or superstition. The people saw that when he prayed for rain, rain came without the assistance of the rainmakers, who were greatly feared.'[53]

The following letter that *Mukama* Paulo Tabaro addressed to the head of the region (spiritually), Rev A. Apolo Kivebulaya, on 30 August 1926 clearly shows the victory of Apolo's authority over the traditional religion:

I ask you to pray for me that God may give me wisdom as he has given to you my father to do everything in great wisdom; that I may trust in Him and he may look

---

[50] Eglise Anglicane du Zaïre, *Kwa Imani Apolo*, 60.

[51] Eglise Anglicane du Zaïre, *Kwa Imani Apolo*, 61.

[52] Luck, *African Saint*, 156.

[53] Luck, *African Saint*, 156.

after all my doing in return; that He may make me grow up and lead his sheep in a right way, as I look after them. That He may go with me in all my leadership among His people, so that I may be a good leader of the country and make it able to develop. May the Lord be my guide in everything, and may his blessings always go with me. Dear Sir, do not forget to pray these things for me your servant.[54]

In this prayer, it is not clear whether the *Mukama* considered God, the source of Apolo's power, as the God from whom his power in traditional religion came from. But for him, Apolo's God is the source of wisdom, good order, growth and all blessings. The subjects of Apolo are God's people. However, the question remained, how did this 'people of God' carry out this 'new mysterious' authority?

Hema Supremacy

Hema, right at the beginning of their settling down in the areas of Boga, managed to impose their domination on the neighbouring ethnic groups such as Nande, Lese, Lendu, Talinga and Mbuba. Their supremacy was mostly due to having been livestock farmers. They therefore used their neighbours as 'workers' in their fields and exploited them by paying them very little. Many forest folk such as Mbuba and Lese came to Boga while it was still within the British sphere of influence, and had 'sold' their children to the Hema as slaves in exchange for food and ground to cultivate. Nasani explained, 'These slaves became a kind of currency, that could be exchanged for a plot of potatoes, a boy or a girl as needed, not that they were ill used, for they lived with the people, but they were in servitude.'[55] But during evangelisation in the forest, these Mbuba slaves were used as 'interpreters', for the forest people around Boga had a working knowledge of each other's languages.

The spread of Christianity from Boga gave opportunity to the Hema to confirm their authority over other tribes. It must be remembered here that as *Mukama* Tabaro 'brought' the Anglican Church into Congo, it was considered as Hema religion, and therefore also seen as representing British power in Semliki area. As the first missionaries of Anglicanism in Congo, the Hema imposed their language Lunyoro on other tribes. Liturgy, services and catechism were all in Lunyoro, and other tribes had to worship and read the Bible in a language they did not know. The prayer book in *Lunyoro* was translated into Swahili only in 1973. Many *Lunyoro* words imposed on other tribes have survived in Anglican language until now: *Kihanda* for priest, *sabadikoni* for archdeacon, *obulisa* for parish, *endoboro,* the basket for offering. They introduced Swahili in Kisangani, and imposed Swahili in Aru in 1980. Since then, in Aru, Swahili has become the

---

[54] Luck, *African Saint,* 138.
[55] Luck, *African Saint,* 116.

official language for services, meetings and administration among Lugbara, Kakwa and Aluru, who are Bangala speakers. Hema supremacy is especially felt in administration. Boga wanted to keep the privilege of remaining as the centre for decision-making[56] and was called the 'Jerusalem' of Congo. However, Hema's supremacy has been seriously questioned and challenged by other tribes and dioceses which are fighting for their autonomy.

Conclusion

The study of authority in the earlier Anglican Church of Congo has proved that the political background of the Church of Uganda has had an impact on the exercise of authority within the EAC. Right at the beginning, Mutesa's desire to have Christianity was not religious, but political. In this sense, the introduction of Christianity in Buganda is seen not only in the context of the political forces prevailing at Mutesa's court, but also against a background of the competing foreign influences to which Mutesa was exposed. Of course, the missionaries were in theory devoted to the task of bringing Christianity as much to ordinary people as to powerful men. The Protestant missionaries held the view that they were evangelists and servants of God, and not representatives of the British crown. The Catholics missionaries, too, regarded themselves as propagators of the religion of the Church of Rome. But in practice, both the Protestant and Catholic missionaries became involved in a political relationship with *Kabaka* and his court, and subsequently with the colonial administrators.

The chiefly institution became the target of the church in its aim to christianise the traditional centre of power. The Anglican Church clung to the old pattern of the Anglican-monarchic model in its dealings with the institution of the kingship. At the same time the political leaders were aware of the possibility of using the mission and the church for their own purposes. The planting of churches in new areas was the work of the native evangelists who faced savage conditions of life, a strange language, shortage of food, exile and persecution in the cause of Christ and they won through. However, the spread of Christianity went hand-in-hand with the political expansion of kingdoms represented by powerful ethnic groups. It was in this religio-political hybridisation that authority developed in the earlier Anglican Church of Congo, as it remained more than seven decades under the Church of Uganda. This hybridisation of authority in the Anglican-monarchic model became an impetus for the EAC to fit into the

---

[56] Dirokpa Balufuga, 'Liturgie Anglicane et inculturation, hier, aujourd'hui et demain', 36.

post-colonial socio-political situation for its survival, as the next chapter will illuminate.

Chapter Four

Self-understanding of Authority in the Anglican Church of Congo

Is the understanding of authority in the Anglican Church of Congo (EAC) different from other Christian churches? Although every church would claim to be part of the one, holy, catholic and apostolic church, there are various factors that have shaped them as particular Christian traditions, Roman Catholic, Orthodox, Anglican, Methodist, Baptist, etc. For instance, the Roman Catholic Church has a central teaching office (Magisterium) and a clearly defined body of doctrine stated in authoritative documents; whereas the Anglican Communion makes a virtue of dispersed authority and gives a constitutional role to laity and clergy in structures of representative church government.

Moreover, within the Anglican Communion itself, the Lambeth Conference of bishops at its first meeting in 1867 said, 'The Anglican Communion of today is a federation of churches, some national, some regional, but no longer predominantly Anglo-Saxon in race, nor can it be expected that it will attach special value to Anglo-Saxon traditions.'[1]

In fact, as Anglicans, we attach importance to our common past and seek to find in it a continuing bond. Unfortunately, this bond is becoming more questionable. At the same time, we are aware of cultural and socio-political factors which have shaped the identity of Anglican local communities. This is why the EAC changed from the Anglican Church in Congo to Anglican Church of Congo. This chapter aims to analyse the self-understanding of authority within the EAC, as a local church within its own cultural and socio-political context. In fact, oral expression and communication are still the major means of sharing and spreading ideas and experiences in the Congo. This section aims to argue that the

---

[1] Church of England, *The Report of the Lambeth Conference 1948* (London: SPCK, 1948), 82.

self-understanding of authority in the EAC consists of 'informal theology' which
has been developed through informal conversations, and is based on political
dynamics. This 'informal theology' discloses attitudes and opinions regarding
authority in the EAC. The EAC certainly has its literate theological dimension
which, unfortunately, consists of documents written from outside, except for a
few dissertations produced each year by the students at the Anglican theological
college. The chapter will first consider the EAC's internal authority structures
and the EAC's theological interpretation of the use and experience of authority
and how that authority has been carried out into the world. The chapter will
mostly be based on interviews and church documents such as constitutions,
canons, meeting records and personal letters.

Theological Understanding of Authority

This section intends to explore the definition and source of authority in the EAC,
and examine how it has affected the use of authority in the EAC.

Definition and Source

Christians in the EAC, like other Christians, agree that the source of Christian
authority is divine, that the Father sent the Son into the world with authority as
Lord. This statement was clearly expressed by Njojo Byankya, the former
Archbishop of Congo, when he said,

> Our Lord Jesus Christ who is the founder of the Church installed the authority of
> God on the earth. Jesus in his turn installed apostles and went to heaven. The
> apostles, thus, began to evangelise because they had received authority from Jesus
> to spread the Gospel (Mt. 28.18).[2]

Here in fact, authority as derived from God is conceived as a legitimate
permission to preach the word of God, powerful enough to convert the sinners
and bring them back under God's authority. Furthermore, authority in the EAC is
seen not simply as permission, but as power from God to enable someone for a
particular ministry in the church. It is received through God's election and call,[3]
as Esther Ang'omoko, the president of the Mothers' Union in Mahagi, put it. It
means authority comes straight from God to the leaders through the Christ.
Dieudonné Adubango, the leader of Youth in Mahagi, made it clearer when he
said that authority is power from God who chooses and calls for the ministry, and
it is only in that work the power is revealed.[4] According to Kiiza Jacques, the

---

[2] Njojo Byankya, oral interview, Boga, August 2000.
[3] Esther Ang'omoko, oral interview, Mahagi, August 2001.
[4] Dieudonné Adubang'o, oral interview, Mahagi, August 2001.

power received consists of the right someone has over others to decide and to rule. It makes him a 'big man' and gives him the right to make the last decision in all issues.[5] This statement, radical as it seems to be, is Kiiza's definition of authority, deduced from his observation of the use of authority in the EAC as institution. Authority in the EAC is the power in titles which allows somebody to do his own will and thus, has only to give account to his superiors. There is 'double consciousness' of authority, one linked to the spiritual aspect of the work, and the other linked to the institutional consideration of the church.

Authority is also the church structure in itself with its aim to keep order in the Lord's ministry in the church. This structure is seen as God's gift to the church. This structural authority is confused with the person who holds a position in the structure. 'You are the authority because you have authority.' Respondents to our questionnaire, when referring to leaders, often used the word authority in French. It means the French word *autorité* has also had an influence on this understanding of authority as the person who has authority in politics. *Autorité* means power, but also the person in charge. However, although some languages in Congo have different words for authority and the leader, cultures seemed to define leader as someone who owns authority. For instance *Lugbara* use the word *okpo* to talk of power and authority. The chief is *Opi*, the owner of *okpo*. This shows that many cultural, political and religious factors have contributed in building up the understanding of authority as the person who holds it.

Therefore, authority in the EAC is believed to have a divine source, channelled to leaders through Christ. It is the power of the Risen Lord to keep order in the church. However from personal observation and experience, authority is conceived as a coercive structural power and a person who manages the structure.

Transmission of Authority

The EAC confesses that Christ is the Life, and his authority is never cut off from its source, the Father who sent him into the world as Lord. Christ's authority flows into the world perpetually in the continuing life of the people of God, making leaders its channels. In other words, Christ's authority gives life through those appointed by Him to the members of the church. It is that unchangeable authority of the Lord given to apostles. Njojo expressed it in this way, 'After Jesus had formed the Church, he conferred the power to the apostles to be used in the Church. To ensure the continuity and succession, the apostles passed that power on to their successors up to the present day.'[6] Thus, authority in the church is seen as an 'appropriation' of the Lord's authority, guided by the Holy Spirit through structures. Officers of these structures are 'God's representatives or

[5] Kiiza Jacques, oral interview, Bunia, January 2002.
[6] Njojo Byankya, oral interview, Boga, August 2000.

ambassadors.'[7] They are visible signs of the invisible authority of God. This hierarchically transmissible power is independent of the congregation.

In fact, ordered structures are needed to protect and safeguard the harmony of the universe. The structure is sacred because it channels the divine authority. Therefore the holders of offices are believed to be 'holy'. It is functional holiness, for someone is holy because he is priest, archdeacon or bishop. All officers are thus hierarchically in communion with each other, which in fact is a structural communion.

The fact that Jesus received his authority from the Father means that authority is transmissible through ordination by laying on of hands. Ordination is conceived as conferring a personal power which the ordained minister subsequently exercises for life in his or her own right. A bishop must perform this ordination in apostolic succession, as it is the exclusive and sole secure test of ministerial and ecclesial validity. For instance, in the Episcopal ministry of Ciakudia, a Congolese Anglican priest was rejected because in 1986 he declared himself the Archbishop of the Anglican Church, and he ordained some bishops with the aim of forming his own province. He intended in vain to be part of the Anglican Communion.

Ordination is sometimes given a cultural legitimacy. Muhindo Ise-somo acknowledged the hereditary character of authority through ordination when he said,

> I remember Jesus Christ saying, 'All authority has been given to me by God'. It was the same in our African culture where the 'big man' is the one who ordains and gives permission to do something. In Nande, it is *akalanda landa*, which means hereditary or infinitely transmissible.[8]

As a result of this understanding of authority given at ordination, the transmission of authority is considered to assume the continuity of Christ's life in the church through a 'sacred elite'.

Primacy of Bishops

Indeed, the office of bishop has proved crucial in the Anglican pattern of three-fold ministry of bishops, priests and deacons. It was recognised to be so in the Chicago-Lambeth Quadrilateral of 1888, which placed 'the historic episcopate' alongside scripture, the creeds and the sacraments as the foursquare basis on which the Church rests. The Quadrilateral has been frequently reaffirmed, even by the 1998 Lambeth Conference, and is firmly considered as the established authority for Anglican tradition. EAC has fully committed itself

---

[7] Ukelo John, oral interview, Bunia, December 2001.

[8] Muhindo Ise-somo, oral interview, November 2001.

to this 'tradition'. The EAC affirms the importance of the primacy of the Scriptures, the tradition of the church, the authority of the creeds, and the continuity of apostolic succession in the consecration of bishops. Therefore the three-fold ministry in historical succession is part of the foundational ideology of Anglicanism in Congo, as stipulated in the constitution,

> The church of this province declares the titles of the bishop, the priest or deacon are to conform to the Holy Scriptures. Nobody will legally be considered as bishop, priest, and deacon in the church of this province or allowed to exercise these ministries unless he is ordained in accordance with the canons of this province or ordained in another church whose orders are accepted by this province.[9]

It is in fact the 'Episcopal succession model' where bishops are 'essential' to the existence of the church, as Paul Avis said.[10] Priests and Christians recognize that a bishop's authority is from God, as Kangamina Sadiki underlines it, 'It is God who by his Spirit has established bishops in the church (Acts 20.28).'[11] If it is true that bishops are 'essential' to the very existence of the church, does that mean they are the church? During the workshop for the new Congolese Prayer Book in 1997 in Bukavu, while discussing whether the ordinand should stand before God and the church or before God and the Bishop, the bishops present at the workshop hastily responded, 'Before the bishop for he is the church'. However, the bishops of EAC are not clear on the extent to which bishops, who are holy by their function, are seen as in essence necessary for the church. There is of course a link between this idea of the bishop being the church and the bishop as symbol of unity in his diocese. Many people in the EAC are convinced that the fact that the bishop is the symbol of unity means he is the church. Sinzahera stated it as follows, 'The bishop is the church for he is the unity of people. The bishop is the symbol of unity. There cannot be two bishops in the same diocese. It means if there is division in the church, it is the bishop's duty to bring people back together.'[12]

This understanding of the bishop's role certainly gives him full authority in decision making, even over the diocesan synod decisions. In fact, it is common in Congo to assimilate the leader to the institution. At the national level, bishops are gathered in a college which assumes the oneness of all bishops within the province. According to the provincial canon, the bishop's college, independently from other Anglican provinces, is the only legitimate court not only for discipline matters, but also to solve doctrinal disputes:

---

[9] Province de l'Eglise Anglicane du Congo, *Constitution,* 2.
[10] Paul Avis, *The Anglican Understanding of the Church: an Introduction* (London: SPCK, 2000), 19.
[11] Kangamina Sadiki, oral interview, Kisangani, December 2001.
[12] Sinzahera Uwimana, oral interview, Bunia, December 2001.

The provincial court is composed of the archbishop as president and all diocesan bishops. The provincial court has to audit and determine the sanctions against a bishop of the province, and to take actions against anyone concerning the use of ecclesiastical laws, organisation and administration of the province, and preservation of the doctrine and order of services.[13]

However, this 'Episcopal primacy' has overshadowed the initial principles of their official documents. The provincial and diocesan charts give the synods' authority in decision-making. These synods are composed of lay and ordained minister representatives. These synods should be the fundamental organs of decisions and control. The college of bishops comes after the executive council. And at each level of the diocesan structure, councils have authority over leaders as individuals. But in practice, individuals have authority over their councils. Isingoma Kahwa's cry for reform is revealing, 'We must turn back to the principles, the principles of these organs, to make the provincial synod at the top of the chart; and let the executive council play its role as executant; and leave the college of bishops the role of solving bishops' matters only.'[14]

One wonders why bishops keep the documents such as Constitution, Canon and Statutes in the church when they do not apply their principles to lead the church. Surely these texts have been reinterpreted in a new socio-political context. A new mechanism of authorising seems to have taken place outside of the official documents. Ise-somo expressed the same frustration in these terms, 'the role of the bishop should be to maintain spirituality, orthodox doctrine against heresies and discipline or order in the church ... but they are often busy with confirmation ... and do not even have a clear vision for their work.'[15] Isingoma Kahwa has also discovered that many problems remain unsolved in the province because the college of bishops has failed to replace the provincial synod as it intended to do.[16] However, regarding the question whether the college of bishops should be banned to let other organs play their role, Isingoma underlined that, as a kind of Lambeth in miniature, it must be maintained for the communion of bishops. But as we shall find out later, Congolese bishops in communion has always been a 'myth'. By 'sacralising' a bishop's ministry too much, they ended up 'desacralising' it. This means the primacy of bishops as a sacred symbol is developed out of the 'official' interpretation of the church documents. A new unwritten interpretation has taken place to accommodate the authority of the local cultural and socio-political context.

---

[13] Province de l'Eglise Anglicane du Zaïre, *Canons*, Canon 1b, d, 1.
[14] Isingoma Kahwa, oral interview, Bunia, November 2001.
[15] Muhindo Ise-semo, oral interview, Bunia, November 2001.
[16] Isingoma Kahwa, oral interview, Bunia, November 2001.

Utii Theology

I cannot refuse to do what my boss asks me to do, because I know that I am *mutumishi* (servant) and he is my head (boss). If they have already taken a decision, the only thing I can do is to obey (kutii) and force the members of my archdeaconry to do it.[17]

Archdeacon Kabarole's argument for submission above might have been influenced by different factors. Firstly, obedience to authority is inculcated within African cultures. Authority is conveyed from the top down. One standing above the recipient in the hierarchy of leaders is superior and this gives him the right to be obeyed by his subjects. Moreover, the whole teaching method in Congo, both in churches and the state education system, does not encourage reflection and questioning. It is often an exercise in rote learning which can then be repeated back to examiners on examination day. Furthermore, unquestioning submission to leaders' authority is reinterpreted as a constitutional recommendation within the EAC. The constitution clearly stipulates, 'The bishops of this province must promise obedience, according to the canons of the church, to the archbishop. The priests or deacons who receive authority for their ministry in whichever diocese of this province must promise obedience to the diocesan bishops.'[18] It is of worthy note that obedience implies unquestioning submission in African cultures.

A Swahili word much used to designate the leaders is *muchungaji* (shepherd). The use of the word *muchungaji* is based on the relationship which exists between the shepherd, an intelligent human being, and the sheep, a non-intelligent animal. 'Sheep' in some Congolese tribes is allegorically used to designate somebody who is 'humble' and follows without questioning. For instance, Lugbara used to label women as sheep, not because of their humility, but because they are thought to be 'humble' and blindly adhere to ideologies like sheep that blindly follow each other without noticing where they are driven. Therefore, *muchungaji* has authority to lead *wakristo* (Christians), the sheep, and give them direction. In return, *wakristo* must obey their master *muchungaji*. This understanding of *muchungaji* is a distortion of the biblical image of Jesus as the good shepherd and the 'Lamb of God' that we shall mention in the last chapter of this work.

During their consecration, bishops are given a crook as symbol of shepherding. They use the crook to shepherd *Wakristo* who represent the sheep. It is noteworthy that the initial meaning of the crook has changed. It was for pulling straying sheep out of difficult places. In Congo, it used to help the livestock farmer to fight the wild animals such as lions that may attack the sheep.

---

[17] Kabarole Baguma, oral interview, Aru, August 2001.

[18] Province de l'Eglise Anglicane du congo, *Constitution*, 2001, 2.

A serious change has taken place, 'now the crook is used to harm the flock.'[19] Even in schools, teachers use the stick to harm pupils to maintain discipline and order for a 'better' education. Parents also use the stick to punish their children, and men do the same to their wives. Again it is the stick which is used by tribal fighters. Even Mobutu used to always hold his cane as the leader. This common use of the 'cane' has affected the use of the symbolic crook as tool for maintaining order in the church. Leaders do not protect their flock against socio-political violence for instance, but still recommend their submission to the hierarchy. In fact, these biblical symbols are overused and reinterpreted in the local context.

Furthermore, the issue of fatherhood is another point of structural submission. As previously said, the role of father was significant in most of African cultures. The father's position at the head of the nuclear family made him the first concrete representation of authority. Authority in the *Bula Matari* state, both pre-independence and postcolonial, was also much dominated by the 'fatherhood model'. It is the same in the EAC, where the holder of a hierarchically superior office becomes 'father' in relation to his 'sons' who hold subordinate positions. When talking to a superior, it is polite to use Baba *Askofu* (father bishop), *baba* coordinator, *baba* or papa pastor. In the EAC, as in the political and cultural spheres, it is a defamation to call an office-holder by his name. It proves that authority symbolically lies in titles. *Monseigneur* (my lord), *Son excellence* (especially used for governors, ministers and the president in the government), venerable, canon, reverend are the most used in the EAC.

Therefore, as in the *Bula Matari* tradition, fatherhood is the principle of unity of command, and reinforces unity of view and action. Authority is one and indivisible. It is the bishop's authority with proprietary authority, delegated to others from above to below. At each level, the Christian family is unified under the leadership of its 'father'. Thus, 'respect of hierarchy, order and discipline are fundamental in the EAC for the growth of the church,' according to Molanga Botola, the provincial secretary.[20] In fact, this is an exaggerated stress on the unexamined concept of hierarchy. *Utii* theology, which values a blind obedience to the Lord's servants reinterprets and adapts biblical and cultural symbols in a new context.

Legitimacy

What are the criteria of legitimacy in the EAC? Who has authority to judge legitimacy? In the EAC, the Episcopal system that is the continuity of the historic episcopate constitutes in itself the criteria. All ministers ordained according to the traditional Anglican rites are legitimate leaders. Any abuse of authority is

---

[19] Rwakaikara Amoti, oral interview, Bunia, July 2001.

[20] Mulanga Botola, oral interview, Bunia, July 2001.

covered by the slogan, 'It is the Episcopal system.' Therefore the supremacy of episcopacy has overwhelmed other biblical criteria.

Isingoma Kawha, the bishop of Boga, recognises that it should be for organs such as synod, other church committees, or the constitution, to approve the legitimacy of an office-holder, with clear criteria set up on biblical principles. Isingoma's suggestion shows that there are other mechanisms of authorizing apart from the principles that are drawn from church documents which the leaders do not apply.

If there is a lack of clear criteria of legitimacy, can then Christians remove an 'undesirable' leader? All our respondents agree that Christians are not permitted to refuse a minister they think 'undesirable' for so many reasons that we can touch on just a few. Firstly it is because of the understanding of the leader as 'ambassador' of God. Anna Kaliru thinks it is not a good witness for the church to get rid of its minister,[21] while Otua Edyoma finds it difficult only because of the Congolese system, because according to him, the removal of a minister could happen in the Anglican Church of Uganda.[22] In fact, even though Christians were able to challenge the minister, the final decision still belongs to the hierarchy. Furthermore, there is mutual support among the leaders despite the complaints of the community.[23] This is why the constitution, as we shall see later, is left intentionally sketchy and vague. This deliberate vagueness protects the authority from being challenged. Therefore, the leaders' right to exercise authority within the EAC is based on unclear criteria, and mutual support of leaders makes them 'invulnerable'.

Authority and Wealth

In the EAC, justified by divine ordination, authority is personalized and exercised through a patron-client network. Consequently, pastors consider it wise to obey the bishop because their livelihood depends on his goodwill. This patron-client network in the church, as in *Bula Matari* model, has led to exploitation and corruption. In fact, the lifestyle of the bishops and other church leaders has alienated them from the mass of people who are struggling for life. What was said of the Roman Catholic Church can be applied to the EAC: 'Having access to foreign currency for projects, many church leaders developed lifestyles that alienated them from the struggles of the common people and made them appear as part of the exploitative upper class.'[24]

---

[21] Anna Kaliru, oral interview, Kumuru, July 2001.

[22] Otua Edyoma, oral interview, Ekanga, August 2001.

[23] Sabiti Tibafa, oral interview, Bunia, November 2001.

[24] S. Wolfgang, 'What does the Rwanda tragedy say to AMECEA churches?' in *AMECEA* (Documentation Service no 424, Nairobi, Kenya, 17/1994), 4.

The exploitative structural network is outside of the diocesan 'financial committee' and diocesan synod control. There is no clear account of the church income and its expenditure given to the community. The details of donations from abroad are rarely disclosed. Hence, Christians regard with suspicion the management of church resources by local church leaders. So the bishops are counting on the people's trust, which is not there. The gifts from abroad have become a manipulating tool for power. Bishops often distribute these gifts to some parishes during the 'big party' after the confirmation service. It is the gift from *Baba* (father) bishop to his beloved children, who in return must express their deep gratitude to their spiritual 'father'. This practice has led the church to remain in continual, total and blind dependence. It is founded on the state's strategy of manipulation to control all resources and to be the ultimate distributor.

This exploitative network has taken a structural legitimacy, and at each level, authority consists of amassing wealth. The target of the ministry has shifted from salvation of the people of God to the Episcopal office, and it has caused competition and hatred among church leaders with destructive effects on the church. Therefore, one wonders if the open letter written by Odette Kakuze to the bishops attending the African synod in Rwanda was also surreptitiously addressed to the EAC leaders,

> You who are our pastors, how many times have you visited the people who are poor, sick and suffering? Do you know where they live, the condition of their houses, what they eat, the things they are in need of? Can you, yourselves, identify with their problems, the scale of these problems? Why do you make friends only with the well-off people, the oppressors of the workers? Your very affluent style of life (luxury cars, fashionable clothes, expensive houses) increases the gap between you and us ordinary people, and this adds to our lack of confidence in you. The Christians feel abandoned, whereas you priests ought to be the voice of the voiceless, the outcasts, and serve the common folks.[25]

Authority and Conflict

Congolese society has always suffered from conflicts and tensions, sometimes with bitter consequences. The Congolese national dilemma has always been the building of the national consciousness for unity of command, but at the same time using the 'divide and rule' policy, which aims to weaken the powerful tribes. As a result, conflict and tensions are provoked and exploited for political reasons. Of course, it is utopia to have a human society without tension or

---

[25] Quoted in Roger Bowen, 'Rwanda: Missionary Reflections on a Catastrophe, J.C. Jones Lecture 1995', in *Anvil* (Vol. 13, No. 1, 1996), 33-44, 41.

conflict. The question remains about the causes of tension and conflict, and how to tackle them.

EAC is facing conflicts and divisions in different dioceses. For instance, in the diocese of Boga, Hema and Lendu they are divided; and in Mahagi the church split into two, for a small group of *wokovu* (revival group from Uganda, known as *Balokole*) have left the church. In the diocese of Kisangani, a group of Christians left the diocese to form their own church. The diocese of North-Kivu is under fire as well, for the bishop's group is facing rejection by other Christians within the diocese. In the diocese of Katanga, Kasai people are not getting on well with Katangese. The question is why all these conflicts and divisions in the EAC? From our respondents, we received different answers.

One of causes is ethnicism or clanism. Ethnocentrism, which is still strongly developed in the Congo, has also affected the church. The supremacy of some ethnic groups has given them the advantage to rule the church, often because they were the first to welcome the EAC in their areas. For instance, in Irumu zone, Hema and Ngiti have been fighting each other for decades. Hema, the pastoralists, despise Ngiti whom they use for manual work such as digging, building houses, etc. In fact, EAC started among Hema, who in their turn, went to evangelise Ngiti. Since then they have maintained their control over them. Ngiti still suffer from an inferiority complex, and they are deprived of key positions in the diocese. The cultural context has made the reconciliation difficult and church leaders are dominated by the cultural aspect, as Byakisaka Deogratias expressed it, 'We, Hema, like hiding problems. If you offend me now, I will keep it deep in my heart for years, although we can meet and talk. And this is our attitude which has been transferred into the church.'[26]

The other cause emphasized, but linked to ethnicism, is the *episcopose* which is an excessive and uncontrolled desire to be bishop, and that desire becomes an incurable disease. As the criticism of the ministry seems to aim at episcopacy, people gossip too much about it. Too often in the EAC people are consumed (gossip about etc.) with the issues of power – who will be the next Archdeacon, etc. As a result of the EAC structure, ministry is seen less in terms of Christian service, by which others are served, and more in obtaining a title which one expects to serve you.

In fact, there is a general tendency to want to be 'the boss' or 'the boss' must come from 'our' ethnic group or 'our' clan. For instance, in Kinshasa when Beni Bataaga arrived to work as the archdeacon, Lumbala, the first priest, left the church with a group of Christians, appropriating the church compound near the university of Kinshasa, because he considered himself in a good position to be the archdeacon.[27] It was the same when Mavatikwa arrived to be the first assistant bishop of Kinshasa. Rev Nzinga left the church with a group of

---

[26] Byakisaka Deogratias, oral interview, Bunia, December 2001.

[27] Eugène Lokangaka, personal communication, Bunia, 22/11/01.

Christians because he had expected to become bishop. In these cases, division was due to the extreme desire to make further steps in the leadership structure. In Kisangani, in 2000, after they had elected a new bishop, Musafiri Ndela, the 'unsuccessful' candidate' left the church with a number of Christians. Molanga Botola stated that this division happened because of the *episcopose* the 'unsuccessful' candidate was suffering from,[28] while Muloy Batibuha has shown a different point of view, 'The former bishop failed to fulfil his promise to promote some pastors as bishops.' He also blamed 'the non-transparency (openness) of elections in the EAC because of tribalism.'[29] The arguments depend on which tribe the person is from. The former is a Topoke, the bishop's tribe, while the latter is from another tribe.

Another aspect raised is the fact that Christians are now re-reading the Bible according to the changing socio-political, economic and religious context in the country. New winds of democracy are blowing all over the country The 'new churches' by their emphasis on freedom of actions based on the action of the Holy Spirit are very attractive. All the above factors are making a considerable impact on *Wakristo* and the leaders who think their superiors have infringed their rights. The dream of a renewed Anglican church with new visions is frequently heard in people's comments. Thus there is a sense of rejection of authority and the genuine desire for freedom of thought, expression and action.

A Case Study of the Conflict Resolution in North-Kivu Diocese

North-Kivu diocese, inaugurated on 23 February 1992 in Butembo, is situated in east Congo and includes the zones of Lubero and Beni. Most of the population are Nande, but there are also Talinga and Nyali. Kainama which has shared with Boga for a long time the history of the Anglican Church of Congo is the point of departure for the creation of other parishes of the actual diocese of North-Kivu. Kainama, the first Anglican chapel in North-Kivu opened by Apolo Kivebulaya in 1921, is of great importance for it is the current bishop's village. The diocese is made up of six archdeaconries and 35 parishes. Most of the population are farmers and few are traders.

Since the year 2000, there has been a serious threat of division within the diocese. It started with the memorandum of 23 January 2000 written by Christians to the Archbishop of the EAC. The memorandum, signed by pastors and Christians, expresses the fear of members seeing their diocese progressing in 'darkness' when its emblem is *sisi ni nuru ya dunia* (we are light of the world).[30]

The chief accusations are as follows: The Bishop is accused of false teaching, by saying that salvation can be achieved through good works, that animals have

---

[28] Mulanga Botola, oral interview, Bunia, October 2001.
[29] Muloy Batibuha, oral interview, Bunia, November 2001.
[30] 'Memorandum ya Wakristo ya Nord-Kivu kwa Archbishop,' Butembo, 23.01.2000, 1.

the Holy Spirit and that the Holy Spirit can leave a Christian who has sinned.[31] The question of post-baptismal sin, known to be an issue in the early church, is still alive and well in Congo. Another accusation is that the bishop is a bad leader, using a dictatorial manner during meetings. He may leave the chair and walk out, or he may bang the table when he is angry and so on. He also makes a lot of unrealisable promises. He is also accused of adultery, embezzlement and tribalism. It is stipulated that most of the departments well supported financially are led by the bishop's relatives from Kainama. The memorandum mentioned that tribalism has caused much darkness in the diocese for all grants are used to build Kainama.

The bishop is also accused of having said that 'he is the cock and all Christians are hens; and hens do not lay eggs without the cock.' It means there is no life without the bishop who is a powerful life-giver. It is worth noticing here that the word *Jogo* (cock) in Swahili and its equivalents in other local languages is used to show the power of a person, and his power to give life. It may be used also to describe someone who is obsessed with sex.

The last point of accusation concerns the name of the Bishop, Munzenda Syavuleka, which means 'chief of the village'. According to Munzenda, a witch gave him the name Syavuleka when he was a baby. The witch offered him a big throne and said, 'you will have a throne like this in your life.' From his explanation, Christians concluded that the throne he has in the cathedral must be the fulfilment of the witch's prediction. Therefore his call as bishop is not from God, but from witches.[32] Another point raised was the fact that the bishop often says to the priests that they have to suffer because he had really suffered himself before he became the bishop.

Many efforts and strategies have been adopted to solve this uprising of Christians and pastors. One of the tools used to solve the crisis was intimidation. The bishop, after he had received a delegation from church members warning him against adultery, convoked a three day meeting and considered the Christian action as a plot against him. He suspended the vicar of Butembo and the church elders and sacked the parents of the victim of his adultery from their posts in the health care service.[33] Indeed the provincial team joined in the investigation, and in the end the college of bishops suspended the bishop of North-Kivu for one year.[34] In fact, intimidation, revocations and suspensions, as used by Munzenda, are frequently used in Congo when a leader, religious or political, is under threat.

The Bible was also used as a tool for intimidation and culpability. This is clearly seen in the pastoral letter written by Dirokpa Balufuga, as the Archbishop of the province and former Bishop of Kivu area, in support of bishop of

---

[31] 'Memorandum', Butembo, 2.
[32] 'Memorandum', Butembo, 8.
[33] 'Memorandum', Butembo, 7.
[34] Compte-rendu du Comité de discipline, Kampala 2000.

North-Kivu. Firstly, the pastoral letter is the expression of the provincial delegation's indignation. It is said that they were received in Butembo 'without respect for provincial hierarchy, refusal of the retreat and the word of God, which is our help at any time (Heb. 4:16) and the fact that the provincial decision was contested.'[35] The pastoral letter also underlined that respect of authority is important to maintain order in the community. Many biblical passages are quoted calling for submission to authority,

> In fact, it is for others that God has placed authority not only in the churches, but also in all human organisations. Therefore the apostle Paul said, 'Everyone must submit himself to the governing authorities, for there is no authority except that which God has established. The authorities that exist have been established by God (Rom. 13,1); 'Consequently, he who rebels against the authority is rebelling against what God has instituted, and those who do so will bring judgement on themselves' (Rom. 13,2); 'Slaves, obey your earthly masters in everything; and do it, not when their eye is on you and to win their favour, but with sincerity of heart and reverence for the Lord' (Col. 3,22).[36]

It is striking to see how the pastoral letter associates these passages which recommend submission to political leaders with submission to church leaders. The letter also bases its appeal for submission on Anglican history. Anglicans of North-Kivu must follow 'Anglican tradition' for 'its emphasis on the respect of hierarchy helped to maintain its unity through centuries, despite the waves in the history which led to division of protestant churches.'[37] Thus, the letter warns the church against the threat to the future of episcopacy if actions are not taken in time to fight it. Therefore biblical passages and church history are used not merely as tranquillizers, but also for intimidation and culpability.

The other means used to tackle the uprising was violence. Rebel soldiers were used by the archbishop's delegation to reopen the door of the Cathedral after it had been locked by a group of thirty-two women as an expression of their rejection of the provincial decision to bring back the suspended bishop. This was then followed by physical violence. The bishop's opponents were frequently taken to prison and were tortured by soldiers. It should be noticed that diocesan and tribal advisers also constituted a valid 'defence' force to commit atrocities on their fellow citizens.

Furthermore, the principle of 'mutual support' was also in action. Although the executive council was called in October 2001 to discuss the crisis of North-Kivu, the college of bishops decided to handle the case in private and publish only the final decision, welcoming back the suspended bishop for the

---

[35] Dirokpa Balufuga, 'Pastoral letter addressed to leaders and Christians of North-Kivu', Bukavu, 27/10/01
[36] Balufuga, Pastoral letter, 14-15.
[37] Balufuga, Pastoral letter, 15.

ministry. This principle of 'mutual support' is expressed in Dirokpa's letter to Philip Bingham, Church Mission Society's regional manager at that time, 'There is a risk of destroying the church of God, thinking that we are building it. Today it is Munzenda who is harassed. Tomorrow it will be someone else. Will you ask everybody to quit because of a small opposition for which reasons are obscure?'[38]

Intimidation, revocation, suspension and culpability are the common means used to track the opposition within society and the church in the Congo. Biblical passages are interpreted out of their original context to back actions for submission to the authority. They have, thus, developed an 'informal' theology which in fact is oral theology, unassisted by critical discernment and hermeneutical skills of biblical interpretation. This has surely led to a weakening of the biblical understanding of authority.

Ecclesiology of Ethnocentrism

Ethnic consciousness has developed in Congo, and since political independence, politicians have exploited it in order to achieve their own ambitions. There have been tensions, hatred and violence between tribes during the postcolonial period, and those tensions are still explored for political causes. Often provinces or territories are set up according to ethnic considerations. Dominant tribes take part in ruling government and exploit government resources for the interest of their own people. Therefore, ethnicism has often satisfied the greediness and selfishness of individuals. Ethnic groups are manipulated for individual interest. The church in Congo has not escaped from this 'disease'.

Ethnic consciousness was deepened as a consequence of the Edinburgh conference in 1910. Although the conference did not have any power to enforce decisions, missionaries in Congo used its recommendations to attribute different parts of the mission field to mission societies, and it often coincided with ethnic groupings. Probably the missionaries saw this as a sensible division of work at the time. However denominations were planted and received as ethnic churches. The various Western Protestant missionary societies confined their activities to the agreed areas. Since then, these first ethnic groups to have received the Gospel became missionaries who spread their denomination to other places. The usual language is 'our church', which gives supremacy to ethnic rather than denominational factors. Denominationalism has thus become the label of ethnic identity. For instance, it is known that the Baptist church belongs to Nande, Anglican to Hema farmers, Brethren church to Hema pastoralists, Evangelical Church-CECA 20 to people from the north (Lubgara, Logo, Kakwa, Alur).

When people move to other cities or towns, ethnic identity continues to be of prime importance. Thus, they set up a *mutualité* (social organisation for mutual

---

[38] Dirokpa Balufuga, letter to Philip Bingham, Bukavu, 30 December 2001.

help). These *mutualités* have a cultural emphasis although they sometimes have political aspirations. Migrants often start 'their church' and keep in touch with the 'mother church' from home for administration. It often takes a long time for members of other ethnic groups to join these churches, for they will still be labelled with the names of their ethnic group or region: Hema church, Nande church, the church of people of Isiro, etc. The concept of the 'tribal church' is mainly seen here from a sociological point of view. The church sociologically belongs to the whole society or ethnic group which in return has power over it. Members expect to have church leaders from their own society and be the first beneficiaries of their church's resources.

This fight for 'our church' is found all over the EAC. For instance, in the diocese of Katanga, there are Lubakati from Katanga and Luba from Kasai who have been together for a long time. In the church Lubakati do not like Luba from Kasai to take responsibilities in the church for it is not their church.[39] It is worth noticing here that bishops from other provinces have always led this diocese of Katanga since the 1950s, and the Katangese have often tried in vain to take over the administration of 'their' diocese. For instance, in 1980, Sakambuya proclaimed himself the archbishop and the supreme chief of the Anglican Church of Congo. He did not succeed, but his followers are still making trouble in the church on an ethnic basis.[40] Again in 1986 Rev. Lumbala declared himself the bishop of Anglican Church in Kinshasa, then the bishop of Oriental Kasai in Mbujimayi. Moreover, when Kindu was still under Bukavu, Makungu Mangozi, a deacon, proclaimed himself bishop of Maniema and caused all Anglican Christians to rebel against the bishop of Bukavu.[41]

The 'ethnic church' has also developed in the diocese of Boga. The Anglican Church, which started in Boga in 1896, is known by Lendu as the church of Hema. The Hema have been fighting violently with their neighbours, the Lendu, for decades. The tension between these two societies automatically affects the church. The church of Ngiti fights for its independence, to have their own diocese, using their own people. The threat is not only from church members, but also from the whole society. In fact Ngiti are not on the diocesan staff and very few are trained at university level although their church was planted immediately after Boga. The claim for 'our' parish or 'our' archdeaconry is heard from the entire diocese. The end result has been to create archdeaconries on an ethnic basis. Boga now has archdeaconries of Hema, Lendu, Alur, Lugbara, Kakwa and the archdeaconry of the forest, although the viability of some of them is doubtful. The battle that is still going on is for each archdeaconry to have an archdeacon from the same tribe. Will the next step be to have dioceses for each tribe?

---

[39] Sabiti Tibafa, oral interview, Bunia, November 2001.
[40] Dirokpa Balufuga, letter to Isingoma Kawha, Bukavu, 10 January 2002, 7.
[41] Balufuga, letter to Isingoma, 7.

Within the same tribe, clans are also considered. Njojo expressed the tension within his own ethnic group between clans when he said, 'the clan of *Baboro* would like to lead the church of Boga as they lead the *collectivité* of Hema. They want a bishop from their clan. This could help to handle both religious and political areas.'[42] *Baboro* is the clan of the current chief. Therefore, ethnicism in Congo is a key factor in shaping the understanding of the church and the exercise of authority in the church. Parallels are easily drawn between what is happening in the political area and that is happening in the church. 'Our' church is a deep concept which causes tensions and violence between ethnic groups and clans; and causes the church to be understood in terms of ethnic considerations. But what is the experience of authority in this Anglican Church, 'our' church?

The Experience of Authority in the EAC

The Anglican Communion shares certain experiences through certain documents such as Prayer Books and Articles. The EAC has adopted as one of the norms of the faith 'the Book of Common Prayer of 1662 with its ordinal and its Thirty-nine Articles.'[43] In addition to these documents, there are some events which have contributed to form the EAC as a body and they shed light on the experience of authority in the EAC. In this context, this section aims to examine how authority is experienced through church documents, laity, youth groups, women's ministry and 'foreign' mission partnership.

Church Documents

In this Twenty-first century, it seems ridiculous to the world to see that there are still institutions that people want to lead in an African traditional way, without reference to any text.[44]

In the EAC, it is 'taboo' to have access to church documents.[45]

These two quotations show the dilemma the church has to solve. They want to update the institution to a 'modern' standard, where texts constitute an alternative to the oral tradition of African traditional society, which Dirokpa sees as 'ridiculous'. Authority in traditional society was in oral words rather than in written words. At the same time, it is a 'taboo' to make those documents available, which ensures that leaders have a monopoly on information. Why this dilemma and what are the texts for in the EAC?

---

[42] Njojo Byankya, oral interview, Boga, August 2000.
[43] Province de l'Eglise Anglicane du Congo, *Constitution,* 2001, art. 3, 3.
[44] Dirokpa Balufuga, letter to Isingoma Kawha, Bukavu, 10 January 2002, 5.
[45] Kithoko Kabangi, oral interview, Kisangani, December 2001.

The EAC has adopted, as previously said, the Book of Common Prayer of 1662 with its ordinal and Thirty-nine Articles. As norms of faith, they have authority. However, the Thirty-nine Articles, in their original form as adopted, are not available and Christians are completely ignorant of their existence. Students at the Anglican Theological College pay little attention to the Articles, which are printed in French in the Canadian Common Prayer Book, used in the college.

The ordinal reproduced from ancient documents into the new Congolese Prayer Book gives clear evidence of a hierarchical pattern of authority and obedience of bishops to archbishop, priests and deacons to bishops and other chief ministers. Priests and bishops are required to promise that they will study the Scripture and dispute erroneous opinions.[46] Bishops are also expected to govern the church, to interpret the Scriptures in disputes, and to exercise authority in a gentle and constructive manner. The overarching authority of the Scriptures is symbolised in the presentation of a New Testament or a Bible to each ordinand.

The Congolese Prayer Book abundantly illustrates the pattern of authority by the roles it gives to the minister in divine service and the administration of the sacraments. They have power in absolution of sins, ordination, confirmation and admission to the Lord's Supper. The Prayer Book also gives authority only to ordained ministers for the public reading of the Gospels, which are consequently seen by *Wakristo*[47] as a 'canon' within the canon. However, the authority of the Prayer Book has been challenged by *Wakristo*, influenced by the charismatic movement which emphasizes the role of the Holy Spirit through oral prayers from the 'heart' of individuals. The current generation of Congolese Anglicans feel very comfortable without the Prayer Book. Is that also due to the influence of other Protestant churches around?

Furthermore, there are *Canons*, *Constitution* and the *Statut* (statutes), which determine the laws, the duties and responsibilities of each office in the EAC. Unfortunately, these documents are not available for everyone to read. These sketchy documents are copies from the Church of Uganda. As in many developing countries, even meeting records are stored in the offices, and are badly preserved. To the question whether Christians have access to official church documents, the respondents' response can be summarized thus, 'We do not know anything about these documents. We have heard there are some documents, but we have never seen them.'

Most of the priests also do not have access to the church documents. The testimony of Sadiki is revealing,

---

[46] Province de l'Eglise Anglicane du Congo, 'Kitabu cha Sala kwa watu wote', imprimerie Rethy, 170.

[47] *Wakristo*, Swahili word for Christians is often used in the EAC to make a difference between the church leaders and other church members.

I have been priest since 1995. I had access to the Canon for the first time in Bunia during my training at Anglican College. I had had no access to the Canon and the constitution in my diocese. The priests do not have access to these documents, and the policy of our bishops is to keep people in ignorance.[48]

To keep people in ignorance has always been a fundamental strategy of domination in *Bula Matari*'s state. Although the statistics show 71% literacy in Congo, very few have access to books and newspapers. Mobutu used to gather thousands of people and could harangue the crowd for hours. Discourses are more important than texts, and people are confident in, and sensitive to, the 'oral word'. Discourses have authority and people often refer to 'what has been said'. This is the traditional value still in action, where the elder used to hold oral discourse around the fire to instruct his people. Does it mean that Scriptures do not have authority in the EAC? It does in theory, but still people are confident in its oral interpretation. 'What is said' has an impact on their daily life. This is why the leaders deliberately keep texts sketchy, vague and hidden so they can give interpretation according to their own presuppositions. So, the authority is not in texts, but in words.

Indeed, leaders often justify their actions by quoting texts. However, these texts are not authoritative as they do not have an 'orthodox' interpretation common to all church leaders. The simple following example can illustrate this. Dirokpa in his letter written on the crisis of North-Kivu stated, 'Then, you recognise that authority in the province lies in the college of bishops. This is again the sign of maturity from your side.'[49] But Isingoma's reaction shows a different reading of the constitution, 'As I know, the provincial constitution, for a case like this, gives much responsibility to the provincial synod, the diocesan synod, church court and the archbishop as the "chief pastor" rather than to the college of bishops.'[50] Therefore, official documents are kept hidden, short and imprecise; and they are used and interpreted in a manipulative manner to take advantage of people's enforced ignorance. How can the laity possess authority when they are kept in ignorance?

Youth Ministry

The EAC is divided into two groups, ordained and non-ordained persons. Lay people have been involved in the ministry, as previously said, since the beginning of the church. They are members of the provincial and diocesan synods, and they have their representatives in all committees. They work as catechists and lead sub-parishes, but they do not exercise the 'holy ministry'.

---

[48] Sadiki Kangamina, oral interview, Kisangani, December 2001.

[49] Dirokpa Balufuga, letter to Philip Bingham, Bukavu, 30 December 2001, 5.

[50] Isingoma Kahwa, interviewed in Bunia, 12 November 2001.

They simply fit as subordinates on the lowest level in view of the hierarchical pattern of ministry. The contribution of the laity is more developed in youth and women's ministry.

'You are the church of tomorrow.' This is a common statement of leaders, not only in the EAC, but also in many other denominations in Congo. It is about the theology of age. In traditional Congolese society, maturity was linked to marriage and age. Old people were mature enough to assess other's wisdom in the society. Marriage introduces someone to the stage where he or she can prove wisdom by leading the family and serving the elders. It is in this sense that youth could participate in elders meetings and take some responsibilities under their control. However, the society has changed and youth has become an unavoidable agent of those changes. In Congo, the national youth organisation is a challenging force and seen by the government as a threat to its authority. They are called *force vive* (dynamic force) of the nation. They are very motivated for the development of the country, but also committed to fighting dictatorship. They often hold demonstrations called *marche de colère* to express their bitterness over the bad management of the country. They frequently use violence to fight their cause.

In rural areas, they are challenging elders' authority. For instance in Onibha in Aru zone, youths have discovered that elders are a dividing instrument in the community. The latter always tell old stories of hatred between clans and families and these stories have damaged the unity of local communities. Thus, youths have taken over the leadership of the village and they consult elders if necessary. Solomoni said, 'Since we have taken over the leadership from our elders, the result is marvellous for the history does not have any influence on us anymore; and different clans are now working together for the welfare of the whole village.'[51] Two elements are important here: age as criteria of maturity and youth as *force vive* for change in society.

Authority structured according to age has greatly affected mission and ministry in the church. In many Protestant churches in Congo, only someone who is an old person can be ordained for the 'holy orders' and be called 'reverend'; otherwise it is said, 'You are too young to take responsibility'. Often 1 Timothy 5:22 is quoted to back the principle of the theology of age, 'Do not ordain anyone hastily, and do not participate in the sins of others; keep yourself pure'. While old age is considered as a sign of maturity and holiness, youth is seen as a 'sinful period' which can affect 'holy orders.' Yiki Solomoni has found in the parish of Ekanga in Aru a tension between youth, morality and holiness. He said, 'Youth of Ekanga are very committed to the development of the parish, but they are only used by the church for manual work. They cannot stand before the congregation and use the Bible for sermons or to do the Bible reading

---

[51] Yiki Solomoni, oral interview, Ekanga, August 2001.

because of their doubtful morality.' [52] The 'sinful period' refers to experimentation with alcohol, adultery and cigarettes.

Ageism was also a reason why the Maniema group left *Communauté Libre Methodiste au Centre de l'Afrique,* as narrated by Kalobya Matumba: 'There was segregation because only people of Shabunda were the big pastors; they did not like our pastors of Maniema to have the pastoral collar. To have the collar you must be old, incapable and without good sight. What can you do at this age?'[53] Although the main reason could be ethnicism, there is reaction against the ordination of old people who have ceased to be *force vive* within the church. In fact, youth in the EAC are now much involved in the ministry. Gathered in youth organisation called *Agape,* young people meet for Bible studies, prayers, evangelism, games and pastoral visits. They sing in the choir during Sunday services, funeral services, etc. However, very few preach and lead the service on Sundays.

Furthermore, they work as agents of reconciliation. For instance in Bunia, youth have run seminars to bring together Hema and Ngiti who have been fighting for years, as Judy Acheson, EAC's Provincial Coordinator of the Youth, shows in her prayer letter,

> Deo, Sinza, Richard and Jijika have continued to reach out and preach to displaced people and to run seminars on reconciliation with amazing results. Many have become Christians, others have repented of their involvement ... and others have decided to take the message of reconciliation to Lendu fighters in the hills to encourage them to give up fighting ... continue to pray for their safety.[54]

In Ekanga, youth have encouraged a good relationship between Anglicans and the Evangelical Church (CECA-20).[55] It is striking to see in the case of Ekanga that youth who participated in Holy Communion were very submissive for they feared suspension. But those who did not participate in Holy Communion were free to speak out and challenge the church leaders. This helped bring people together from these two Christian denominations.

Youth also work as *force vive* for change in the church. Beni Baataga has observed this in Boga and said,

> The church in Boga is somehow a traditionalist church, they don't really want to change. So, for instance, this jumping, clapping hands and dancing in the church, all those kinds of things. Some people, some leaders don't really want this in the church ... but still it is coming because of the influence of Bunia young people going to Boga, sometimes they go to Boga. So they go with their youth spirit, what

---

[52] Yiki Solomoni, oral interview, Ekanga, 2001.
[53] Kalobya Matumba, oral interview, Kalima Maniema, August 1998.
[54] Judy Acheson's Prayer letter, personal communication, November 2002, 1.
[55] Kaliru Anna, oral interview, Ekanga, August 2001.

they have in the worship here they take it there. You know, it becomes something new. And some young people there, they are realising it, they are doing it.[56]

Youth, in fact, are against the theology of age which gives them little power for the ministry. With the influence of the charismatic movement, the emphasis of teaching has moved from 'special gift' of the Holy Spirit given to the 'elite cast' for the ministry to the gift of the Holy Spirit to every believer to build the body of Christ, the Church. The emphasis is on the continuing experience of the Holy Spirit through his faithful people in the church. Youth thus question the supremacy of elders' authority for ministry.

Therefore, the youth in EAC is a *force vive*, able to challenge 'authority' in the church, but also to work for the well being of the people of God in this changing society. But the elders reluctantly integrate this change. The young people in the church are also members of the youth national organisation in Congolese society. Thus, national and local youth organisations, and other religious movements are influential in making Anglican youth, women and men, a *force vive* in the church, agents of change with a critical discernment of history and its weakness.

Women's Ministry

The position of women in Congolese tribes is culturally similar to other tribes in Africa where a wife is expected to submit to her husband. In return she receives protection from her husband against external attacks. The goals of marriage are the procreation of children and the promotion of the economic well-being of the family. Procreation and economy are key factors for life. It does not concern only women, but also men. In traditional Congo, the families both of the bride and the bridegroom had to make sure that they were good people,[57] and would collaborate to build their family. The spirit of complementarity within the family was recommended according to the roles each spouse had to play for the well-being of their family. It is with this spirit of complementarity that women have ensured the survival of the family these days when many people suffer from unpaid salaries and unemployment in Congo. Therefore, what Musimbi Kanyoro said about the whole of Africa can be applied in the Congolese situation,

> Women are the key actors in the economic system, often inventing various ways of working as small business entrepreneurs. Women control the non-monetary economy (subsistence agriculture, bearing and rearing of children, domestic

---

[56] Beni Bataaga, oral interview, Bunia, September 2000.
[57] Good girl or boy: someone who is a hard worker, welcoming, polite, wise, admired by others because of the moral standard required by the society.

labour) and 80% of economically active women are involved in agriculture, being 60% of the informal sector producers, and producing over 80% of food in Africa.[58]

Indeed, Kanyoro talks of women as marginalized people, but very engaged in the country's economic life for survival. However, in Congo women are engaged in the economy as committed members of their families. This corresponds to traditional education which sees it an honour in society to serve others.

Even religion in traditional society was not a private matter, but a community concern. Religion covered the whole of life. In fact women played a significant role in the community's worship life. Acts of healing, chasing away evil spirits, promoting fertility and success in life were performed both by priestesses and priests. A chief priestess or priest of a particular deity trained everybody involved in these activities. Priestesses were also known by the name of the deity they served. A woman could be regarded with respect if ancestors used her name to communicate with people.[59] For instance, Hema called their deified ancestors *Bacwezi*. The chief *Bacwezi* are Wamara, Ndahura, Kanyoro and Kyomya. Hema offer the goat Rutanga to these 'male' spirits. But there is also Kaikara, goddess of fertility, to whom is offered a black nanny goat which is kept in the kitchen.[60] The kitchen is not a despised place for it is the heart of family life. Thus, women as well as men were venerated as having supernatural powers.

Furthermore, for Hema, as other Africans, religion is not primarily about a belief in God, but about opposition to evil. Religion does not end with winning a place in heaven, but in maintaining the social and cosmic harmony here and now. For this reason, *wafumu* (witch-doctors) were very important to fight hidden forces of evil. Many of these *wafumu* are women, trusted and consulted by the population because of their 'spiritual' or supernatural power. Also, old women could perform some tasks in society and their voice could be heard. They could participate in certain reunions where only the wise men of the village were seated for solving problems.

The EAC, right from the beginning, recognised the ministry of women, as we said in the third chapter. They were pioneers with the founder Apolo Kivebulaya. They went with him to do the pastoral task and evangelism. It meant there were women catechists capable of teaching and evangelising; and Apolo took turns with them as he wrote himself, 'In February 1924, I began to visit the churches in Bukima, Tchabi, Bundingiri … We went with two lady teachers, Meri and

---

[58] Musimbi Kanyoro, 'Thinking Mission in Africa', in *International Review of Mission* (Vol. LXXXVIII no 345), 229.

[59] Muhindo Tsongo, 'The Role of Women in the Anglican Church of Congo: A Case Study of the Diocese of North Kivu' (MA dissertation, Trinity College, Bristol, July 2000), 8.

[60] Titre Ande, 'Le Christianisme face au Système d'Héritage chez les Bahema de Boga' (Mémoire de Licence, Bunia, 1994), 57.

Yunia. In Tchabi we gathered twenty people and preached the gospel.'[61] Women, since the beginning of the EAC, have enjoyed the authority to preach the gospel.

Furthermore, women were also involved in teaching to equip the people of God for ministry. For example, after the death of Apolo, a woman called Dolisi arrived at Boga from Uganda to work as a teacher at the Bible school. Interestingly, there was no criticism of women's ministry for it fitted with the women's role in the traditional religious world. Both men and women were given opportunity to study, and to serve in the church. The EAC constitution has also warned against any discrimination within the church,

> In conformity with the Christian pre-established doctrine, the EAC proclaim and support that all people have equal value, equal rights and equal dignity before God. The EAC will not allow any discrimination against its members or in its government on the basis of colour, race or tribe.[62]

Certainly here, colour, race and tribe are underlined to avoid any discrimination. Has gender been deliberately omitted? If so, is it because this kind of discrimination is not in people's minds? Or is it because bishops who wrote the constitution wanted to be careful about women's ordination to 'holy' ministry as they have based their argument on Christian pre-established doctrine? However, the constitution supports the idea of equal values, rights and dignity before God. Although the real sense of the above-mentioned statement has never been clearly defined in theological and ecclesiological terms, it has at least favoured the acceptance of women's ministry at different levels.

Moreover, a women's organisation, known as the Mothers' Union, has contributed much in making the diocese a society where people take joy in working together. Women play a variety of roles. They read the Bible and do evangelism. As in North-Kivu diocese,

> After they have acquired this biblical knowledge, however minimal it may be, the mothers are full of zeal and generosity to go and share it with others. This is the way for them to respond to the Lord's missionary command given in Mt 28:19-20. So the mothers organise evangelistic campaigns across the parishes and archdeaconries, and make individual visits in the name of evangelism. Those who cannot read the Bible share their witness. This evangelism helps towards the building up and reawakening of those women and men who have gone cold in their faith, and also to give new converts to the church.[63]

---

[61] Eglise Anglicane du Zaire, *Kwa Imani Apolo: Maisha ya Apolo Kivebulaya,* n.p, 1984, 41.

[62] Province de l'Eglise Anglicane du Congo, *Constitution,* 2001, Art. 4, 2

[63] Tsongo, 'The Role of Women in the Anglican Church of Congo', 17.

During the services, the women take the Bible readings, collect offerings, pray, teach in Sunday schools, preach and serve as churchwardens. Like other lay people, they are not allowed to read the Gospel or to distribute the Holy Communion.

More important is the role women play at ecumenical level. EAC is a member of the Church of Christ in Congo which gathers over sixty-four Protestant churches. For instance in North-Kivu, as Joyce Muhindo has noticed, 'The Anglican church was accused of having false doctrine and resembling the Roman Catholic Church in its liturgy; and of encouraging immorality. Although this false propaganda had no foundation, it has blocked the means of gaining new members for a long time.'[64] But the mothers are integrated into the federation of Protestant women and they share in all activities. They meet in churches on a rota basis that allows other denominations to come and pray with the Anglicans. These meetings help to remove the popular conception that Anglicans are as wolves among lambs.

Apart from pastoral work, women also learn practical skills, for self-development and to bring change in the local community, through small projects aiming at the holistic social and economic development of each member. Women are also used in different departments, whether at provincial or diocesan level. They are represented in all church meetings. But the Mothers' Union, because of its strong emphasis on the family, sidelines certain categories of women such as single mothers.

However, although women's authority has never been openly questioned for non-ordained ministry, there have still been some cultural and religious points which have destroyed women's self-esteem and forced some women and men to regard with suspicion women's authority for the ministry. As expressed by Esther Angomoko, 'People used to despise women's leadership, but they have finally accepted it. Women prefer men's leadership.'[65] Esther as an Alur might have been influenced by some traditional stories. Adubango related the story of Anyume, a woman who was chief of Alur. Women were unhappy with the leadership of a woman, and used to carry her on a *typoy*. One day they deliberately threw her into the river at Kaboti. Since then, elders have refused to have a woman chief.[66] This traditional story is well known in Alur zone. It might be a myth intended to reinforce male supremacy and it has destroyed women's self-esteem.

Christianity has also made women's leadership authority a complex issue in the church. Many biblical passages are quoted and interpreted as evidence of the illegitimacy of women's leadership in the church. For instance, 'The man is the head of woman' (1Cor. 11:3); 'I do not permit a woman to teach or to have

---

[64] Tsongo, 'The Role of Women in the Anglican Church of Congo', 18.

[65] Esther Ang'omoko, oral interview, Mahagi, August 2001.

[66] Adubango Dieudonné, oral interview, Mahagi, August, 2001.

authority over a man; she must be silent' (1 Tim. 2.12); Jesus never had women apostles; women were created after men (Gen. 2.22), etc. These arguments based on particular conservative and sacerdotal reading of Judeo-Christian religion came to obscure the positive reading people would have had of the traditional role of women in Congolese society.

Today the core issue of women's concern is the access to 'holy ministry'. According to G.R. Evans, 'In ordination three things come together: the gift of the Holy Spirit; the community's acceptance of the new minister's standing in a special relationship to the community; the bringing of the candidate into a recognised place in the church's order, with offices, tasks and responsibility.'[67] Surely, the members of the EAC would agree that the gift of the Holy Spirit for the office and work of a priest or bishop in the church is not based on gender, although it is considered as a 'special' one. As the acceptance of beliefs and practices in traditional religion was unquestionable, members would accept the church's teaching and tradition without questioning. However, the lack of unanimity about the legitimacy of women's ordination might have been partly influenced by some Christian denominations in Congo which had a negative view of woman's ordination which is in accordance with the previous Anglican position. The issue of woman's ordination had been postponed for a long time in both provincial and diocesan synods. Now it has been accepted.

It is worth noting that there has never been a serious and deep theological and ecclesiological debate on the issue of women's ordination in the EAC. The argument for women's ordination is often, 'We are late for other Anglicans have already done it. Even in Congolese society, women are occupying all levels.' Is the lack of this debate due to the academic level of church leaders? However, the members of the EAC will have to submit to the bishops' decision.

Therefore, although women are involved in church ministry, they do not have full access to all offices. There is still some uncertainty on their authority to act as priests and bishops. Although in theory, their authority has been recognised, still in practice, they are not well equipped to take the 'new responsibility'. Thus, the EAC has to take into account the challenge raised by Damali, as it is the case in many African countries:

> Our problem is that we are willing to do those things, but we don't have the capability of doing it because we didn't go for studies. When the time comes for choosing people to go and study they look at the men ... So we feel that we don't have the real training which should help us in our groups. But we pray to God that one day he will open for us a way so that we can also be studying different things. Leadership, theology, and everything that the men can do, I think we can do it.[68]

---

[67] G.R. Evans, *Authority in the Church: A challenge for Anglicans* (Norwich: The Canterbury Press, 1990), 79.
[68] Damali Sabiti, oral interview, Mukono (Uganda), October 2000.

The EAC and Society

The church members engage in mission or evangelisation because in this way they follow Jesus and are privileged to share in his mission and his life's work. This mission consists not only in building up the church both in its community and its institutional aspects, but also in promoting the reign of God by giving witness to certain key Christian values. It is to share Christ's good news with others. God, who was in Christ, entered the world and lived, loved and suffered in the midst of realities. Through his very nature he has shown his concern for the world and has also challenged the world. The church has to follow this path to be faithful both to the divine concern and the divine challenge. In this context, how does the EAC give expression to this incarnational basis of its faith?

Socio-political Context

People have tried to do everything within their means to secure a bright future for themselves; they have created all sorts of institutions to ensure that life is orderly and efficient. Economically, people have exploited, sometimes plundered, nature to enable them to have a comfortable life; they have excelled in military build up; but today we live in a world where for the majority, life is meaningless and the future hopeless.

In the Congo, economic, political and military power is wielded today within the country in the interest of a particular group of people who get rich and maintain power at the expense of neglecting the genuine needs of people. Furthermore, there is no equal treatment in governmental economic and educational policies between classes or ethnic groups. Political structures at national level thus are not still fully in touch with the needs and aspirations of people today.

People still suffer from governmental violation of the integrity of the person, torture, cruel, inhuman or degrading treatment or punishment; arbitrary arrest or imprisonment; denial of fair public trial. Moreover, the country is facing militarism which ensures that the nation's military apparatus has ever-increasing control over the lives and behaviour of its citizens; and military goals and military values increasingly dominate national culture, education, the media, religion, politics and the economy at the expense of civilian institutions. People are deprived of their civil rights that include having a legal and social environment which protects and enhances the healthy development of individuals and groups within the society. This concerns even the right to such vital necessities as food, shelter, health care and education. Yet with the endless 'civil' war, the situation has deteriorated and got worse. Therefore, today life is characterized in the Congo by hopelessness, meaninglessness and despair. That makes people extremely anxious about the future. So, in such a world, what has been the role of the EAC as the Anglican Church of Congo?

Church and Social Transformation

The EAC has discovered that community development and social transformation are legitimate goals and expressions for the church in mission and ministry. The EAC's statutes state it well. 'The association has as goals: evangelisation, education, development, health care, and all other activities related to education and the well being of the population.'[69] Thus the EAC has created in each diocese primary and secondary schools, hospitals and health care centres in rural and urban areas; small projects such as providing clean water, breeding or farming, electric mills, etc.[70] Some literacy training centres are set up to help those in the society who could not go to school. Very few of these centres are now functioning because of the economic problem the country is facing. However, these are not specifically Anglican concerns, for it has become a custom in Congo for all churches to have schools, hospitals, guesthouses, and community development to gain recognition of those churches by society. The target is not primarily the well being of the population, but to build up greater membership in the church.

The EAC also offers education on social issues such as child mortality, sexual abuse, alcohol abuse, AIDS, and teenage pregnancies and child and youth delinquency, through youth and Sunday school groups.[71] However, the EAC pays less attention to other issues such as unemployment due to the economic recession, domestic violence, lack of relevant educational facilities, abandoned children, parental violence, orphans, and so on.

Moreover, the EAC helps in fighting environmental problems: soil erosion and deforestation. Many local parishes are involved in the afforestation policy. However, the state has taken advantage of church concerns for social transformation as an excuse to abdicate from its responsibility, and at the same time scrutinise the church's involvement. It is in this sense that Likambo Araba, the chief of Kumuru, reminded the church of its responsibility and opportunity to demonstrate to the nation the reconciling power of the gospel in a multi-ethnic society where ethnic groups suffer violence and discrimination.[72] Indeed, the EAC should concentrate on community building by creating supportive social systems which enable individuals and families to survive, to grow towards God and towards one another, and to enable communities to become welcoming and inclusive. Unfortunately the EAC is also facing internal conflicts.

---

[69] 'Statuts de l'Association sans but lucrative, Communauté Anglicane du Zaire', Art 3, 1.
[70] Makuru Mpabaise, personal communication, Kisangani, 13 December 2001.
[71] Sinziri Onadra, interviewed in Kumuru, 30 July 2001.
[72] Likambo Araba in an interview with 12 people, Kumuru, 29 July 2001.

The EAC and Dominating Power

As one of the leaders, I have found that the church has not engaged yet with the socio-political issues of the country. The social actions done are destroyed by the new policy of war. We must also engage with this new policy of war. How? We have never met to discuss it and to put together our forces. Everybody is on his own. It is not like Roman Catholic bishops, when one of them speaks up, others support him. The politicians who know the Anglican Church expect in vain something from it. We will never meet to discuss political issues because we think it is evil.[73]

Isingoma Kahwa has clearly stated that the EAC does not engage with political issues, yet it should be in the forefront in challenging those who hold political power and office to ensure that the rights of people are protected and safeguarded at all times. Isingoma's lamentation was the same as most of our respondents. 'It is true that our church is among the silent churches.'[74] 'The church does not look after the state, but the state observes the church, controls church's activities and its sermons. Is there any limit for the state in church's affairs?'[75] Thus, the EAC has not gathered to consider the real problems and dilemmas that people are facing.

Different reasons have been given for the fact that the church is not morally impelled to intervene when people's rights are violated, and remains inactive. Many people think it is because of a fear of retaliation from the government that church leaders have not reacted with moral outrage to the violation of human rights. Ise-somo also explained, 'It is true that leaders fear to denounce the evil work of political leaders because, during the former government, you might have had a problem if you tried to challenge them. These days they welcome everybody, but still the church is careful because the government is changing everyday.'[76]

The fear is also cultural. For instance, there is an adage from Hema which says, '*ngo umwantukire abantu mbaseka ento bwantumwanzi e bantu bakoe*' (people laugh at a fearful person, but people cry over courageous persons). Lubgara say, '*omba dria otuko*' (death to the courageous people). It means the one who fears saves his life and the one who is courageous risks his life. This explains why many Congolese do not like to take risks and challenge political leaders. Talking of life, Ukelo said, 'Once a Roman Catholic becomes a priest, he gives his life to others, while in our church, pastors want to conserve their lives, and there is no self-sacrifice.'[77] The comparison of Anglican leaders with Roman Catholics is striking, and it appeared in every interview.

---

[73] Isingoma Kahwa, personal communication, Bunia, 12 November 2001.

[74] Young people in towns were strongly against the EAC having being silent, while people in rural areas were reserved.

[75] Sinzahera Uwimana, personal communication, Bunia, 15/12/01.

[76] Ise-somo Muhindo, oral interview in Bunia, 29 November 2001.

[77] Ukelo Unen, interviewed in Bunia, 15 December 2001.

One of the reasons is that the Anglicans lack international backing while Roman Catholics are enjoying it through their network from Rome.[78] But the reaction from others is that EAC should take advantage of being a member of the Anglican Communion.[79] The argument is that Roman Catholics are 'well educated because they pass through different levels of training, while our leaders have limited access to training opportunities.'[80] However, Ise-somo sees a change in the attitude, 'Because of some educated people, our leaders have reluctantly started to speak, and have managed to write a memorandum.'[81] Indeed, the unique memorandum written by Anglican bishops was a big step in the EAC's history towards its prophetic ministry. However, the memorandum was written to denounce the aggression of the Congo by neighbouring countries, and did not challenge the Congolese government. The memorandum states,

> We declare that we are unanimously against this bloody war, against balkanisation, against the policy of exclusion; and we denounce the foreign and illegal occupation of the Congolese territory, the accomplice passivity of UN and the whole international community, and the naivety of some Congolese politicians. Our brothers and sisters, remain stuck together during this hard period for our homeland, the Democratic Republic of Congo, speaking the same language relying on our Lord Jesus Christ who liberates and procures real peace.[82]

This memorandum has an interesting background. In 1998, all Congolese Anglican bishops attended the Lambeth Conference and they delayed coming back to Congo because the second 'rebellion' against the Kabila's regime had started. The Ugandan newspaper *New Vision* criticised the Congolese bishops' delay, accusing them of being against Kabila's regime. Bishops were then expecting retaliation from the government. This memorandum came, in fact, to refute that, and show their support to Kabila's government. No clear action was suggested in the memorandum. The five recommendations urged the help of the Anglican Communion, the need for an immediate stop to war, respect for the Lusaka accord, inter-Congolese dialogue and national and international fasting for peace in Congo. Nothing is new in this memorandum, except the call for the support of the Anglican Communion and international fasting. The call for fasting was already common within independent church circles. The rest of the language is borrowed from politicians themselves, even the 'naivety of some Congolese politicians' was the term used by the government to point at the 'rebel leaders' considered to be treacherous puppets. Therefore the EAC has adopted the policy of accommodation.

---

[78] Sabiti Tibafa, interviewed in Bunia, 24/11/01.

[79] Again this argument is much supported by the youth.

[80] Musinge Tibafa, personal communication, Kisangani, 14/12/01.

[81] Ise-somo Muhindo, interviewed in Bunia, 29/11/01.

[82] 'Memorandum ya Wakristo ya Nord-Kivu kwa Archbishop,' 23 January 2001, 1.

In fact, there is an historical link between the EAC and the political leaders. Henry VIII's involvement in the foundation of the Anglican Church sticks in people's minds. It is also significant that the Anglican Church was introduced into Congo on *Mukama* Tabaro's demand. Although Apolo Kivebulaya, one of the first Ugandan missionaries, used to challenge the *Mukama*, the latter has retained its honoured place in the church. For instance, in the Cathedral of Boga, the *Mukama* has his throne or seat still near the altar and nobody else is allowed to use it when the *Mukama* is absent. The *Mukama* is welcomed with his team at the New Year services. As a source of happiness for his people, he dedicates the offering to God.[83] Therefore, this historical link with the power structure together with the different causes of fear we have described above has forced the EAC to accommodate itself to the state policy and ideologies.

The EAC's Policy of Adaptation

The EAC's policy of accommodation or adaptation has led the church to blindly copy the *Bula Matari*'s model of authority. These two following quotations give a good summary of what many people think of this accommodation.

> The authorities of the EAC seek to equal the political authorities, to take advantage of what they gain, they want to have the equivalent. An archdeacon will mobilise all pastors, Christians and choirs to welcome him. It is normal to welcome, but the disciplinary measures are applied if there is no warm welcome.[84]

The authority in the EAC is the reproduction of the state, while it was for the state to copy the church. It is as if we have a burgomaster, the reverend pastor will like to copy what the burgomaster does. It is like that up to the top. It is as if the church is now taught by the state instead of the state being taught by the church.[85]

In fact the way the church leaders are welcomed is not simply cultural, but an adaptation to *Bula Matari*'s model. For instance, the church leaders enjoy the songs of welcome sung in their honour with their names, immersing themselves in the crowd of Christians waving flowers, and walking on the clothes laid on their path by Christians. During their visit to parishes or sub-parishes, nobody is allowed to talk to the leaders, except through the protocol.[86] This is exactly what the politicians do in the Congo. The dictatorship is another example of adaptation. People are happy to see their church leaders behaving like political dictators. One of the accusations against Bishop Munzenda by his colleagues and

---

[83] Titre Ande, 'Le Christianisme face au Système d'Héritage chez les Bahema de Boga', 28.

[84] Muhondi Mubakabakaba, personal communication, Kisangani, 14 December 2001.

[85] André Changaila, personal communication, Kisangani, 14 December 2001.

[86] Kangamina Sadiki, personal communication, 13 December 2001.

church members was that 'he is used to and speaks to everybody, even children. He does not know he is bishop.'[87]

Church members see this adaptation as a 'good relationship' between the church and the state, which are one body, but with different roles. Asiiki's statement shows it well,

> The EAC has no problem with the state because the EAC has its own authority in its work and cannot forget the state because the EAC goes together with the state. When the EAC wants to do something, for example a party, they cannot forget the state. The EAC has seen the importance of the state, because they know that the state guides us physically and the EAC guides us spiritually they are one body, so they have to move together in all they do.[88]

'One body, but different roles' is a common slogan in the EAC to describe the good relationship between the state and the EAC; and it has led to the theology of 'accommodation'. Romans 13.1-7 and 1 Peter 2.13-17 have become the endless slogan to back the submission to civil authority with a biblical basis. Even though it is a biblical concept that governments and leaders are ordained by God to ensure that justice is maintained in society and nation, they themselves also need to be kept in check, or otherwise they may go beyond the prescribed limits of their authority, thus becoming oppressive. In the Congolese violent and oppressive society, the church should plead for a culture of non-violence as a force for change and liberation. Instead of accommodating itself to that culture of violence, the church should give up any theological or other justification for the use of oppressive power, and develop just and peaceful ministries.

Conclusion

This chapter has found that the self-understanding of authority within the EAC is built on historical, cultural and political assumptions rather than a systematic written theology of authority. Authority is believed to have a divine source, channelled to leaders through Christ. But authority is conceived as a coercive structural power and as the person who manages the structure. In a world of conflicts caused by tribalism and *episcopose*, authority is personalized and exercised through an exploitative structural network. A new unwritten interpretation of biblical passages and symbols has developed to value *utii* theology in an uncertain socio-political climate. However, the challenge is that there is a sense of rejection of authority and the genuine desire for freedom of thought, expression and action, for this unsystematic understanding of authority has had little to contribute to those to whom it should be ministering, and the dynamics at work are very different from the principles of documents. The

---

[87] Memorandum of North Kivu, 23 January 2001.

[88] Asiiki David, oral interview, Mahagi, 09 August 2001.

written theology does not engage with the grassroots where authority is expressed verbally and behaviourally.

Therefore, the system of authority in the EAC does not practically meet the needs of Congolese Christians marked by hopelessness, meaningless and despair of life. As a reproduction of political manipulative interpretation of the culture and biblical passages, the understanding of authority in the EAC is not theologically in harmony with what we understand to be Christian authority. Thus, there is a need for re-evaluation and rediscovering of unconscious traditional values of authority and a vital, dynamic and biblical theology of authority.

Chapter Five

Liberating Authority in African Communion Models

Authority in Communion Ecclesiology

African theologians such as Sawyerr, Pobee, Dickson, Mbiti and Idowu, have stated that African culture and religion have been utterly ignored by the colonizing powers that saw an African as an object of no intrinsic value. Consequently, true African liberation is not possible without rediscovering deeply rooted traditional cultural values. African churches thus have an important role to play in this process of inculturation. Economic performance and politics accordingly require an inculturation that is truly permeated by African thinking and living.

In fact, it is essential that the impact of a truly inculturated Christianity should be made plainly manifest to the Africans who have been and still are prey to injustice, disease and other social evils. The question to solve still remains 'who Christ is and what impact he has on the Africans'. This need for Christianity, 'truly' African and considering its cultural values, was already expressed by African students in Paris in their publication *Des Prêtres Noirs S'interrogent* in 1957, then by Pope Paul in Kampala in 1969 when he challenged Africans by stating, 'You may and must have an African Christianity.'[1]

African Roman Catholic theologians have since then seriously considered this challenge. Vatican II and various subsequent conferences have underlined the importance of the local church, resulting in a plea for the doctrine of subsidiarity, which means that a higher level should not decide what could be handled at a lower level. In this case, the best of African theology is to rethink the established

---

[1] Patrick Ryan, 'Introduction', in Patrick Ryan (ed), *The Model of 'Church-as-Family':
Meeting the African Challenge* (Nairobi: CUEA Publications, 1999), ii.

models of the church. It is a 'theology that calls for a re-articulation of ecclesiology in a way that speaks forcefully to the milieu of Africa. It speaks to the distinctive challenges, perceptions, and profound lifestyle of this age.'[2]

In approaching the meaning of the Church in practical, concrete ways, African theologians have used metaphors to bring down to earth the 'people of God Theology'. We will deal only with three of these metaphors: the Church as Clan, the Proto-Ancestor model and the Church-as-Family model. We will also examine the sense of community according to Kwesi Dickson and John Pobee. We will end the chapter with an analysis of the Anglican paradigm of 'communion-through-baptism'. We argue that any African category uncritically used for the church will result in a violent, discriminating and dominant model. This section aims to examine whether these models provide relevant values to incarnate Christ's authority, as 'authority of Life-for-life'.

Authority in Clan Ecclesiology

Laurenti Magesa, one of Africa's foremost exponents of the liberation genre of theology has proposed the African Clan as a paradigm for democracy in the church and in the world. Magesa built his argument for the proposed clan model on the life of the historical Jesus. According to Magesa, power and the exercise of authority are important elements in any social organisation, and the entire life and preaching of Jesus were aimed at rejecting and breaking down the pyramidal social structure of his day.[3] Jesus' authority is one of service; it is recognised in service. Service is thus the manifestation of the power of Jesus' Spirit which distinguishes both Christian leadership and all human relationships. Christian authority is properly one of service and vulnerability or the authority of 'washing each other's feet', as John 13.1-20 puts it, after the example of Jesus himself.[4]

Magesa thus suggested that Clan was a good model of the Church in Africa for it adheres to important theological principles and time honoured mechanisms of subsidiarity, solidarity, participation and socialization in Church life and practice; and he argued that it mandates the practices of democracy in a Church faithful to its calling to bring about and witness to the fullness of life in the world.

In fact, Magesa is confident that, in Africa in general, the institution of the clan may be said to be the best expression of Jesus' commitment to egalitarian social relations, and its spirituality consists in participation-sharing which is the central principle for human existence, the mark of true humanity. This principle

---

[2] Ryan, 'Introduction', ii.

[3] Laurenti Magesa, 'Christ's Spirit as Empowerment of the Church-as-Family', in Ryan (ed), *The Model of 'Church-as-Family'*, 19-35, 21

[4] Laurenti Magesa, 'Theology of Democracy', in Laurenti Magesa and Zablon Nthamburi (eds), *Democracy and Reconciliation: A Challenge for African Christianity* (Nairobi: Acton Publishers, 1999), 121.

provides a person with the right to be listened to and respected as a member of the community. This right is accorded usually in the measure such an individual contributes to the community. Thus it also places a strong demand on every member of the community to contribute to the enhancement of its 'vital force'. It is here as well that the community's ancestors and other spiritual forces are directly involved in clan structures and activities.[5]

Of special significance in the clan structure and operation is the aspect and role of leadership. The most important obligation of every leader is to do whatever is in his/her power to protect and prolong the life of the clan-community according to the order established by the ancestors and transmitted by tradition. The leader's authority and respect depend on how such a leader executes the responsibility entrusted to him/her. Authority is 'authority-for-life', for reconciliation and unity. Abusive power is, in the end, null and void.

What the clan seeks to preserve by its structure of leadership and operation are, therefore, unity, justice, service, honour to God and the ancestors, the correct transmission of tradition, and the widening of the clan through marriage and the formation of friendships and alliances so that the life of the clan and its happiness might be assured. The operational structures of the clan are thus embodied in the central concern of the historical Jesus which consisted in liberating people. Therefore, democracy within the church embodies the four basic and most important aspects of Jesus' exercise of authority that Justin S. Ukpong lists: 'authority in service'; 'authority in humility'; 'authority in obedience of God'; and 'authority in enabling activity.'[6] However, quoting Ukpong, Magesa agreed that enabling is particularly important for pastoral ministry:

> Jesus' ministry and life with his disciples bring home more concretely the use of how he exercised his authority in an enabling creative way. The miracles of his earthly ministry were meant to enable the blind, the lame, the deaf, those possessed by demons and the marginalized in society to regain their self-worth and be re-integrated into society … This was in fulfilment of his declared mission which was to bring the good news to the poor and afflicted.[7]

John Waliggo has also developed the Clan ecclesiology, but based on the fifty-two clan system of the Baganda Ethnic Group, which is the largest group in Uganda. According to the clan system in Buganda today, Waliggo found out that clan is highly ecumenical, embracing members of all faiths. Its leadership is for service. It has a very clear division of labour in which every member participates. It values community and reconciliation. It promotes sincere concern of everyone for each other. It caters for the integral growth of each and every member. Above

---

[5] Magesa, 'Theology of Democracy', 124.
[6] J.S. Ukpong quoted by Magesa, 'Theology of Democracy', 130.
[7] Magesa, 'Theology of Democracy', 130.

all, it allows a lot of initiatives and fulfils the search for authentic inculturation. Thus, 'the clan's openness, democratic nature, concern for the weaker and disadvantaged of its members, structures of participation in decision making are', in Waliggo's words, 'advantages to taking the clan system as a model for the living Church.'[8]

However, although clan has been described as the basis of the African experience of unity, harmony and solidarity, it was a closed social unit where non-members of the clan were excluded. The overriding concern of the clan unit was the protection of the whole unit's integrity and economic welfare in the most satisfactory way possible. When it became necessary to co-operate with other clans, it was because there was a common objective to be achieved or a common danger to be averted. But such objective or danger had to be of equal concern. It is not clear in which sense Magesa exactly uses 'democracy' for there is no guarantee that the positions of minorities or those who are on the losing end of a vote will be respected. Thus, the idea of church as clan will simply reinforce clanism and tribalism. The frequent cases of violent clashes between clans and tribes, their selfishness and greediness as seen in previous chapters will make the church more vulnerable than before, and its image will be blackened.

Church as Great Family

Ancestors are thought to be central to the African concept of life. They are seen as the intermediaries between God and men, and they are considered as members of the extended family. African theologians have proposed many models which will incorporate ancestors as members of the Christian family. Among these models of the church, this section will only examine the church as great family and proto-ancestor models.

In 1960, Bengt Sundkler, in his book *The Christian Ministry in Africa*, suggested:

> There is possibility ... that the African Protestant theologians of the future will build on [the] fact of the family as one of the main pillars of his theology, particularly of his ecclesiology. He may come to regard it as his particular task to see the Church in terms of the Great Family.'[9]

In fact, Harry Sawyerr took seriously Sundkler's suggestion and expanded on the concept of the church as 'the Great Family'. His aim was to relate ecclesiology to African kinship structures. Looking at Paul's ecclesiology,

---

[8] J. Mary Waliggo, 'The African Clan as the True Model of the African Church', in Mugambi and Magesa (eds), *The Church in African Christianity: Innovative Essays in Ecclesiology* (Nairobi: Initiatives Publishers, 1990), 122-124.

[9] Bengt Sundkler, *The Christian Ministry in Africa* (Swedish Institute of Missionary Research: Uppsala, 1960), 289.

Sawyerr notes that for the apostle, the Christians are all 'one man' in Christ (Galatians 3.28; Ephesians 2.11-22); they drink of one Spirit (1Cor. 12.13) and they share one body and blood of Christ (1 Corinthians 10.16). The oneness of the church leads him to the concept of the church as the whole Christ, which he relates to the church as the Great Family in the following manner:

> The church as the whole Christ, members of the Body integrated in to the Head ...,
> is therefore, in our opinion, more likely to appeal to the true feelings of the African
> because the idea of Jesus Christ as the first-born among many brethren can readily
> be introduced in this context.[10]

The tendency here is to compare 'Christ as first-born' to 'Christ as Ancestor'. For Sawyerr, 'the African community embraces the living, the unborn and the dead.' It is essential somehow to relate ecclesiology to the bloodline family ties which are very important to Africans. He refers the reader to Matthew 27.52; 1 Corinthians 15.29 (baptism for the dead); 1Peter 3.18 (descent into hell); 1 Thessalonians 4.14-18; and the great cloud of witnesses in Hebrews 11. According to him, these texts show that Christians of New Testament times had a real concern for their relatives and compatriots who had died either before the establishment of the Christian church (in the case of non-Christians) or before the parousia (in the case of Christians). He thus concludes:

> We would, therefore, go on to suggest that the prayers of African Christians might,
> in the providence of God, lead to the salvation of their pagan ancestors. Indeed, we
> must justifiably add that it is highly probable that some of the dead for whom the
> early Christians were baptized had never heard of the promise of salvation through
> Jesus Christ.[11]

Therefore, as 'African people live with their dead', Sawyerr suggested:
In the present context, therefore, Christian doctrinal teaching should be directed towards, first, presenting the church as a corporate body with a unique solidarity transcending by far anything akin to it in pagan African society; and, second, discovering a means of preserving the tribe, solidarity of living and dead, as Africans understand that relationship, but in a new idiom, that of the community of the church. In any case, ancestors are thought of in relation to their tribes or clans or families. They could, therefore, be readily embraced within the framework of the universal church and be included within the communion of saints.[12]

Dirokpa Balufuga, the Anglican archbishop of Congo, suggested the same idea of embracing the ancestors in the framework of the Church:

---

[10] Harry Sawyerr, *Creative Evangelism: Towards a New Christian Encounter with Africa* (London: Lutterworth Press, 1968), 79.

[11] Sawyerr, *Creative Evangelism*, 95.

[12] Sawyerr, *Creative Evangelism*, 95.

The inculturated liturgy should give an important place to the ancestors as in the African traditional society. In doing so, it is important to begin the service with the invocation of ancestors, even during other moments of the celebration. They are the intercessors that oversee the behaviour of the community and they are '*traits d'union*' (hyphen) between their descendants and supernatural beings.[13]

Another African theologian who links ancestor veneration, the communion of saints and ecclesiology is E.W. Fasholé-Luke. He built his theology on the finding of anthropologists that 'ancestral cults are expressions of the family and tribal solidarity and continuity.'[14] He aims to see the church developing a theology of the communion of saints that will satisfy the passionate desire of Africans, Christians and non-Christians alike, to be linked with their dead ancestors.

For African ancestors who were not Christians to be embraced within the framework of the universal church and included in the communion of saints, Fasholé-Luke emphasized a more profound appraisal of the situation and a deeper theological interpretation of the beliefs about the fate of the departed. He based his interpretation of the *sanctorum communio* of the creeds of Karl Barth to mean fellowship with holy people of all ages and the whole company of heaven through participation in the holy sacraments. First, at baptism Christians are made members of the universal church, and are therefore able to have fellowship with Christians of every age, and are linked with the faithful departed since the fellowship within the church is not limited by time or space and this fellowship is not broken by death. Then, at Eucharist Christians join the whole company of heaven, the faithful departed, the angels and archangels, to praise and glorify God. Can the perpetual memorial of Christ's death thus link with non-Christian ancestors? Fasholé-Luke expressed his position as follows:

> We believe that the death of Christ is for the whole world and no one either living or dead is outside the scope of the merits of Christ's death. Thus both Christians and non-Christians receive salvation through Christ's death and are linked with him through the sacrament which he himself instituted. This view is supported by the fact that in his roll of heroes of faith, the author of Hebrews includes non-Christians whose faith was not perfect. We would equally affirm that the African ancestors could also be included in the Communion of Saints in this way, since they had a faith which was not perfect; but the death of Christ can make perfect the feeble faith which they had and thus incorporate them into his Body the Church.[15]

---

[13] Dirokpa Balufuga, 'Liturgie Anglicane et inculturation, hier, aujourd'hui et demain', 239.

[14] E.W. Fasholé-Luke, 'Ancestor Veneration and the Communion of Saints', in M. E. Glasswell and E.W. Fasholé-Luke (eds), *New Testament Christianity for Africa and the World* (London: SPCK, 1974), 209.

[15] Fasholé-Luke, 'Ancestor Veneration and the Communion of Saints', 217.

Therefore Sawyerr and Fasholé-Luke agree that the concept of the family is the best category for African ecclesiology, for it incorporates ancestors into the church and grants them salvation. In our view, it is doubtful that such a view of Sawyerr and Fashole-Luke may have a positive impact on mission. It is just a device to make Christianity more palatable to Africans. In this case, can the theology of ancestors serve as a starting-point of ecclesiology in Africa? This question leads us to examine proto-ancestor ecclesiology.

Proto-Ancestor Model

In his book *African Theology in Its Social Context,* Bénézet Bujo, a Catholic theologian from north east Congo, is convinced that African theology has a contribution to make to the liberation of all people towards life in its fullness. This liberation can be effective only if the Black African rediscovers his roots so that the ancestral tradition may enrich post-colonial people and make them adopt a critical attitude towards modern society which is, in Bujo's words, 'responsible for a tragic situation of dictatorship, both domestic and foreign'.[16] The ancestor model thus became Bujo's fundamental concept to elucidate Christology and ecclesiology in the context of African culture.

Bujo based his proto-ancestor ecclesiology argument on the African concept of life. Life is a participation in God, but hierarchically ordered. It means God is the source of all life, and ancestors are the indispensable channels through which this divine life-force reaches the living members. This divine life can be enjoyed in its fullness when the ancestors are remembered and honoured. It is life as unity in its wholeness, for Africa knows no distinction between individual, social, religious and political life. Although life is always mediated by one standing above the recipient in the hierarchy of being, it is not life merely seen in a biological sense, but it is a metaphysical concept. Ancestors who lived exemplary lives had laid down laws, and established customs, which embodied their own experiences, and which they passed on to their descendants as a precious legacy.[17]

The descendants remain in living communion both with the ancestor and their own living kin when they make the experience of the ancestor their own. African society is a real 'mystical body', encompassing both dead and living members, in which every member has an obligation to every other. The living members of this 'mystical body' have an inalienable responsibility for protecting and prolonging the life of the community. The past has a supreme importance for Africans, for the secret of life is found in ancestral heritage. The life-giving traditions of the past determine the present and the future. Bujo thus rejects John Mbiti's idea of

---

[16] Bénézet Bujo, *African Theology in Its Social Context* (Saint Paul Communications, 1992), 15.

[17] Bujo, *African Theology in Its Social Context,* 11.

'backwardness of history'. For Bujo, the 'circular thinking' of the compulsory repetition of ancestral heritage means that people looked to the past for salvation. This life-giving tradition which is, in fact, the ancestral heritage, constitutes a sort of 'narrative theology'. The repetition of rituals is a way of remembering and re-enacting the past and it is a guarantee of prosperity for the future. This recalling of the history of ancestors is a kind of 'Exodus Theology'. Salvation must be grounded in ancestral tradition and the future depends on the actualisation of ancestral heritage.

Bujo expressed the African way of looking at things as anthropocentric, for African religion focuses on the mystery of life and death. Thus humankind itself is naturally the centre of concern, and the moral orders are seen simply as the relationships between human beings themselves. [18] While Bujo accuses missionaries of destroying many vital elements in African culture, he also rebukes African theologians for having failed to translate the traditional dimension of liberation into the modern situation in order to achieve a balanced life. Thus the Christian church has a responsibility to raise a new society by incarnating the ancestral world into modern society. This involves a complete reconstruction of the current dominant church, which must be based on ancestors' concepts and practices. It is to recognise the authority of 'ancestral heritage' in modern society.

According to Bujo, the African concept of life must be the corner-stone of an African ecclesiology, and any attempt to formulate an African ecclesiology which leaves this concept out of account is in danger of remaining superficial and of talking over the heads of the Africans. [19] Bujo's Christology aims to recover the genuinely human dimension of Jesus so that his message may really meet modern people and modern problems. He found the titles bestowed upon Jesus by the first Christians reflect the situation of the Risen Christ, and must be reinterpreted in the African modern context as they were borrowed from their own contemporary culture.

In fact, Bujo believes that the historical Jesus of Nazareth brought life in its fullness, working miracles, healing the sick, opening the eyes of the blind and raising the dead to life. All these qualities and virtues Jesus manifested are those which Africans like to attribute to their ancestors and which lead them to invoke the ancestors in daily life. Therefore Jesus is the Proto-Ancestor, life-giver which is the central theme of the New Testament. This is a Christology 'from below' for the African context, for theology can only speak of God in human terms and Jesus himself described God in terms drawn from human experience. [20]

However, Bujo is conscious that the term 'ancestor' can only be applied to Jesus in an analogical way, since to treat him otherwise would be to make of him

---

[18] Bujo, *African Theology in Its Social Context,* 32.
[19] Bujo, *African Theology in Its Social Context,* 92.
[20] Bujo, *African Theology in Its Social Context,* 80.

only one founding ancestor among many. He stated that to treat Jesus as an ancestor is not in any crudely biological sense. To regard him as the ancestor par excellence means he begets in us a mystical and supernatural life. This uniqueness of Jesus signifies that Jesus realized the authentic ideal of ancestors, but furthermore he infinitely transcended that ideal and brought them to a new completion.[21] According to Bujo, the title proto-ancestor given to Jesus Christ is not a mere label, but expresses the very essence of the Word becoming human. It means that in the mystery of the incarnation, God so truly became human that God is identified with humankind, and has become a part of this world, part of the reality and of the history of the cosmos.

Therefore, the concept of life, according to Bujo, is fundamental to understand 'proto-ancestor' ecclesiology, for Jesus is the means by which God imparts his divine life to the world. Bujo based this on Pauline theology and the gospel of John: Jesus as the second Adam (1 Corinthians 15.45ff), the First-Born from the dead, the Head of the Body, the Church (Colossians 1.18), Giver of life in abundance (John 10.10). Thus, Jesus is the pre-eminent source of life for the world. The fact that Jesus is the Bread of Life and source of eternal life means that the Eucharist stands at the very heart of African ecclesiology. The Eucharist is the very life of the church and the source of its growth. It nourishes and renews the life of the community. Thus, the proto-ancestor Jesus bestows life to all the community, and they become channels of life within the church and the clan or nation. This truly African church, built on the proto-ancestral meal as the foundation stone, has important prophetic consequences for the whole social and community life of modern Africa.

In this proto-ancestor ecclesiology, church leaders are called to transmit more deeply to others the life of Jesus Christ, the Proto-Ancestor. Authority is a matter of service, and all clericalism and episcopalism must be destroyed together with the abandonment of a pyramidal model of the church. The laity must fully participate in decision-making in their own church. Therefore, as John Parratt summarised it, 'Bujo's ecclesiology is the one based on the religious experience of the significance of the ancestors, and founded on the biblical concept of the word life, which brings life to his people and leads them through the spirit into fellowship with the Father.'[22]

Indeed, Bujo is right that life should be taken seriously as a core issue of theology in Africa. As African religion is potentially liberating, theology in Africa must be liberating in all aspects of life. This liberation concerns men and women, both at personal and social levels. Therefore, Africa needs 'practical ecclesiology' which relates not only to selfhood and identity, but also takes seriously the local socio-political situation. However, Bujo's consideration for the authority of ancestral heritage and for the ancestors who did not witness the

---

[21] Bujo, *African Theology in Its Social Context*, 80.

[22] Parratt, *Reinventing Christianity*, 134.

Gospel has serious theological implications for the understanding of the church that we will discuss later.

Ecclesiology of Church-as-Family

John Paul II suggested that the church in Africa should be designated by the word 'family' which implies 'care for others, warmth in human relationships, openness, dialogue and acceptance, avoiding ethnocentrism and particularism, promoting reconciliation and community.'[23] Unfortunately the threat to the family had already overshadowed its traditional values and families can sometimes be terribly exclusive. But the African Synod, which African Catholic theologians think was an event of fundamental importance for the church in Africa, evolved the concept of a new model of church, 'church-as-family', developed from and built on the image of the people of God. This ecclesiology of church-as-family emphasises the warmth of love among widely extended relationships and an authority that finds its proper context in service. It must be rooted, not in biological kinship, but in the Trinity, as a Christian community in some way should reflect the Trinitarian communion which is its source and the ecclesial communion which is its sign.

Indeed, confusion could arise from the concept of family as human institution and the church-as-family model. Magesa tried to analyse the difference when he said,

> The aspects of solidarity, unity and communion form the difference between family as merely human institution and the church as a church-as-family. When the African Synod used the latter image, it sought to eliminate any elements that circumscribe, and therefore limit, the extent, depth and quality of unity and communion that characterise human families. Quite distinct, or really different, from the understanding of the structure and functioning of human families, the church-as-family embraces everyone irrespective of class, gender, race or ability. This means that the church-as-family is a universal communion in which humanity, fully common to all human beings, is the basic and most important element or measure.[24]

Therefore, solidarity, unity and communion must shape the visible structure of the church. However, the difference does not seem to be well understood. As Uzukwa observes, 'Only a short time after the Synod, there was already the tendency to link the notion of family with a spiritual "paternity" of priests! But

---

[23] Ryan, 'Introduction', in Patrick Ryan', ii
[24] Magesa, 'Christ's Spirit as Empowerment of the Church-as-family', 29.

the Christian value and power of the model becomes evident only when it is stripped of all characteristics of patriarchal dominance.'[25]

Furthermore, Waliggo has also warned against paternal authority in the family model. He cautions that the family of God should not be a patriarchal structure in which bishops, priests and religious are the parents and the laity are children:

> The family of God in Africa has to be redesigned in order to give the laity – and especially lay women- their rightful responsibility. The theology of church-as-family is a two-edged sword. It can be profitably used but may also lead to benign paternalism. Before it is applied, the image of the family must be fully liberated. We should not once again end up with a pyramid structure of the church but rather a circular one of communion.[26]

It is worth noticing here that the African family has continually undergone changes that continue to shift people's perceptions of this 'family'. Different societies have different types of families based on adaptations made to enhance survival in their environments.' Therefore, in the African context there is a general understanding of what constitutes family but no single specific form exists.

Extended family systems are common and extensively widespread in African societies. But due to pressures of cultural and social changes caused by industrialisation, urbanisation and education, composite family systems have continued to exist in different forms from those in African traditional societies. Furthermore, many families are cutting links with extended families because of economic hardship and social constraints such as high expenses and housing. Therefore the pressures on the family are many: dispersal of family members, the generation gap, urbanisation, unstable partnerships, new forms of family unions, and so on.

Moreover, the current modern African family is neither wholly traditional nor wholly Western, for African traditional systems have been able to borrow some aspects of Western family life and yet retain aspects of their own traditional values. This has placed the family in a dynamic socio-cultural context. Therefore the important theoretical issue which needs serious consideration is which particular type of family would be ideal, and what modalities would be put into operation to ensure that this ideal African family would be realised. We need to deliberate on whether such a common ideal is feasible and necessary. Moreover, the image of 'family' and 'father' have been exploited to establish a *Bula Matari* model of authority in the Congolese state and within the church. Will the image

---

[25] Elochukwu E. Uzukwa, *A Listening Church: Autonomy and Communion in the African Churches* (New York: Orbis, 1996), 66.

[26] Waliggo, 'The African Clan as the True Model of the African Church', 147.

of the family not serve again as 'the manipulative tool' for misuse of authority and power?

Another issue is that the church is composed of people of different ethnic groups. The tragic contemporary examples in Africa show civil wars and ethnic group clashes. The recent bloody clashes between different tribes in the Ituri and Kivu regions, also in Kenya with savage killings after the presidential elections update the issue. Can the church-as-family or clan help Christian faith to overcome tribalism, racism and other forms of discrimination? Will the African theology and praxis of church-as-family not overshadow the mystery of the church as the Body of Christ? We shall come back to these concerns in the last chapter.

Communitarian Models

It is often said that Africans are a communitarian people. A person's life is geared to the well-being of the community. The 'person-in-community' is considered a very important reality in African societies. A person is first a member of the community, and secondly an individual. This has led some theologians to use the word community instead of family. We will examine the sense of community according to Kwesi Dickson and John Pobee, and the Small Christian Communities proposed as the New Being of the church.

Dickson's Concept of Community

Kwesi Dickson is a Ghanaian Methodist who has taught for many years at the University of Ghana, first as professor of Theology and Religion, then as Director of the Institute of African studies. A former president of the Methodist Conference of Ghana, he is currently the president of the All Africa Conference of Churches. In his book *Theology in Africa*, Dickson's emphasis is on the importance of the cultural context in doing theology. He wrote, 'Theology is done most meaningfully in a particular setting: the cultural particularity is indispensable because theology is done by flesh and blood.'[27] Therefore, there is a need to develop Christian theologies with reference to the cultural contexts.

According to Dickson, 'It is commonplace that the sense of community is strong in Africa.[28] In his Akan religio-cultural context, the beliefs, attitudes and values laid down by ancestors are held in common within a community, and they shape its identity, and thereby the identity of its members. The ancestors are regarded as part of the community, and their authority legitimises the code of conduct. The honour that is shown to them reflects the solidarity of the community as a whole. Dickson believes that 'the community is made up of the

---

[27] Kwesi Dickson, *Theology in Africa* (London: Darton, Longman and Todd, 1984), 4.
[28] Dickson, *Theology in Africa,* 62.

unborn, the living and the dead. The child is believed to be one of the departed members of the family who has been reborn, and until the spirit was reborn it was a member of the spirit world, a world that, it is believed, overlaps very significantly with the physical world. In fact, Dickson's view refers to the theory of reincarnation.

Moreover, the spirits of ancestors who lived praiseworthy lives use their power for the well-being of the community. Therefore social structure and religious practice are closely related to the ancestors who are regarded as part of the community, and by their presence they express the solidarity of the community. The African concept of community may be seen as a limiting factor upon the individual's self-expression. But for Dickson, the sense of community requires the self-awareness of the individual and a sense of individual responsibility towards other members of the community.

The self-awareness of the individual shows that the community consists of a social system developed amongst people who have a sense of belonging together and of mutual interdependence. In Willmott's words, it is a 'community of attachment'.[29] In this community, people know each other on a personal level. It is not a collective, but consists of individuals freely interacting with each other and finding their identity in what they have in common. The sense of identity in a community of attachment may be associated with a particular locality, and with particular interests, beliefs, attitudes and values that are held in common.

The sense of community identified by Dickson is similarly to be recognised within a sufficiently small group of people for there to be personal interactions between them, but is also claimed to express the feelings of people in relation to the wider groups of which they are members. Their sense of identity is to some extent formed by beliefs, attitudes and values that they share with all other people in the Akan cultural context. Dickson thinks this is the type of community model for what the church and human society are intended to be.

Moreover, in Dickson's community, humans and other created things are interdependent and humans can have a sense of belonging to the natural world as a whole (the stone, the sea, the tree and generally the various elements in the human environment). Dickson stated, 'Man is in concert with nature; not only is he subject to Nature's fierce wrath, but also he is sustained by Nature's bounty and shares kinship with the things that make up Nature.'[30]

The death of Christ is a source of life in Dickson's community. The solidarity of the human community may be maintained by the life which is made available through the death of Christ. And the communal meal in which Christians recall and celebrate the death of Christ is a vivid expression of this life. In fact, from

---

[29] Quoted in Peter Fulljames, *God and Creation in Inter-Cultural Perspective: A Comparative Study of the Theologies of Barth, Dickson, Pobee, Nyamiti and Pannenberg* (PhD dissertation, University of Birmingham, July, 1991)

[30] Dickson, *Theology in Africa,* 161.

Dickson's sense of community, some points may be drawn. Firstly, the dead are part of the community. However, Christian community consists of the living and the dead in Christ, and the authority of ancestors does not legitimate the code of conduct in the Christian community. Secondly, Dickson recognizes that relationships between humans and other living things and inanimate objects are clearly not the same as relationships amongst humans themselves. But the interdependence of humans and other things and the sense of belonging to the natural world may contribute to an understanding of human identity in which the value of human life is complemented by the value of other created things. However, although Dickson's assumption may sound strange in other societies like Hema and Nande, the value of all created things is to be affirmed, and it is not only humans that have a place in the purpose of God. This could help the authorities in Congo to see the value of all created things and fight for the protection of the environment and the responsible use of resources. Thirdly, Dickson links the source of life in the community to the death of Christ for there is no Akan category for the resurrection of Christ. This helps him to find a place for ancestral authority in Christian theology as sustainers of life within the community. But life in a Christian community should originate from the resurrection of Christ which crowns his death and crucifixion. This new life rooted in the Risen Lord is holistic, as the next section will argue.

Pobee's View of Community

John Pobee was professor of New Testament and Church History in the University of Ghana, and Associate Director of the Programme in Theological Education in the World Council of Churches in Geneva. In his book *Towards an African Theology,* Pobee underlines that theology needs to be developed in terms of a particular cultural context rather than the African cultural context in general. He thus based his study on Akan culture, although he sometimes refers to Africa in general. In relation to our study, we will examine two of his themes: the sense of community and fullness of life.

The starting-point of Pobee's sense of community is *'Cognatus ergo sum'*, which means 'I am related by blood, therefore I exist' or more clearly expressed 'I exist because I belong to a family.'[31] It is not Descartes's *Cogito ergo sum*, which means 'I think, therefore I exist'. Therefore, Pobee conceives community as the sense of belonging together and of mutual interdependence associated with the recognition of common interests, attitudes, beliefs and values in the smallest group of the family and within wider groups. Any action that threatens the sense of belonging together and mutual interdependence of humans in a community is considered a sin. For instance, in Akan society, 'the essence of sin is an anti-social act. It is not an abstract transgression of law, rather it is a factual

---

[31] John S. Pobee, *Towards an African Theology* (Nashville: Abingdon, 1979), 49.

contradiction of established order.'[32] In fact, this idea of the essence of sin as an anti-social act is widespread in Africa. For instance, among the Lendu and Hema in the Ituri region, everyone must participate in tribal clashes. Not to revenge a murdered 'sister' or 'brother' is seen as sin, regardless of the origin or the causes of the fighting.

For Pobee, humans, created in the image of God, are created for community and human life in community is a response to the initiative of God, but it still is relational understanding of human personality. However, Pobee states that the relationship in the human community is possible only because of God. This implies that the well-being of the community depends on God. And this well-being is fullness of life.

According to Pobee, life is the well-being of people in society, while death is anything that weakens the relationships within the community. But life in its fullness is offered to people through Jesus Christ, who is himself the supreme example of life for he is in perfect relationship with others in the human community.[33] Therefore the church is the community of those who accept the sovereignty of Christ, and the identity of the church is intimately related to the identity of Christ. However, fullness of life is identified with the well-being of people as they are related to each other in the community.

Pobee, like Dickson, aims to respond positively to the religious dimension of the cultural context. But Pobee gives serious attention to political and economic aspects for well-being is as physical as it is spiritual. As God is the Sovereign Lord of all life, political life cannot be excluded from the sovereignty of God. Thus, Christian involvement in politics is non-negotiable, and 'where two or three are gathered in connexion with the society there is politics.'[34] Pobee from Akan society suggested, 'as Christians we ought to ensure that our affirmation about humans bearing the *imago Dei* and the *sensus communis* as well as the holistic approach to life are fed into political life and the creation of a national ethics in a plural society and world.'[35] As power and authority are exercised in a real world which is characterized by sin, Pobee warned against their abuse that Power tends to corrupt, absolute power corrupts absolutely. As in the Akan society, power has to be used for the good of the people, for authority is received from God and the ancestors, the twin pillars of Akan religion. Thus religious beliefs and practices have had a significant role in legitimazing political structures and authority. He rejects a complete identification of the church with the political structures, and the government should obtain religious legitimation for its policies. Power can work for life and peace only if it is informed by

---

[32] Pobee, *Towards an African Theology*, 42.

[33] Pobee, *Towards an African Theology*, 8.

[34] Pobee, *Towards an African Theology*, 25.

[35] John S. Pobee, 'Life and Peace', in John S. Pobee and Carl F. Hallencreutz (eds), *Variations in Christian Theology in Africa* (Nairobi: Uzima Press, 1986), 25.

Christian notions of *imago Dei* and love.[36] The church has to act as 'the conscience of society'. However, to act as 'the conscience of society' is to bring the ancestral heritage, church leaders and political leaders under the rule of God. It is to experience the newness of life in Christ at a most local level.

Small Christian Community

The Small Christian Community (SCC) movement in Eastern Africa started during the AMECEA Catechetical Conference 'Towards Adult Christian Community' of 1973 and the AMECEA plenary Assemblies of 1973, 1976 and 1979. These conferences laid the foundations for a movement which met with varying degrees of success in different dioceses and countries such as the Congo. It has been strongly endorsed as a pastoral strategy, both by the AMECEA bishops and by the 1994 African Synod itself. But the building of SCC was preceded and inspired by several pastoral and secular experiments. We will only examine the *Ujamaa* and *kumi-kumi* system.

Ujamaa, used by Julius Nyerere for his philosophy of African Socialism, means 'familyhood'. He took the African Family as a model for community cooperation at village level and other levels. Thus other citizens were to be treated in the same way as one treats the members of one's own family, as 'traditionally, we lived as families with individuals helping and supporting each other on terms of equality,' said Nyerere.[37] It was to apply the principles of the family to the wider society of the neighbourhood and village.

The response of Catholic Church leaders to *ujamaa* was favourable. This could be seen in Christopher Mwoleka, Bishop of Rulenge's article which described *Ujamaa* as a practical, down-to-earth method of imitating the life of the Holy Trinity, the life shared by all Christians as members of God's family.[38] Even in November 1975, the Tanzanian Episcopal Conference directed its National Committee on Liturgical Research to prepare an '*Ujamaa* Eucharistic Prayer.'

However *Ujamaa* did not help to install a familial society in Tanzania, one in which the family should be strengthened as an institution, and its values such as equality, freedom, sharing and love are promoted. Although an African sense of family was the starting-point, the emphasis was on the village. The entire country was divided into cells of ten households, known as *kumi-kumi*. Although the

---

[36] Pobee, 'Life and Peace', 26.

[37] Anylward Shorter, 'The Family as a Model for Social Reconstruction in Africa', in Leonard Paul, Maurice Schepers, Aylward Shorter and others, *Theology of the Church as Family of God* (Nariobi: Paulines Publications Africa, 1997), 31.

[38] Christopher Mwoleka, 'Trinity and Community', in Christopher Mwoleka and Fr.Joseph Healey (eds), *Ujamaa and Christian Communities* (Eldoret, Kenya: Gaba Publications, 1976), 15.

kumi-kumi system was an outstanding political achievement and a highly efficient instrument for mobilizing the population for elections or census enumeration, it did not enable clusters of families to exert an influence on local development and decision making. The *kumi-kumi* turned out to be a totalitarian device for ensuring that households obeyed the 'top-down' directives of higher authority, attended political meetings and participated in collective projects. However, the *kumi-kumi* system was a salutary challenge to the church itself.

In the late 1960s, missionaries, inspired by the *kumi-kumi* system, started to form clusters of Catholic households and to turn them into embryonic basic communities. The communities were conceived as groups of families, but the social configuration of the village ensured that the families in each cluster were related to each other. This was due to the villagers' preference for blood relatives as neighbours. It is difficult to set up SCCs as surrogate 'families' in the spiritual sense, for in rural Africa there is a tendency for extended families and clans to be given corporate and territorial expression. Although the urban parish in Africa is often a place of social and ethnic integration, the reality in countries like Congo shows that the tendency is to join the 'ethnic church' where brothers and sisters from the same ethnic group are. Of course on the one hand, there is the natural tendency to seek out people like us, but on the other hand there is the danger that people's perspectives will be narrowed in the process. The challenge thus is, as we shall see in the next chapter, to move from contextualisation to universalisation.

The African Synod stated that the church as family cannot reach her full potential as church unless she is divided into communities small enough to foster close human relationships. The Special Assembly for Africa of the Synod of Bishops of the Roman Catholic Church in 1994 stated in its final report:

> Primarily they should be places engaged in evangelising themselves, so that subsequently they can bring the Good News to others; they should moreover be communities which pray and listen to God's Word, encourage the members themselves to take on responsibility, learn to live an ecclesial life and reflect on different human problems in the light of the Gospel. Above all, these communities are to be committed to living Christ's love for everybody, a love which transcends the limits of natural solidarity of clans, tribes or other interest groups.[39]

It means these SCC are cells within which love of God is inseparable from love of neighbour, and in which the tendencies to disunity, egoism, and ethnicism are discerned and overcome. It is a concrete expression of Being Church at a most local level. The church life is based on the communities in which everyday life and work take place, those basic and manageable social

---

[39] Joseph Healey and Donald Sybertz, *Towards an African Narrative Theology* (Nairobi: Paulines Publications Africa, 1999), 148.

groups whose members can experience real inter-personal relationships and feel a sense of communal belonging, both in living and working.

The SCC model of church is based on the church as communion (koinonia). It is part of Trinitarian communion ecclesiology. The Triune God wants to share divine life with human beings. As Mwoleka said, 'The right approach to the mystery is to imitate the life of the Trinity which is life of sharing.[40] Thus, the unity of the Father, Son and Holy Spirit is not only the source, but also the model of the unity of the church and of all large and small communities. The Christian journey is to enter into and imitate the union, communion and relationships of the Three Divine Persons. Leadership and structures reflect the emphasis on Trinitarian communion and ministries are expanded to everyone. The African communitarian values of fraternity, solidarity, openness and inclusiveness are emphasized.

However, the daily evidence of the disintegration of the African family and the decline of family institutions, such as traditional marriage, make the implementation of SCC on the basis of the family model hard. During the last tribal clashes in Bunia, the SCC members failed to protect members of enemy tribes. It means the SCC still has a difficult task to overcome ethnicism and clanism. SCC built among families with ties of consanguinity may easily reinforce the selfishness of clans and ethnic groups. Although this could help with inculturation as they share similar cultural traits, SCC will not be a 'communion of communities.'

Implication of the Use of African Categories

The African metaphors of the church we have analysed can contribute a lot in the building of the church in Africa. They all put communion at the centre of the church, and everything is done in order to strengthen it. The human dignity and equality of each member are stressed. Participation-sharing is fundamental for the life of the community where laity must have a role to play in decision-making. There is a real need of 'circular' authority that finds its proper context in service.

All the metaphors analysed refer to the church in terms of the natural family. The church as family means that in local churches trust, mutual sharing of burdens, concerns and joys are developed in a spirit of kinship. Moreover, the family metaphor offers 'organizing power and integrating vision' to members. However, the metaphor reinforces the community's highly stratified hierarchy of power and privilege. It often transfers the father metaphor from the divine to the human realm to legitimize the authority of local church leadership. It concerns the rhetorical-manipulative use of religious symbols, both by church leaders and political leaders.

---

[40] Mwoleka, 'Trinity and Community', 15.

Furthermore, as Tite Tiénou noted, 'Understanding the church as the Great Family in the African context can lead only to incorporating the ancestors into the church, thereby granting them salvation.'[41] Indeed, theologians such as Bujo and Sawyerr are aware that God's household cannot be identical with the natural family. Even so, they see God's household as a mystical body including ancestors who did not receive the gospel. In this case, Christ is the mystical elder-brother or proto-ancestor. This certainly raises the issue of the authority of ancestors and the authority of Jesus Christ in the life of the church in Africa. If it is possible to see some similarities between Christ and ancestors, there are nevertheless major differences which should prevent hasty extrapolations.

As John Parratt said, the question is 'if Jesus is the mystical and spiritual proto-ancestor, how can he be related to biological ancestors who are not strictly within the community bound together by faith?'[42] Any Christo-centred theology must keep a good balance between Christ as man and Christ as God. To stress the historical Jesus as the first-born and the elder brother may lead to the risk of considering Jesus as one of the African divinities. God rules over them and is the source of whatever power and authority they may have. In fact the community of faith comprises the living and the dead in Christ. But their communion is through Christ. It would be unbiblical to expand that communion to the ancestors who had not received the gospel. Indeed the knowledge of God was possible through nature and conscience, but man has turned to the worship of creation rather than the Creator (Romans 1.18-23). Furthermore, a wrong conception of sin results in a wrong view of salvation. In ancestral theology, sin is societal. Sin is an antisocial act, and salvation can be procured by satisfying social demands. African Theology seems to strongly agree with the societal essence of sin.[43] As sin is a profound philosophical and theological concept, it warrants particular attention for research which is beyond the scope of this book. Indeed, sin has both a personal element and a societal element, and both personal and societal sins are ultimately judged by God. The African emphasis on the societal aspects of sin does find resonance in the New Testament, for example in Jesus' parables of the rich fool, and the rich man and Lazarus, but does not encompass the attention given to individual dimension of sin. This remains a challenge for African Theology.

According to New Testament writings on individual sin, salvation is not based on works of kindness (Ephesians 2.8-9), but on God's grace and can be accepted only by faith. Good works follow, but do not precede nor produce salvation.

---

[41] Tite Tiénou, 'The Church in African Theology: Description and Analysis of Hermeneutical Presuppositions', in D.A. Carson (ed), *Biblical Interpretation and the Church: Text and the Context* (Exeter: The Paternoster Press, 1984), 161.

[42] Parratt, *Reinventing Christianity*, 135.

[43] See Pobee, *Towards an African Theology*; Dickson, *Theology in Africa*; Sawyerr, *Creative Evangelism.*

Since the original fall, the total race of Adam has been condemned to death (Romans 3.23; 6.23). Salvation in the Christian sense of the term is manifested in and through, and constituted on the basis of the life, death and resurrection of Jesus Christ. Salvation is the passing out of the prison of death (John 5. 24) into the dimension of life.

Therefore the Church in Africa must not be under the authority of ancestral heritage, but under Christ's authority. The natural family is not identical with God's household. When Paul and the writer to the Hebrews used the term 'household' for the Church, they almost always qualify it with 'faith' or 'God'. So, one can legitimately be a member of God's household by faith in Christ, for the Church is God's household (Ephesians 2:19; 1 Timothy 3.15), or the 'household of faith' (Galatians 6:10). Therefore, the church is like family because the solidarity that binds it together can be better expressed in terms of kinship; but the family of God can never be identical with any natural family. Christian's membership in the body of Christ should supersede his ties to his natural family. Jesus said, 'Whosoever does the will of God; he is my brother and sister and mother (Mark 3.35). This radical view of Jesus in its time shows the distinctive nature of Jesus' perspective on the natural family.

Therefore, it can be argued that the New Testament avoids any kind of kinship imagery. Indeed, Jesus used the cultural language about people of God in formulating his conception of a 'family of faith'. However, Jesus reoriented the cultural language to explain the distinctive nature of his community, which assumes a shift of loyalties resulting in significant relational fallout in the natural family. He foresees the day when 'brother will betray brother to death, and a father his child, and children will rise against parents and have them put to death; and you will be hated by all because of me' (Mark 12-13). Theology in Africa must realise that shift of loyalty from ancestral heritage to Christ-centred community.

In fact, Jesus has made God known in a particular and specific manner and it is the self-revelation of God, a personal revelation which cannot be detached from the person of God. He is redeemer, and he defines the shape of the redeemed life. Thus, Jesus makes life possible, but that life must be conformed to Christ. Therefore the person of Jesus Christ is of central importance to any Christian theology. Jesus Christ is the historical point of departure for Christianity, and Christian theology is obliged to return to him in the course of its reflection. Theology in Africa must avoid turning more to African traditional religion as a source of theology than to the Scriptures. The use of African categories to integrate the non-Christian dead has no clear biblical support, and seems to deny Christ's centrality to the church. Therefore, care must be taken in using African categories to bring down to earth the reality and mystery of incarnation into the Body of Christ. This will help to meet Pobee's challenge for

Africanisation to couch 'Christian theology in genuinely African terms and categories without losing an iota of authentic and essential Christianity.'[44]

It must also be noticed that as young people are not grounded in their traditional cultures, a relevant African Christianity and theology should consider the challenges of the new generation and new African values. A group of African theologians and others, while pleading for an integrated approach, expressed their view as follows:

> Inculturation should draw from the traditional values which have continued to influence people's lives and world-view. At the same time it must draw from the present African experience, brought about by cultural contacts, rapidity of change and the entire socio-economic and political realities in Africa and elsewhere.[45]

We conclude by saying that theology in Africa must be Christ centred. If life is the cornerstone for African ecclesiology, the church must be Life-Community, living the life of Christ in its fullness and sharing Christ's life with others. Authority within the Church must be 'authority-for-life', not in the sense of dictation for life, but in the sense of 'authority for enhancing life'.

Conclusion

The study of African communion ecclesiologies has proved that life, as inherited from God and daily lived, must be the cornerstone in understanding the church in Africa. The claim is that the church should involve non-Christian departed who are still in communion with their descendants. The authority of ancestral heritage is thus claimed to be considered in building the life of the community. However, the experience of blood relationships has proved exclusivist, resulting in violence, clanism and ethnicism. Uncritical and rhetorico-manipulative use of African categories has been practised both by church leaders and political leaders. The suggestion is that African categories should be carefully and critically selected in shaping the understanding of the church as they tend to compromise the centrality of Christ. Authority must be Christ-centred and must be authority for life. Jesus as the Life must supersede life conceived in terms of blood family, creating Life-Community where those marked by hopelessness, meaningless and despair of life would live Christ's life in its fullness, and share it with others.

In this Life-Community which is the concern of the final chapter, Christ-centred people of authority have to unmask the ideological use of theological and biblical concepts, and take a positive political responsibility for

---

[44] Pobee, *Towards an African Theology,* 79.
[45] Joseph Healey and Donald Sybertz, *Towards an African Narrative Theology* (Nairobi: Paulines Publications Africa, 1996), 39.

the faith. They will be able to detect, and fight for remedying, social and political sins and be a real conscience of the society which needs a transformation of conscience.

Chapter Six

Liberating Authority in
Life-Community Ecclesiology

The Concept of Community

African theologians, as previously discussed, have claimed that the concept of life should be a key factor for ecclesiology, providing effective and vitalistic authority for the community. In fact, the study of the African traditional worldview showed that the concept of life is fundamental. Life is a gift from God, it is essentially relational and communitarian. Consequently, life is understood as blood relationship and determines the community. Thus, although it is thought to be theo-centric, the African concept of life is 'man-centred' and needs to be theologically re-oriented.

In this chapter, we suggest that Life-Community which is Christ-centred potentially constitutes a fundamental power base for authority to be exercised for the good of the people of God. It thus can help to build Christ-centred authority within the community which is inclusive, providing a holistic sense of life in its fullness for the society as a whole. The chapter will first examine the concept of community, and then underline the centrality of Christ as Life of the Church on a Trinitarian basis with a liberating authority within the church and the society.

The studies of some African scholars such as John Pobee, Kwesi Dickson and Laurenti Magesa have shown that communality, relationality and fundamental interconnections are still crucial to the African worldview. As Kwesi A. Dickson expressed it, 'It is commonplace that the sense of community is strong in Africa.'[1] Although Dickson's statement may assume that everyone knows what

---

[1] Dickson, *Theology in Africa,* 62.

community means, the reality is that community is defined according to the context.

A. Okechukwu Ogbonnaya, in his book *On Communitarian Divinity: An African Interpretation of the Trinity,* has attempted to demonstrate how the communal orientation of the African worldview applied to Divinity would contribute in developing Christian theological thought. Interacting with non-African authors such as Ferdinand Toennies and John Cobb, Ogbonnaya discovered that participation, openness, freedom and common responsibility are fundamental for community. In fact, in a sociological context, for Toennies, community is determined by simple and direct face-to-face relations with each other, while participation, common responsibility and respect for diverse individuality are the three criteria that determine genuine commonality for Cobb and Daly:

> A society [community] should not be called a community unless (1) there is extensive participation by its members in the decisions by which its life is governed, (2) the society [community] as a whole takes responsibility for the members, (3) this responsibility includes respect for the diverse individuality of its membership.[2]

This is a very Western democratic view of society which would exclude most countries in the world. Further, it does not take into account the spiritual aspect within the society. Ogbonnaya noted this spiritual aspect when he said, 'Although for Africans the face-to-face encounter is vital for community, the existence and perpetuation of community depend on more than physical encounter, and spiritual ties to the community always exist.'[3] He acknowledges that the African communal orientation tends to be based squarely on tribal loyalty, but that the African metaphysical orientation demands the community be more than a physical face-to-faceness. It is based on 'a common union, a union grounded on the fact that humanity shares a common nature that connects them to one another.'[4]

Members of community share in one power, yet because of the unique expression of spirit in each person this power allows each member an exercise of freedom. This freedom might lead persons to take a variety of roles in the community. So for the contribution of the person to be effective, the community must be open to new possibilities of creativity. Therefore, openness becomes a fundamental principle. In fact, Ogbonnaya's view of community is not as simply sociological as Toennies' or socio-economic, but his emphasis on spiritual ties is important. However, Ogbonnaya's approach, as with many Trinitarian theories,

---

[2] A. Okechukwu Ognonnaya, *On Communitarian Divinity: An African Interpretation of the Trinity* (United States: Paragon House, 1994), 2.

[3] Ognonnaya, *On Communitarian Divinity,* 7.

[4] Ognonnaya, *On Communitarian Divinity,* 8.

suggests the African worldview to be a basis for discussing the Trinity. It is to understand the Trinity from the African community, rather than understanding African community from the doctrine of the Trinity.

Furthermore, Life-Community is not politically motivated. Indeed community is not a new concept within the *Eglise du Christ au Congo* (ECC). The *Conseil Protestant du Congo,* which was founded in 1923, became *Eglise du Christ au Zaïre* (ECZ) by a legal decree of 31 December 1971.[5] ECZ then became the sole framework of the existence of Protestant churches in the Congo. As the socio-political context was marked by a radical centralisation of national institutions and the personalisation of power in the person of the President Mobutu, the ECZ modelled its structure and administration on the state's presidential monarchism. Therefore, leaders of ECZ at each level became *président,* and each Protestant church changed to *Communauté,* led by a *président communautaire.* Each *Communauté* has a registration number within the ECZ. Thus, the Anglican Church became eleventh *Communauté Anglicane du Congo* (CAC).

In fact, *Communautés* were created in order to bring all Protestant denominations under one umbrella to stand against the Roman Catholic Church, but with the additional aim of fitting into the 'new' socio-political context, which saw the reunification of the nation as urgent in order to restore 'order, peace and unity'. But this politically motivated unity did not help the churches to solve their internal divisions and conflicts or to have a real communion between communities within the ECC.

Life-Community has the potential to be a power base for unity as it is not simply a loose-knit collection of human beings in a geographical space or a direct biological relational community. Moreover, it is not built on the principle 'I am because we are', which, in fact, is man-centred. It is built on the centrality of Christ in a Trinitarian basis. Therefore, Life-Community is not sociologically, politically and economically motivated, but it is a theological concept mostly Christ-centred on a Trinitarian basis, with sociological, economic and political implications.

Centrality of Christ

Life-Community, contrary to African communion ecclesiology, should be built on Christ, the Life and the source of authority, as the following section will argue. Our approach presupposes a view of the New Testament as the basic source of authority. This does not exclude the Old Testament which is fulfilled in the New Testament. To express Christian authority in a truly African context is to begin with the study of authority in the Bible and allow it to judge authority as understood in political and traditional society. Otherwise, the manipulated values

---

[5] Mbaya, *L'Eglise du Christ au Zaire,* 290.

of authority will take precedence over authority in the Church. As Kwesi Dickson said, 'It would be inexcusable to fail to give biblical teaching pride of place in this quest for African theology.'[6] The importance of the Bible for African Theology was stressed in 1977 during the Pan-African Conference of Third World Theologians, 'The Bible is the basic source of African theology, because it is the primary witness of God's revelation in Jesus Christ. No theology can retain its Christian identity apart from Scripture.'[7]

Christ, the Life

In the New Testament, the term 'life' is found frequently in Paul's letters and Johannine literature, including Revelation, but only occasionally in the other New Testament books. *Bios* is used to designate the conduct of life (Luke 8:14; 2 Timothy 2:4), while, according to *New Bible Dictionary*, *zoe* tends to mean natural vitality (Acts 8:33) or resurrection, life in Johannine literature. [8] It designates human existence and connotes also 'health' (Mark 5:23 John. 4:50).[9] We will refer more to life in the sense of *zoe* which results in *bios* as conduct of life.

Life in the New Testament, as in the Old Testament, is properly the life of God, the Ever-Living one (Romans 5:21) who has life in himself and the life of God is manifest in Jesus Christ.[10] The 'natural life' is considered as the perversion of the divine gift, and it is by divine act of redemption embracing the whole human race that true life in the individual can be set free.[11] This is done by Jesus, who gave his life for the forgiveness of humanity's sin (Mark 10.45; Galatians 3.13; Ephesians 5.2). Through his resurrection, Christ has become the author of a new life for humanity. Christ is God's living power, conquering death and raising the dead (2 Corinthians 13.4). Life is Christ's everlasting life, life from the dead and beyond the grave.

John presents the Word as being eternal life even before his incarnation. He has lived eternally with God and for the benefit of men (John 1.4; 1 John. 1.1). He is the source of divine life and power both in the old and in the new creation.

---

[6] Kwesi A. Dickson, 'Towards a Theologia Africana', in M.E Glaswell and Edward W. Fasholé-Luke (eds), *New Testament Christianity for Africa and the World* (London: SPCK, 1974), 198.

[7] Kofi Appiah-Kubi and Sergio Torres, 'Theological Sources', in Kofi Appiah-Kubi and Sergio Torres (eds), *African Theology en Route* (Maryknoll (NY): Orbis Books, 1979), 81.

[8] D.R.W. Wood (ed), *New Bible Dictionary* (Third edition: Leicester, England, 1996), 688.

[9] George Arthur Buttrick (ed), *The Interpreter's Dictionary of the Bible* (Vol 3, Nashville, New York: Abingdon Press, 1962), 127.

[10] Wood (ed), *New Bible Dictionary,* 689.

[11] Buttrick (ed), *The Interpreter's Dictionary of the Bible,* 127.

In his incarnation, he is the revelation of God, but he not only brings eternal life by his word (John 6.68; 10.28; 12.50), he himself is the true life (1 John 5.20), the bread of life (John 6.35, 48), 'the resurrection and the life' (John 11.25), 'the way, the truth and the life' (John 14.6).[12] So, the pre-existent Son of the eternal Father is sent into the world to give life to men both by his word and in his own person (John 6.33; 10.10; 1 Jn. 4.9).

The life of Christ is mediated to Christians by the word of life (Philippians 2.16) and by the creative power of the Spirit (Romans 8.2,6,10; 1 Corinthians 15.45). The life of Christians is not their own life, but the life of Christ for Christ lives in them (Galatians 2.20, Philippians 1.21) and they live the life of Christ (2 Corinthians 4.10). But, as Colin Brown expressed it, 'The life of Christ is mediated to Christians neither as a power (as with the Gnostics), nor through mystic union, but by the word of life (Philippians 2.16, 2 Timothy 1.10) and by the creative power of the Spirit (Romans 8.2,6).'[13] The life of Christ is not mediated as 'vital force' from God in a biological way in the African world. The life of God is received by faith (1 John 5.12). It is not only for the believer to look at Jesus' life as the highest type of life, but also to follow him in order to be transformed into the likeness of his life (Matthew 10.25; John 5.39-40). Through Jesus' redemptive life, the perverted life of people can be renewed and regenerated (John 3.3-8; 1 Peter 1.3). It is not simply a change of conduct, but of status. Life is a voluntary subjection of one's existence to God's plans, and it is not merely 'confined to a special psychological sphere of "spiritual life", but rather manifests itself as a special quality which informs a person's whole life (Matthew 7.21; Luke 6.46)'.[14] The new life is capable of bearing fruit (Matthew 7.16-20), and does not try to escape from everyday life. It is compatible with sins (Romans 7.15-20) and spiritual weakness (Matthew 17.20; 26.30-35), caused by infirmity of human flesh (Matthew 26.41; Romans 7.18). However, although this life is constantly threatened by enemies such as the devil, law and death, the power of Christ can overcome them (Romans 8.37-39). Life is not lived in self-chosen freedom but rather in God's service (John 12.50; 4.34; 5.19-20). Thereby Jesus brought to light a new feature of life, destined to be lived for mutual help. The believer is a new creature, and life in its freedom (John 8.32,36; Romans 6.18) bears witness to the God who gave it, and refutes fatalism. Having this power of Christ in themselves, believers are therefore capable of influencing the course of this world (John 15.4).

---

[12] Wood (ed), *New Bible Dictionary*, 689.

[13] Colin Brown, *New Testament Theology* (Volume 2: G-Pre. Exeter: The Paternoster Press, 1976), 481.

[14] Buttrick (ed), *The Interpreter's Dictionary of the Bible*, 127.

Christ, Source of Authority

In their attempt to reinterpret biblical and historical Christological dogma in categories that are both traditionally African and at the same time relevant to the Africa of today, African theologians have proposed different Christologies: Jesus as Clan-founder, Black, Proto-Ancestor, First-Born, Liberator, Healer, Elder Brother, Great Chief, etc. Moreover, Christology has been developed to sustain the continuity between African religions and Christianity. For instance, Gwinyai H. Muzorewa interprets the concept of the 'pre-existent Christ' to argue that African traditional theology already knew of Jesus in pre-Christian ages.[15] Based on Shone and Ndebele beliefs that God is conceived as Father, Son and Mother, Muzorewa concludes that 'the African concept of a Trinitarian God is prior to Christianity and it renders the traditional African culture "Christian" in a peculiar sense.'[16] Therefore, according to Muzorewa, the work of Christ in Africa would have to be rediscovered, and the meaning of the incarnation, rather than its history, would become the essence of Christianity.[17]

An African 'original' experience thus is emphasized by Muzorewa to articulate 'Christian' faith. According to this view the humanity of Jesus is stressed to underline the authority of ancestral heritage. It is about what God was doing with Jesus and through him rather than in terms of who ontologically Jesus was. In fact, the African concept of a Trinitarian God prior to Christianity is very controversial and does not apply to most of Africa. The problem for African theology is that African traditional religions lack historical roots, as Parratt has stated:

> African religions are not 'historical' in the sense that they find their *raison d'être* in a historical founder, nor they have a tradition of 'sacred history'. Their foundations are to be sought elsewhere, in the authority of the ancestors in the case of most Bantu systems, or in the combined authority of ancestors and deities in many parts of West Africa.[18]

This inclination for continuity is what Ali A. Mazrui called 'tribal tradition' that is 'conservative ethnicist which prefers continuity to change, where change is necessary, they would insist upon gradualism.'[19] It is reliance on experience rather than theory.

---

[15] Gwinyai H. Muzorewa, *The Origins and Development of African Theology* (Maryknoll, New York: Orbis Books, 1985), 85.

[16] Muzorewa, *The Origins and Development of African Theology*, 85.

[17] Muzorewa, *The Origins and Development of African Theology*, 85.

[18] Parratt, *Reinventing Christianity: African Theology Today*, 78.

[19] Ali A. Mazrui, 'Ideology and African Political culture', in Teodros Kiros (ed), *Explorations in African Political Thought: Identity, Community, Ethics* (New York: Routledge, 2001), 100.

In this sense, the role of Jesus in the New Testament is seen as accomplished in salvation history rather that what he was in himself ontologically or metaphysically. As the Christian faith is rooted in events that involved a specific person at a specific time in human history, theology in Africa must consider functional and ontological Christology. Christ said, 'All authority in heaven and on earth has been given to me' (Matthew 28.19b). It is commonly thought that Matthew draws this passage from LXX Daniel 7.14. But as Robert H. Gundry suggested, in this passage of Matthew we do not discover a forward reference to the *parousia* in accord with other allusions to Daniel 7.13-14. Therefore it is better to say that Matthew takes his passage from the tradition behind Luke 4.6b, 'to you I will give all this authority.'[20] The emphasis rests on the universal authority delegated to Jesus by God. It is not based on Jesus' resurrection or his exaltation to heaven, for he had this authority before his resurrection (Matthew 7.29; 9.8; 21.23). So, Christ is the source of every authority and the basis for Christian theological reflection. This also underlines the authority of the Scriptures which bring us to knowledge of Jesus Christ who reveals God and is bearer of salvation, manifested in and through, and constituted on the basis of, the life, death, and resurrection of Jesus Christ. Therefore, Christological determination of ecclesiology is important to recognise Christ as the source of authority-for-life. This Christology has to be developed in the context of the Holy Trinity. The church in Congo claims to possess divine authority. But a more strongly clerical ecclesiology has emerged from the assumption that clergy have received the authority of disciples of Christ over the community. By contrast, Life-Community is Christologically oriented and the ontological inspiration of its authority is based on the Holy Trinity.

Trinitarian Basis of Authority in Life-Community

Trinity, the Uultimate Koinonia

In recent years, an effort has been made to re-examine what the British Council of Churches has called 'the forgotten jewel of Christian theology.'[21] Many theologians have attempted to re-examine the centrality of the Trinity to Christian life, as stated by the British Council of Churches' document:

> Such eminent theologians of this century as the Roman Catholic Karl Rahner and the Protestant Karl Barth have made the doctrine of the Trinity the corner-stone of their theology. Their interest, and that of many other theologians, suggests that the

---

[20] Robert H. Gundry, *Matthew: A Commentary on His Handbook for a Mixed Church under Persecution* (Second edition, Grand Rapids, Michigan (USA): Wm. B. Eerdmans Publishing Co, 1994), 595.

[21] British Council of Churches, *The Forgotten Trinity* (London: BBC/CCBI, 1991), 1.

triune God is not merely an intellectual speculation or an optional extra, but the very foundation of our lives as Christians.[22]

However, the worldviews of those interpreting the doctrine has sometimes made it more of a paradigm for exclusion and social intolerance. But for theologians such as Leonardo Boff and Jurgen Moltmann, the Trinity comes as an answer to the problem of pluralism confronting the current generation. For instance, Boff stated:

> The Trinity, as a prototype of human community has social and political implications, especially in providing a model of inclusiveness and communion in communities where similarities and differences are present. It serves both as a critique and inspiration of society, becoming the basis for an inclusive universal fellowship.[23]

Thus, for these theologians the Trinity is a symbol of unity in diversity and illuminates what it means to be a just and truly humane society.

It is also in a multi-religious and multi cultural context that some African theologians such as Kwesi Dickson and Christopher Mwoleka have developed Trinitarian communion ecclesiology. For them, communion refers to the very essence of the church, and it is a 'matter of our communion with God through Jesus Christ in the Holy Spirit'.[24] They believe that the Holy Trinity is the greatest mystery in the Christian faith. The triune God wants to share divine life with human beings. Thus the Christian journey is to enter into and imitate the union, communion and relationship of the three Divine persons.[25] The ultimate Koinonia is thus that of God's own triune life. The unity of the Father, Son and Holy Spirit is not only the source, but also the model of the unity of the church locally and universally. The African communitarian values of fraternity, solidarity, openness and inclusiveness are emphasized. However, as said in the previous chapter, the aim of communion based on the life of Trinity was to legitimate the communion with the ancestors in African traditional religions. Therefore, care should be taken to use Christian Trinitarian theology to back African communion ecclesiology which values African ancestral heritage.

Indeed, the example of the EAC testifies the difference between theory and practice of the implication of the Trinity. Like the Anglican Church in Britain, EAC has a Trinity Sunday, when the doctrine is 'taken out of deep storage, briefly given an airing, and then returned to its hiding place until the same time

---

[22] British Council of Churches, *The Forgotten Trinity*, 2.

[23] Leonardo Boff, *Trinity and Society* (Kent, Great Britain: Burns and Oates, 1988), 147-148.

[24] Final Report of the 1985 Extraordinary Synod of Bishops, England, no C, 1.

[25] Final Report of the 1985 Extraordinary Synod of Bishops, 132.

next year.'[26] The Trinity is also regularly invoked at the conclusion of formal prayers. However, as in the Church of England, it remains 'merely a doctrine somehow suspended over heads as a logical abstraction without either real content or relevance to everyday lives.'[27] The same idea was expressed by Mwoleka when he said, 'Many Christians do not know what to do with it [Trinity] except that it must be believed. It is a dogma they cannot apply to their daily life. So they push it aside to look for interesting devotions elsewhere.'[28] But the doctrine of the Trinity should be a practical doctrine with far reaching consequences for the Christian life. As Leonardo Boff put it, 'The mystery of the Trinity should be the deepest source, closest inspiration and brightest illumination of the meaning of life that we can imagine.'[29] The practical implications of Trinitarian doctrine flow directly from God's salvific activity through the cross of Christ as Jürgen Moltmann argued in his *The Crucified God*, 'The doctrine of the Trinity is no longer an exorbitant and impractical speculation about God, but is nothing other than a shorter version of the passion narrative of Christ in its significance for the eschatological freedom of faith and the life of oppressed nature.'[30] Unfortunately in the EAC, as the church has its being from its relation to a hierarchical head, the emphasis is on ontological grading of persons modelled on the Trinity simply understood as patricentric Trinity, where relations are conceived in terms of structural communion as in traditional society and in the *Bula Matari* model. Thus, a close examination of who and what kind of being Christ is in relation to God the Father and the Holy Spirit, and the rest of the human race is needed, if authority is to be based on the Trinity.

The doctrine of Trinity, indeed, is not explicit in the New Testament, for it is a later theological construction by patristic writers. It is the fruit of a long process of reflection on the events of Christ's life and experience of God's mercy. It was trying to clarify the implication of what God had done among people through the coming of Jesus Christ and the Holy Spirit. So, though the doctrine is not explicitly biblical, it is enshrined in the Bible in a number of passages both in the Old and New Testaments. Trinity is so crucial and central to Christian faith and has made important contributions to worship, prayer and spirituality. Indeed, Life-Community grounded on the doctrine of Trinity can make a remarkable contribution on the issue of authority for the well being of the whole society. As

---

[26] The British Council of Churches, *The Forgotten Trinity*, 1.
[27] The British Council of Churches, *The Forgotten Trinity*, 1.
[28] Mwoleka, 'Trinity and Community', 15.
[29] Boff, *Trinity and Society*, 111.
[30] Jurgen Moltmann, *The Crucified God: The Cross of Christ as the Foundation and Criticism of Christian Theology* (London: SCM, 1974), 246.

John Zizioulas said, 'The nature of God is communion.'[31] This means the ontological basis for church is the communion of the 'Father-Son-Spirit' model.

The Communion of the Trinity as Basis of Life-Community

Life is attributed to God, so the supreme goal of human life is represented as sharing in divine life (1Peter 1.4). Jesus presented himself as life personified (John 11.25; 14.6; 5.26). His mission consists in bringing life abundantly (Jn. 10.10). Anyone who shares in Christ partakes of a 'new creation' (2 Corinthians 5.17). Here God means the Father, Son and Holy Spirit in the presence of one another for each other, by each other, in each other and with one another. As Leonardo Boff put it, 'The essential characteristic of each person is to be for the others, through the others, with the others and in the others. They do not exist in themselves for themselves: the "in themselves" is "for the others".'[32] The unity of the three persons expresses the infinite dynamism of eternal communion, sharing life of one with the others, the interpenetration and coinherence of the three. All are equally eternal, infinite and loving in communion.

Of course, communion implies intimacy, transparency of intention, and union of hearts, convergence of interests. This is what Life-Community intends for personal and social well-being, and it comes only from bonds of communion between all parts. Moreover, openness as a mark of Spirit is important to build a community. It implies feeling oneself referred outside oneself. Without this openness, there is no acceptance. Therefore, the Holy Trinity is not merely a society in the sense of a collectivity; God is communion of love and unbroken personal relationships. As the personal nature of God is fellowship, to have a personal relationship with God is 'a question of being caught up into the fellowship of God which is always personal but never individualistic'.[33] The Trinitarian ontology helps us to appropriate something of the richness and openness. Trinity is to be put before men 'not in abstract ideas', as Mwoleka said, 'but in concrete facts of our human earthly life: present the Life of the Trinity as shared and lived by us Christians here and now.'[34] Therefore, the church is called to be the kind of reality at a finite level that God is in eternity, as this provides the basis for the personal dynamics of the community as people of God.

---

[31] John Zizioulas, *Being as Communion: Studies in Personhood and the Church* (London: Darton, Longman and Todd, 1985), 134.

[32] Boff, *Trinity and Society*, 127.

[33] The British Council of Churches, *The Forgotten Trinity*, 27.

[34] Mwoleka, 'Trinity and Community', 16.

Laos of God

Life-Community is the *laos* of God. 'People', *laos* in Greek, serves in the NT to emphasise Christians as drawn from Gentiles as well as Jews (Acts 15.14). It may simply refer to the church as in Acts 18.10. Appropriating the covenant language of Exodus 19.5-6, 1 Peter 2.9-10 claims the full title 'people of God' for Christians:

> You are a chosen race, a royal priesthood, a holy nation, God's own people, in order that you may proclaim the mighty acts of him who called you out of darkness into his marvellous light. Once you were not a people, but now you are God's people. Once you had not received mercy, but now you have received mercy.

As the *laos* is the whole people, Life-Community does not make a distinction between laity and the clergy. Life-Community is a chosen people, a people with a special status and dignity because of their relationship with God. As Everett Ferguson expressed it, 'to be the *laos* of God gives a sense of importance, identity and purpose to life, and the free grace of God in Christ removes any basis for pride and contributes to a humble acknowledgement of dependence on God.'[35] Life-Community is a congregation which is to be fashioned into the image of Christ and called to proclaim the mighty acts of God. It transcends the unity based on identity from citizenship in a nation, being of the same race, sharing a certain occupation, and participating in a certain social class. Life-Community is the people of God because of now being in Christ.

The Community of the Spirit

Life-Community is a community which arises through the common participation in the Holy Spirit that brings people together (2 Corinthians 13.13). It is as a fellowship created by the Spirit, a 'Spirit-filled community', as Hans Küng put it.[36] Thus, the church in its very essence is a divine creation for it is a community, a fellowship, through the divine Spirit. John Zizioulas stated, 'The Spirit is not what animates an already existing church, but the Spirit makes the church to be.'[37] It means that the church was not first a body into which God poured the Spirit as the living context. No, it was the coming of the Spirit that created the church. The Spirit continues to give life to the church, and it is the life of Christ. Therefore, the church is the community of the Spirit. The unity and equality within Life-Community comes from the fact that all members possess the same

---

[35] Everett Ferguson, *The Church of Christ: A Biblical Ecclesiology for Today* (Cambridge: William B. Eerdmans Publishing Company, 1996), 90.

[36] Hans Kung, *The Church* (London: Burns and Oates, 1967), 162-179.

[37] Zizioulas, *Being as Communion,* 132.

Spirit (1 Corinthians 12.13) with diversity of function which does not exalt one group above others.

This can be understood from the biblical metaphor of the church as the 'Body of Christ'. It is about the close interdependence between the parts or members of the body. Each member has been given particular gifts for the sake of the whole body and the whole has a duty to care for one another and to nurture the gifts that each has been given. Nevertheless, static perception of the body metaphor must be avoided as each member or part has its appointed place and this should not be used to justify a rigidly hierarchical church.

However, Life-Community, as the community of the Spirit or the body of Christ, does not tend to 'divinise' the church. It is aware of its weakness. Therefore, it is 'an ever-reforming body', constantly needing to submit to God's word, to repent and to change. It is truly *ecclesia semper reformanda*. Consequently, authority must be checked and constantly submit to God's word, ready to change when it is needed.

The Liberative Power of Jesus

This section aims to revisit the role of ministry within the church that will lead to the ministry of the whole people of God in Christ. It is to work for a dynamic hierarchy built on the liberating power of Jesus.

Authority within the Christian community is grounded in Jesus Christ: 'All authority in heaven and on earth has been given to me' (Matthew 28.18b). In Jesus' own exercise of his authority, there are certain crucial features which led to a new faith-praxis with a radically reformed understanding of religious authority. He used his power to confront evil and to challenge untruth; he acted in service to his brothers and sisters, he valued humility highly and includes those whom society cast out to margins. His saving and caring power was for the good of people. It was authority in humility and service. He clearly expressed it after the incident of the request of the mother of Zebedee's sons:

> You know that among the gentiles the rulers lord it over them, and great men make their authority felt. Among you this is not to happen. No, anyone who wants to become great among you must be your servant, and anyone who wants to be first among you must be your slave, just as the son of man came not to be served but to serve, and to give his life as a ransom for many (Matthew 20.25-28).

The authority of Christ himself, and therefore of all who share in it, is an authority only for the sake of service; an authority to care for others and to consider their interests. In the Life-Community, authority is not to be exercised in manipulative and oppressive ways. It takes seriously Jesus' warning: 'It shall not be so among you.' Authority brings salvation and liberation of people from all that enslaves them. It challenges and transforms the whole notion of 'legitimation of authority' informed by 'worldly' models available in societies.

Therefore, authority-for-life in Life-Community has to challenge the *Bula Matari* model within the church. It has to use the structures as vitalistic means of exercising authority for the 'common good' of God's people.

A Dynamic Hierarchy for a New People

A Christian community, like any other human community, needs some structures and clearly designed social functions in order to minimise possible tensions. As T.I. Ball put it, 'A society of men cannot exercise any authority that belongs to it in *confuso*; it must exercise it through the proper officers of the society.'[38] For instance, the Anglican Church developed a static hierarchical system of episcopacy where everyone knows officially where the power lies. This monarchical system within the Episcopal system resulted from an understanding of the concept of a single divine source of authority:

> Authority, as inherited by the Anglican Communion from the undivided Church of the early centuries of the Christian era, is a single Divine source, and reflects within itself the richness and historicity of the Divine revelation, the authority of the eternal Father, the incarnate Son, and the life-giving Spirit.[39]

This hierarchical understanding of authority led many churches to the understanding that the higher a man is in the ecclesiastical hierarchy the closer he is to God, and that his function is to mediate the grace of God to those lower down the scale. It leads to exaggerated stress on the unexamined concept of hierarchy. The focus of the exercise of authority is on leaders rather than upon Jesus Christ who is its source and the foundation of the unity of the church. This, in fact, is a serious distortion of the principles of the New Testament which are central for the true idea of the church: Christ is the sole mediator between God and humanity (1 Timothy 2.5; Acts 4.12); and he identifies himself with all who believe in him and are gathered together in his name (Matthew 18.20).

The development of ecclesiology in many churches was influenced by the local culture and local styles of leadership and structures of authority. These churches belong to the paradigm of the traditional authority which perpetuates the primitive Christian community and that its leaders stand in a succession that goes back to the apostles.

Status rather than role is the key to traditional authority within the church. It follows the traditional ecclesiology as described by Paul Avis: firstly, status is hierarchical in that the concept of hierarchy is written into the trust deeds of the church, from the Lord's commission to Peter onwards, in such a way that for the

---

[38] G.R. Evans, *Authority in the Church: A challenge for Anglicans* (Norwich: The Canterbury Press, 1990), 19.
[39] Evans, *Authority in the Church,* 19.

church to cease to be hierarchical would be for the church to cease to be the church. Secondly, it is essential for it is the channel through which sacramental grace is mediated to the church for the salvation of souls. Thirdly, it is sacred in that it is not only the channel of the sacred but is sacred itself. It is untouchable and no candidate for reform.[40] Life-Community provides a dynamic hierarchy that goes beyond the above traditional ecclesiology. In doing so, the role of Episcopal ministry needs to be revisited in the context of a corporate apostolic succession.

Corporate Apostolic Succession

According to John Home, there has been a tendency, among Anglicans, for bishops particularly to be seen as a class apart who are the Church 'par excellence.'[41] The report of the Archbishop's Group on The Episcopate in 1990 demonstrated how, through the office of a bishop, the church is maintained and strengthened in unity in its service to God and its witness to the world. They stated:

> In the local church the bishop focuses and nurtures the unity of his people; in his sharing in the collegiality of bishops the local church is bound together with other local churches; and, through the succession of bishops the local community is related to the Church through the ages. Thus the bishop in his own person in his diocese; and in his collegial relations in the wider church; and through his place in the succession of bishops in their communities in faithfulness to the Gospel, is sign and focus of the unity of the Church.[42]

They thus concluded that 'the loss of a common episcopate, the resulting existence of parallel episcopates and divisively diverse forms of oversight ministries, diminishes the sign of unity and continuity.'[43] Here the stress is on the bishop as sign and agent of unity and continuity within the diocese and within the whole church. Anglicanism has firmly committed itself to constitutional episcopacy in which the government of the church by the bishops is limited and supported by synods, canons, and other methods whereby the whole Church, clergy and laity, participate in its government and mission.[44]

---

[40] Paul Avis, *Authority, Leadership and Conflict in the Church* (London: Mowbray, 1992), 59.

[41] John Home, *Highways and Edges: Anglicanism and the Universal Church* (London: CIO Publishing, 1985), 47.

[42] Church of England, *Episcopal Ministry: The Report of the Archbishops' Group on The Episcopate* (London: Church House Publishing, 1990), 160.

[43] Church of England, *Episcopal Ministry*, 161.

[44] Lambeth Conference, *The Report of Lambeth Conference 1978* (London: CIO Publishing, 1978), 77.

However, the theology of gracious gift developed by the Report of the Archbishops' Commission on the Organisation of the Church of England, *Working as One Body*, is important. The authors are convinced that God in his goodness has already given to the church the resources it needs to be God's people, and to live and work to his praise and glory.[45] Thus, God has given the church various gifts, to be used in love for the good of the whole, including the gift of leadership. So the church has to recognise the many diverse gifts graciously given to God's people, to be used co-operatively to his glory and for the salvation of humanity. In this sense, the office of the bishop is personal (God-given personal responsibility), collegial and communal in unbreakable relationship to the whole community of the baptised. They built their proposals on the conciliar model of the Bishop-in-Synod. The Church of England is currently spoken of 'episcopally led and synodically governed'. The document stated the importance of the synod:

> Ordination is one of the gifts of the Holy Spirit, who gives liberally to every member of the body. But the task of the Church requires the co-ordination of the many gifts of the Spirit, and a synod is one way in which counsel may be taken and consent sought, and the skills and judgement of the whole people of God may be brought to bear on the issues and challenges of the day.[46]

However, the document recognises that the principal purpose of a special or 'ordained' ministry is to serve the continuity and effectiveness of witness to the gospel of Jesus Christ. We agree with G.R. Evans when he says,

> The ordained minister is placed by ordination in a special relationship to the common priesthood, on behalf of the community of which he has pastoral charge. This is not a handing over of authority to be exercised as a personal right, but an entrusting of responsibility answerable to Christ and to the community. What is involved is a service to the community, and it is always exercised from within the community and on its behalf, and thus it can have no independent authority. Such office is not an open-ended gift of power, but an entrusting of authority for a limited purpose within the *koinonia*, or fellowship.[47]

Leadership is a function of the Christian community and not a status over against it. Church as Life-Community emphasizes the bishop's function, beyond the strange notion of episcope that focuses the church in himself and creates the church by virtue of his power to ordain and confirm. The corporate apostolic

---

[45] Church of England, *Working as One Body: The Report of the Archbishop Commission on the Organisation of the Church of England* (London: Church House Publishing, 1995), 4.
[46] Church of England, *Working as One Body*, 7.
[47] Evans, *Authority in the Church*, 23.

succession of the church, rather than the bishops, makes the Life-Community universal and inclusive for the unity of the Church.

A Renewed Episcopacy

The Virginia Report acknowledged that where the principle of the ministry of all the people of God has taken root, it is still too often seen in terms of back-up support for the 'real' (ordained) ministry, so that the Church remains in many places a community gathered round a minister instead of being the ministering community it is called to be.[48] The Report underlined that the ministry of the baptised is the fundamental ministry of the Church, with the function of ordained ministry being to serve, equip and enable this ministry to take place. The Report sadly noticed that the tendency today is to start with the ordained ministry and to see lay ministry as in some way derived. It suggested that the ministry of the whole body should come first.

In Church as Life-Community, the bishop is a person of God among the people and should be accessible to people instead of hiding behind a heavy protocol, as leaders often do in the state. The bishop as the president of the council gives direction and vision with the consent of members. The bishop is 'chief' pastor in the sense of role, not status. Pastors are called for the ministry by Christ, but commissioned on behalf of the church by the bishop. The bishop is the *symbol* of unity and representative of the diocesan community in the sense of a corporate episcope. The Church of England has formulated it as follows, 'Bishop holds an office which is personal, but also collegial and communal.'[49] Indeed, the 'personal' episcope is not in contradiction with an episcope exercised 'with' all other officers in the diocesan community, and beyond that with the community as a whole. As the Report put it, 'This supremely personal Episcopal ministry at the same time belongs to the whole community … It is the essence of the matter that the authority of a bishop, which is given to him by the community of the church, is returned by him to the community in the exercise of his ministry.'[50] Apostolic succession in its fullest sense is a succession of the whole community, as well as the local churches. In some dioceses of the Anglican Communion, the traditional interpretation of the apostolic succession has been revisited with the integration of women in the 'ordained ministry'. An episcopate inseparable from the community it serves will mean a personal episcopal office handed on by the imposition of hands. However, the bishop, the priest and the deacon remain members of the *laos*. The concept of Council as a 'leading and governing body' diminishes the notion of a single Episcopal head. This makes

---

[48] James M. Rosenthal and Nicola Currie (eds), *Being Anglican in the third millennium* (London: Morehouse Publishing 1997), 115.
[49] Church of England, *Episcopal Ministry*, 175.
[50] Church of England, *Episcopal Ministry*, 176.

the Episcopal office a *shared* ministry. Pastors in parishes share the ministry with the bishop, but their call by Christ must be considered.

The Life-Community as the body of Christ offers a dynamic view of the hierarchy. It is not built on a static view of the body where each member or part has its appointed place, as this has been used to justify a rigid hierarchical church. Dynamic hierarchy consists of close interdependence between the parts or members of the body. Each member has been given particular gifts for the sake of the whole body and all have a duty to care for one another and to nurture the gifts that each has been given. According to the language of priesthood, the whole church can act with authority because of Christ's presence within it (Matthew 18.15-21). The Life-Community ecclesiology considers also the 'head and body' language, not to create a hierarchical structure with a clerical caste at its apex, but to express that Christ is the head of the body (Ephesians 4.15-16; Col. 1.18), and the whole body is ordered towards him and derives its coherence from him.

Life-Community develops the old episcopal power by means of council government representing the voice of the whole people of God. It provides the personal and corporate aspects and ensures that the leadership cannot dominate the people. As Tim Bradshaw said, 'The personal authority within the community is the gift of the HolySpirit, but balanced by the electoral system of councils.'[51] It means the community must recognise the personal authority and allow it to be used within the community.

Councils as Leading and Governing Bodies

Power in an Anglican Province resides in the synod. The synod alone can, by the decision of its members, make canon law and constitutions. Their membership includes bishops, clergy and laity. Synodical government in the Church of England came into operation in 1970 after the Convocation system and the Church Assembly, as a result of the Enabling Act 1919, which allowed the lay people to join the clergy in decision-making.

Synod in itself has a noble importance, as John Home stated: 'The very meaning of "synod" is that people, perhaps of several differing views, set out to find how best, in Christ's cause, they can find a way forward together. It is with this conception in view that procedure by synod has its roots in the earliest centuries of the Church.'[52] However, from his own experience, he has noticed that not only does the style in which a synod works differ from one part of the world to another, but also interestingly the style is often inclined to imitate facets

---

[51] Tim Bradshaw, *The Olive Branch: An Evangelical Anglican Doctrine of the Church* (Carlisle: The Paternoster Press, 1992), 261.
[52] Home, *Highways and Edges,* 50.

of the political ordering of the country,[53] which is the case in the EAC. In fact, the synod was introduced into the Congo by the Church of Uganda, a system modelled on the British parliamentary system with the system of houses. Each synod is opened and closed by a civil authority. It is formal and the members sit according to their status: canons nearby the Bishop, then Archdeacons, diocesan staff, priests and other delegates. Members are not elected, but pre-appointed by the constitution according to the position they hold in the church. The synod is, in fact, a 'talking-shop', and the quality of the debates has been seen by many as 'very low' and 'boring'. Despite the vote, the bishops have the right to veto the decisions.

Therefore, the central structure of the EAC needs to be re-ordered in order to make the church Life-Community. The synod must have the sense of council for two reasons. Firstly, the synod as council will allow friendly discussions as brothers and sisters in Christ, as people are used to it in their villages and societies. There will be freedom of opinion that leads to a consensus. Secondly, the same council will *lead* and *govern* the church. Therefore, the Bible-based decisions of the council will be 'final', depriving the leader of the right to veto.

The Diocesan Council will not be only a 'shop-talking' forum, but the principal decision-making body on policy and resources. Legislative power and its control over 'the rules' will give to the council a special degree of authority. The Archbishop would be elected by the provincial synod or council instead of the *Collège des évêques*, for this will allow the Archbishop to be truly accountable to the provincial synod.

Life-Community thus provides a dynamic hierarchy in the sense that bishops, clergy and laity work together as a body linked by the fact that the Holy Spirit has been given to the Church as a whole. It is as in the apostolic age, the life and action of the Church were the life and action of the whole body. The officers acted with, not instead of, the community; and the community acted with, not in mere obedience under, its officers.

Self-critical Church

Stan Nussbaum, working on African Independent Churches (AICs), has proposed the restatement of the three-self formula of Henry Venn: self-governing, self-supporting and self-propagation. Nussbaum has suggested a more dynamic concept of self-motivating instead of self-supporting, for 'motivation causes things to move rather than simply to stand still. A self-motivating church is driven by its past experience of God's action and pulled

---

[53] Home, *Highways and Edges,* 50.

towards the work it is called to do.'[54] Indeed, motivation is needed to make our churches running and moving instead of simply engaging in routine maintenance. Yet self-financial support is important for the 'independence' of the local church. Life-Community is an energetic community where members rely on the action of the Holy Spirit and are motivated for action. Life-Community uses the church tradition for action not for mere maintenance. Nussbaum has also suggested replacing self-governing by self-critical. However, self-criticism is an aspect of self-governing. It is open to prophetic voices in how affairs are conducted, with mission rather than maintenance of the structure as the overriding concern. This openness should start within the church itself before it carries the prophetic voice to society as a whole.

As previously said, church leaders do not appreciate 'opposition', and anyone who has a different view is treated with suspicion. It is the same discourse as Mobutu's that 'there is no opposition in traditional Africa'.[55] Life-Community should first use its authority as community to liberate its members from their submissive attitude. It is to combat *utii* theology that consists of blind obedience based on the *Bula Matari* model and cultural assumption of the 'sacred hierarchy'. In this sense, the use of local titles such as *Atalau* (chief) for leaders should be avoided in the church in order to avoid confusion in people's mind. Titles in the church must relate to humility in service. Therefore leaders will be honoured by the titles of their functions such as Archbishop, Bishop, Archdeacon, and Pastor. As the metaphor of 'father' has been misused in Congo to back the abuse of authority both in the church and in the state, the term *Baba* (father) should be discouraged in the church as it favours the dependence of members on the leader and induces unquestionable submission to the leader.

Authority in the church must also liberate people from ignorance. Church documents such as constitutions, canons, notes of meetings, etc., should be in the local language and made available to all members. Official documents should be detailed and clear on 'orthodox' interpretation in order to avoid any misunderstanding. These documents must reflect the doctrine, theology and discipline of the local church so that there is no difference between the 'textual' theology and oral theology. Care should be taken not to conform blindly the action in the church to 'foreign ideologies' from the state. In doing so, the church has to prioritise education and develop creativity and a critical spirit in Bible schools and theological colleges. It is a liberating education which is, in Paulo Freire's words, 'the practice of freedom as opposed to education as the practice of domination.'[56] It is to create men and women who are creative and who are

---

[54] San Nussbaum, quoted by John Pobee and Gabriel Ositelu II, *African Initiatives in Christianity: The growth, gifts and diversities of indigenous African churches. A challenge to the ecumenical movement* (Geneva: WCC Publications, 1998), 56.

[55] Michel, *Mobutu, Dignité pour l'Afrique*, 87.

[56] Paulo Freire, *Pedagogy of the Oppressed* (London: Penguin Books, 1996), 62.

discoverers. Liberating education forms minds which can be critical, can verify and not simply accept things as they are offered. This education is a dialogue between human beings, as to speak is not the privilege of some few persons, but the right of everyone. The members of the church thus should be equipped to question the *status quo* in the church and make a critical assessment of the situation. The church in Africa and particularly in the Congo carefully needs to develop a constructive criticism not under the influence of ethnicism or jealousy, but under the guidance of the Holy Spirit. As Sykes said, 'Criticism is, of course, uncomfortable, and creates conflict. Criticism may be mistaken; it may be based on jealousy; it may lead to resentment. But it is again my conviction that the manifold and changing needs of, and challenges to, the Christian Church require both the discriminating exercise of authority and the discriminating exercise of criticism if Christ's work is to be done in the world.[57]

In this self-criticism the authority of scholarship should be acknowledged. There is a need to form a *Commission Théologique,* that is, a body to provide detailed clarification regarding not only the standing of doctrine, but also the real nature of the church. This *Commission Théologique* will function as the 'wisdom' of the church councils in order to avoid the current vague and ambiguous generalities of synods pronouncements. The EAC has always avoided creating a *Commission Théologique.* In fact, Musolo was right to say, 'Africans hate more what they need more.'[58] There is a need to train more people in the key areas of Christian theology. Therefore, liberating authority is, as Paul Avis said, 'A concept of authority that brings out its root meaning of enabling rather than dominating, and finds its justification in a spiritual and theological competence that invites voluntary acknowledgement rather than in hierarchical or bureaucratic demands for acquiescence.'[59]

Global Dynamic

Authority-for-life in Life-Community ecclesiology is universally oriented. It passes from ethnicism to inter-ethnic consciousness, and from contextualisation to vitalistic globalisation.

Inter-Ethnocentrism

It is an illusion to attempt to create a global society which is totally homogeneous and non-argumentative. Conflict is inescapable in human relations. But it becomes endemic within a community where no real sense of community exists.

[57] Stephen Sykes, *Unashamed Anglicanism* (London: Darton, Longman and Todd, 1995), 162.
[58] Masolo, *African Philosophy in Search of Identity,* 50.
[59] Avis, *Authority, Leadership and Conflict in the Church,* x.

For instance in the EAC, we have said that the whole province is facing conflicts and division, caused not only by ethnocentrism and clanism, but also by *episcopose*, lack of freedom and the 'truth'. It has developed an authority marked by self-centredness and hatred. It is a competitive and aggressive authority. Wilful distortion of biblical interpretation, intimidation, revocation, suspension and culpability are deliberately used to tackle any 'opposition' in aiming to restore 'order'. But Authority-for-life creates inter-ethnic consciousness. This functions through deep conversion which consists of true change of mind and spirit and adoption of a new direction of life under the lordship of Christ. It is authority modelled on Christ's authority, as Avis has stated, 'Through a life totally open to God and wholly at God's disposal, a life in which God was incarnate, his authority was the authority of God. It reveals the authority of God to be in no way oppressive, inhibiting, external, alienating, heteronymous, but rather liberating, enabling, personal, sustaining and creative.' [60] It is the consciousness of belonging to a 'new' community that is a supra-ethnic community. Authority-for-life must help the new convert to open his/her life wholly to God, so that he or she can grow and become the agent of 'ethnic conversion' into inter-ethnic consciousness. Authority-for-life creates, enables and sustains an inter-ethnic consciousness. To achieve this, the church should avoid setting up new parishes, archdeaconries and dioceses on an ethnic or clan basis, or appointing ministers on ethnic criteria. Church offices should be inter-clanic within the same ethnic group, and inter-ethnic within a pluralistic society. The appointment of leaders should be based not only on spiritual and vocational factors, but also on competence in management.

From Contextualisation to Vitalistic Globalisation

The problem of the relationship between Gospel and culture presents a challenge to the church and to Christians at all times and in all places. The chief concern of most African theologians is that Western missionaries transferred to Africa forms of Christianity determined by their own philosophical and socio-cultural understandings. They thus plead for the African worldview to be taken seriously. For instance, Harry Sawyerr clearly expressed it in these terms:

> Christian African leaders seem however not to have felt fully at home with the 'imported' forms of worship. Today, African Christians and missionaries alike are calling for an intensive study of the ingredients of the indigenous religious

---

[60] Avis, *Authority, Leadership and Conflict in the Church,* 125.

thought-forms and practices in order to ensure a truly effective communication of the Gospel.[61]

Indeed, local context is very important if the Gospel has to be incarnated in the heart of God's people. Jesus must speak to people in their current context so that Christians can 'feel at home'. Local life values such as solidarity, harmony, unity, participation-sharing must be promoted in the church. The Gospel will have to speak the local cultural language to incarnate the message. Natural family values such as warmth of love, care for others, openness and acceptance must help to build the Christian authority that finds its proper context in service. However, this 'localisation' of Christianity must avoid isolating the church in the local context. As Life-Community is universal in its nature, localisation should operate in a global context, or should have a global dynamic.

On the other hand, 'localisation' should avoid the use of local language such as metaphors to legitimate the manipulative and oppressive authority of local church leadership. For instance, in the Democratic Republic of Congo, President Mobutu emphasized nationalism, which consisted of an anticolonial movement intending to restore the old political order based on precolonial principles. Cultural Revolution based on nationalism and *authenticité* became an alienating tool using the past to introduce new elements for domination and exploitation. Unfortunately, as said in Chapter Two of this work, the rhetorical-manipulative use of religious symbols by church and political leaders has led the church to 'clone authority' as the churches were institutionalised and legitimated by the state. It was a 'competitive authority' for a new dynamic of social integration. Therefore, inculturation has led to manipulative cultural values, and contextualisation has led to 'clone authority'. Imposed nationalism resulted in bloody ethnocentrism. This shows the tension between 'localisation' and globalisation' in Africa. Those in power seek to impose 'globalisation' in order to control people and their wealth, but encourage 'localisation' to weaken the 'global community'. We argue that imposed globalisation will not succeed unless it is built on localisation globally oriented. The local context must be valued in order to develop the global community. It is 'glocalisation' which consists of incarnating the Gospel into the local context with global inclination. It is methodologically from the Gospel to local context towards global community.

As contextualisation has resulted in tribalism and discrimination, Life-Community develops inter-ethnic consciousness through education and practical actions. In doing so, the parish constitutes the basic ecclesial unit where the pastor cares for people from different clans and tribes. In rural areas with

---

[61] Harry Sawyerr, 'What is African Theology?', in John Parratt (ed), *The Practice of Presence: Short Writings of Harry Sawyerr* (Michigan: Wm.B. Eerdmans Publishing Co, 1996), 85-99, 99.

mono-ethnic social groups, interclan activities should be prioritised. As activities such as marriages, funerals, dance, and sport bring people together despite their social groups, the church should encourage participation-sharing on these bases. Evangelism, conferences, training and other religious activities should be organised frequently on an interethnic basis. Exchange of workers in different ministries will serve to build bridges between different groups.

In urban areas, the experience will be slightly different. The church should discourage its members from adhering to *mutualités* (co-operatives) based on ethnicity or regional origin. *Mutualité* is a social organisation of people from the same tribe or from the same social class based on the work place, study and so on. The aim is for mutual help and support. In Congo, they have often become ethnic groupings with political aspiration. For instance, different current rebel groups in east Congo have originated from *mutualités*. Most of their members were Christians and all meetings began with a Christian service. The churches have had also their *mutualités* based on language or regional origin. These *mutualités* are completely exclusive. Of course, people are afraid of losing their identity and would like to value their language. However, one's identity must introduce one to the identity of others.

'Our' church as 'ethnic church' must be an inclusive and welcoming church, showing the love of Christ and openness to others. 'Our' church must develop in a global context. Furthermore, language in 'our' church should be considered as a gift of God for communication and not simply for conforming to ethnic identity as this leads to ethnocentrism and exclusion. Newcomers often join 'theirs' because of language. In an inter-ethnic community, the use of a national language would be recommended, as often the majority group tries to impose their language as the main language of the church. Care must be taken concerning small Christian groups, which often in Congo result in autonomous churches, and encourage more divisions in the Church. Moreover, theological colleges and Bible schools must be inclusive and build a strong relationship between students while on the campus. The church should improve facilities to help students to live on the campus so they can improve their participation-sharing abilities. Therefore, it is in this global context that the church can redeem the 'dying' societies in Congo.

Redemption of Society

'Enough is enough. We do not like to bury again the dead. We want to live in peace and work together for our common future. The Congolese people will not accept to be manipulated again'[62] This was the message of the Roman Catholic

---

[62] La Tempête de Tropiques, 'Le Cardinal Etsou et les Chrétiens Catholiques dénoncent la guerre et prient pour la paix en RDC et en Irak,' Kinshasa 31/03/03/ politics, http://www.digitalcongo.net/fullstory.

Archbishop, Cardinal Etsou, to the Congolese in South Africa during the National Dialogue in March 2003. 'Enough is enough' attests that the situation is desperate and calls for immediate action. The two first chapters of this book have argued that the state in the Congo has collapsed with all its structures. The so-called 'African First World War', the climax of the Congolese turmoil, has had a devastating impact on thousands of lives. Meanwhile, the churches in general have failed in their prophetic obligation to subject the political systems to the judgement of the word of God, for they were blinded by Cultural Revolution built on Africanisation and nationalism. They opted to clone the *Bula Matari* model. It is the same situation in other African countries such as Zimbabwe and recently Kenya. The collapse of the state 'authority' thus has entailed the failure of the 'authority' in the Church. As the gospel of Jesus Christ demands our participation in the struggle to free people from all kinds of dehumanisation, the Church in Africa should stand against oppression in any form. African societies have to be redeemed, not only through social service, but also through social action. This is why the following section proposes practical action that will sustain authority within Life-Community as an agent of transformation and fullness of life.

Social Service

It was said in Chapter Four that the EAC has been involved much in social transformation by providing education, health care and different projects for the welfare of the population. However, these activities need to be redefined and reoriented, for the simple care for the poor must move towards the improvement or transformation of economic and political systems for their liberation from poverty and oppression. The church as Life-Community's best contribution to the wider society is made by being the community of salvation. Salvation is not simply, as John Stott stated, 'a self-reformation, or the forgiveness of sins, or a personal passport to paradise, or a private mystical experience without social or moral consequences.'[63] Salvation is the blessing of God's rule. Isaiah 52.7 states, 'Beautiful on the mountains are the feet of those who bring good news, who proclaim salvation, who say to Zion, "Your God reigns!"' Salvation is thus not separated from the Kingdom of God, which is God's dynamic rule, breaking into human history through Jesus, confronting, combating and overcoming evil, spreading the wholeness of personal and communal well-being, taking possession of his people in total blessing and total demand. Therefore Life-Community seen in the sense of the Kingdom of God provides a model of what a human community should look like when it comes under the rule of God, and offers a challenging alternative to secular society.

---

[63] John Stott, *New Issues Facing Christians Today* (London: Marshall Pickering, 1999), 27.

In fact the Christian task consists of bringing individuals as well as the whole society under God's rule. Individuals must be responsible for their acts for social transformation, and authority in the church has to deal with the collective evil present in the world, built into the organized structures. The church's task is not simply one of making disciples, but also of transforming the whole society, as the living God of the Bible is not only concerned with his covenant people, but with all people. This point is made by John Gladwin: 'It is because this is God's world, and he cared for it to the point of incarnation and crucifixion, that we are inevitably committed to work for God's justice in the face of oppression, for God's truth in the face of lies and deceits, for service in the face of the abuse of power, for love in the face of selfishness, for cooperation in the face of destructive antagonism, and for reconciliation in the face of division and hostility.'[64] It means true faith issues in love, and true love issues in service. True faith leads to practical action.

Kairotic Moment

'Kairotic moments' are moments of God's judgement as well as God's grace, moments in which the reign of God breaks afresh into history, judging human injustice, but also creating opportunities which are liberating and redemptive.[65] The study of authority in postcolonial Congo argued that the *Bula Matari* model of the use of power has resulted in the crisis or vacuum of authority in the secular society and in the church. The collapse of authority has resulted in confusion, disorder, and breakdown of social, political and economic structures, violence, rebellions and million of deaths. As other African countries, Congo is, in fact, facing a crisis which calls theology to reconsider again its responsibility for discerning and responding to 'the signs of the times'. The church in Congo must recognise her prophetic role to respond to the crisis, facilitating the *kairos*, a moment of truth. As in South Africa, it is a situation in which an explicit confession for Jesus Christ over against the powers has become inescapable.

The context of political crisis in South Africa was different from what has happened in the Congo. However, although the *Kairos Document* to which we will refer frequently in this section is the self-understanding of the church within South Africa, it has a broad theological impact on the thinking and action of the churches in the world. John Parratt expressed it when he said, 'The document has vital practical implications for many countries in the Third world today.'[66] The

---

[64] John Gladwin, *God's People in God's World: Biblical motives for social involvement* (Leicester: Inter-Varsity Press, 1979), 179.
[65] Kairos Theologians, *Challenge to the Church: A Theological Comment on the Political Crisis in South Africa* (Braanfontein, South Africa: Skotaville Publishers, 1986), 1.
[66] John Parratt, 'Conclusion: Current Issues in African Theology', in John Parratt (ed), *A Reader in African Christian Theology* (London: SPCK, 1997), 149.

crucial point in the struggle of the church is not the tension between black and white as such, but the tension between an oppressed majority and a privileged minority. It is in this sense that the document can speak to the church of Congo in its own situation.

God has inaugurated a just new world order in Jesus. The proclamation of the good news of God's reign in Jesus Christ must thus address the situation of social crisis with peculiar directness. It is to denounce the reign of terror and dictatorship marked by an inherent ungovernability. Authority-for-life in Africa should speak as God did to Assyria: 'Woe to the city of blood, full of lies, full of plunder, never without victims!' (Nahum 3.1); 'I am against you' (2.13; 3.5); '… for who has not felt your endless cruelty?' (3.19). Jesus himself understood his mission as liberating, 'The Spirit of the Lord is on me, because he has anointed me to preach good news to the poor. He has sent me to proclaim freedom for the prisoners and recovery of sight for the blind, to release the oppressed, to proclaim the year of the Lord's favour' (Luke 4.18-19). The mission of Jesus was not a simple evangelistic message of repentance and faith in Christ, it is a message which embraces the whole of society: poverty, captivity, blindness and oppression are to be confronted. A 'Kairotic moment' is a call to action, but it requires a clear understanding of the situation in its socio-economic, cultural and political context.

Social Analysis

Authority in Life-Community proclaims the unity of God's rule in Christ, and recognises that the Kingdom brought by Christ himself was 'political and spiritual'. The church in Congo should make a serious effort to understand the socio-economic and political situation, as committed action comes from analysis and discernment.

Social analysis is 'the effort to obtain a more complete picture of a social situation by exploring its historical and structural relationships.'[67] It studies the changes of a social system through time, and 'unmasks the underlying values that shape the perspectives and decisions of those acting within a given situation.'[68] It unfolds the context within which a programme for social change can be outlined, although it does not provide a blueprint for action. Therefore social analysis focuses on issues, policies and structures, but also on economic and political systems, and the institutional concentrations of power within a community are called into question.

However, this must begin with conscientization in a country like Congo, where people have been kept in ignorance for a long time and are used to

---

[67] Joe Holland and Peter Henriot, *Social Analysis: Linking Faith and Justice* (Maryknoll, New York: Orbis Books, 1983), 14.
[68] Holland and Henriot, *Social Analysis,* 15.

political, cultural and religious manipulation. This conscientization is not a popular harangue as in political parties; it involves, as Duncan B. Forrester put it, 'a critical and active grappling with reality understood in the light of a form of social analysis which interprets the situation in terms of oppression and calls for the overthrow of all oppressive structures.'[69]

As social analysis is indispensable for effective action on behalf of justice, it will assist the church in the process of corporate discernment in the fulfilment of its apostolic mission. This theological process, which begins with conscientization, must lead to 'theological reflection' and pastoral planning. However, the aim of analysis is not a continual questioning and doubt, but to constantly adapt the analysis to the new situations, and remaining open to critical assessment. But caution must also be taken against any political manipulation of the African holistic concept of authority.

Relevant Political Theology

In Africa, confusion may be noticed between political theology and 'theological politics'. As seen in Chapter Two, the states use theological discourse to promote political ideologies, and the church falls into the trap of borrowing political ideologies to support their theological thinking. The language used by church leaders is often 'as the president of state has said'. The fact that the presidents often identify themselves as Christians gives church leaders a blind confidence to copy uncritically the political discourse. The analysis of 'state theology' and 'church theology' done in the *Kairos Document* is a good example applicable to situation in many African countries.

Firstly, the document underlines that 'State Theology' is simply the theological justification of the status quo, for it 'blesses injustice, canonises the will of the powerful and reduces the poor to passivity, obedience and apathy.'[70] It twists Scriptures and misuses theological and biblical concepts such as Law and Order to serve its purposes. The state is not at the service of the people through promotion and protection of human rights, safeguarding the lives and liberties of all people. Instead, the state is deified. Thus, the state 'is not merely an idol or false god, it is the devil disguised as Almighty God, the antichrist.'[71] Theological and biblical arguments merely become 'ideological' in the interest of the minority and lead to heretical and blasphemous theology. The document continues with a theological-ethical discussion of the 'illegitimate' nature of a state which has betrayed its proper function of 'rewarding the good and

---

[69] Duncan B. Forrester, *Theology and Politics* (Oxford: Basil Blackwell, 1988), 155.
[70] The Kairos Theologians, *Challenge to the Church*, 3.
[71] The Kairos Theologians, *Challenge to the Church*, 8.

punishing the evildoers', and has become *hostis boni communis*, an enemy of the common good.[72] It means that a tyrannical regime has no moral legitimacy.

Secondly, 'Church Theology' represents the reflections and attitudes of the churches which did not engage in a serious enough analysis of the signs of the times, and thus 'relies upon a few stock ideas derived from Christian tradition and then uncritically and repeatedly applies them to our situation.'[73] It has little understanding of politics and political strategy, and seeks an easy and uncostly road to reform. It uses Christian ideas such as reconciliation, peace, justice and non-violence in superficial and inadequate ways. This type of theology in the service of politics rests on a fundamentally inadequate understanding of the faith and spirituality, as having little to do with the life of the world. As Forrester has put it, 'It regards passivity as virtue.'[74] Theological politics which has submitted theological reflections to political ideologies remains a challenge to theology in Africa. The *Kairos Document* thus calls for a relevant political theology which would offer the means to unmask and remove 'the devil disguised as Almighty God' not only in the state, but also in the church.

Prophetic Theology: Call for Action

The church in Africa really is in need of 'Prophetic Theology', just as it was specifically needed in South Africa. The church needs *Kairos* theologians to unmask the ideological use of theology, and to point to a positive political responsibility of the faith. Prophetic Theology is a call to action, as stated by *Kairos* theologians:

> Our present KAIROS calls for a response from Christians that is biblical, spiritual, pastoral and, above all, prophetic. It is not enough in these circumstances to repeat generalised Christian principles. We need a bold and incisive response that is prophetic because it speaks to the particular circumstances of this crisis, a response that does not give the impression of sitting on the fence but is clearly and unambiguously taking a stand.[75]

Prophetic Theology is a commitment to change. It is to put words or deeds into action, as Paulo Freire said:

> When a word is deprived of its dimension of action, reflection automatically suffers as well; and the word is changed into idle chatter, into verbalism, into an alienated

---

[72] The Kairos Theologians, *Challenge to the Church*, 8.
[73] The Kairos Theologians, *Challenge to the Church*, 9.
[74] Forrester, *Theology and Politics*, 165.
[75] World Council of Churches, Challenge to the Church: Theological Comment on the Political Crisis in South Africa, the Kairos Document and Commentries', in PCR Information, 1985, 23.

and alienating 'blah.' It becomes an empty word, one which cannot denounce the world, for denunciation is impossible without a commitment to transform, and there is no transformation without action.[76]

To take action is often seen as a 'rebellion'. But obedience entails also a rebellion of conscience illuminated by the Spirit of God. Julius Nyerere, considering the church as the conscience of humanity and prophetic, recognised that 'the church must not be afraid to advocate 'rebellion', the rebellion of the children of God against spiritual as well as physical slums.'[77] So, the church is to detect, and fight for remedying, the social and political sins and ills of the society. As in the midst of crisis people look to the church for moral guidance, Life-Community should adopt what the *Kairos* theologians underlined,

> It [the church] has a message of the cross that inspires us to make sacrifices for justice and liberation. It has a message of hope that challenges us to wake up and to act with hope and confidence. The church must preach this message not only in words and sermons and statements but also through its actions, programmes, campaigns and divine services.[78]

Some practical actions should be taken for liberation, justice and peace, for the well-being of people in the kingdom of God.

Firstly, Life-community must encourage a commitment to faithful and integral prayer. Jesus consecrated his life fully in prayers and asked his followers to dwell in prayers. However, prayers are not simply a Christian formality aiming to recite what has been learnt. Prayer must name the evil. It must be as clear as when Apolo prayed, 'Father, remove this bad chief and help us quickly.'[79] Reacting to the political turmoil in Congo which has caused unimaginable loss of lives, Cardinal Etsou of Kinshasa stated, 'The time of praying without action is not only out of date, but this type of prayer is contrary to the gospel Christ gave us, He who came that we might have life and have it in abundance.' Unfortunately when there is a crisis, the church quickly requires prayer meetings without an adequate analysis of the situation. Indeed, it is a biblical recommendation to pray for political leaders, but it does not give political leaders authority to plan prayers and church services for their purposes as they do in Congo. The rebels who have committed horrible atrocities have also imposed prayers on the church members, not because they seek God's guidance, but simply as a means of political propaganda. The church should be careful

[76] Freire, *Pedagogy of the Oppressed,* 68.
[77] Julius Nyerere, *Man and Development* (Dar se Salaam: Oxford University Press, 1974), 82.
[78] Kairos Theologians, *Challenge to the Church,* 30.
[79] Eglise Anglicane du Zaire, *Kwa Imani Apolo: Maisha ya Apolo Kivebulaya* (printed in Great Britain by Paradigm Print, Gateshead, Tyne and Wear, 1984), 28.

about this kind of manipulation. Where 'NO' is needed, the church should say 'NO', despite the cost.

Moreover, some churches have created their department for justice and peace. However, these departments often fail to function because of lack of the commitment for justice and peace. The commission for justice and peace built on self-determination is urgently needed at each level of the church's structure. Its task would be to analyse issues pertaining to social justice, to draw up suitable programmes for people, and to see that the programmes are carried out. The church should provide formation for social justice, not only for an educated elite, but also for the whole society. In doing so, the church should also develop other means of communication such as booklets, reviews and bulletins which deal both with theological issues, and political ideologies.

Another point is that the Roman Catholic Church in Congo has developed a new ministry called *L'Apostolat des Dirigeants, Entrepreneurs et Cadres Catholiques [Apostolate of Catholic Leaders, Entrepreneurs and Managers (ADEC)]*. It is a committed group of people who have accepted Christ as Saviour through the Catholic church which brings together three categories of people: political leaders, entrepreneurs (business men and women) and managers and executives in public administration, and in public, private and mixed economy firms. The objectives of ADEC are: training of the members through dynamic and committed pastoral care within the church in order to help them better live out the Christian faith in their responsibilities and their management of public and private affairs; accompanying members in their steps towards true and authentic conversion, deepening of their faith and real life experience of faith. Their motto is based on love, work and sharing. The church should develop this kind of ministry that will make an impact on good management in the country, not only in private matters, but also in public affairs.

Finally, the church should follow the path of its Master for the 'Cleansing of the Temple'. The physical assault of Jesus to clear the Temple is revealing. He drove out the 'traders' and overturned the tables and chairs that they used. Of course, the church's task is not to lead protests against any institution, but to support practical efforts aimed at affirming love, justice, freedom and human dignity. However, the church may be irrelevant when it doesn't take action for freedom where it is necessary, as Julius Nyerere said: 'Unless we participate actively in the rebellion against those social structures and economic organizations which condemn men to poverty, humiliation and degradation, then the Church will become irrelevant to man.'[80] Of course, Christians are called to love their enemies (Matthew 5.44), but the latter must be identified. As *Kairos* theologians proposed, 'The most loving thing we can do for both the oppressed and for our enemies who are oppressors is to eliminate the oppression, remove

---

[80] Nyerere, *Man and Development*, 85.

the tyrants from power and establish a just government for the common good of all the people.'[81]

The church is a guide of the people on the road to true humanity and this implies service. The church exists for the people. 'Its love', as Nyerere said, 'must be expressed in action against evil, and for good. For, if the church acquiesces in established evils, it is identifying itself and the Christian religion with injustice by its continuing presence.'[82] Therefore, there are times when the church will use the 'cleansing of the Temple' principle to remove the 'evil' leaders, not only in the state, but also in the church. Even in traditional society, a bad chief who did not work for the common good had to be removed. In situations like the Congo, Zimbabwe and many other countries, where hopeless people are abandoned to fend for themselves, and the use of violence has become the standard of leadership, the church will allow its members to take action in self-defence. Therefore, Authority in Life-Community must read the 'signs of time', wisely subjecting the cultural and political systems to the judgement of the word of God, and disobeying and resisting any malevolent power, visible or invisible, for the sake of the Kingdom of God.

---

[81] Kairos Theologians, *Challenge to the Church,* 23.
[82] Nyerere, *Man and Development,* 17.

Conclusion

Yahweh reigns! He is the God of righteousness and justice. He champions the cause of the weak and the oppressed (Deuteronomy 4:32). In Genesis 18:20-21, the Lord said, 'The outcry against Sodom and Gomorrah is so great and their sin is so grievous that I will go down and see if what they have done is as bad as the outcry that has reached me.' As explained by Richard Nelson Boyce, 'Outcry' is a technical word for the cry of pain or the cry for help from those who are being oppressed or violated. It is the 'cry for help' addressed to the authorities by the needy.[1] Indeed, what the God of righteousness heard from Sodom was not just 'an outcry' but specifically 'a cry for help' addressed to himself as the ultimate 'Judge of all the earth.' In this case, God's intervention to destroy the cities would be seen as breaking their power over the poor and oppressed in the surrounding area, an act of biblical justice. Sodom was used as a paradigm, a model of human society at its worst and of the inevitable and comprehensive judgement of God on such wickedness. It was a place filled with oppression, cruelty, violence, perverted sexuality, idolatry, pride, greedy consumption and void of compassion or care for the needy.

The Sodom paradigm is not different from the *Bula Matari* model, marked by its cruelty, terror, greediness and the personalisation of power. As mentioned in the introduction of this book, African governments have caused at least as much suffering as the colonial rulers before them. They are responsible for more hunger, poverty, repression, injustice and loss of Africa's resources. If Africa is to overcome the present crisis and know lasting peace and prosperity, African Christians must become more active participants in the economic, political and social development of their nations. This involvement implies that theology in Africa must strongly deal with not only African cultures, but also with political power. Unfortunately, this book has sought to demonstrate that, in the process of Africanisation, cultural theology worked with cultural revolution as advocated by political leaders in reinventing traditions and a pattern of behaviour, using African traditional categories of authority as a tool of manipulation. This led to the domination of 'Africans by Africans', not only within the society, but even within the church. Inculturation thus led to domination and exclusivism.

Does this mean inculturation is not needed in doing theology in Africa? Of course inculturation is needed as the gospel must be incarnated into the local context. Contextualisation is the dynamic process whereby the constant message of the gospel interacts with specific, relative human situation. It is concerned

---

[1] Richard Nelson Boyce, *The Cry to God in the Old Testament* (Atlanta: Scholars Press, 1988)

with presenting Christianity in such a way that it meets peoples' deepest needs and penetrates their worldviews, thus allowing them to follow Christ and remain in their own cultures. Although the gospel is unchanging, the contexts in which it must be related will be regularly changing. It must be communicable for it to be good news. The creation of humankind in God's image means that there is no culture that lacks virtuous elements in terms of which the gospel can be expressed. At the same time the fall of humankind from grace means that no culture is completely virtuous. The coming of the gospel from outside the cultural context gives it the ability to affirm those aspects of every culture that agree with God's purposes, which predispose members of that culture to comprehend the gospel. But the gospel also comes to judge the evil elements in every society that are contrary to God's will. Therefore, each generation of Christian people need to understand the times and the culture in which it is set and respond accordingly, drawing from and seeing to be true to both the Scriptures and the tradition.

The example of the Church in Congo, as in other African countries, shows that, instead of reading the signs of time, theology has tended to give support to the ruling governments. The leadership values which underpin the church ministries have been those of unquestioning obedience within an organisation in order to achieve a desired end. To enable the Church to be effective in its mission to the whole community, the Church must communicate the faith in deep and life-changing ways to those who come to be baptised. Hence, as the Congolese Bishop Tshibangu said, 'A theology of concrete socio-political commitment is needed if we are to appreciate values that are in a constant state of flux, determine the proper criteria for passing moral judgment on new social phenomena, and morally evaluate the means to be used in pursuing the aims of development.'[2]

The forces for change affecting our society must not affect the whole way we are church, the way we engage as churches in the mission of God; and therefore must not affect the nature and task of those who are ordained ministers. We are explicitly told not to model ourselves on society around us in the way power is used. However, there is much that the Church can learn from good practice developed over many years in the public sector. But when insights gained from these worlds are adopted uncritically by the Church, there are dangers. Uncritical adoption of *Bula Matari* model of authority is not the answer to our need for a new paradigm of Christian ministry in this changing world. There is a great deal in the Scriptures about the way in which the power should be exercised within the Christian community and by those who would be leaders. Insights flowing from the world need to engage with and be checked against insights of Scripture before they are incorporated wholesale into the life of the people of God.

---

[2] T. Tsibangu, *La Théologie Africaine: Manifeste et Programme pour le développement des activités théologiques en Afrique* (Kinshasa: Editions Saint Paul Afrique, 1987), 17.

The values of worldly leadership carry with them a particular view of the world and of humanity which clashes in significant ways with the New Testament view. The secular concepts of authority cannot do justice to the whole of what it means to be in authority nor must we allow them uncritically to shape our understanding of Christian ministry. We need to listen to the lessons of the world around us, but we need also to attend to our own inheritance if a new and healthy understanding of what it means to be in authority is to emerge.

Life-Community as a 'practical ecclesiology' offers a good power basis in the sense that it relates not only to selfhood or identity, but also it takes seriously the local socio-political situation. In Life-Community ecclesiology, Christians are to assume a critical stance vis-à-vis the authorities, traditions and institutions of this world. They undersand that nothing needs to remain the way it is as the death, resurrection, and ascension of Christ had inaugurated the great renewal of the history. They are aware of the principle *ecclesia semper reformanda* and carefully apply it when necessary. The gospel entrusted to the church has the power to transform Africa into a caring, just, peaceful and morally healthy society. Therefore, authority in Life-Community is to be capable of integrating proclamation, discipleship and engaging in social, economic and political liberation in a comprehensive dynamic and consistent witness. We thus emphasize that theology in Africa should equip the Church in its role of liberation. As Nyerere put it:

> The Church has to help men to rebel against their slums; it has to help them to do this in the most effective way it can be done. But most of all the Church must be obviously and openly fighting all those institutions, and power groups, which contribute to the existence and maintenance of the physical and spiritual slums regardless of the consequences to itself or it members. And, wherever and however circumstances make it possible, the Church must work with the people in the positive tasks of building a future based on social justice. It must participate actively in initiating, securing and creating the changes which are necessary and which will inevitably take place.[3]

The Church must contribute actively and effectively in building a just and fair society in the Kingdom of God. Therefore, the creation of a more just and equal society, not only in the wider society but also in the church, remains a big challenge for theology in Africa.

---

[3] Nyerere, *Man and Development,* 115.

Bibliography

Primary sources

Alphabetic list of the informants

Adhaku Georges: member of youth group Aru, Aru, 07/08/01.
Adjionzi Adjiko: nurse and member of the CAC Aru, Aru, 07/08/01.
Adoroti Ombabhua: Anglican priest, Aru, 06/08/01.
Adubang'o Dieudonné: president of youth group, Mahagi, 08/08/01
Adyaa Yassam: trader, Aru, 10/10/01.
Aria Rose: member of Mother's Union Kumuru, 30/07/01.
Asiiki David: archdeacon of Mahagi, 09/08/01.
Bahemuka Mugenyi: priest and student at Uganda Christian University, 05/01/02.
Balinda Tito: Anglican priest and the president of Engabu, Boga, 16/08/00.
Bataaga Beni: priest and provincial coordinator of communication, Bunia, 15/09/00.
Batibuha Muloy: member of the diocese of Kisangani, 14/12/01.
Birizene Mutchinda: student at ISThA and member of the diocese of Bukavu, Bunia, 13/09/02.
Businge Tibafa: chief stock keeper of *médecins sans frontières*, Kisangani, 14/12/01.
Byakisaka Deogratias: diocesan leader of youth group, Bunia, 01/12/01.
Changaila André: member of the diocese of Kisangani, 13/12/01.
Damalie Sabiti: provincial secretary of Mother's Union, Kampala, 12/11/00.
Esther Ang'omoko: president of Mother's Union, Mahagi, 08/08/01.
Ise-Somo Muhindo: provincial co-ordinator of evangelism, Bunia, 29/11/01.
Isingoma Kahwa: Anglican Bishop of Katanga, Bunia, 12/11/01.
Kabarole Baguma: archdeacon of Aru, 06/08/01.
Kahwa Njojo: priest and lecturer at ISThA, Bunia, 12/09/02.
Kaliru Anna: member of Mother's Union Ekanga, Ekanga, 01/08/01.
Kalobya Matumba: member of de diocese of Kindu, Kalima, 30/08/00.
Kandole Bamuraki: trader, Bunia, 12/09/02.
Kangamina Sadiki: Anglican Priest, Kisangani, 13/12/01.
Kapita Selemani: member of youth group Mahagi, 08/08/01.
Kiiza Jacques: youth leader for evangelism, Diocese of Boga, Bunia, 03/01/02.
Kithoko Kabangi: diocesan Secretary of Kisangani, Kisangani, 13/12/01.
Kyayama Pierre: student in the University of Kisangani, 13/12/01.
Likambo Araba: chief of Kakwa, Kumuru, 29/07/01.

Likambo Tamaru:	Anglican priest of Isiro, Boga, 14/08/00.
Lokangaka Eugène:	member of the archdeaconry of Kinshasa, Bunia, 12/09/02.
Lukambula Kihanda:	director of the Bible school of Mbau, Nord-Kivu, 10/10/00.
Makuru Mpabaise:	lecturer at the University of Kisangani and Président des laics of the diocese of Kisangani, 13/12/01.
Mamba Selemani:	social worker, Bunia, 16/07/01.
Mateso Akeso:	member and teacher of secondary school, Bunia, 16/07/01.
Molanga Botola:	Provincial Secretary of the Anglican Church of Congo, Bunia, 15/07.01.
Mukambilwa:	*Conseiller* of the Anglican schools of the diocese of Kindu, Bunia, 27/08/02.
Munege Kabarole:	archdeacon of Bunia, diocese of Boga, Bunia, 15/12/01.
Mupagazi Bwanamuzuri,	Anglican priest, Nord-Kivu, 13/08/00.
Mutshindu Achille:	member of the archdeaconry of Kinshasa.29/08/02.
Ndirito Paul:	member of youth group, Mahagi, diocese of Boga, 08/08/01.
Nganka Edrungi:	the army's Chaplain in Bunia, Bunia, 26/08/02
Nguba Bahigwa:	Lecturer at Anglican Theological College in Bunia, 27/08/02.
Njojo Byankya:	former Archbishop of Congo and the Bishop of Boga, Boga,15/08/00.
Otua:	*président des chrétiens* Ekanga, Ekanga, 02/08/01.
Pasheni Adubango:	member of youth group, Mahagi, 09/08/01.
Rwakaikara Amoti:	member and *président des chrétiens* Yambi, Bunia,
Sabiti Tibafa:	lecturer at ISThA, Bunia, 24/11/01.
Sinzahera Uwimana:	youth leader for agricultural project, diocese of Boga, Bunia, 15/12/01.
Sinziri Onadra:	Archdeacon of Kumuru, diocese of Boga, Kumuru, 30/07/01.
Thuambe Ferdinard:	*Président des Chrétiens*, Mahagi, 29/08/00.
Ubaya Uchaki:	Anglican priest of Mahagi, 29/08/00.
Ugen Lambert:	member of the parish of Mahagi, 29/08/00.
Ukelo John:	*président* of Christians, Archdeaconry of Bunia, 15/12/01.
Uma Jean:	Anglican priest of Avari, 03/08/01.
Uweka Marie:	member of Mother's Union, Mahagi, 29/08/00
Yiki Solomoni:	youth leader, parish Ekanga, Boga, 01/08/01.
Nzapi Yangalayo:	Former *Commissaire de District* of Ituri, 05/08/00.

Written Sources

Acheson, Judy. Prayer letter, November 2002, CMS Missionary in Bunia, CONGO.
Ande, Titre. 'Le Christianisme Face au Système d'Héritage chez les Bahema de Boga.' Bunia, Mémoire de Licence, Juillet 1994.

Balufuga, Dirokpa. 'Liturgie Anglicane et Inculturation, hier, aujourd'hui et demain: regard sur la célébration eucharistique en République Démocratique du Congo'. PhD Thesis, Université de Laval, Quebec, Avril 2001.

Letter to Philip Bingham, 30 December 2001, archives provincial office of the CAC in Bunia, Congo

Letter to Isingoma Kawha, 10 January 2002, archives provincial office of the CAC in Bunia, Congo.

Pastoral letter addressed to leaders and Christians of North Kivu, 27.10.03.

Bakole wa Ilunga. 'Parole de vie aux Chrétiens de l'Archdiocèse de Kananga,' 11 February 1975.

College des Eveques. Le rapport du *Collège des Evêques*, 1-2 September 1997 in Kindu (D.R.congo).

Compte-rendu du Comité de discipline, Kampala 2000.

Compte-rendu du *Collège des Evêques*:
— Du 25-26 Janvier 1994, Bunia.
— Du 28 Janvier 1995, Bunia.
— Du 1-2 Septembre 1997, Kindu.
— Du 6–8 Septembre 1997, Lubumbasi.
— Du 29-30 Septembre 1999, Kampala.
— Du 26 Juillet 2000, Kampala.
— Du 8–9 Octobre 2000, Boga.

Diocese de Boga-Zaire. *Sinodi ya tatu ya uaskofu wa Boga-Zaire ya tarehe 12mpaka 15 Septemba 1984*, Boga, 1984.

— 'Constitution', in *Sinodi ya tatu ya uaskofu wa Boga-Zaire ya tarehe 12 mpaka 15 Septemba 1984*, Boga, 1984.

Eglise Anglicane du Zaire. *Kwa Imani Apolo: Maisha ya Apolo Kivebulaya,* Printed in Great Britain by Paradigm Print, Gateshead, Tyne and Wear, 1986.

— *Kitabu cha Sala kwa watu wote*. Rethy, Bunia, 1998.

ISTHA. A Brief History of the Anglican Church in Zaire 1986-1996, booklet edited by ISTHA, 1996.

Kabanga. 'Je suis un homme', pastoral letter for Lent, Archevêché de Lubumbashi, March 1976.

Kahwa, Isingoma. 'La Notion Traditionnelle de la Communauté en Afrique Noir et son intégration dans la vie Ecclésiale: Cas de Banyoro en République du Zaire.' Bangui: Mémoire de Maitrise, 1989.

— Vision Missionnaire pour la PEAC: Remarques et propositions. Paper presented to the College of Bishops, 23 Septembre 2001.

'Lettre Pastorale des Evêques du Zaire,' 25 February 1977, in *Documentation et Information*, 28 June 1978, pp.590-597.

Mathe, M.M. 'Evolution des Problèmes Politiques Administratives entre les Batangi-Mbau et Mbabuba de la Collectivité de Beni.' ISP/Bunia, dissertation, 1990.

Memorandum ya Wakristo ya Nord-Kivu kwa Archbishop, 23.01.2000, archives in provincial office, Bunia, Congo.

Province de l'Eglise Anglicane du Congo: Canons.

Province de l'Eglise Anglicane du Congo. *Constitution*, ed. Revisée 2001.

— *Statuts de l'Association sans but lucratif*

— *Report of the College des Evêques, 1-2 Septembre 1997* in Kindu (D.R. Congo)

Tsongo, M. 'The Role of Women in the Anglican Church of Congo: A Case Study of the Diocese of North Kivu.' MA dissertation, Trinity College, Bristol, July 2000.

Secondary Sources

Africa, no 62(1), 1992.

An-na'im, Abdullahi A., ed. *Cultural Transformation and Human Rights in Africa.* London: Zed Book Ltd, 2002.

Anstey, Roger. *King Leopold's Legacy: The Congo Under Belgian Rule 1908-1960.*London: Oxford University Press, 1966.

Appiah-kubi, Kofi. 'Theological Sources', in Kofi Appiah-Kubi and Sergio Torres, eds. *African Theology en Route.* Maryknoll (NY): Orbis Books, 1979.

Appiah-kubi, Kofi and TORRES, Sergio, eds. *African Theology en Route.* Maryknoll (NY): Orbis Books, 1979.

Asani, Yabili. *Code de la Zairianisation.* Lubumbashi: Editeur 'Mwanga-Hebdo,' 1975.

Asch, S. *L'Eglise du Prophète Kimbangu: de ses origines à son rôle actuel au Zaïre.* Paris: Karthala, 1983.

Avis, Paul. *Christians in Communion.* London: Geoffrey Chapman Mowbray, 1990. *Authority, Leadership and Conflict in the Church.* London: Mowbray, 1992.
— *The Anglican Understanding of the Church: an introduction.* London: SPCK, 2000.

Ayiteyy, George B.N. Africa Betrayed. New York: St Martin's Press, 1992. *Africa in Chaos.* London: Macmillan Press, 1999.

Balandier, G. *Sociologie Actuelle de l'Afrique noire.* Paris: P.U.F, 1955.

Battle, Michael. 'The Ubuntu Theology of Desmond Tutu', in Leonard Hulley, Louise Kretzschmar and Luke Lungile Pato. *Archbishop Tutu: Prophetic Witness in South Africa.* Cape Town: Human and Rousseau, 1996.

Baxter, P.T.W and Butt, Audrey. *The Azande, and Related Peoples of the Anglo-Egyptian Sudan and Belgian Congo.* London: International African Institute, 1953.

Bayart, Jean-Francois, ELLIS, Stephen and HIBOU, Beatrice. *The Criminalization of the State in Africa.* Oxford: James Currey Press, 1999.
— *The State in Africa: The Politics of the Belly.* London and New York: Longman, 1993.

Bernardin. *L'Ecole Congolaise: Eléments d'Organisation Scolaires.* Bondo: Frères de St-Gabriel, 1958.

Biaya, Tshikala K. 'Postcolonial State Strategies, Sacralization of Power and Popular Proselytization in Congo-Zaïre, 1960-1995', in Abdullahi Ahmed An-Na'im, ed. *Proselytization and Communal Self-Determination in Africa.* Maryknoll, New York: Orbis Books, 1999.

Birmingham, David and Martin, Phyllis, eds. *History of Central Africa. The Contemporary Years Since 1950.* London: Longman, 1998.

Boateng, O. 'The poison designed to produce an African disease', in *New African*, no 390, November 2000.

Bobb, F. Scott. *Historical Dictionary of Democratic Republic of the Congo (Zaïre),* Revised edition of *Historical Dictionary of Zaïre.* Lanham, Maryland, and London: The Scarecrow Press, 1999.

Boissonade, Euloge. *Le Mal Zairois.* Paris: Herme, 1990.

Bowen, Roger. 'Rwanda: Missionary Reflections on a Catastrophe, J.C. Jones Lecture 1995', in *Anvil* vol. 13. no 1, 1996.

Boff, Leonardo. *Ecclesio Genesis: The base communities reinvent the church*. London: Collins, 1986.

Boff, Leonardo. *Trinity and Society*. Kent (Great Britain): Burns and Oates, 1988.

Bradshaw, Tim. *The Olive Branch: An Evangelical Anglican Doctrine of the Church*. Carlisle: The Paternoster Press, 1992.

Braeckman, Colette. *L'Enjeu Congolais: L'Afrique Centrale après Mobutu*. Fayard, 1999.

British Council of Churches. *The Foegetten Trinity*. London: BBC/CCBI, 1991.

Brown, Colin. *New Testament Theology*. Volume 2: G-Pre. Exeter: The Paternoster Press, 1976.

Buakasa, Gerard. *Réinventer l'Afrique de la Tradition à la Modernité*. Paris: L'Harmattan, 1996.

Bujo, Bénézet. *African Theology in Its Social Context*. Saint Paul Communications, 1992.

Busia, K.A. *The Position of the Chief in the Modern Political System of Ashanti*. London: Frank Cass, 1951.

Buttrick, Arthur George, ed. *The Interpreter's Dictionary of the Bible*. Vol. 3, Nashville, New York: Abingdon Press, 1962.

Carson, D.A. ed. *Biblical Interpretation and the Church: Text and the Context*. Exeter: The Paternoster Press, 1984.

Cathier, Felicien. *Droit et Administration de l'Etat Indépendent du Congo*. Brussels, 1898.

Catholic Bishops of Congo. *Final Report of the 1985 Extraordinary Synod of Bishops*, no C.

Centre de Recherche et d'Information Socio-Politique. *Congo*. Brussels: Centre de Recherche et d'Information Socio-Politique, 1966.

Chabal, Patrick. *Power in Africa, An Essay in Political Interpretation*. New York: St. Martin's Press, 1994.

Chabal, Patrick. and DALOZ, J-P. *Africa Works: Disorder as Political Instrument*. Indiana: Indiana University Press, 1999.

Church of England. *The Report of the Joint Committee of the Convocation of Canterbury*, no 365, 1902, reprinted by the Church Information Board, 1953.

— *The Report of the Lambeth Conference 1978*. *London*: CIO Publishing, 1978. *Eames Report: Report of the Archbishop of Canterbury's Commission on Communion and Women in the Episcopate*. London: Church House Publishing, 1989.

— *Episcopal Ministry: The Report of the Archbishops' Group on The Episcopate*. London: Church House Publishing, 1990.

— *Working as One Body: The Report of the Archbishop Commission on the Organisation of the Church of England*. London: Church House Publishing, 1995.

Coleman, Roger, ed. Resolutions of the Twelve Lambeth Conferences 1867 – 1988. Toronto, Canada: Anglican Book Centre, 1992.

Coquery-Vidrovitch, C., FOREST, A. and WEISS, H. eds. *Rebellions-Révolution au Zaïre 1963-1965*. Paris: L'Harmattan, 1987.

Cronin, Thomas E. 'Reflections on Leadership', in Rosenback, William E. Rosenbach and Robert L. Taylor, eds. *Contemporary Issues in Leadership*. Oxford: Westview Press, 1993.

Davis, W.D. and Allison, D.C. *The International Critical Commentary: Matthew.* Volume III. Edinburgh: T & T Clark, 1997.

De Boek, Philip. 'Postcolonialism, Power and Identity: local and globalperspectives from Zaïre', in Richard Werbner and Terence Ranger, eds. *Postcolonial Identities in Africa.* London and New Jersey: Zed Books, 1996.

Depelchin, Jacques. *De l'état indépendant du Congo au Zaïre contemporain (1885 – 1974).* Paris: Karthala, 1992.

Diangenda, K. *L'Histoire du Kimbanguisme.* Kinshasa: Editions Kimbanguistes, 1984.

Dickson, Kwesi. 'Towards a Theologia Africana', in M.E. Glaswell and Edward W. Fasholé-Luke, eds. *New Testament Christianity for Africa and the World.* London: SPCK, 1974.

Dickson, Kwesi A. *Theology in Africa.* London: Darton, Longman and Todd, 1984.

Doornbos, R. Martin. *The Ankole Kingship Controversy: Regalia Galore Revised.* Kampala, Uganda: Fountain Publishers Ltd, 2001.

Du Boulay, Shirley. *Tutu: Voice of the Voiceless.* London: Hodder and Stoughton.

Dulles, Avery S.J. *Models of the Church: A Critical Assessment of the Church in all its aspects.* Dublin: Gill and Macmillan, 1976.

Dunbar, A.R. *A History of Bunyoro-Kitara.* Nairobi: Oxford University Press, published on behalf of The Makerere Institute of Social Research, 1965.

Dupont, E. *Lettres sur le Congo.* Paris: Reinwaild, 1889.

Eglise Du Christ au Congo. *Procès Verbal, 31 session du Comité Exécutif National.* Kinshasa 24 Septembre – 8 Octobre 2000.

— *Le recours à la Bible pour un Christianisme authentique',* Procès Verbal du Synode National de l'ECC, 1973.

— *Procès Verbal du Synode National de l'ECC,* 1989.

— *La vie en abondance en Christ',* Procès Verbal du Synode National de l'ECC, 1971.

— *Process Verbal du Synode National de l'ECC,* 1975.

— *Un commandement nouveau: Aimez-vous les uns les autres'.* Procès Verbal du Synode National de l'ECC, 1981.

Ekanga, B. *Cultural Policy in the Republic of Zaire.* Paris: UNESCO, 1976.

Ela, Jean-Marc. *African Cry.* Maryknoll, New York: Orbis Books, 1986.

Ellis, Stephen, ed. *Africa Now: People, Police and Institutions.* The Hague: Ministry of Foreign Affairs, London: James Currey, 1996.

Evans, G.R. *Authority in the Church: A challenge for Anglicans.* Norwich: The Canterbury Press, 1990.

Eze, Emmanuel Chukwudi, ed. *Postcolonial African Philosophy: A Critical Reader.* Oxford: Blackwell Publishers, 1997.

Fashole-Luke, Edward, W. 'Ancestor Veneration and the Communion of Saints', in M.E. Glasswell and E.W. Fasole-Luke, eds. *New Testament Christianity for Africa and the World.* London: SPCK, 1974.

Ferguson, Everett. *The Church of Christ: A Biblical Ecclesiology for Today.* Cambridge: William B. Eerdmans Publishing Company, 1996.

Forrester, Duncan.B. *Theology and Politics.* Oxford: Basil Blackwell, 1988.

Freire, Paulo. *Pedagogy of the Oppressed.* London: Penguin Books, 1996.

Friedman, K. Ekholm. *Catastrophe and Creation: The Transformation of African Culture.* Chur, Switzerland: Harwood Academic Publishers, 1991.

Fulljames, Peter. 'God and Creation in Inter-Cultural Perspective: A Comparative Study of the Theologies of Barth, Dickson, Pobee, Nyamiti and Pannenberg.' PhD dissertation, University of Birmingham, July, 1991.

— *God and Creation in Inter-Cultural Perspective: Dialogue between the Theologies of Barth, Dickson, Pobee, Nyamiti and Pannenberg*. Frankfurt am Main: Peter Lang, 1993.

Gbabendu, E. and EFOLO, N. *Volonté de Changement au Zaïre: De l'Acte de la Souveraineté en Acte*. Paris: Harmattan, 1991.

Gichuhu, G.N. 'The Spirituality of SCCs in Eastern Africa', in *SPEARHEAD* no 85. Nakuru, Kenya: Gaba Publications, February 1985.

Girard, Patrick. 'Washington dans l'embarras', in *Jeune Afrique, Hebdomadaire International Independent*, no 1614, 4 au 10 Decembre 1991.

Gladwin, John. *God's People in God's World: Biblical motives for social involvement*. Inter-Varsity Press, 1979.

Glasswell, M.E. and FASHOLE-LUKE, E.W. eds. *New Testament Christianity for Africa and the World*. London: SPCK, 1974.

Golding, John. *Authority and Ministry*. Bramcote Notts: Grove Books, 1976.

Greenland, J. 'Western Education in Burundi 1916-1973: The Consequences of Instrumentalism', in *Cahiers du CEDAF*, nos. 2-3, 1980.

Gundry, Robert. H. *Matthew: A Commentary on his Handbook for a Mixed Church and Persecution*. Grand Rapids, Michigan (USA): Wm.B.Eerdmans Publishing Co, 1994.

Gunton, C.E. and Hardy, D.W. eds. *On Being the Church*. Edinburgh: T & T Clark, 1989.

Hannaford, R. ed. *A Church for 21st Century: Agenda for the Church of England*. 1998.

Hansen, Holger Bernt. *Mission, Church and State in a Colonial Setting: Uganda 1890-1925*. London: Heinemann, 1984.

Hansen, Holger Bernt and TWADDLE, Michael. eds. *Christian Missionaries and the State in the Third World*. Oxford: James Currey, 2002.

Hansen, Holger Bernt. 'The Colonial State's Policy Towards Foreign Missions in Uganda', in Hansen, Holger Bernt and Twaddle, Michael, eds. *Christian Missionaries and the State in the Third World*. Oxford: James Currey, 2002.

Harrison Paul M. *Authority and Power in the Free Church Tradition: A Social Case Study of the American Baptist Convention*. Princeton: Princeton University Press, 1959.

Hastings, Adrian. *The Church in Africa 1450-1950*. New York: Oxford University Press, 1994.

Hastings, Adrian. ed. *A World History of Christianity*. London: Cassell, 1999.

Healey, Joseph and SYBERTZ, Donald. *Towards an African Narrative Theology*. Limuru, Kenya: Paulines Publications Africa, 1996.

Helfers, Norman H. 'Leadership of the Church', in *Africa Journal of Evangelical Theology*. Volume 19.1, 2000.

Helgesen, Geir. *Democracy and Authority in Korea: The Cultural Dimension in Korean Politics*. Richmond, Surrey: Curzon Press, 1998.

Hodgson, Janet. 'African and Aglican', in Leonard Hulley, Louise Kretzschmar and Luke Lungile Pato. *Archbishop Tutu: Prophetic Witness in South Africa*. Cape Town: Human and Rousseau, 1996, pp.106-128.

Hoedmaker, Bert. 'The Kairos Document: A Challenge to the Ecumenical Movement', in World Council of Churches. *Challenge to the Church: A Theological Comment on the Political Crisis in South Africa, the Kairos Document and Commentaries,* in PCR information, 1985.

Holland, Joe and Henriot, Peter. *Social Analysis: Linking Faith and Justice.* Washington: Orbis Books, 1984.

Home, J. *Highways and Edges: Anglicanism and the Universal Church.* London: CIO Publishing, 1985.

HulleY, Leonard, Kretzschmar, Louise and PATO, Luke Lungile. *Archbishop Tutu: Prophetic Witness in South Africa.* Cape Town: Human and Rousseau, 1996.

Ingham, Keneth. *The Kingdom of Toro in Uganda.* London: Methuen, 1975.

— *Politics in Modern Africa: The Uneven Tribal Dimension.* London: Routledge, 1990.

Institut Makanda Kabobi. *Histoire du MPR.* Kinshasa: Institut Makanda Kabobi, 1975.

Jacobs, Eva, ed. *Voltaire, Zaire.* London: Hodder and Stoughton, 1975.

Jacob, W.M. *The Making of the Anglican Church Worldwide.* London: SPCK, 1997.

Jeffery, R., ed. *By What Authority?* Oxford: Mowbray, 1987.

Jeune Afrique, Hebdomadaire International Independent, no 1614, 4 au 10 Décembre 1991.

— no 1958 du 21 au 27 Juillet 1998.

— no 1968 du 29 Septembre au 5 October 1998.

— no 1980-1981 du 22 Décembre 1998 au 4 Janvier 1999.

— no 1984 du 19 au 25 Janvier 1999.

— no 1986 du 2 au 8 Février 1999.

— no 1989 du 23 Février au 01 Mars 1999.

— no 2000-2001 du 11 au 24 Mai 1999.

Journal Officiel de la République du Zaïre, Constitution de la République du Zaire, 27 Juin 1988.

Kairos Theologians. *The Kairos Document: A theological comment on the political crisis in South Africa*, Second Revised Edition. Braamfontein, South Africa: Skotaville Publishers, 1986.

Kamitatu, O. *La Grande Mystification.* Paris: Maspero, 1971.

Kanyoro, Musimbi. 'Thinking Mission in Africa', in *International Review of Mission.* Vol. LXXXVIII no 345.

Kanza, T. 'Le Zairois serait-il maudit, inconscient? In *Elima*, Kishasa, 19 Septembre, 1991.

Kaplan, I. ed. *Zaire: a country study.* Washington: The American University, 1979.

Kaputo, Samba. *Phénomène d'Ethnicité et Conflits Ethno-politiques en Afrique Post-coloniale.* Kinshasa: Presses Universitaires du Zaire, 1982.

Karugire, S.R. *A political History of Uganda.* Nairobi: Heinemann Educational Books, 1980.

Kenya Catholic Secretariat. *The Catholic Family: A Source Book for Every Catholic Family, for Youth and Married Couples.* Nairobi, 1985.

Kiros, Teodros, ed. *Explorations in African Political Thought: Identity, Community, Ethics.* New York, London: Routledge, 2001.

Klaiber, Jeffrey. *The Church, Dictatorship and Democracy in Latin America.* Maryknoll, New York: Orbis Books, 1998.

Kofi, Quashigah Edward and Chinedu, Okafor Obiora, eds. *Legitimate Governance in Africa: International and Domestic Legal Perspectives.* The Hague, The Netherlands: Kluwer Law International, 1999.

Kung, Hans. *The Church.* London: Burns and Oates, 1967.

Kwesi, K.P. Prah. *Beyond the Color Line.* Africa World Press, 1998.

LagerGren, David. *Mission and State in the Congo: A study of the relations between Protestant missions and the Congo Independent State authorities with special reference to the Equator District, 1885-1903.* Uppsala: Gleerup, 1970.

Lasswell, Harold D. and Kaplan Abraham. *Power and Society.* New Haven: Yale University Press, 1950.

Levy Jr. Mario J. *The Structure of Society.* Princeton: Princeton University Press, 1952.

Lewa, Francois-Marie et GESLIN, Dominique. 'Kabila: Ombres et Lumières', in *Jeune Afrique*, no 1980 – 1981, du 22 Décembre 1998 au 4 Janvier 1999.

Loyd, A.B. *Apolo the Pathfinder: Who follows.* London, CMS, 1934.

Luck, A. *African Saint: The Story of Apolo Kivebulaya.* London: SCM Press, 1963.

Lufuluabo, Francois-Marie. *Perspective Théologique Bantoue et Théologie Scolastique.* Malines, Belgique: Imprimerie St. Francois, 1966.

Luntandila. *Libération et Dévelopment du Kimbanguisme 1921-1960.* Kinshasa, 1971.

Magesa, Laurenti. 'Theology of Democracy', in Laurent Magesa and Zabulon Nthamburi, eds. *Democracy and Reconciliation: A Challenge for African Christianity.* Nairobi: Acton Publishers, 1999.

— 'Christ's Spirit as Empowernment of the Church-as-Family', in Patrick Ryan, ed. *The Model of the 'Church-as-Family': Meeting the African Challenge.* Nairobi: CUEA Publications, 1999.

Magesa, Laurenti and NTHAMBURI, Zabulon, eds. *Democracy andReconciliation: A Challenge for African Christianity.* Nairobi: Acton Publishers, 1999.

MakanzU, M. *L'Eglise du Christ au Zaire, son passé, son present et son avenir.* Kinshasa, ECZ, 1975.

— *L'Eglise et l'Authenticité Zairoise.* Brochure published by CEDI, Kinshasa, 1973.

Malina, Bruce J. *The Social Gospel of Jesus: The kingdom of God in Mediterranean Perspective.* Minneapolis: Fortress Press, 2001.

Martelli, G. *Leopold to Lumumba.* London: Chapman & Hall, 1962.

Martin, M-L. *Kimbangu: An African Prophet and his Church.* Oxford: Basil Blackwell, 1975.

Masolo, D. *African Philosophy in Search of Identity.* Indiana: Indian University Press, 1994.

Massina, P. 'De la Souveraineté des Conferences Nationales Africaines', in *Revue Burkinabe de Droit*, 24 Décembre 1991.

Maviiri, John C. 'Suffering: A Theological reflections in the African context', in *African Christian Studies.* Volume 16, no 1, March 2000.

Mazrui, Ali A. 'Ideology and African Political Culture', in Teodros Kiros, ed. *Explorations in African Political Thought; Identity, Community, Ethics.* New York, London: Routledge, 2001.

Mbaya, Kabongo. *L'Eglise du Christ au Zaire: Formation et adaptation d'un Protestantisme en situation de dictature.* Paris: Karthala, 1992.

Mbaya, Kankwenda. Ed. *Zaïre: What Destiny?* Chippenham, England: Codesria, 1993.

Mbiti, John. *African Religion and Philosophy.* London: Heinemann Educational Books, 1961.

M'buyinga, E. *Pan Africanism or Neo-Colonialism: The Bankrupty of the OAU.* London: Zed Press, 1982.

Mccain, Danny. 'The Church in Africa in the Twenty-First Century:Characteristics, Challenges and Opportunities', in *Africa Journal of Evangelical Theology*, Volume 19.2, 2000.

Medart, Jean Francois. 'The Underdeveloped State in Tropical Africa: Political Clientelism or No-Patrimonialism', in Clapman, C. *Private Patronage and Public Power*. London: Trances, Pincer, 1982.

Michel, Albin. *Mobutu, Dignité pour l'Afrique*. Paris: Albin Michel, 1989.

Mobutu, S. *Discours a l'O.N.U*, 1973.

Molyneux, Gordon. *African Christian Theology: The Quest for Selfhood*. San Fransico: Mellen Research University Press, 1993.

Mugambi, J.N.K., ed. *Christian Mission and Social Transformation: A Kenyan Perspective*. Nairobi: National Council of Churches of Kenya, 1989.

— 'The Contribution to African Theology of the Faculté de Théologie Catholique in Kinshasa, Zaire', in *Africa Journal of Evangelical Theology*. Vol 11.2, 1992.

Mugambi, J.N.K. and Magesa, L. eds. *Jesus in African Christianity: Experimentation and Diversity in African Christology*. Nairobi (Kenya): Initiatives Publishers, 1989.

Mugambi, J.N.K and Magesa, Laurenti, eds. *The Church in African Christianity: Innovative Essays in Ecclesiology*. Nairobi: Initiative, 1990.

Mulago, Vincent. *Un Visage Africain du Christianisme: L'union vitale Bantu face à l'Unité ecclesiale*. Paris: Présence Africaine, 1962.

Muli, Alfred. 'The Modern Quest for an African Theology Revised in the Light of Romans 1: 18-25: An Exegesis of the Text (part 2): Implications for African Theology', in *Africa Journal of Evangelical Theology*, Volume 16.2, 1997.

Musopole, Augustine C. *Being Human in Africa: Toward an African Christian Anthropology*. New York: Peter Lang, 1994.

Muzorewa, Gwinyai H. *The Origins and Development of African Theology*. Maryknoll, NY: Orbis Books, 1985.

Mwaria, Cherl B., Federic, Silvia and Mclaren, Joseph, eds. *African Visions*. London: Greenwood Press, 2000.

Mwoleka, C. and Healey, J.G. *Ujamaa and Christian Communities*. Eldoret, Kenya: Gaba Publications, 1976.

Ndaywel A Nzian, Isidore. *Histoire Générale du Congo: De l'héritage ancien à la République Démocratique*. Paris, Bruxelles: De Boeck et Larcier, 1998.

Ngamayamu, Manduku Dagoga. 'A Propos de l'Organisation de l'Eglise du Christ au Zaire (8 Mars 1970 – 24 Avril 1990)', in *Revue Zairoise the Théologie Protestante*, no 6 publication annuelle, 6e annee 1992, Kinshasa, Centre Protestant d'Edition et de Diffusion, pp. 65-87.

Ngoie, J. 'Situation Salariale au RDC 1966-1970', in *Cahiers Economiques et Sociaux*, 8 no 2, June 1970.

Ngindu, Mushete. 'Le propos du recours à l'authenticité et le Christianisme au Zaire', in *CRA* Vol. 8, no 16, 1974.

Ngolet, Francois. 'Democratization and Interventionism in Francophone Sub-Saharan Africa', in Mwaria Cheryl B., Federici, Silvia and McLaren Joseph, eds. *African Visions: Literary Images, Political Change, and Social Struggle in Contemporary Africa*. London: Greenwood Press, 2000.

N'kanza, L.Z. 'The Social Origins of Political Underdevelopment in the ex-Belgian Congo (Zaire).' PhD dissertation, Harvard University, 1976.

Nkrumah, Kwame. *Ghana: An Autobiography*. London: Nelson, 1957.

Nkurunziza, Deusdedit R. K. *Bantu Philosophy of Life in the Light of the Christian Message: A basis for an African vitalistic theology*. Frankfurt am Main: Peter Lang, 1989.

Ntalonga, N. 'The Continuing Struggle for National Liberation in Zaire', in *Journal of Modern African Studies* 17, no 4, December 1979.

Nthamburi, Zablon. 'Theology and Politics in Africa', in Laurenti Magesa and Zablon Nthamburi, eds. *Democracy and Reconciliation: A Challenge for African Christianity.* Nairobi: Acton Publishers, 1999.

Nussbaum, Stan, ed. *Freedom and Independence.* Nairobi: OAIC, 1994.

— 'African Independent churches and a Call for a New Three-Self Formula for Mission', in Stan Nussbaum, ed. *Freedom and Independence.* Nairobi: OAIC, 1994.

Nyamiti, Charles. *Christ as our Ancestor: Christology from an African Perspective.* Harare (Zimbabwe): Mambo Press, 1984.

Nyerere, Julius. *Man and Development.* Dar se Salaam: Oxford University Press, 1974.

Obert, K. 'The Kingdom of Ankole in Uganda', in M. Fortes and E.E. Evans-Pritchard, eds. *African Political Systems.* London: Oxford University Press, 1969.

Odetola, T.O., Oloruntimehin, O. and Aweda, D.A. *Man and Society inAfrica: An Introduction to Sociology.* London: Longman, 1983.

O'Donovan, Olivier. *The Desire of the Nations: Rediscovering the roots of political theology.* Cambridge: Cambridge University Press, 1996.

O'Donovan, Wilbur. *Biblical Christianty in African Perspective.* Carlisle: Paternoster Press, 1996.

Ogbonnaya, A.Okechukwu. *On Communitarian Divinity: An African Interpretation of the Trinity.* United States: Paragon House, 1994.

Okitakekumba, Longandjo. 'State Power under MPR Control: An Interpretive Essay', in Mbaya, Kankwenda, ed. *Zaire: What Destiny?* Chippenham, England: Codesria, 1993.

Ottaway, M. *Democracy in Africa: The Hard Road Ahead.* London: Lynne Rienner Publishers, 1997.

Oxfam. *Under Fire: the human cost of small arms in north-east Democratic Republic of Congo. A case study.* January 2001.

Parratt, John. *Reinventing Christianity: African Theology Today.* Cambridge: Wm.B.Eerdmans Publishing Co, 1995.

— 'Introduction', in John Parratt, ed. *A Reader in African Christian Theology.* London: SPCK, 1997.

— 'Conclusion: Current Issues in African Theology', in John Parratt, ed. *A Reader in African Christian Theology.* London: SPCK, 1997.

Parratt, John. ed. *The Practice of Presence: Short Writings of Harry Sawyerr.* Michigan: Wm.B.Eerdmans Publishing Co, 1996.

Parratt, John. ed. *A Reader in African Christian Theology.* London: SPCK, 1997.

Paul, L. ed. *Theology of the Church as Family of God.* Nairobi: Paulines Publications Africa, 1997.

Pearce, G.J.M. *Congo Background.* London: The Carey Kingsgate Press, 1954.

Percy, Martyn. 'A Theology of Change for the Church' in G.R. Evans and Martyn Percy, eds. *Managing the Church? Order and Organisation in a Secular Age.* Sheffield, England: Sheffield Academic Press, 2000, pp. 174-190.

Platten, Stephen. *Augustine's Legacy: Authority and Leadership in the Anglican Communion.* London: Darton, Longman & Todd, 1997.

Pobee, John. *Toward an African Theology.* Nashville: Abingdon, 1979.   *Jesus Christ, the Life of the World: an African Perspective,* 1983.

— 'Life and Peace: an African Perspective' in John Pobee and Carl F. Hallencreutz, eds. *Variations in Christian Theology in Africa.* Nairobi: Uzima Press, 1986.

Pobee, John. 'Take Thou Authority: An African Perspective', in Sykes, Stephen, ed. *Authority in the Anglican Communion*. Toronto: Anglican Book Centre, 1987.

Pobee, John. and Hallencreutz, C.F. *Variations in Christian Theology in Africa*. Nairobi: Uzima Press, 1986.

Pobee, John and Ositelu II, Gabriel. *African Initiatives in Christianity: The growth, gifts and diversities of indigenous African churches. A challenge to the ecumenical movement*. Geneva: WCC Publications, 1998.

Politique Africaine 39, 1990.

Potentiel mensuelle de Janvier 1991.

Prah, K.K. Beyond the Color Line: Pan-Africanist disputations, Selected sketches. Trenton, N.J.: Africa world Press, 1998.

Presence Africaine, Primordiale du sixieme jour, 1963.

Prunier, Gerard. 'The Catholic Church and the Kivu Conflict', in *Journal of Religion in frica: Religion and War in the 1990s*, Volume XXX1-2. Leiden: Koninklijke Brill NV, 2001.

Randrianja, Solofo. 'Nationalism, Ethnicity and Democracy', in Stephen Ellis, ed. *Africa Now: People, Policies and Institutions*. The Hague, The Netherlands: Ministry of Foreign Affairs, 1996.

Redfern, Alastair. *Being Anglican*. London: Darton: Longman and Todd, 2000.

Reid, J. Richard. *Political Power in PreColonial Buganda: Economy, Society and Warfare in the Nineteenth Century*. Oxford: James Currey, 2002.

République Démocratique du Zaire. *Manifeste de N'Sele*, N'Sele1967.

Rheenen, Van G. *Church Planting in Uganda: A Comparative Study*. California: Willian Carey Library, 1976.

Rosenback, William E. and TAYLOR, Robert L. eds. *Contemporary Issues in Leadership*. Oxford: Westview Press, 1993.

Rosenthal, James, M. and CURRIE, Nicola, eds. *Being Anglican in the Third Millenium includes The Virginia Report and The Dublin Liturgical Report*. Pennsylvania, USA: Morehouse Publishing, 1997.

Ross, White Stephen. *Authority and Anglicanism*. London: SCM press Ltd, 1996.

Rowe, John. 'Mutesa and the Missionaries: Church and State in Pre-colonial Buganda', in Holger Bernt Hansen and Michael Twaddle, eds. *Christian Missionaries and the State in the Third World*. Oxford: James Currey Ltd, 2000, pp. 52-65.

Rowland, Christopher. 'Introduction: The Theology of Liberation', in C. Rowland, ed. *Liberation Theology*. Cambridge: Cambridge University Press, 1999.

Runcie, Robert. *Authority in Crisis? : An Anglican Response*. London: SCM Press, 1988.

Ryan, Patrick. 'Introduction', in Patrick Ryan, ed. *The Model of 'Church-as-Family': Meeting the African Challenge*. Nairobi: CUEA Publications, 1999.

Ryan, Patrick, ed. *The Model of 'Church-as-Family': Meeting the African Challenge*. Nairobi: CUEA Publications, 1999.

Ryckmans, Pierre. *Dominer pour Servir*. Brussels: Edition Universelle, 1948.

Ryman, Bjorn. 'Empathy and Antipathy in Research: A Ugandan Example', in *SMT*, Vol. 87, no 1, 1999.

Sandbrook, Richard. *The Politics of Africa's Stagnation*. New York: Cambridge University Press, 1993.

Sawyer, Amos. 'Proprietary Authority and Local Administration in Liberia', in Wunsch, J. and Olowu, D., eds. *The Failure of the Centralized State: Institutions and Self-Governance in Africa*. Oxford: Westview Press, 1990.

Sawyerr, Harry. *Creative Evangelism: Towards a New Christian Encounter with Africa.* London: Lutterworth Press, 1968.

'What is African Theology?' in John Parratt, ed. *The Practice of Presence: Short Writings of Harry Sawyerr.* Michigan: Wm.B. Eerdmans Publishing Co, 1996.

Schatzberg, M.M. 'Bureaucracy, Business, Beer: The Political Dynamics of Class Formation in Lisala, Zaire.' PhD dissertation, University of Wisconsin-Madison, 1977.

— *The Dialects of Oppression in Zaire.* Bloomington: Indiana University Press, 1988.

— 'Highjacking Change: Zaire's "Transition" in Comparative Perspective', in Ottaway, Marina, ed. *Democracy in Africa: The Hard Road Ahead.* London: Lynne Rienner Publishers, 1997.

Shorter Anylward. 'The Family as a Model for Social Reconstruction in Africa', in Leonard Paul, Maurice Schepers, Aylward Shorter and others. *Theology of the Church as Family of God.* Nairobi: Paulines Publications Africa, 1997.

Shutz, John. *Paul and the Anatomy of Apostolic Authority.* Cambridge: Cambridge University Press, 1975.

Slade, Ruth. *English-Speaking Missions in the Congo Independent Sate (1878-1908).* Brussels: Editions J. Duculot, S.A Gembloux, 1959.

— *The Belgian Congo: Some Recent Changes.* London: Oxford University Press, 1960.

— *King Leopold's Congo.* London: Oxford University Press, 1962.

Stott, John. *New Issues Facing Christians Today.* London: Marshall Pickering, 1999.

Sugden, Chris and Samuel, Vinay, eds. *Anglican Life and Witness: A Reader for the Lambeth Conference of Anglican Bishops 1998.* London: SPCK, 1997.

Sundkler, B. *The Christian Ministry in Africa.* London: 1960.

Sykes, Stephen. *Unashamed Anglicanism.* London: Darton, Longman and Todd, 1995.

— 'Authority in the Church of England', in Robert Jeffery, ed. *By What Authority?* Oxford: Mowbray, 1987.

Sykes, Stephen, ed. *Authority in the Anglican Communion.* Toronto: Anglican Book Centre, 1987.

Taylor, J.V. *The Growth of the Church in Buganda.* Edinburg: T.A Constable, 1958.

Tempels, Placide. *Bantu Philosophy.* Paris: Présence Africaine, 1959.

Teodros K., ed. *Explorations in African Political Thought: Identity, Community, Ethics.* New York: Routledge, 2001.

The Doctrine Commission of the Church of England. *We Believe in God.* London: Church House Publishing, 1991.

The Kairos Theologians. *Challenge to the Church: A Theological Comment on the Political Crisis in South Africa.* 1986.

The Secretary General of the Anglican Consultative Council. *The Truth Shall make you free. The Lambeth Conference: The Reports, Resolutions and Pastoral Letters from the Bishops.* London: Church House Publishing, 1988.

Tienou, Tite. 'The Church in African Theology: Description and Analysis of Hermeneutical Presuppositions', in D.A. Carson, ed. *Biblical Interpretation and the Church: Text and the Context.* Exeter. The Paternoster Press, 1984.

Tshonda, Omasombo Jean, ed. *Le Zaire à l'épreuve de l'histoire immédiate.* Paris: Karthala, 1993.

Tsibangu, T. *La Théologie Africaine: Manifeste et Programme pour le développement des activités théologiques en Afrique.* Kinshasa: Editions Saint Paul Afrique, 1987.

Tuma, A.D.T. *Building a Ugandan Church: African Participation in Church Growth and Expansion in Busoga 1891-1940.* Nairobi: Kenya Literature Bureau, 1980.

Twaddle, Michael. *Kakungulu and the Creation of Uganda 1868 – 1928.* London: James Currey, 1993.

Uzukwa, E.E. *A Listening Church: Autonomy and Communion in the African Churches.* New York: Orbis, 1996.

Waliggo, Mary J. 'The African Clan as the True Model of the African Church', in J.N.K. Mugambi and Laurenti Magesa, eds. *The Church in African Christianity: Innovative Essays in Ecclesiology.* Nairobi: Initiatives Publishers, 1990.

Ward, Kevin 'The Church of Uganda and the Exile of Kabaka Mutesa II, 1953-55', in *Journal of Religion in Africa,* volume XXVIII, Leiden, The Netherlands: Brill, 1998, pp. 411-449.

— '"The Armies of the Lord": Christianity, Rebels and the State in Northern Uganda, 1986-1999', in *Journal of Religion in Africa: Religion and War in the 1990's,* Volume xxx1-2. Leiden: Koninklijke Brill NV, 2201, pp. 187-221.

Weber, Max. *The Theory of Social and Economic Organization.* New York: Free Press, 1964.

Weiss, Herbert. 'Zaire: Collapsed Society, Surviving State, Future Polity', in Zartman I. William, ed. *Collapsed States: The Desintegration and Restoration of Legitimate Authority.* Boulder: Lynn Rienner, 1995.

Welbourne, F.B. *East African Rebels.* London: Oxford University Press, 1961.

Werbner, R. and Ranger, T. *Postcolonial Identities in Africa.* London: Zed Books, 1996.

Wild, Emma. 'Is it Witchcraft? Is it Satan? It is a Miracle.' Mai-Mai Soldiers and Christian Concepts of Evil in North-East Congo', in *Journal of Religion in Africa,* Volume XXVIII. Leiden, The Netherlands: Kninklijke Brill NV, 1998, pp. 450-467.

Willame, Jean-Claude. *L'Automne d'un Despotisme: Pouvoir, Argent et Obéissance dans le Zaire des Années Quatre-Vight.* Paris: Karthala, 1992.

Patrimonialism and Political Change in the Congo. Stanford, California: Stanford University Press, 1972.

Wiredu, Kwasi. 'Democracy and Consensus in African Traditional Politics: A plead for Non-Party Polity', in Eze, Emmanuel Chukwudi. Ed. *Postcolonial African Philosophy: A Critical Reader.* Oxford: Backwell Publishers Ltd, 1997.

Wolfgang, S. 'What does the Rwanda tragedy say to AMECEA churches?' *AMCEA Documentation service,* Nairobi Kenya, 17/1994, no 424.

Wood, D.R.W., ed. *New Bible Dictionary.* Third edition. Leicester, England, 1996.

World Council of Churches. 'Challenge to the Church: Theological Comment on the political Crisis in South Africa, the Kairos Document and Commentaries', in *PCR information,* 1985.

Wunsch, S. James and Olowu, Dele, eds. *The Failure of the Centralized State: Institutions and Self-Governance in Africa.* Oxford: Westview Press, 1990.

Young, Crawford. *Politics in the Congo: Decolonization and Independence.* Princeton, New Jersey: Princeton University Press, 1965.

— 'Zaire: the anatomy of a failed state', in David Birmingham and Phyllis Martin, eds. *History of Central Africa: The Contemporary years since 1960.* London and New York: Addison Wesley Longman, 1998.

Young, Crawford and Turner, Thomas. *The Rise and Decline of the Zairian State.* Madison, Wisconsin: The University of Wisconsin Press, 1985.

Zartman, I.William, ed. *Collapsed States: The Disintegration and Restoration of Legitimate Authority*. Boulder: Lynn Rienner, 1995.

Zizioulas, John. *Being as Communion: Studies in Personhood and the Church*. London: Darton, Longman and Todd, 1985.

Index of Names and Subjects

This combined index covers the main subjects dealt with, and includes the names of people mentioned or quoted in the text.

REGNUM STUDIES IN GLOBAL CHRISTIANITY
(Previously GLOBAL THEOLOGICAL VOICES series)
Series Listing

David Emmanuuel Singh (ed.)
Jesus and the Cross
Reflections of Christians from Islamic Contexts
2008 / 978-1-870345-65-1 / x + 226pp

The Cross reminds us that the sins of the world are not borne through the exercise of power but through Jesus Christ's submission to the will of the Father. The papers in this volume are organised in three parts: scriptural, contextual and theological. The central question being addressed is: how do Christians living in contexts, where Islam is a majority or minority religion, experience, express or think of the Cross? This is, therefore, an exercise in listening. As the contexts from where these engagements arise are varied, the papers in drawing scriptural, contextual and theological reflections offer a cross-section of Christian thinking about Jesus and the Cross.

Sung-wook Hong
Naming God in Korea
The Case of Protestant Christianity
2008 / 978-1-870345-66-8 / xiv + 170pp

Since Christianity was introduced to Korea more than a century ago, one of the most controversial issue has been the Korean term for the Christian 'God'. This issue is not merely about naming the Christian God in Korean language, but it relates to the question of theological contextualization—the relationship between the gospel and culture—and the question of Korean Christian identity. This book examines the theological contextualization of the concept of 'God' in the contemporary Korean context and applies the translatability of Christianity to that context. It also demonstrates the nature of the gospel in relation to cultures, i.e., the universality of the gospel expressed in all human cultures.

Hubert van Beek (ed.)
Revisioning Christian Unity
The Global Christian Forum
2009 / 978-1-870345-74-3 / xx + 288pp

This book contains the records of the Global Christian Forum gathering held in Limuru near Nairobi, Kenya, on 6 – 9 November 2007 as well as the papers presented at that historic event. Also included are a summary of the Global Christian Forum process from its inception until the 2007 gathering and the reports of the evaluation of the process that was carried out in 2008.

Paul Hang-Sik Cho
Eschatology and Ecology
The Case of the Protestant Church in Korea
2010 / 978-1-870345-75-0/

This book raises the question of why Korean people, and Korean Protestant Christians in particular, pay so little attention (in theory or practice) to ecological issues. The author argues that there is an important connection (or elective affinity) between this lack of attention and the other-worldly eschatology that is so dominant within Korean Protestant Christianity. Dispensational premillennialism, originally imported by American missionaries, resonated with traditional religious beliefs in Korea and soon came to dominate much of Korean Protestantism. This book argues that this, of all forms of millennialism, is the most damaging to ecological concerns.

REGNUM STUDIES IN MISSION
Series Listing

Kwame Bediako
Theology and Identity
*The Impact of Culture upon Christian Thought
in the Second Century and in Modern Africa
1992 / 1-870345-10-X / xviii + 508pp*

The author examines the question of Christian identity in the context of the Graeco–Roman culture of the early Roman Empire. He then addresses the modern African predicament of quests for identity and integration.

Christopher Sugden
Seeking the Asian Face of Jesus
*The Practice and Theology of Christian Social Witness
in Indonesia and India 1974–1996
1997 / 1-870345-26-6 / xx + 496pp*

This study focuses on contemporary holistic mission with the poor in India and Indonesia combined with the call to transformation of all life in Christ with micro-credit enterprise schemes. 'The literature on contextual theology now has a new standard to rise to' – Lamin Sanneh (Yale University, USA).

Hwa Yung
Mangoes or Bananas?
*The Quest for an Authentic Asian Christian Theology
1997 / 1-870345-25-8 / xii + 274pp*

Asian Christian thought remains largely captive to Greek dualism and Enlightenment rationalism because of the overwhelming dominance of Western culture. Authentic contextual Christian theologies will emerge within Asian Christianity with a dual recovery of confidence in culture and the gospel.

Keith E. Eitel
Paradigm Wars
*The Southern Baptist International Mission Board
Faces the Third Millennium
1999 / 1-870345-12-6 / x + 140pp*

The International Mission Board of the Southern Baptist Convention is the largest denominational mission agency in North America. This volume chronicles the historic and contemporary forces that led to the IMB's recent extensive reorganization, providing the most comprehensive case study to date of a historic mission agency restructuring to continue its mission purpose into the twenty-first century more effectively.

Samuel Jayakumar
Dalit Consciousness and Christian Conversion
Historical Resources for a Contemporary Debate
1999 / 81-7214-497-0 / xxiv + 434pp
(Published jointly with ISPCK)
The main focus of this historical study is social change and transformation among the Dalit Christian communities in India. Historiography tests the evidence in the light of the conclusions of the modern Dalit liberation theologians.

Vinay Samuel and Christopher Sugden (eds.)
Mission as Transformation
A Theology of the Whole Gospel
1999/ 0870345133/522pp
This book brings together in one volume twenty five years of biblical reflection on mission practice with the poor from around the world. The approach of holistic mission, which integrates proclamation, evangelism, church planting and social transformation seamlessly as a whole, has been adopted since 1983 by most evangelical development agencies, most indigenous mission agencies and many Pentecostal churches. This volume helps anyone understand how evangelicals, struggling to unite evangelism and social action, found their way in the last twenty five years to the biblical view of mission in which God calls all human beings to love God and their neighbour; never creating a separation between the two.

Christopher Sugden
Gospel, Culture and Transformation
2000 / 1-870345-32-0 / viii + 152pp
A Reprint, with a New Introduction of Part Two of *Seeking the Asian Face of Jesus Gospel, Culture and Transformation* explores the practice of mission especially in relation to transforming cultures and communities - 'Transformation is to enable God's vision of society to be actualised in all relationships: social, economic and spiritual, so that God's will may be reflected in human society and his love experienced by all communities, especially the poor.'

Bernhard Ott
Beyond Fragmentation: Integrating Mission and Theological Education
A Critical Assessment of some Recent Developments
in Evangelical Theological Education
2001 / 1-870345-14-2 / xxviii + 382pp

Beyond Fragmentation is an enquiry into the development of Mission Studies in evangelical theological education in Germany and German-speaking Switzerland between 1960 and 1995. This is carried out by a detailed examination of the paradigm shifts which have taken place in recent years in both the theology of mission and the understanding of theological education.

Gideon Githiga
The Church as the Bulwark against Authoritarianism
Development of Church and State Relations in Kenya, with Particular
Reference to the Years after Political Independence 1963-1992
2002 / 1-870345-38-X / xviii + 218pp

'All who care for love, peace and unity in Kenyan society will want to read this careful history by Bishop Githiga of how Kenyan Christians, drawing on the Bible, have sought to share the love of God, bring his peace and build up the unity of the nation, often in the face of great difficulties and opposition.' Canon Dr Chris Sugden, Oxford Centre for Mission Studies.

Myung Sung-Hoon, Hong Young-Gi (eds.)
Charis and Charisma
David Yonggi Cho and the Growth of Yoido Full Gospel Church
2003 / 1-870345-45-2 / xxii + 218pp

This book discusses the factors responsible for the growth of the world's largest church. It expounds the role of the Holy Spirit, the leadership, prayer, preaching, cell groups and creativity in promoting church growth. It focuses on God's grace (charis) and inspiring leadership (charisma) as the two essential factors and the book's purpose is to present a model for church growth worldwide.

Samuel Jayakumar
Mission Reader
Historical Models for Wholistic Mission in the Indian Context
2003 / 1-870345-42-8 / x + 250pp
(Published jointly with ISPCK)

This book is written from an evangelical point of view revalidating and reaffirming the Christian commitment to wholistic mission. The roots of the 'wholistic mission' combining 'evangelism and social concerns' are to be located in the history and tradition of Christian evangelism in the past; and the civilizing purpose of evangelism is compatible with modernity as an instrument in nation building.

Bob Robinson
Christians Meeting Hindus
An Analysis and Theological Critique of the Hindu-Christian
Encounter in India
2004 / 1-870345-39-8 / xviii + 392pp
This book focuses on the Hindu-Christian encounter, especially the intentional meeting called dialogue, mainly during the last four decades of the twentieth century, and mainly in India itself.

Gene Early
Leadership Expectations
How Executive Expectations are Created and Used in a Non-Profit Setting
2005 / 1-870345-30-4 / xxiv + 276pp
The author creates an Expectation Enactment Analysis to study the role of the Chancellor of the University of the Nations-Kona, Hawaii, and is grounded in the field of managerial work, jobs, and behaviour, drawing on symbolic interactionism, role theory, role identity theory and enactment theory. The result is a conceptual framework for further developing an understanding of managerial roles.

Tharcisse Gatwa
The Churches and Ethnic Ideology in the Rwandan Crises 1900-1994
2005 / 1-870345-24-X / approx 300pp
Since the early years of the twentieth century Christianity has become a new factor in Rwandan society. This book investigates the role Christian churches played in the formulation and development of the racial ideology that culminated in the 1994 genocide.

Julie Ma
Mission Possible
Biblical Strategies for Reaching the Lost
2005 / 1-870345-37-1 / xvi + 142pp
This is a missiology book for the church which liberates missiology from the specialists for every believer. It also serves as a textbook that is simple and friendly, and yet solid in biblical interpretation. This book links the biblical teaching to the actual and contemporary missiological settings with examples, thus making the Bible come alive to the reader.

Allan Anderson, Edmond Tang (eds.)
Asian and Pentecostal
The Charismatic Face of Christianity in Asia
2005 / 1-870345-43-6 / xiv + 596pp
(Published jointly with APTS Press)
This book provides a thematic discussion and pioneering case studies on the history and development of Pentecostal and Charismatic churches in the countries of South Asia, South East Asia and East Asia.

I. Mark Beaumont
Christology in Dialogue with Muslims
A Critical Analysis of Christian Presentations of Christ for Muslims from the Ninth and Twentieth Centuries
2005 / 1-870345-46-0 / xxvi + 228pp
This book analyses Christian presentations of Christ for Muslims in the most creative periods of Christian-Muslim dialogue, the first half of the ninth century and the second half of the twentieth century. In these two periods, Christians made serious attempts to present their faith in Christ in terms that take into account Muslim perceptions of him, with a view to bridging the gap between Muslim and Christian convictions.

Thomas Czövek,
Three Seasons of Charismatic Leadership
A Literary-Critical and Theological Interpretation of the Narrative of Saul, David and Solomon
2006 / 978-1-870345484 / 272pp
This book investigates the charismatic leadership of Saul, David and Solomon. It suggests that charismatic leaders emerge in crisis situations in order to resolve the crisis by the charisma granted by God. Regarding Saul, the book argues that he proved himself as a charismatic leader as long as he acted resolutely and independently from Samuel his mentor. He failed, however, because in Samuel's shadow he could not establish himself as a charismatic leader.

Jemima Atieno Oluoch
The Christian Political Theology of Dr. John Henry Okullu
2006 / 1-870345-51-7 / xx + 137pp
This book reconstructs the Christian political theology of Bishop John Henry Okullu, DD, through establishing what motivated him and the biblical basis for his socio-political activities. It also attempts to reconstruct the socio-political environment that nurtured Dr Okullu's prophetic ministry.

Richard Burgess
Nigeria's Christian Revolution
The Civil War Revival and Its Pentecostal Progeny (1967-2006)
2008 / 978-1-870345-63-7 / xxii + 347pp

This book describes the revival that occurred among the Igbo people of Eastern Nigeria and the new Pentecostal churches it generated, and documents the changes that have occurred as the movement has responded to global flows and local demands. As such, it explores the nature of revivalist and Pentecostal experience, but does so against the backdrop of local socio-political and economic developments, such as decolonisation and civil war, as well as broader processes, such as modernisation and globalisation.

David Emmanuel Singh & Bernard C Farr (eds.)
Christianity and Cultures
Shaping Christian Thinking in Context
2008 / 978-1-870345-69-9 / x + 260pp

This volume is a way of marking an important milestone, 25th anniversary, of the Oxford Centre for Mission Studies (OCMS). The papers here have been exclusively sourced from Transformation, a quarterly journal of OCMS, and seek to provide a tripartite view of Christianity's engagement with cultures by focusing on the question: how is Christian thinking being formed or reformed through its interaction with the varied contexts it encounters? The subject matters include different strands of theological-missiological thinking, socio-political engagements and forms of family relationships in interaction with the host cultures.

Tormod Engelsviken, Ernst Harbakk, Rolv Olsen, Thor Strandenæs (eds.)
Mission to the World
Communicating the Gospel in the 21st Century:
Essays in Honour of Knud Jørgensen
2008 / 978-1-870345-64-4 / 472pp

Knud Jørgensen is Director of Areopagos and Associate Professor of Missiology at MF Norwegian School of Theology. This book reflects the various main areas of Jørgensen's commitment to mission. At the same time it focuses on the main frontier of mission, the world, the content of mission, the Gospel, the fact that the Gospel has to be communicated, and the context of contemporary mission in the 21st century.

Al Tizon
Transformation after Lausanne
Radical Evangelical Mission in Global-Local Perspective
2008 / 978-1-870345-68-2 / xx + 281pp

After Lausanne '74, a worldwide network of radical evangelical mission theologians and practitioners use the notion of "Mission as Transformation" to integrate evangelism and social concern together, thus lifting theological voices from the Two Thirds World to places of prominence. This book documents the definitive gatherings, theological tensions, and social forces within and without evangelicalism that led up to Mission as Transformation. And it does so through a global-local grid that points the way toward greater holistic mission in the 21st century.

Bambang Budijanto
Values and Participation
Development in Rural Indonesia
2009 / 978-1-870345-70-5 / x + 237pp

Socio-religious values and socio-economic development are inter-dependant, inter-related and are constantly changing in the context of macro political structures, economic policy, religious organizations and globalization; and micro influences such as local affinities, identity, politics, leadership and beliefs. The three Lopait communities in Central Java, Indonesia provide an excellent model of the rich and complex negotiations and interactions among all the above factors. The book argues that the comprehensive approach in understanding the socio-religious values of each local community is essential to accurately describing their respective identity which will help institutions and agencies, both governmental and non-governmental, to relate to these communities with dignity and respect.

Young-hoon Lee
The Holy Spirit Movement in Korea
Its Historical and Theological Development
2009 / 978-1-870345-67-5 / x + 174pp

This book traces the historical and theological development of the Holy Spirit Movement in Korea through six successive periods (from 1900 to the present time). These periods are characterized by repentance and revival (1900-20), persecution and suffering under Japanese occupation (1920-40), confusion and division (1940-60), explosive revival in which the Pentecostal movement played a major role in the rapid growth of Korean churches (1960-80), the movement reaching out to all denominations (1980-2000), and the new context demanding the Holy Spirit movement to open new horizons in its mission engagement (2000-). The volume also discusses the relationship between this movement and other religions such as shamanism, and looks forward to further engagement with issues of concern in the larger society.

Alan R. Johnson
Leadership in a Slum
A Bangkok Case Study
2009 / 978-1-870345-71-2 xx + 238pp

This book looks at leadership in the social context of a slum in Bangkok from an angle different from traditional studies which measure well educated Thais on leadership scales derived in the West. Using both systematic data collection and participant observation, it develops a culturally preferred model as well as a set of models based in Thai concepts that reflect on-the-ground realities. This work challenges the dominance of the patron-client rubric for understanding all forms of Thai leadership and offers a view for understanding leadership rooted in local social systems, contrary to approaches that assume the universal applicability of leadership research findings across all cultural settings. It concludes by looking at the implications of the anthropological approach for those who are involved in leadership training in Thai settings and beyond.

Ande Titre
Leadership and Authority
Bula Matari and Life - Community Ecclesiology in Congo
2010 / 978-1-870345-72-9

This book proposes that Christian theology in Africa can make a significant development if a critical understanding of the socio-political context in contemporary Africa is taken seriously. The Christian leadership in post-colonial Africa has cloned its understanding and use of authority on the Bula Matari model, issued from the brutality of colonialism and political absolutism in post-colonial Africa. This model has caused many problems in churches, including dysfunctions, conflicts, divisions and lack of prophetic ministry. The book proposes a Life-Community ecclesiology for liberating authority, where leadership is a function, not a status, and 'apostolic succession' belongs to all the people of God.

Frank Adams
Odwira and the Gospel
A Study of the Asante Odwira Festival and Its Significance for Christianity in
Ghana
2010/978-1-870345-59-0

The study of the Odwira festival is the key to the understanding of Asante
religious and political life in Ghana. The book explores the nature of the Odwira
festival longitudinally - in pre-colonial, colonial and post-independence Ghana -
and examines the Odwira ideology and its implications for understanding the
Asante self-identity. The book also discusses how some elements of faith
portrayed in the Odwira festival could provide a framework for Christianity to
engage with Asante culture at a greater depth. Theological themes in Asante
belief that have emerged from this study include the theology of sacrament,
ecclesiology, eschatology, Christology and a complex concept of time. The
author argues that Asante cultural identity lies at the heart of the process by
which the Asante Christian faith is carried forward.

OTHER REGNUM TITLES

Peter Johnson, Chris Sugden (eds.)
Markets, Fair Trade and the Kingdom of God
Essays to Celebrate Traidcraft's 21st Birthday
2001 / 1870345193 / xii+155pp

Deryke Belshaw, Robert Calderisi, Chris Sugden (eds.)
Faith in Development
Partnership Between the World Bank and the Churches of Africa
2001 / 978-0821348482 / 246pp

Robert Hillman, Coral Chamberlain, Linda Harding
Healing & Wholeness
Reflections on the Healing Ministry
2002 / 978-1- 870345-35- 4 / xvii+283pp

David Bussau, Russell Mask
Christian Microenterprise Development
An Introduction
2003 / 1870345282 / xiii+142pp

David Singh
Sainthood and Revelatory Discourse
An Examination of the Basis for the Authority of Bayan in Mahdawi Islam
2003 / 8172147285 / xxiv+485pp

For the up-to-date listing of the Regnum books see
www.ocms.ac.uk/regnum

regnum

Regnum Books International

Regnum is an Imprint of The Oxford Centre for Mission Studies
St. Philip and St. James Church
Woodstock Road
Oxford, OX2 6HR

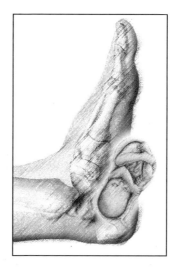

Maternity
Reflexology
a guide for reflexologists

Compiled by
Elsa Reid
R.N., C.M., Grad. Dip. Nursing (Women's Health)
Certificate of Reflexology
Certificate of Medical Hypnosis

and

Susanne Enzer
R.N., R.S.C.N. (UK), S.C.M. (UK)
Reflex Zone Therapist

Design by Louisa Bevege BVA.GD
Certificate of Reflexology

Published by
Born to be Free and Soul to Sole Reflexology
1997

Elsa Reid and Susanne Enzer
Maternity Reflexology – a guide for reflexologists

ISBN 0 646 31392 4

Published 1997
Reprint 1997
by Born to be Free and Soul to Sole Reflexology

For further information regarding this book contact the authors:
Elsa Reid
24 Pamela Crescent
BOWEN MOUNTAIN
NSW 2753
0245 721 666

Susanne Enzer
14 Bourke Street
PYMBLE
NSW 2073
(02) 9144 6390

Designed by Louisa Bevege

Photography by Warren Norris, Turramurra, NSW.

Printed in Australia by Bridge Printery Pty Ltd.

Maternity Reflexology - a guide for reflexologists is designed as a guide for reflexologists who work with maternity clients. It is suggested complementary health support for maternity clients, it is not a substitute for professional obstetric care.

For our beloved daughters
Amira and Kate

We appreciate and wish to acknowledge the love and encouragement of all those who have supported us with our book. Special thank-yous to Erica who helped get the words in the right place, and Darren who helped get the bones in the right place!

contents

preconception

antenatal

contents

contents

postnatal

contents

footnotes from the authors

Elsa's Notes

As we learn we change. Obstetric care-givers and reflexologists change their care as they and their specialities evolve. For this reason it is important to realise that the information contained in this publication is correct for the authors at the time of printing. We have aimed to broaden information to fit rural, interstate and overseas reflexologists, despite certain facts varying from place to place (eg in New South Wales a foetus is viable from 20 weeks gestation, while in the UK viability is from 24 weeks gestation).

This workbook is a comprehensive but not exhaustive list of common conditions related to "maternity time". In this publication we refer to the obstetric care-giver as the person in charge of a woman's obstetric care. The obstetric care-giver may be an obstetrician, a midwife, a general practitioner, a nurse, a hospital medical officer or, as with "shared care", a combination of professionals. If we have stipulated an obstetrician's care and/or advice, this indicates that a pregnancy specialist should be involved in the woman's care in addition to her obstetric care-giver.

It is absolutely essential for responsible practice that the reflexology practitioner is aware that certain maternity conditions contraindicate reflexology. Other conditions are compatible with reflexology only when approved by the obstetric care-giver. Warnings and contraindications are clearly noted in the text and diagrams pertaining to these conditions. For legal, ethical and safety reasons reflexologists are encouraged to work with the client's approval and also, where relevant her obstetric caregiver's approval. The practitioner's intuition needs to be heeded - listen to the inner voice which says "be wary". Appropriate referral is always good practice.

We have purposely worded the information contained within these pages to be client and practitioner friendly. For clarity we have referred to the mother as "she", while baby, partner and care-givers are "he". We have avoided calling an unborn baby "foetus" as mothers feel offended by language that does not acknowledge their baby as a person before the birth.

In addition to simple terminology in the text a glossary of terms and abbreviations has been included, to help reflexology practitioners to "translate" terms and conditions into easily understood simple language for their clients.

Providing reflexology care to maternity clients can be as wonderful an experience as being the recipient of maternity reflexology. Being involved with maternity clients offers a unique opportunity to be involved in the evolution of a family, whilst the love, care, nurturing and healing offered with reflexology provides immeasurable benefits to all.

We hope this book helps clients and practitioners enjoy being part of such a special life event.

Susanne's Notes

This workbook contains a lot of information presented in a condensed form. It is designed for reflexologists who work with maternity clients.

MATERNITY
For the purposes of this book "Maternity time" is defined as: from a few months before conception, throughout pregnancy, labour and the puerperium.

The maternity information has been compiled by the authors, both of whom are midwives. All midwives have a core of specialised maternity knowledge, common to all, and tailor their advice and practice to the perceived needs of the mother, their client.

For the reflexologist working with maternity clients, whenever there is any doubt, anxiety or queries contact the client's obstetric care-giver and always work within your own modality, abilities and knowledge.

There is a glossary of maternity terms and abbreviations on page 184

REFLEXOLOGY
Suggestions for reflexology therapy techniques have been acquired from my accumulated knowledge, experience and practice and includes other reflexology sources which I have found to be valuable. I make the assumption reflexology therapists are familiar with the majority of the work, although they may have many additional techniques and different terminology for the

same technique. There is a glossary on page 188 which gives lesser known terms used in this book, any known alternate terms for the same technique, explanation of some techniques which I have found especially useful and the sources of this information. The term "REFLECTION ZONE" has been used throughout in preference to "REFLEX ZONE" as I believe that there are other exquisite subtle energies of the feet at work here - especially in maternity reflexology.

THE BOOK
The book is arranged in three sections :

Preconception pages 12 - 25
Antenatal pages 26 - 131
Postnatal pages 132 - 183

On each left hand page the heading indicates a condition which may occur during the "maternity time". Preconceptual care conditions are arranged in order of possible occurrence. The conditions of antenatal care and postnatal care are arranged in alphabetical order. The maternity information is at the top of the left page. A reflexology response follows in an easy to understand grid. Each reflection zone named in the grid is highlighted on the diagram on the facing page. A footnote with the symbol of two feet gives some tips for the reflexology practitioner and other points of interest.

preconception
preconceptual care

When a couple are planning to have a baby it is sensible for both of them to first get in good shape, not only physically but also mentally and spiritually - there will be many unplanned surprises along the way. Be prepared!

general well being

Recommend a full reflexology session each week prior to conception for both partners.

reflection zone	*technique*	*intent*
reflexology	full reflexology session	to attain and maintain health and well-being to balance any disordered zones

 Reflexology is an excellent preparation for childbearing.

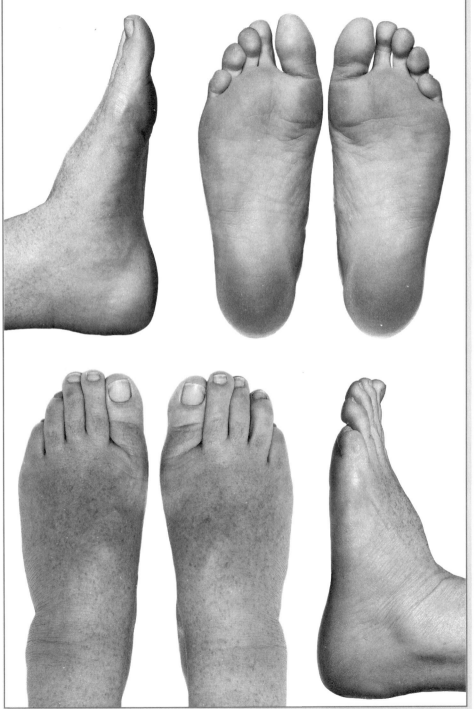

preconception
ovulation &
menstruation cycles

A complete well balanced cycle repeats every 29 to 32 days. Ovulation occurs 14 days before menstruation which lasts 3 to 5 days with a moderate flow. The many disorders of the ovulation/menstrual cycles are too numerous to list in this book. (They are the subject of another book!)

reflection zone	*technique*	*intent*
reflexology	full reflexology sessions	to balance the cycles to maintain regular cycles

1ST AID FOR PAINFUL PERIODS (DYSMENORRHOEA)

reflection zone	*technique*	*intent*
uterus	bimanual sedation grip	to relieve the pain and decrease the tension release trapped energy

 often when rebalancing the cycles they appear more disordered before they settle into a new balanced pattern.

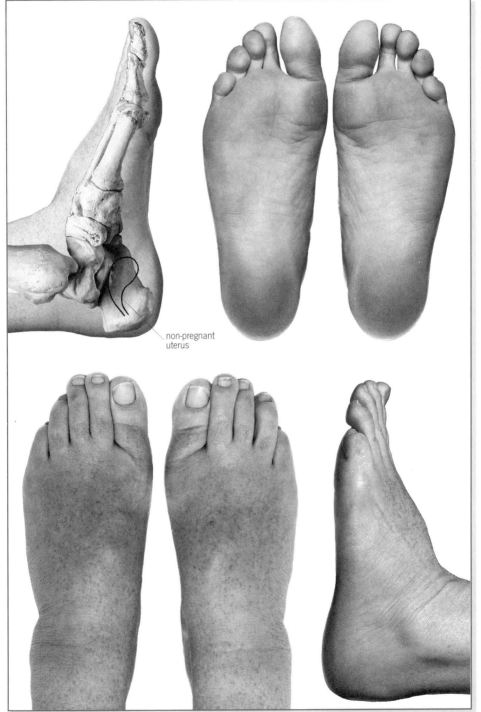

non-pregnant uterus

preconception
infertility

A couple may become very distressed at failure to conceive. Suggest reflexology therapy for both partners - an intensive regime of twice a week for six weeks, thereafter once a week.

reflection zone	*technique*	*intent*
entire body	full reflexology session	to balance body mind and spirit to observe imbalances and correct them
endocrine system	endocrine balance	to normalise and harmonise the body's chemical messengers
solar plexus	bimanual thumb hold	to clear the creative energy flow
uterus	stimulate	to enliven the area
pelvis	ankle boogie ankle rotations	to relax and open up the area
lymphatic system	lymphatic drainage massage	to assist removal of toxins and improve cell health

Even if there are physical reasons why a couple cannot conceive, reflexology therapy will help to balance them so that if they choose other methods of becoming pregnant they will be better prepared.

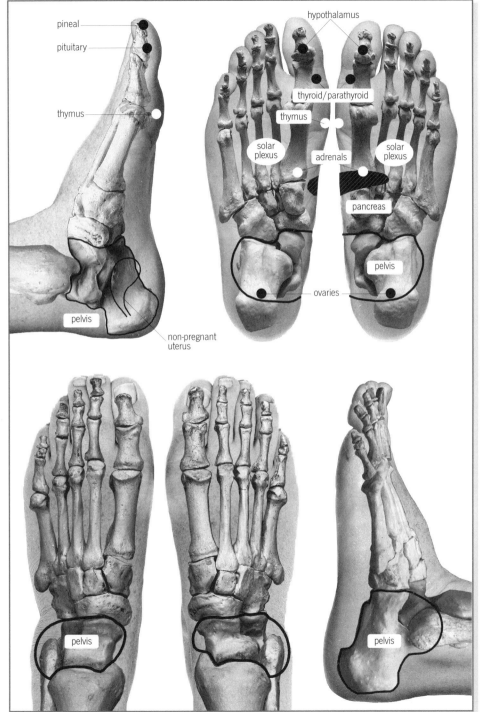

preconception
miscarriage
threatened

Threatened miscarriage is diagnosed when vaginal bleeding occurs before twenty weeks gestation. The bleeding is usually not severe, the cervix remains closed and providing the pregnancy is not expelled the baby is not effected. Mild pain/cramping may occur. Medical advice usually includes the woman remaining in bed until the bleeding has stopped. She may be prescribed a sedative medication to encourage relaxation. After 48 hours without blood loss gentle ambulation can recommence.

reflection zone	*technique*	*intent*
solar plexus	bimanual thumb hold	to calm and relieve anxiety

Advise the woman to follow her doctor's advice or to consult a doctor if she hasn't already done so.

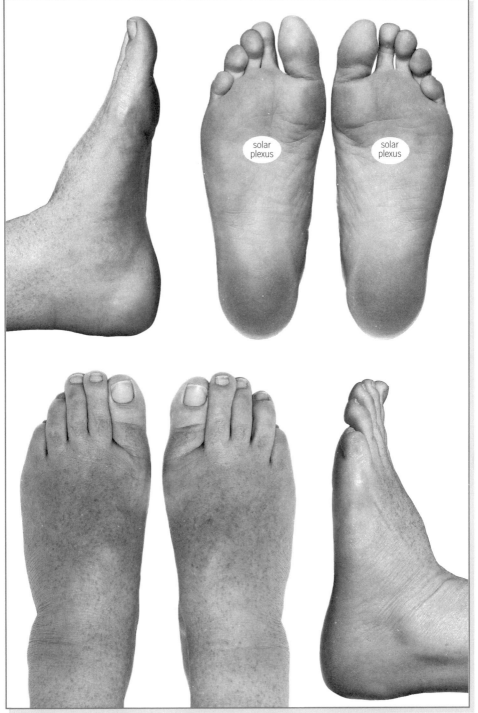

solar
plexus

solar
plexus

preconception
miscarriage
inevitable, incomplete

Inevitable miscarriage is the diagnosis given to a pregnancy that cannot possibly continue ie when the baby has died or a large portion of the placenta has separated from the uterine wall. Blood loss is usually plentiful, the cervix opens and often the membranes rupture. Pain is usually more acute than when miscarriage is threatened and rhythmical cramp and/or contractions may be felt. Medical advice usually includes an ultrasound to confirm to the parents that the miscarriage is inevitable ie that the baby's heartbeat is absent. Ultrasound is also useful in determining if the miscarriage is complete or incomplete ie if all products of conception have been expelled from the uterus. An incomplete miscarriage usually requires a dilation and curettage (D&C), commonly known as "clean out" of the womb.

reflection zone	*technique*	*intent*
entire body	full reflexology session	to balance the being
solar plexus	bimanual thumb hold	to calm and relieve anxiety and balance the energy of creation
endocrine system	endocrine balance	to restore balance
uterus indirect ovary	linking technique	to link the energy of female reproduction
spleen	gently stimulate	to provide adequate blood supply
lymphatic system	lymphatic drainage massage	to assist removal of waste matter

 By the time the client presents with a diagnosis of inevitable miscarriage she will be in the care of a doctor. If not encourage her to consult a doctor. Counsell the couple. It is important that there are no misunderstandings about what has happened. Be supportive. Use listening and counselling skills.

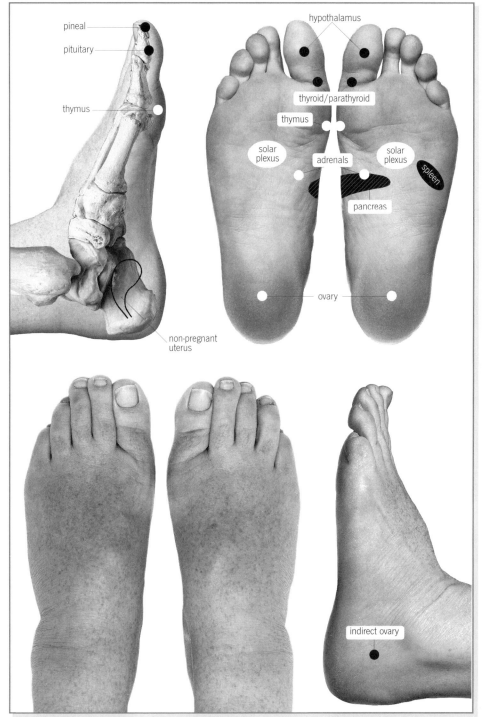

preconception
miscarriage
habitual, recurrent

Some women have no problem with conceiving, but cannot carry a pregnancy past the first trimester of pregnancy. Habitual or recurrent miscarriage is the term used after the woman has had three consecutive miscarriages. Sometimes the baby has a chromosomal abnormality, sometimes the mother has a hormonal imbalance and sometimes there is no obvious reason. This is always distressing to the couple, they will require specialist investigation and counselling.

REFLEXOLOGY CONTRAINDICATED

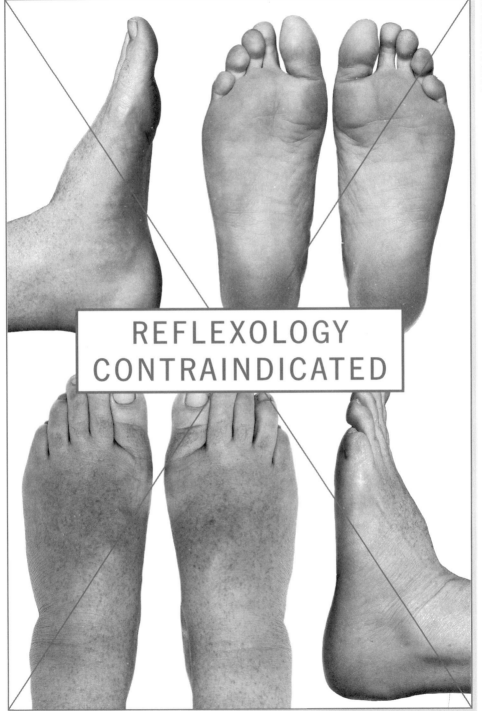

REFLEXOLOGY
CONTRAINDICATED

preconception
after miscarriage or termination of pregnancy

Losing a baby is always an emotional time. A period of grieving is to be expected when feelings of denial, anger and/or guilt are expressed. Reflexology should start as soon as possible to help with the emotional and physical adjustment of losing a baby. Short daily sessions are recommended.

reflection zone	*technique*	*intent*
entire body	full reflexology session	to balance
endocrine system	endocrine balance	to restore non-pregnant hormonal balance
hypothalamus "sense of self"	linking technique	to restore the person
uterus indirect ovary solar plexus	linking technique	to restore femininity to the female
solar plexus	bimanual thumb hold	to calm, centre and restore the creative life force
lower abdomen and internal pelvis	healing hold	to help prevent feelings of guilt settling
lymphatic system	lymphatic drainage massage	to help cleanse the body

 Use listening, calming, relaxing and healing skills. Be supportive and understanding. To the best of your ability, explain whatever the client wants and needs to know. Repetition of information is sometimes necessary before realisation sinks in. Be patient. Be honest, and keep your own limitations in mind.

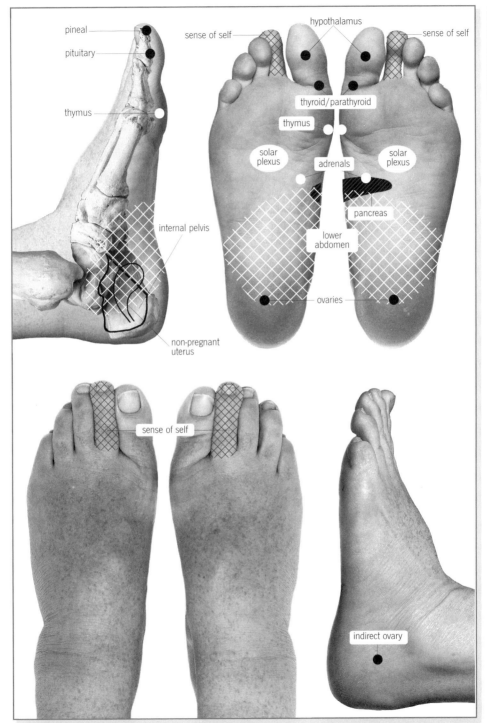

pineal

pituitary

thymus

hypothalamus

sense of self

sense of self

thyroid/parathyroid

thymus

solar plexus

solar plexus

adrenals

pancreas

internal pelvis

lower abdomen

non-pregnant uterus

ovaries

sense of self

indirect ovary

antenatal care

From the moment of conception (for some women before that moment) huge changes in the being are the norm. Mind, body and spirit are all involved. With an incoming soul manifesting physically within her the woman's sensitivity and intuitiveness are on "high voltage", her body adapts to the stresses of physical change and her mind keeps coping with it all. A modality such as reflexology is excellent to maintain equilibrium during the changing balance of pregnancy.

The skill of the reflexologist is to balance and harmonise the whole being. Many of the minor ailments of pregnancy respond well to reflexology therapy. It is important to work within one's own ability and to know when the specialised skills of the obstetric caregiver are needed. The complications and disorders of pregnancy must have expert medical attention.

general well-being

A full reflexology session each week throughout pregnancy is ideal to maintain balance and harmony during the changes of pregnancy.

Ensure each session includes:

• an endocrine system balance
• lymphatic drainage massage
• bimanual solar plexus balance
• reflexology therapy for any specific condition

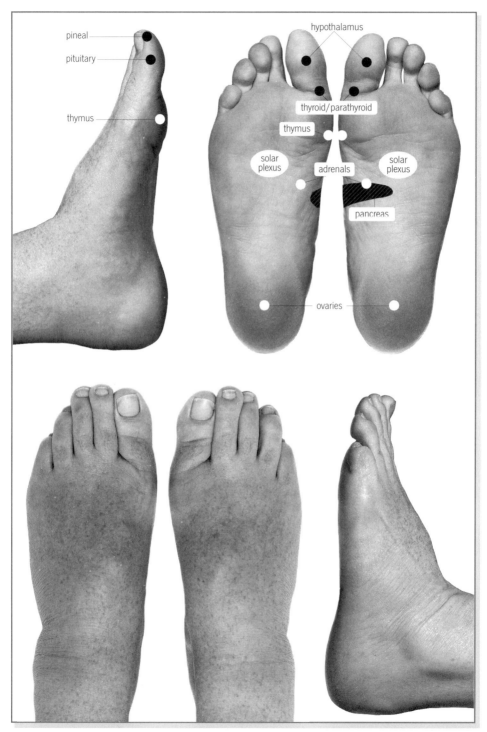

pineal

pituitary

thymus

hypothalamus

thyroid/parathyroid

thymus

solar plexus

adrenals

solar plexus

pancreas

ovaries

antenatal

anaemia

(physiological anaemia & iron deficiency anaemia)

During pregnancy blood haemoglobin concentrations drop slightly as the blood volume increases disproportionately to haemoglobin increases. This is known as physiological anaemia and is to be expected with pregnancy. When haemoglobin levels drop significantly, faintness, lethargy and breathlessness can result, causing physical stresses on mother and baby. Medical treatment usually involves the prescription of iron tablets, rest and regular blood tests to monitor haemoglobin levels.

reflection zone	*technique*	*intent*
spleen	gently stimulate	to encourage red blood cell vitality
liver	gently stimulate	to encourage blood health
heart	moderately stimulate	to promote joy

Explain the difference between physiological and iron deficiency anaemia. Recommend a dietary intake of iron-rich foods eg leafy green vegetables, red meats etc. If the client is reluctant to take additional iron due to constipation, suggest foods high in vitamin C can be taken at the same time as iron tablets (vitamin C increases the body's uptake of iron). Remind the client also that an iron tablet twice a week is better than none

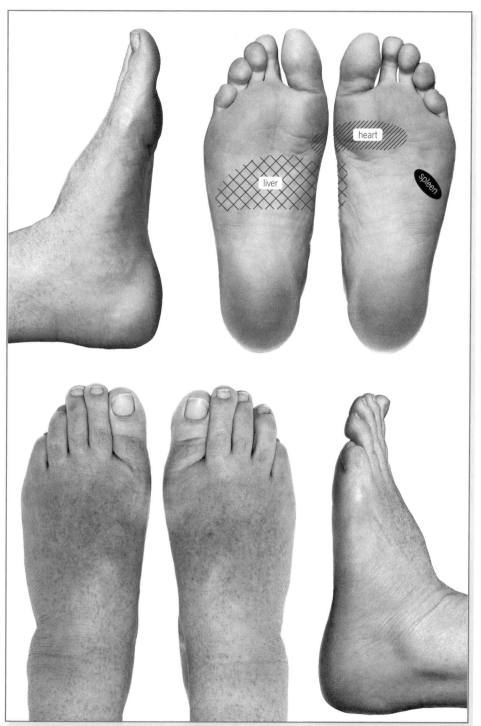

antenatal
appetite

During pregnancy the growth and physical changes which occur in a woman's body require good nutrition and additional energy. Pregnant women often experience huge appetite increases, desires for particular foods and even cravings for bizarre substances eg garden soil. Obstetric caregivers recommend that a wide variety of nutritious foods are eaten and that a woman's weight gain, whilst minimal during the first 20 weeks, should be a steady gain during the second half of pregnancy.

reflection zone	technique	intent
endocrine system	endocrine balance	to support the body through rapidly changing hormone levels
pancreas	gentle stimulation	to help replace energy being used by the growing foetus

If the client describes food cravings, help her to determine the nutrients which she is needing and acceptable foods which provide those nutrients. For most women minerals in the form of tablets would be a more acceptable alternative to garden soil! It is interesting to note that if there is an urgency to eat a certain food it is the baby who needs that particular nutrient.

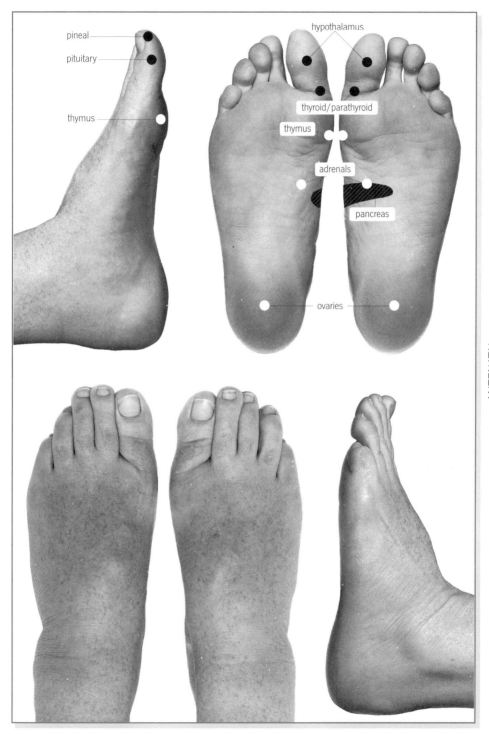

pineal

pituitary

thymus

hypothalamus

thyroid/parathyroid

thymus

adrenals

pancreas

ovaries

antenatal
backache

During pregnancy hormones are released to relax the pelvic joints allowing the baby more space through the birth canal. Unfortunately these hormones cannot be totally selective, causing relaxation of all joints. As well as altering a woman's gait (walk) unstable pelvic joints often result in ligament pain and backache. As the baby grows, a shift in the centre of gravity occurs tilting the pelvis forward. To compensate the woman will lean backwards to maintain her balance. The consequence is extra curvature of the lumbar spine and a tendency towards backache.

reflection zone	*technique*	*intent*
spine	spine stretches gentle spinal twist thumb walk	to ease the discomfort to keep the joints supple to re-establish support
head and neck	stretch and rotate	to lengthen the spine
diaphragm	rotate onto thumb	to ease emotional stress to relax the muscle

 Advise client to rest for short periods whenever possible as well as using good lifting techniques at all times. Recommend she practices back, abdomen and pelvic floor exercises regularly.

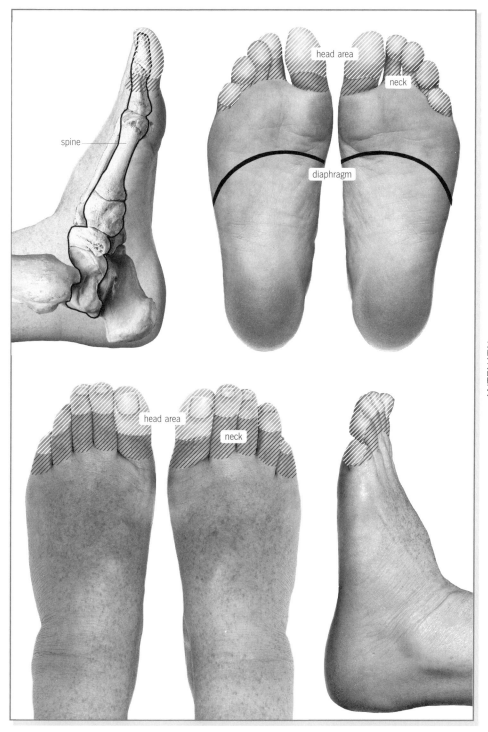

spine

head area

neck

diaphragm

head area

neck

antenatal
bleeding: vaginal

DURING PREGNANCY THERE SHOULD BE NO VAGINAL BLEEDING. IT IS IMPERATIVE THE CLIENT OBTAINS OBSTETRIC CARE.

see also "MISCARRIAGE" pp18 - 22 "LOW LYING PLACENTA" p84 AND "PLACENTAL SEPARATION" p98

DURING THE EARLY STAGES OF LABOUR THE CLIENT WILL HAVE A "SHOW" WHICH IS A PLUG OF BLOOD-STREAKED MUCOUS FROM THE CERVIX. THIS IS NORMAL, AND SHOULD BE REPORTED TO THE OBSTETRIC CARE-GIVER.

REFLEXOLOGY CONTRAINDICATED

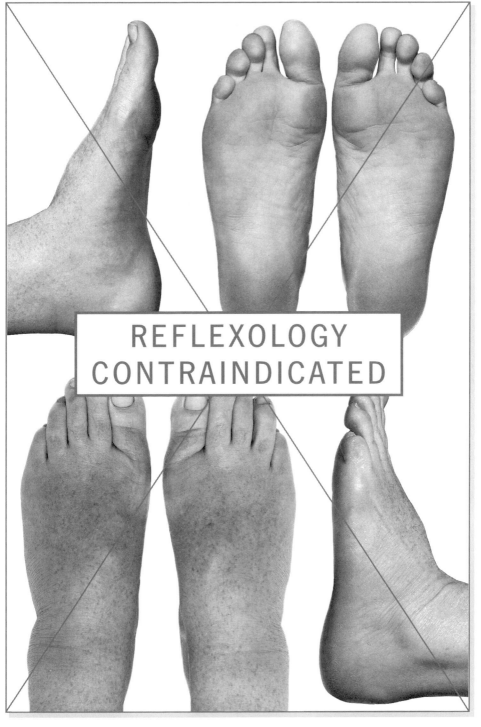

REFLEXOLOGY
CONTRAINDICATED

antenatal
blood pressure: high

Increased body weight, blood volume and cardiac output cause strain on the kidneys sometimes resulting in high blood pressure. Raised blood pressure in early pregnancy is usually due to a tendency towards hypertension regardless of being pregnant. Increased blood pressure in the second half of pregnancy is more likely to be caused by the pregnancy itself. This is referred to as "pregnancy induced hypertension" (PIH) when associated with either oedema or proteinuria. Mild PIH is usually treated with rest at home and more frequent checkups with the obstetric care-giver. Moderate PIH may require hospitalisation. Medical treatment includes regular blood pressure checks, urine tests for protein quantities, blood tests for creatinin levels and regular checks of the baby's heartbeat pattern. Medication has proven beneficial for some blood pressure problems. Mild PIH does not warrant early delivery of the baby. Moderate PIH that does not settle with hospitalisation may be treated by inducing labour near full term if the cervix is favourable or "ripe".

MILD AND MODERATE PIH REFLEXOLOGY WITH OBSTETRIC CARE-GIVER'S PERMISSION

reflection zone	technique	intent
kidneys	very gently bimanually sedate	to ease the tension
urinary system	urinary system flush	to keep the energy moving
endocrine system	endocrine balance	to balance the system
adrenals	very gently sedate	to relieve stress
solar plexus	bimanual thumb hold	to encourage life energy to flow
diaphragm	sedate	to ease out the tension
heart	gently sedate	to revive the spirit
lymphatic system	lymphatic drainage massage	to help remove toxins
chest, shoulders, spine	gentle relaxation techniques	to settle and relax

 Explain, reassure, chat... Women with PIH can feel hyperfit and very healthy, so sitting around on bedrest is extremely frustrating. Remind the client of the benefits of relaxation. Reflexology is an especially effective tool to help balance raised blood pressure.

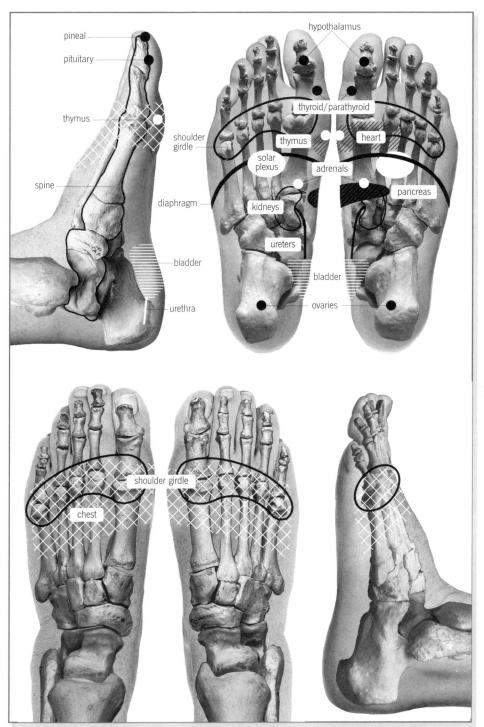

pineal
pituitary
thymus
spine
bladder
urethra

hypothalamus
thyroid/parathyroid
shoulder girdle
thymus
heart
solar plexus
adrenals
diaphragm
kidneys
pancreas
ureters
bladder
ovaries

shoulder girdle
chest

ANTENATAL

antenatal
blood pressure: low

Reduced peripheral resistance in the blood vessels caused by pregnancy hormones results in a lowered blood pressure (hypotension) during pregnancy. This is a normal occurrence with no physical signs of hypotension for the mother. Feelings of dizziness or weakness, which may be associated with hypotension, should not be presumed normal. Postural hypotension, with or without symptoms, occurs easily in the third trimester if the mother lies flat on her back. Pressure from the pregnant uterus on the large blood vessels (inferior vena cava) reduces venous return to the upper body, the consequences of which can be harmful to mother and baby.

NEVER COMMENCE A REFLEXOLOGY SESSION WITH A CLIENT IN THE THIRD TRIMESTER OF PREGNANCY WHERE SHE IS LYING FLAT, EVEN IF SHE SAYS THAT SHE IS COMFORTABLE.

reflection zone	technique	intent
solar plexus	bimanually gently stimulate	to strengthen creative energy flow
kidneys	stimulate gently	to increase vitality
endocrine system	endocrine balance	to balance the system
spine	spinal rub	to encourage energy flow

 Suggest to the client that when she lies down she uses pillows under one side of her body to tilt her. Alternatively use pillows under her shoulders and back to achieve a semi-recumbant position with good head and back support.

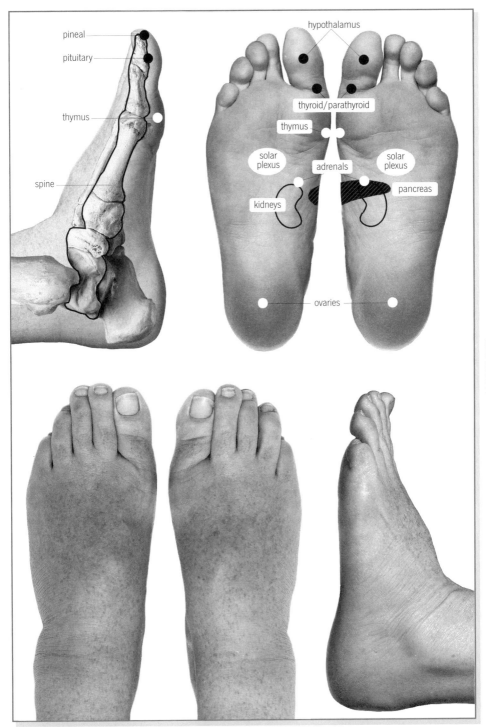

pineal

pituitary

thymus

spine

hypothalamus

thyroid/parathyroid

thymus

solar
plexus

adrenals

solar
plexus

pancreas

kidneys

ovaries

ANTENATAL

antenatal
blood pressure: normal

Slight blood pressure fluctuations may occur during pregnancy. The obstetric care-giver will monitor the blood pressure regularly to ensure it is within normal limits.

reflection zone	technique	intent
endocrine system	endocrine balance	to help the body adapt to the changing balance
kidneys	gently stimulate	to retain strength for the pregnancy
solar plexus	bimanual thumb hold	to keep the energy of procreation flowing freely
heart	gently stimulate	to keep the energy of love and joy flowing well
lymphatic system	lymphatic drainage massage	to ensure efficient removal of increased amount of cell debris

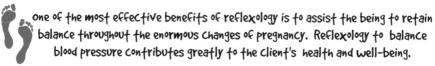

one of the most effective benefits of reflexology is to assist the being to retain balance throughout the enormous changes of pregnancy. Reflexology to balance blood pressure contributes greatly to the client's health and well-being.

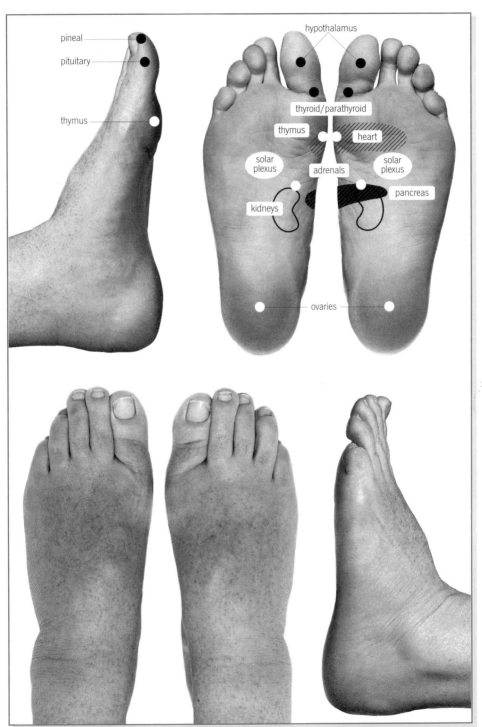

pineal
pituitary
thymus
hypothalamus
thyroid/parathyroid
thymus
heart
solar
plexus
adrenals
solar
plexus
pancreas
kidneys
ovaries

antenatal
blood pressure:
severe pregnancy induced
hypertension (PIH)
(pre-eclampsia/eclampsia/toxaemia)

Severe PIH requires hospitalisation. It probably will be treated with hypertensive drugs and may result in induction of labour, caesarean section and even premature delivery if the baby and/or mother are at risk.

REFLEXOLOGY CONTRAINDICATED

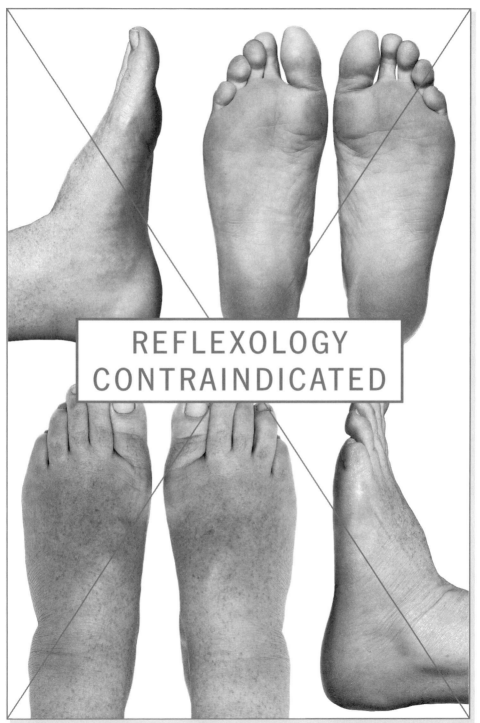

REFLEXOLOGY
CONTRAINDICATED

antenatal
breast changes

One of the first signs of pregnancy that a woman may notice is breast tenderness. A prickling/tingling sensation is often described by women in the first months of pregnancy. This increased level of sensation is often replaced by discomfort or pain at about 6 - 8 weeks gestation as the breasts enlarge, becoming quite tense. Montgomery's tubercles become more prominent and secrete sebum to keep the nipple soft and supple. Surface veins, nipple size and pigmentation all increase during the initial months of pregnancy. From 16 weeks gestation colostrum is produced and may be expressed, or leak from the nipple.

reflection zone	technique	intent
breast direct and indirect	general work out	to promote growth and change to encourage free flow of love energy
endocrine system	endocrine balance	to for easier adaptation to body changes

Remind the client to wear a supportive, comfortable bra while she is pregnant. Her bra should not "ride up" at the back, cut into the shoulders or allow the breast to bulge out of the cups. A formal fitting for a maternity bra at about 5 months of pregnancy is recommended by most obstetric care-givers. To prepare the nipples for breast feeding suggest that the client twiddles and rolls them between finger and thumb.

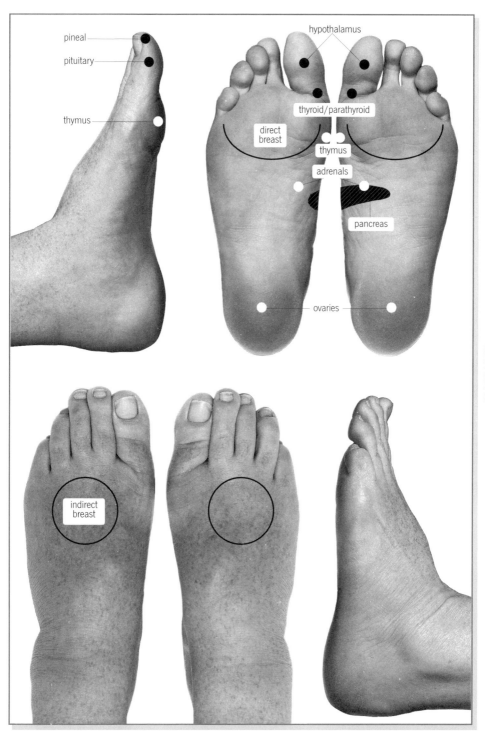

pineal
pituitary
thymus

hypothalamus

thyroid/parathyroid

direct breast
thymus
adrenals
pancreas

ovaries

indirect breast

antenatal
carpal tunnel syndrome

Numbness and/or pins and needles in the hands and fingers is caused by fluid retention in the tissues which in turn encroach on the carpal tunnel of the wrist. Oedematous tissues press on the median nerve making the hand and fingers weak and clumsy. This effect is especially debilitating in the mornings. Medical treatment includes raising the hands on 2 or 3 pillows and wearing wrist splints at night. Cortisone injections and/or diuretics may be prescribed although these treatment options are not usually favoured.

reflection zone	*technique*	*intent*
referral areas: other wrist and ankles	sedate	for pain relief
lymphatic system	lymphatic drainage massage	to lessen oedema
kidneys	if blood pressure is normal: gently stimulate bimanual urinary system flush	to promote kidney function to balance normal fluid levels to promote excretion of urine
solar plexus	light sedation	to ease anxiety

TLC++ and listening skills are essential as this condition is not only uncomfortable but also debilitating and frustrating.

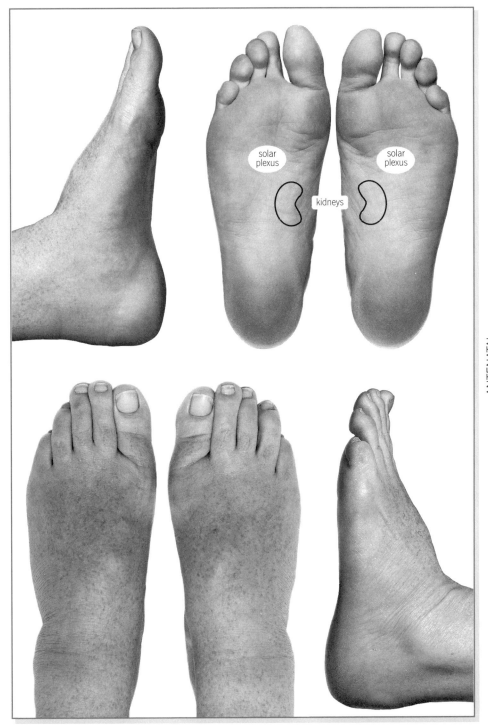

antenatal

constipation

During pregnancy constipation may be caused by hormonal changes, a different diet, fluid retention, pressure from baby on the bowel and most frequently - iron tablets.

reflection zone	technique	intent
STIMULATION OF PELVIC REFLEX ZONES CONTRAINDICATED		
large intestine excluding rectum	gently massage reflecting direction of flow	to improve activity of bowel
small intestine	gently stimulate	to assist digestion and absorption
liver and gall bladder	gently stimulate	to support digestion and absorption help release associated emotions
lower spine and hips	relaxation techniques N.B. ankle boogie very gently	to relax tensions

 Suggest that the client increases her dietary fibre and drinks water in preference to tea, coffee and cordials. It is helpful if she can have a regular time each day to have her bowels open.

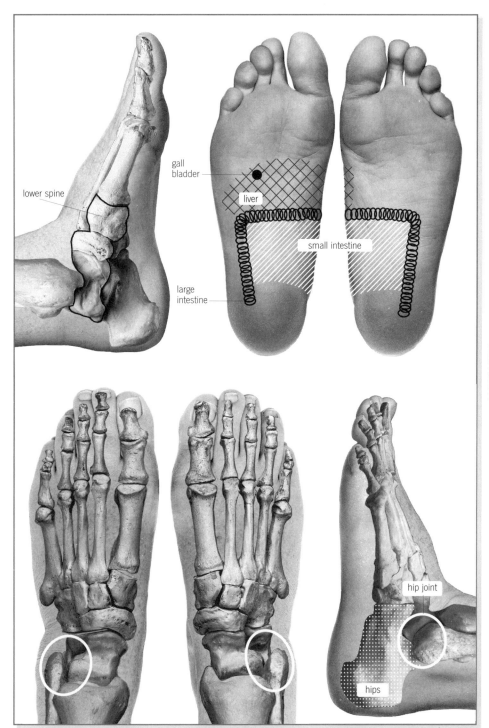

lower spine

gall
bladder

liver

small intestine

large
intestine

hip joint

hips

antenatal
cramps in legs

BE AWARE OF POSSIBLE DEEP VEIN THROMBOSIS

These are not uncommon during pregnancy. Many women will complain of cramps severe enough to wake them at night and prevent further sleep. Cramps are thought to be caused by changes in the pH balance or electrolytes, ischaemia or possibly calcium/salt intake. Medical advice includes, reviewing the diet, raising the foot of the bed approximately 25cms and during a cramp flexing the foot to stretch the affected muscle.

reflection zone	technique	intent
endocrine system	endocrine balance	to balance body chemistry
lymphatic system	lymphatic drainage massage	to promote cell health
solar plexus	bimanual sedation	to relieve anxiety

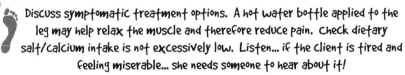

Discuss symptomatic treatment options. A hot water bottle applied to the leg may help relax the muscle and therefore reduce pain. Check dietary salt/calcium intake is not excessively low. Listen... if the client is tired and feeling miserable... she needs someone to hear about it!

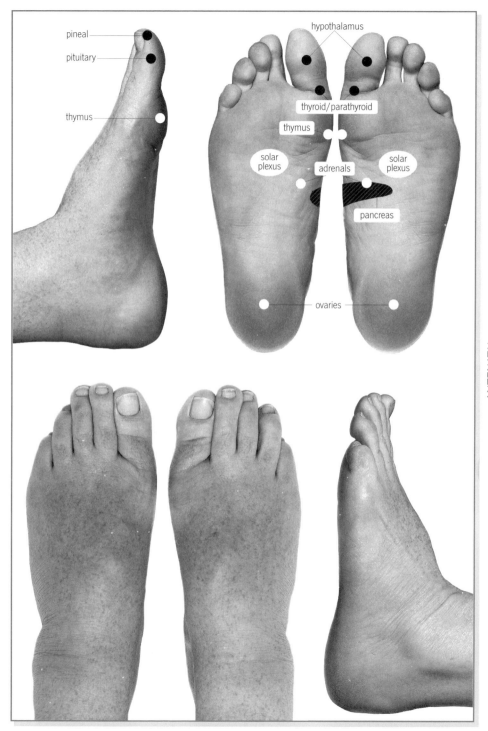

pineal

pituitary

thymus

hypothalamus

thyroid/parathyroid

thymus

solar
plexus

adrenals

solar
plexus

pancreas

ovaries

antenatal
deep vein thrombosis
(DVT)

Blood clots often occur after surgery or prolonged periods of immobilisation. They can also occur during pregnancy. The danger associated with clots in the large blood vessels (deep veins) may occur if a clot dislodges from the vein wall. The clot may float freely through the large vein until it reaches the small vessels of the heart causing an occlusion (complete blockage). This can be fatal. Typical signs of a DVT include sudden onset of leg pain, tenderness, redness, and increased skin temperature in the calf and/or thigh. The pain usually worsens when a muscle is flexed or when pressure is applied over the vein. Occasionally DVTs present without these classic signs and symptoms.

> # REFLEXOLOGY
> # CONTRAINDICATED

 Ensure the client has sought medical treatment.

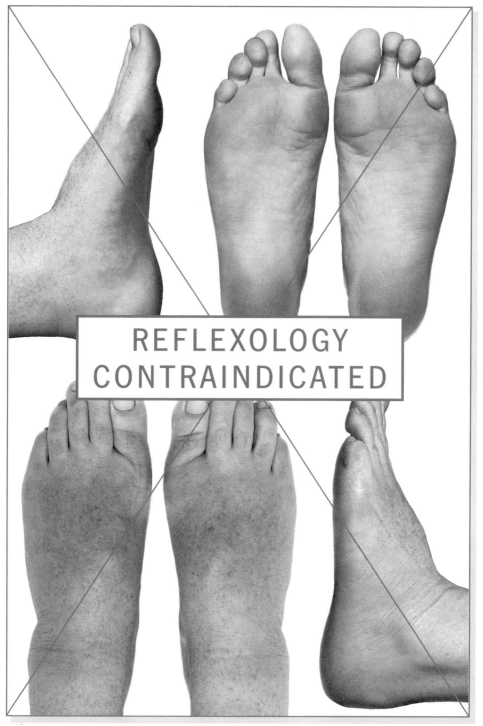

REFLEXOLOGY
CONTRAINDICATED

antenatal
diabetes: caused by pregnancy
(gestational diabetes)

During pregnancy a woman's carbohydrate metabolism changes in order to make glucose more readily available. More insulin is produced by the pancreas to cope with this glucose. These extra demands for insulin (sometimes 2 to 3 times more than when not pregnant) cannot always be met, resulting in sugar intolerance. This is known as gestational diabetes or pregnancy diabetes, effecting approximately 3% of pregnant women. Gestational diabetes is diagnosed with a glucose tolerance test. Most women produce sufficient insulin to metabolise their sugar intake but with the increased insulin demand at around 24 to 26 weeks gestation, some women develop diabetes. Once a woman is diagnosed with gestational diabetes her pregnancy will be monitored more closely, usually by an obstetrician in consultation with an endocrinologist. The aim of medical treatment is to maintain her blood sugar level within the normal range. This is usually achieved by excluding simple sugars and moderating her carbohydrate intake. Giving insulin by injection is unlikely but may be necessary if dietary measures are unsuccessful. Most women with gestational diabetes are taught to test their own blood sugar so that levels can be monitored 2 to 3 times a day at home or at work. Regular checkups with a doctor ensure that unstable blood sugar levels are noticed and treated early. If blood sugars are maintained at a normal level throughout pregnancy, labour and delivery will proceed as if there were no diabetes. If sugar levels are high or unstable the major risk for the mother is a large baby and the associated delivery difficulties. For the baby, large amounts of sugar from mother cease abruptly at birth leading to withdrawal symptoms from their sugar addiction. In extreme cases when untreated this form of hypoglycaemia can be fatal.

reflection zone	technique	intent
endocrine system	endocrine balance	to help the body adjust to changing hormone levels

Reassure the client. Educate where appropriate. Remind her that she is entitled to simple straightforward explanations and information from her doctor relating to health, pregnancy, labour and postnatal management. She may need to ask for this. The physical stress of pregnancy will show up physical weakness such as the woman's potential to blood sugar imbalance. It is interesting to note that the next major change of hormonal balance (excluding pregnancy) is menopause when diabetes may re-occur. It is helpful to suggest that now is an excellent time to modify the diet to support long term health.

54

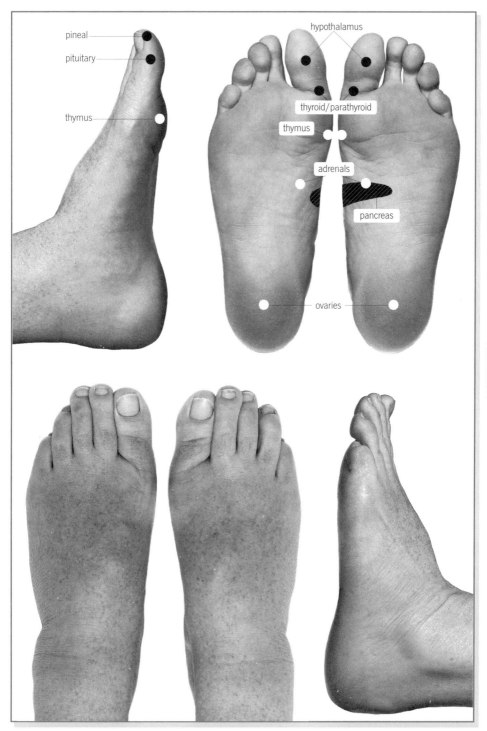

pineal

pituitary

thymus

hypothalamus

thyroid/parathyroid

thymus

adrenals

pancreas

ovaries

ANTENATAL

antenatal
diarrhoea

Diarrhoea can be dangerous during pregnancy for a number of reasons. An irritable bowel can in turn irritate the uterus causing contractions. Fever, a symptom commonly accompanying diarrhoea can also pre-empt premature labour. Dehydration poses a health threat for mother and baby.

Women approaching full term of their pregnancy sometimes report bouts of diarrhoea just prior to the onset of labour. If a woman is otherwise feeling very healthy, this diarrhoea is considered by many obstetric care-givers to be a natural clearing of the bowel prior to labour, a prodromal sign of the onset of labour.

reflection zone	technique	intent
large intestine	sedate	to calm the agitation
solar plexus	bimanual hold	to settle the being
small intestine	sedate	to restore balance

Encourage the client to be reviewed by her obstetric caregiver even if diarrhoea occurs at term. It is the obstetric caregiver's role, not the role of the reflexologist, to determine risk factors for mother's health.

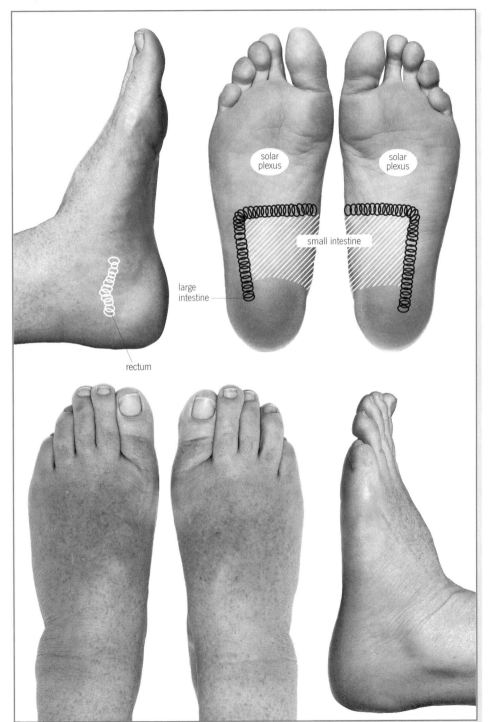

solar plexus

solar plexus

small intestine

large intestine

rectum

antenatal
dizzy spells & fainting

Some women experience feelings of dizziness and may feel faint during pregnancy which may be caused by the pregnancy itself. Occasionally dizzy spells and faintness may progress to episodes of fainting. The obstetric care-giver will determine the cause of these episodes and make appropriate management plans, if any, for the pregnancy. These episodes may be associated with low blood sugar levels, illness or hypotension.

reflection zone	technique	intent
spine	spinal runs	to clear the energy pathway up and down the spine
endocrine system especially pancreas	endocrine balance	to give energy to balance blood sugar levels
internal pelvis hypothalamus	linking	to restore balance

 Help the client to identify activities associated with dizzy spells and encourage her to modify or avoid those activities. Advise her to discuss this problem with her obstetric caregiver. Remind her to stop and rest if she begins to feel dizzy or faint.

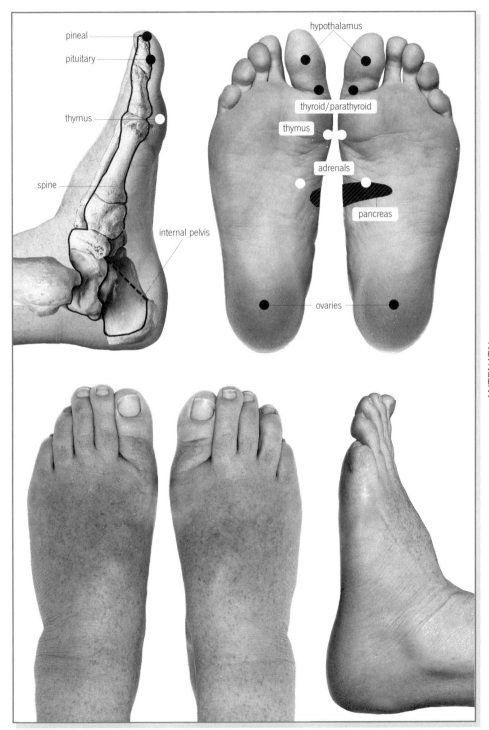

pineal

pituitary

thymus

spine

internal pelvis

hypothalamus

thyroid/parathyroid

thymus

adrenals

pancreas

ovaries

antenatal
dreams & fantasies

Most women report an increased number of dreams and fantasies during pregnancy. With so many changes occurring, this is not surprising. Dreams can be acknowledged as a way of letting subconscious issues rise to the conscious mind. Common themes tend to revolve around motherhood (eg cuddling, feeding and playing with baby), water (eg fish, swimming, ocean), mortality and morbidity of self, partner, baby (eg baby being born deformed, as a monster, miscarriage). Water themes probably relate to the fluidity of life and emotions, while the more morbid themes probably help a woman to realise how precious her family is to her, how vulnerable they are and how attached she is already to her yet to be born baby.

reflection zone	technique	intent
head "sense of self"	linking technique	to honour the dreams and fantasies and accept them as another form of communication

 Reassure the client that dreams and fantasies are a common occurrence and have a purpose. Help her to investigate their purpose ie specific fears, concerns, issues which need to be dealt with. If she becomes obsessed with her dreams, believing them to be premonitions of disaster, suggest that she speaks to her obstetric care-giver or a counsellor about this obsession.

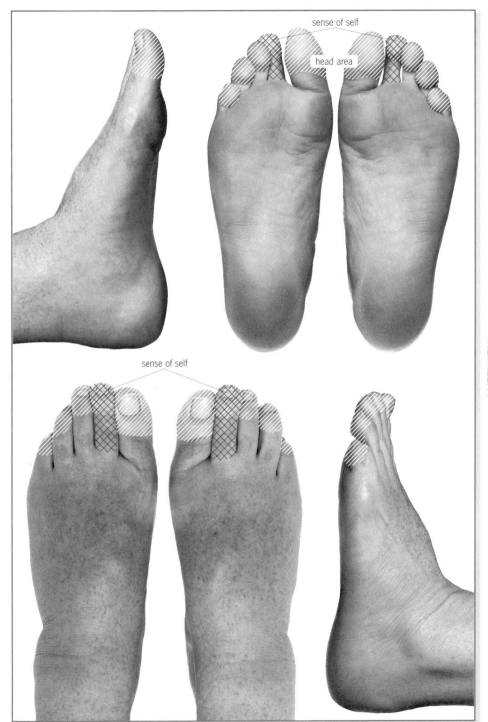

sense of self

head area

sense of self

antenatal
fatigue

The fatigue of early pregnancy often comes as a great surprise to the client. The body seems to need sleep while it is adjusting to its changing hormones and different status. During the last few weeks of pregnancy sleep disturbance, increased weight and day to day activities can be very tiring.

reflection zone	*technique*	*intent*
endocrine system especially pancreas and adrenals	endocrine balance	to balance the being to the rapidly changing hormone levels
spleen	gently stimulate	to encourage the production of red blood cells
solar plexus	gently stimulate	to support the extra demand on life energy
head	Brazilian toe balance	to equalise energies in the longitudinal zones
balance organ	linking technique to hypothalamus	to balance blood pressure

 Discuss the client's lifestyle with her. If she is trying to do too much each day there may be some activities which can be omitted or delegated to others to allow time for more rest. Reassure her that fatigue is a normal reaction to pregnancy.

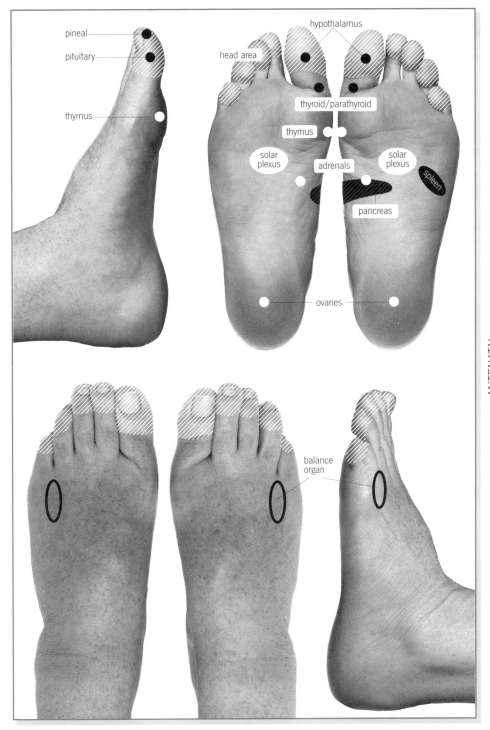

pineal

pituitary

thymus

hypothalamus

head area

thyroid/parathyroid

thymus

solar
plexus

adrenals

solar
plexus

spleen

pancreas

ovaries

balance
organ

antenatal
fluid retention (oedema)
associated with raised blood pressure

Pregnancy Induced Hypertension (PIH) previously known as Pre-Eclampsia is diagnosed when two of the following three symptoms are present: raised blood pressure, oedema, protein in the urine (proteinuria). Danger signs include frontal headaches, blurred vision, heartburn-like sensations. If untreated, PIH can develop into fulminating eclampsia (toxaemia) which is life threatening to both mother and baby. A client with oedema associated with PIH will be in the care of an obstetrician and if not admitted to hospital will be advised to rest in bed at home.

REFLEXOLOGY WITH OBSTETRIC CARE-GIVER'S PERMISSION

reflection zone	technique	intent
lymphatic system	lymphatic drainage massage	to persuade the body to remove excess fluid
kidney/ureter tubes/ bladder/urethra	extremely gentle urinary system flush	to persuade the body to excrete the extra fluid
solar plexus	healing hold	to allow procreative energy to balance

 Lymphatic drainage massage using the foot reflex zones is especially effective for clients with oedema. It may be used as an entire reflexology session to the exclusion of other reflexology techniques. Encourage the client to rest as advised. Women with PIH usually feel very well, which makes rest frustrating.

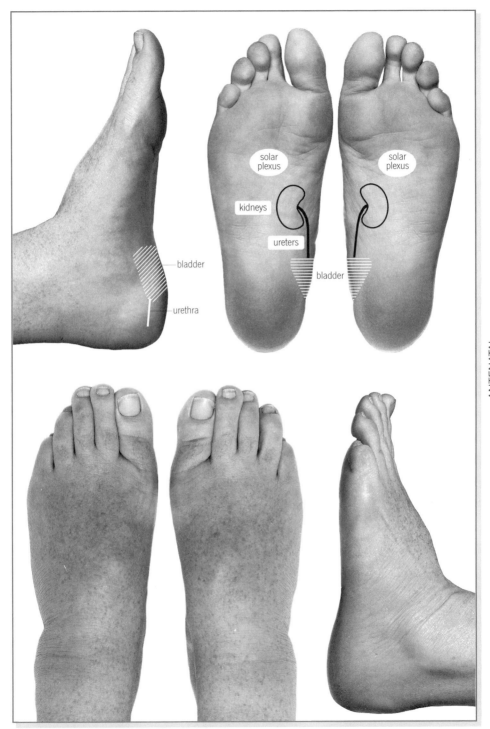

solar
plexus

solar
plexus

kidneys

ureters

bladder

bladder

urethra

antenatal
fluid retention (oedema)
associated with fulminating eclampsia

Oedema, hypertension and proteinuria are three symptoms of pregnancy induced hypertension (PIH), also known as pre-eclampsia and toxaemia. Danger signs include frontal headaches, blurred vision, heartburn-like sensations. If untreated PIH can develop into fulminating eclampsia which is life threatening to both mother and baby. A client with oedema associated with PIH will be in the care of an obstetrician and in hospital.

THIS IS AN OBSTETRIC EMERGENCY

REFLEXOLOGY CONTRAINDICATED

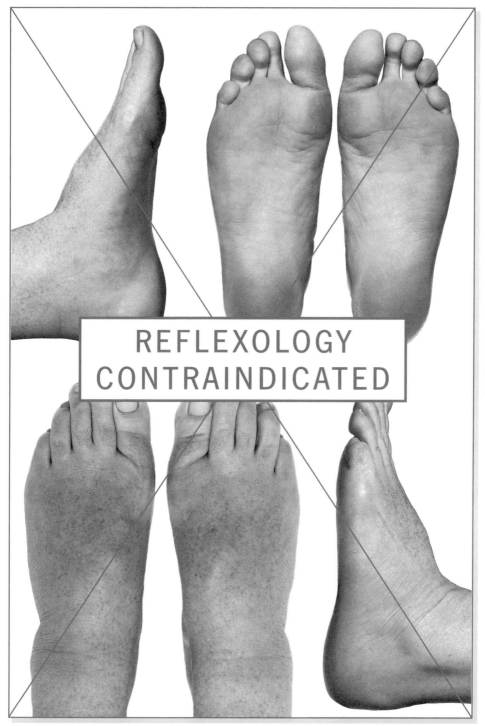

REFLEXOLOGY
CONTRAINDICATED

antenatal
fluid retention
(physiological oedema)

During pregnancy many cells retain a small amount of extra fluid. This is the body's normal response. It is necessary and beneficial and is recognised as part of the "glow" of good health in pregnancy. The amount of retained interstitial fluid increases throughout pregnancy. Physiological oedema of the lower legs is posture-aggravated and worsened with hot weather. Medical advice usually involves maintaining good posture, avoiding prolonged periods of standing and constrictive clothing (eg knee-high stockings), and increasing oral fluid intake as this has a natural diuretic action.

reflection zone	*technique*	*intent*
lymphatic system	lymphatic drainage massage	to retain cell health and nutrition to keep emotions balanced
urinary system	bimanual urinary system flush	to maintain fluid movement

 There is a very fine line between physiological oedema and oedema as an early sign of pre-eclampsia. If the client's rings become too tight on her fingers advise her to take them off and keep them off for the remainder of the pregnancy. Her obstetric caregiver will note this change. Reflexology is an excellent therapy to maintain the fine interstitial fluid balance.

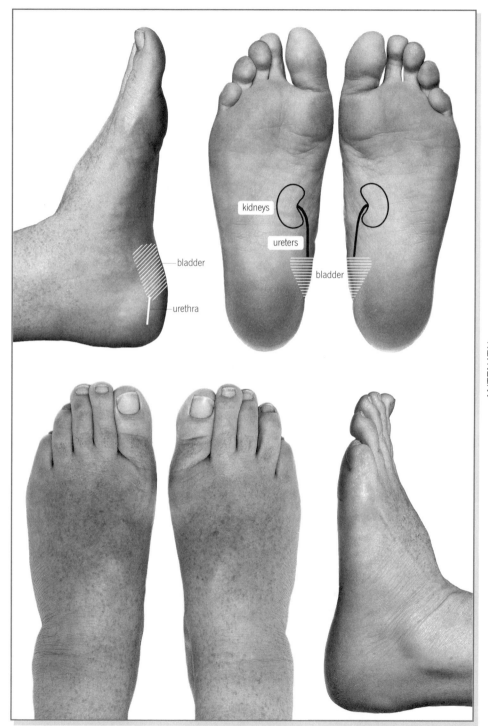

bladder
urethra
kidneys
ureters
bladder

antenatal
groin pain, ligament pain

During pregnancy the uterus expands stretching the ligaments. Rapid growth particularly in the last 2-3 months of pregnancy results in ligament pain especially at the ligament insertion points. The round ligament is notorious for causing concern as the pain associated with its stretching is felt as a sharp vaginal/groin pain.

reflection zone	*technique*	*intent*
groin	bimanually sedate at the epicentre of the reflected pain	to release trapped energies
lower spine	gentle spinal twist	to lessen the tension and increase mobility
hips	gentle ankle boogie	to lessen tension
abdomen	relaxation techniques especially thumb windscreen wiper movements	to relax and allow the ligaments to stretch
solar plexus	bimanual thumb hold	to relieve anxiety

Suggest that your client sees her obstetric caregiver about EVERY abdominal pain. Once the pain has been diagnosed as ligament pain, reflexology may proceed with the obstetric care-giver's permission. Ligament pain is yet another discomfort of pregnancy as your client's body adapts to accommodate her baby. As with other discomforts listen if she needs to off load disappointment or other emotions relating to her expectations of pregnancy.

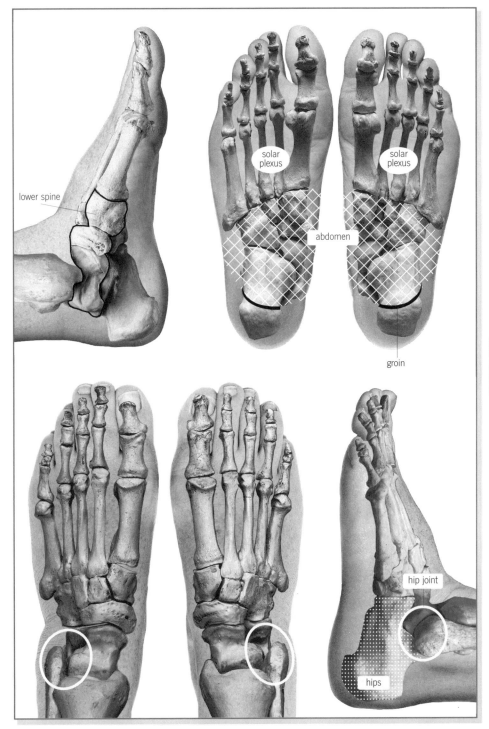

lower spine

solar plexus

solar plexus

abdomen

groin

hip joint

hips

antenatal headaches

Changes in the hormones and the circulatory system cause an increased incidence of tension headaches during pregnancy, especially in the first trimester. In warm weather severe headaches may occur. Headaches may be related to medical conditions eg high blood pressure and therefore a medical consultation is advisable before assuming the headaches to be innocent.

reflection zone	technique	intent
head	toe rotations and stretches	to relax head tension
spine	gentle spinal twist spine runs up and down	to relax back tension to clear energy flow
diaphragm	sedate and rotate onto thumb	to release emotional energy

 Suggest that the client wears cool loose clothing and takes time out to relax. Whenever possible avoid stress, rushing about and feeling hassled.

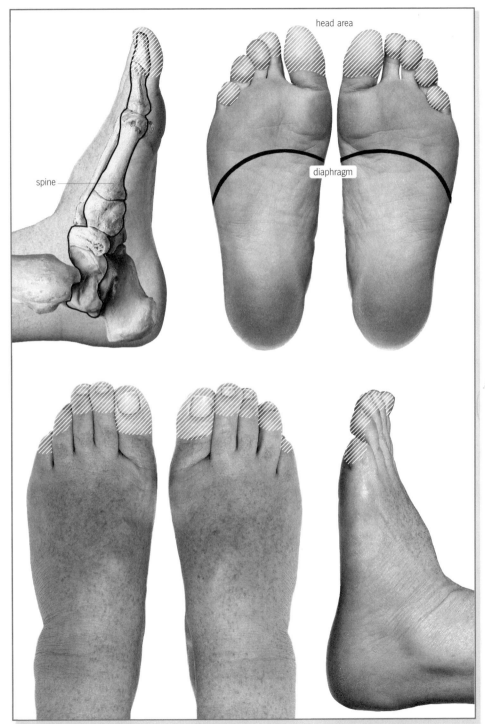

spine

head area

diaphragm

antenatal
headaches
specific headaches

reflection zone	technique	intent
MIGRAINE • temple • head/coccyx	• sedation grip • linking technique	• to ease pain and release tension • to re-establish energy flow
BACK OF HEAD • kidney/ureter tubes/bladder/urethra • lymphatic system	• bimanual urinary system flush • lymphatic drainage massage	• to clear the energies of the urinary system • to help clear toxins from the cells
SIDE OF HEAD • gallbladder	• stimulate	• to clear gallbladder energies
FOREHEAD • stomach	• normalise ie stimulate or sedate as required	• to clear stomach energies
CENTRE OF HEAD • liver	• stimulate	• to clear liver energies

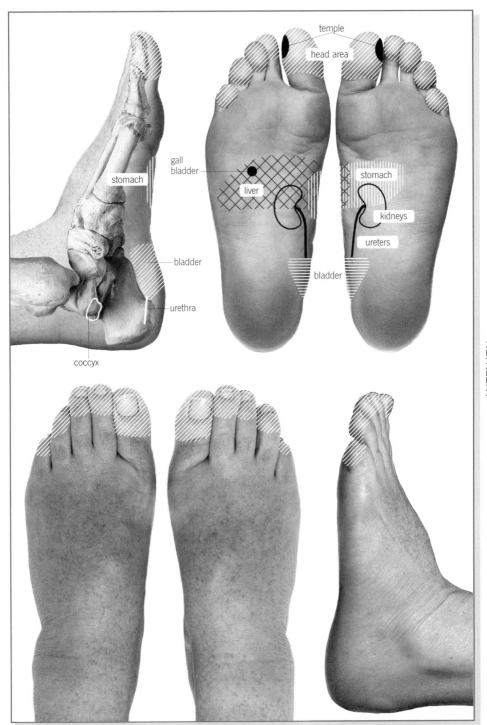

temple
head area
gall
bladder
liver
stomach
kidneys
ureters
stomach
bladder
urethra
coccyx
bladder

antenatal
heartburn

During pregnancy the muscle at the lower end of the oesophagus (gullet) relaxes slightly allowing stomach acid to rise into the oesophagus. The burning affect of the acid which can cause inflammation of the oesophagus is known as heartburn. Early and late pregnancy are the most common times to experience heartburn.

reflection zone	*technique*	*intent*
stomach	sedate	to help prevent over activity
solar plexus	bimanual thumb hold	to calm and relieve anxiety
oesophagus	sedate	to relieve pain

 Recommend to the client that she eats smaller more frequent meals and avoids fatty, spicy or "windy" food which may aggravate the condition. A drink of milk will reduce stomach acidity thereby relieving symptoms. An upright posture after meals will also help.

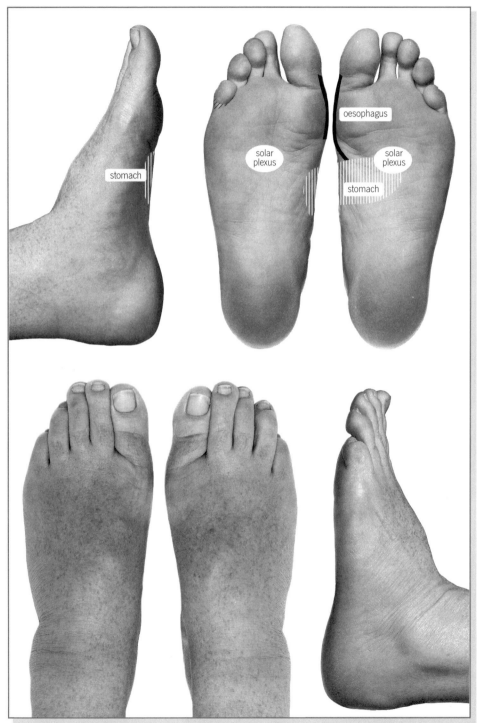

antenatal

itchiness
bottom (vulva & anus)

Itchiness of the bottom is distressing but not uncommon during pregnancy. Itchiness of the vulva is a symptom of thrush (see page 126) and other treatable vaginal conditions. Anal itching may be caused by haemorrhoids (see page 96) or worms.

reflection zone	technique	intent
solar plexus	bimanual thumb hold	to calm agitation
internal pelvis/hip	linking technique	to balance pelvis yin/yang energies
adrenals	stimulate	to stimulate anti-inflammatory hormones if there is an infection
lymphatic system especially pelvic lymphatics	lymphatic drainage massage	to encourage cell health and remove toxins
lower spine	relaxation techniques gentle spinal twist gentle ankle boogie	to encourage calm and reduce itchiness

 Discuss symptoms with client and suggest medical consultation for diagnosis and treatment of all but mild localised itches.

78

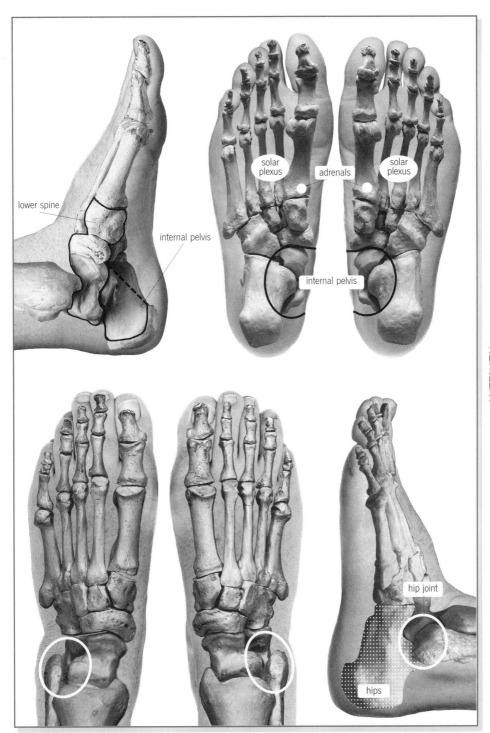

lower spine

internal pelvis

solar plexus

adrenals

solar plexus

internal pelvis

hip joint

hips

antenatal
itchiness
skin

Itchiness is distressing but not uncommon during pregnancy. Confined to the skin of the belly and hips and/or breasts itchiness occurs at times of rapid growth eg late pregnancy. It often precedes the appearance of stretch marks. Severe itching over the entire body is due to an accumulation of bile salts and requires medical advice.

reflection zone	technique	intent
endocrine system	endocrine balance	to try to prevent stretch marks
lymphatic system	lymphatic drainage massage	to help prevent accumulation of bile salts

Discuss symptoms with client and suggest medical consultation for diagnosis and treatment of all but mild localised itches.

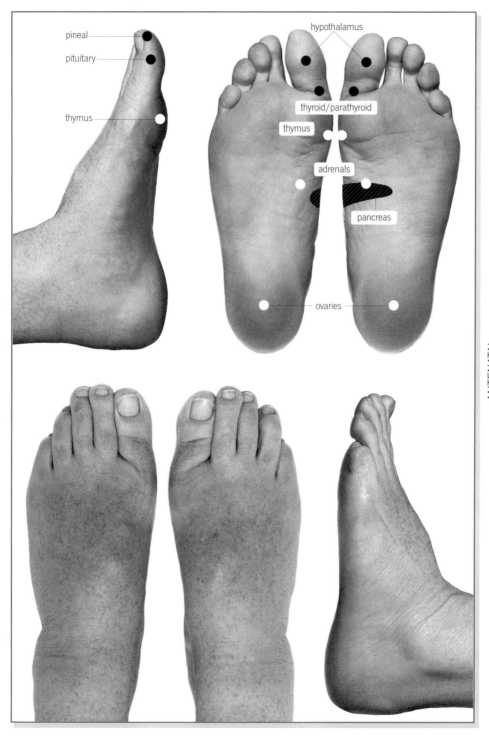

antenatal
labour

The management of normal labour is skilled specialised work for midwives. As a "support person" the reflexologist can offer the benefits of reflexology when appropriate and must be guided by the midwife. Many women prefer to be mobile whilst labouring and many do not liked to be touched, which makes "doing" the feet impossible. However, the relaxation techniques of reflexology are very effective during the first stage of labour.

BETWEEN CONTRACTIONS

reflection zone	*technique*	*intent*
entire body	relaxation techniques: fish movement spinal twist ankle boogie	to relax the shoulder girdle to keep the spine relaxed to relax pelvis and hips
solar plexus	bimanual thumb hold	to help stay centred and relieve anxiety help control fear
lungs/chest	lung press	to normalise breathing
diaphragm	pivot onto thumb the width of the diaphragm	to help control many emotions
coping point	bimanual thumb/finger lightly pinch	to help 'cope' with labour

DURING CONTRACTIONS

solar plexus	bimanual press/relax	to create a rocking rhythm
lung /chest	lung press in time with controlled breathing	to create a calm balanced breathing rate

 Inform the correct authorities of the client's request to have a "support person" attend her labour. Be prepared for an unknown length of labour, any time day or night, within two weeks either side of E.D.D. Take snacks and refresher wipes for yourself.

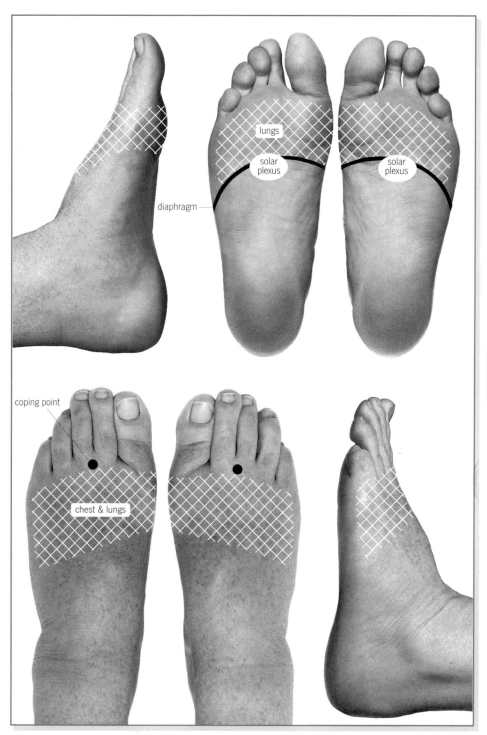

lungs

solar
plexus

solar
plexus

diaphragm

coping point

chest & lungs

antenatal

low lying placenta
(placenta praevia)

The most likely cause of painless bleeding during pregnancy is placenta praevia. Placenta praevia or low lying placenta is usually diagnosed by ultra sound either during a routine scan in the second trimester of pregnancy or after an episode of bleeding in the second half of pregnancy. Placenta praevia is classified into grades 1, 2, 3 and 4 depending on how low the placenta is lying. Grades 1 and 2 with the placenta lying in the lower uterine segment but not covering the cervical opening require hospitalisation only if bleeding occurs.

GENERAL REFLEXOLOGY WITH OBSTETRIC CARE-GIVER'S PERMISSION

Grades 3 and 4 with the cervical opening partially or completely covered by the placenta needs close observation in hospital during the last trimester of pregnancy. Sudden haemmorhage can occur with these grades of placenta praevia as the placenta does not grow as rapidly as the lower segment of the uterus.

REFLEXOLOGY CONTRAINDICATED

Explain in simple terms if the doctor has not already done so. Reiterate his/her explanation. TLC +++. Bleeding or the chance of it during pregnancy is always anxiety provoking.

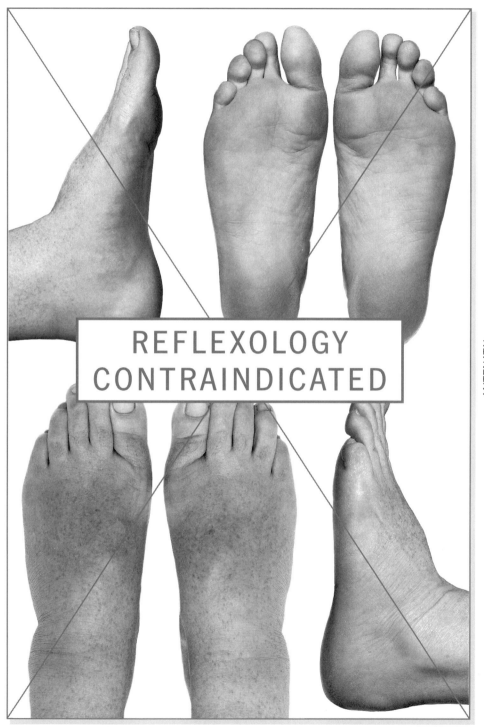

REFLEXOLOGY
CONTRAINDICATED

antenatal
mood swings

Scientific and medical facts have replaced myth and rituals leaving many women of today with the concept that reproduction should not affect her usual coping style and therefore should not disrupt her usual routine. Our society seems to have overlooked the fact that reproduction is a miracle. During this special time the pregnant woman needs to be nurtured and cherished. Lethargy and mood swings may be caused by hormone changes but they also provide reminders of the effort her body is making to ensure optimum conditions for the development of her baby. Partners, family and friends need to keep this in mind while providing a nurturing and supportive environment for mother and baby. The pregnant woman also needs to remember this and not feel guilty or inadequate if she does not maintain her old lifestyle as well as nurturing her baby. Vagueness during pregnancy may well be nature's way of preparing her for the unpredictability of parenting.

reflection zone	technique	intent
solar plexus	bimanual hold	to centre and calm to allow the energy of creation to flow
endocrine system	endocrine balance	to help adjust to the huge changes of pregnancy
balance organ "sense of self"	linking technique	to restore sense of self

 Use listening skills. Listen with "heart" accepting all that is said without judgement or comment.

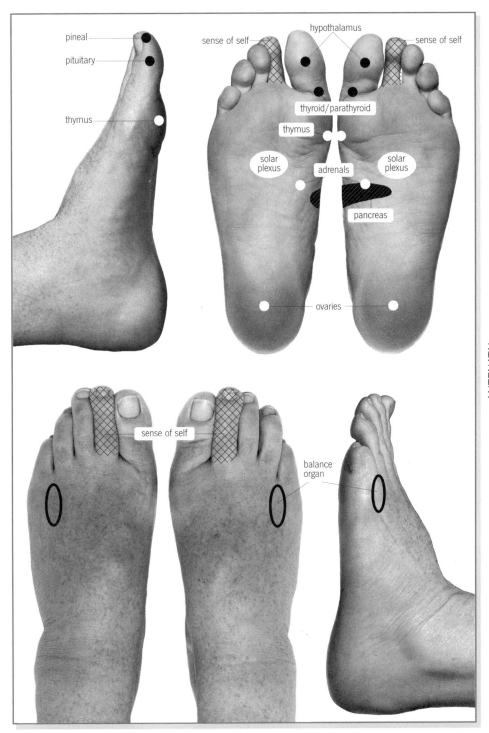

pineal

pituitary

thymus

hypothalamus

sense of self

sense of self

thyroid/parathyroid

thymus

solar
plexus

adrenals

solar
plexus

pancreas

ovaries

sense of self

balance
organ

antenatal
morning sickness

Pregnancy hormones are believed to be responsible for morning sickness. The most common period of morning sickness is experienced between 6 and 16 weeks gestation, although for some women it may persist into the third trimester. Symptoms range from mild nausea to sudden vomiting, occurring at any time of the day or night and can worsen with an empty stomach. The senses already heightened by the pregnancy can be aggravated by various tastes and smells. Severe or persistent vomiting must be treated by the obstetric care-giver.

reflection zone	technique	intent
stomach	sedate	to settle the stomach and allay the "I'm sick of it" feeling
endocrine system	endocrine balance	to help 'cope' with changing hormone balance
pancreas	gentle stimulation	to improve the "sweetness of life" and balance blood sugar levels

 Suggest that the client nibbles on healthy foods little and often. Whilst nutrition is important, if the client is not keeping healthy food down, anything she wants to eat is ok for the time being.

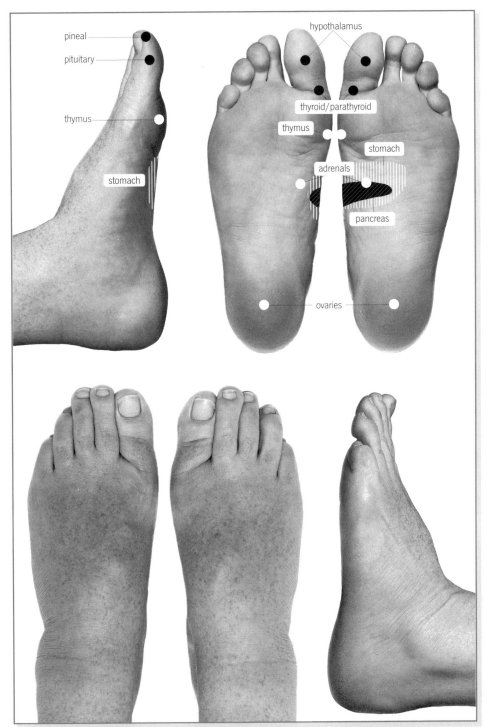

pineal

pituitary

thymus

stomach

hypothalamus

thyroid/parathyroid

thymus

stomach

adrenals

pancreas

ovaries

antenatal
nose bleeds

Pregnancy hormones relax blood vessel walls and increase the blood volume circulating within the body. Nose bleeds are common during pregnancy due to the weakening of the blood vessels and increased blood supply to the nose.

REFLEXOLOGY 1ST AID

reflection zone	*technique*	*intent*
nose reflex	sedation grip	to stop the bleeding

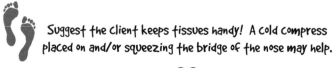

Suggest the client keeps tissues handy! A cold compress placed on and/or squeezing the bridge of the nose may help.

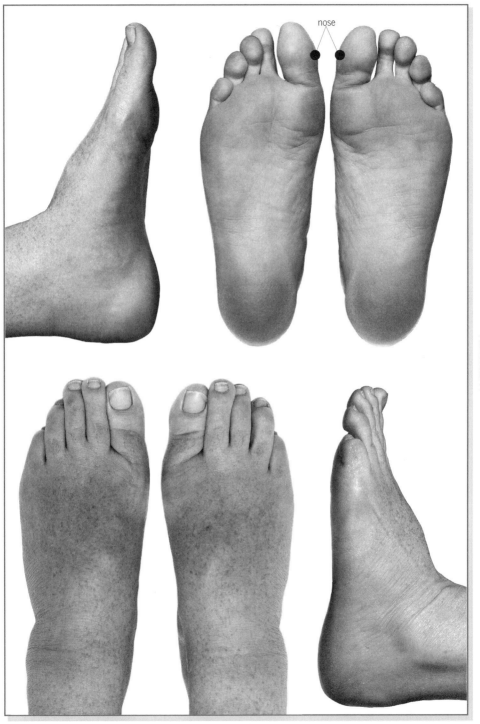

nose

antenatal
palpitations

Some women experience palpitations and feel a pounding pulse due to the increase in blood volume and cardiac output associated with pregnancy. This is known as physiological hypervolaemia. This is normal.

reflection zone	technique	intent
solar plexus	bimanual thumb hold	to decrease anxiety
heart balance organ	linking technique	to regain equilibrium
lymphatic system	lymphatic drainage massage	to help cope with hypervolaemia

Encourage the client to consult her obstetric caregiver for a diagnosis. Once the condition is diagnosed as physiological hypervolaemia reassure her that this is normal.

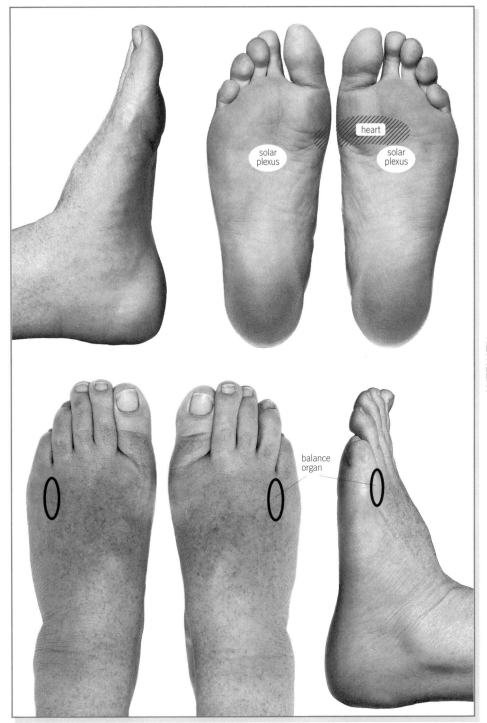

solar
plexus

heart

solar
plexus

balance
organ

antenatal
panic attacks & hyperventilation

While she is pregnant a woman is more likely to experience panic attacks. Hyperventilation is a pattern of frequent rapid breaths resulting in dizziness, fainting, and/or blackouts due to high blood oxygen concentrations. This breathing pattern often accompanies a panic attack or emotional upset, sometimes occurring in labour.

reflection zone	technique	intent
solar plexus	bimanual thumb hold	to calm and settle
shoulder girdle	relaxation techniques: fish movement metatarsal kneading	to ease tension
lungs	relaxation techniques: lung press	to regulate respiration rate

Recognise rising anxiety levels and reassure and calm the client.
If hyperventilation starts encourage the client to take slower breaths and re-breathe exhaled breath by cupping her hands over her nose and mouth.

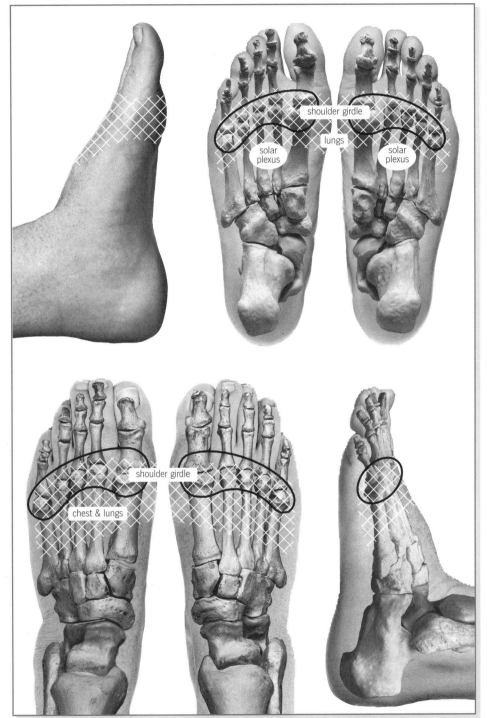

shoulder girdle

lungs

solar plexus

solar plexus

shoulder girdle

chest & lungs

antenatal

piles
(haemorrhoids)

Piles, also known as haemorrhoids, are variscosities of the anal canal. They may be internal or external and are usually first noticed by the client as small lumps at the anal orifice. They may be itchy or bleed slightly. Medical treatment includes avoiding constipation. Haemorrhoidal creams or suppositories may be used to relieve the itch, inflammation and irritation.

reflection zone	technique	intent
lymphatic system	lymphatic drainage massage	to encourage good tone of the system
hips / pelvis	very gentle ankle boogie ankle rotations	to relax the area

Many clients feel more uncomfortable discussing this area than their reproductive regions. Be polite but straightforward when discussing "occult" body bits, as this should relieve the client's distress and allow you to offer information and advice. Ask client about bowel habits. Remind her to increase her fluid and fibrous food intake. Regular gentle exercise and allowing plenty of time to visit the toilet, possibly with relaxation exercises while there, also helps to relieve constipation. A small stool or stack of phone books on either side of the toilet bowl allow a squatting position to be adopted while sitting on the toilet. This posture will help with defecation but may aggravate already severe haemorrhoids.

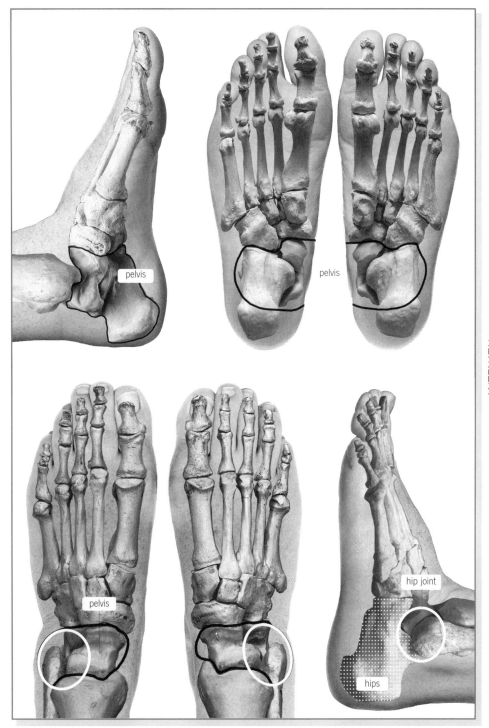

pelvis

pelvis

pelvis

hip joint

hips

antenatal
placental separation
(placental abruption)

The most acute condition that includes vaginal bleeding with associated abdominal pain is a placental abruption, also known as abruptio placenta. In this condition the placenta separates from the wall of the uterus. This most often occurs with major trauma (eg car accident, falling off a horse etc) or with fulminating eclampsia. Blood becomes trapped between the placenta and uterine wall, therefore the amount of vaginal bleeding is not indicative of the degree of placental separation. Pain is a better indicator of separation. Pregnancy may continue to term if a small abruption resolves quickly without damage to mother or baby. Moderate and severe abruptions are obstetric emergencies and must be treated promptly to ensure mother's health. The pregnancy is not likely to continue to a full term delivery of a healthy infant.

REFLEXOLOGY CONTRAINDICATED

Explain in simple terms if the doctor has not already done so. Reiterate his explanation. TLC +++ . Bleeding or the chance of it during pregnancy is always anxiety provoking.

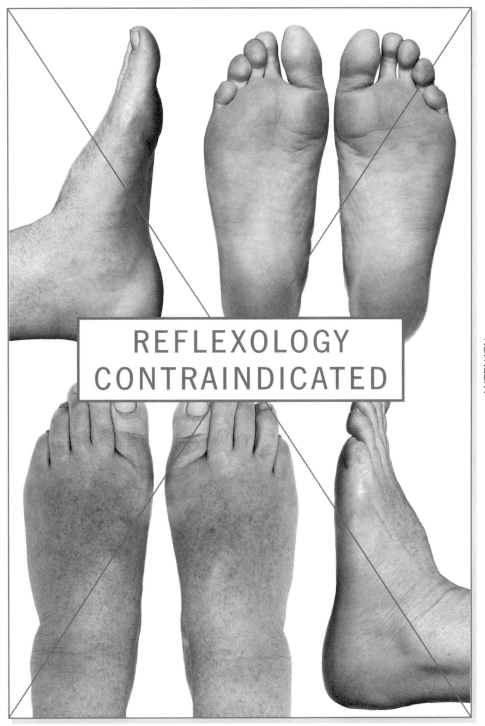

REFLEXOLOGY
CONTRAINDICATED

post maturity &
induction of labour

Providing mother and baby are well and healthy, normal pregnancy can continue up to two weeks beyond the estimated date of delivery (EDD) ie up to forty two weeks of pregnancy. After that time an induction of labour may be considered. There are situations when labour needs to be "brought on" or "induced" in the interest of the health of either mother or baby. Induction of labour may involve a single method or a combination of methods.

INDUCTION OF LABOUR IS NOT A DECISION TO BE MADE BY A REFLEXOLOGY THERAPIST.

If induction of labour is being contemplated
REFLEXOLOGY MAY BE USED WITH OBSTETRIC CARE-GIVER'S PERMISSION.

reflection zone	*technique*	*intent*
hypothalamus	stimulate strongly hook and back up	if possible there will be stimulation - integration - response
pituitary	stimulate strongly hook and back up	to set the body messengers in action
large intestine especially rectum	stimulate strongly	to encourage pelvic outflow action
internal pelvic zones	stimulate strongly	to work up some action
hips and pelvis	vigorous ankle boogie	to shake things up

Natural methods of inducing labour include gentle nipple stimulation (twiddling, rolling, pulling, sucking) to produce oxytocin, and/or sexual intercourse which deposits prostaglandin (a component of semen) at the cervix. These actions will not bring on labour if the client's body is not almost ready to labour spontaneously.

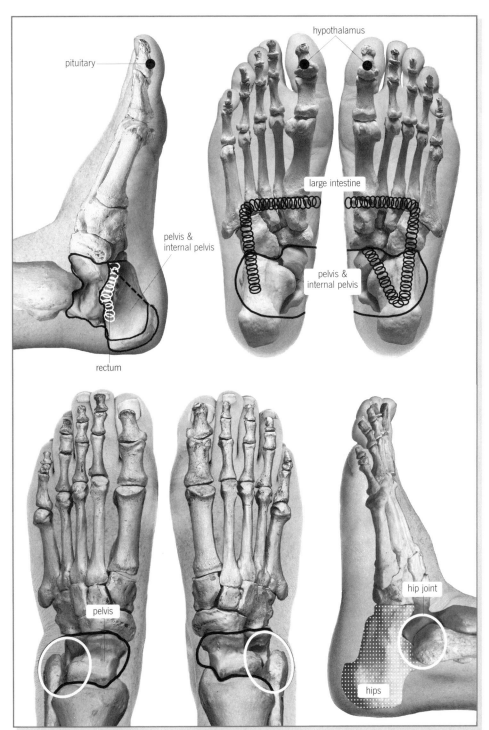

antenatal

pre-term labour:
after 34 weeks gestation

Pregnancy is calculated as 40 weeks from the first day of the last menstrual period (LMP). As much as 2 weeks variation on the expected date of delivery (EDD) is considered normal or "full term". Labour prior to 37 weeks gestation is considered to be premature or "preterm". Medical treatment depends on how premature the labour is as well as the condition of mother and baby. Treatment usually aims at suppressing labour. If labour cannot be suppressed steroid medications may be given to the mother to help mature the baby's lungs. Babies born before 36 weeks gestation are likely to have immature lungs and an immature sucking reflex and consequently will require nursing in a special care nursery.

REFLEXOLOGY ONLY WITH OBSTETRIC CARE GIVER'S PERMISSION

reflection zone	technique	intent
solar plexus	bimanual thumb hold	to attain centering
shoulder girdle spine pelvis	extremely gentle relaxation techniques	to relax the whole being

 These deceptively simple relaxation techniques can be most affective. Expect to use them many times for several days until mother and baby are settled. Give TLC and reassurance. Although an unexpected and unwanted outcome, preterm babies generally do very well.

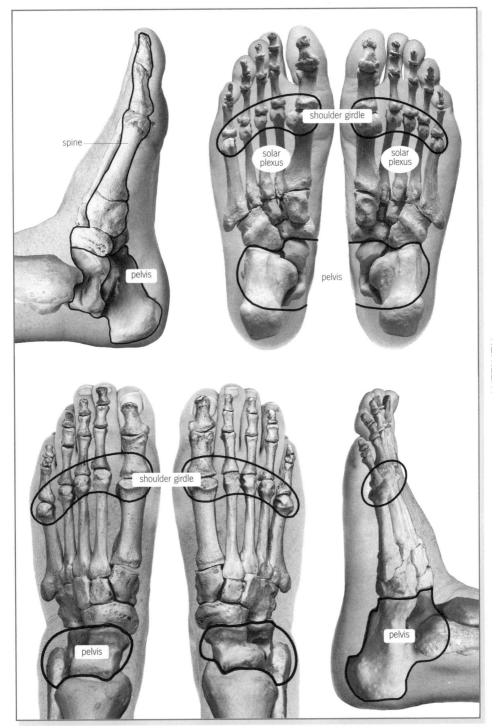

spine

shoulder girdle

solar plexus

solar plexus

pelvis

pelvis

shoulder girdle

pelvis

pelvis

ANTENATAL

antenatal
pre-term labour:
before 34 weeks gestation

Ideal conditions for delivery of the baby is in a hospital with neo-natal intensive care facilities, therefore transfer to another hospital may be necessary. The higher the birth weight of the pre-term baby, the higher the survival rate.

REFLEXOLOGY
CONTRAINDICATED

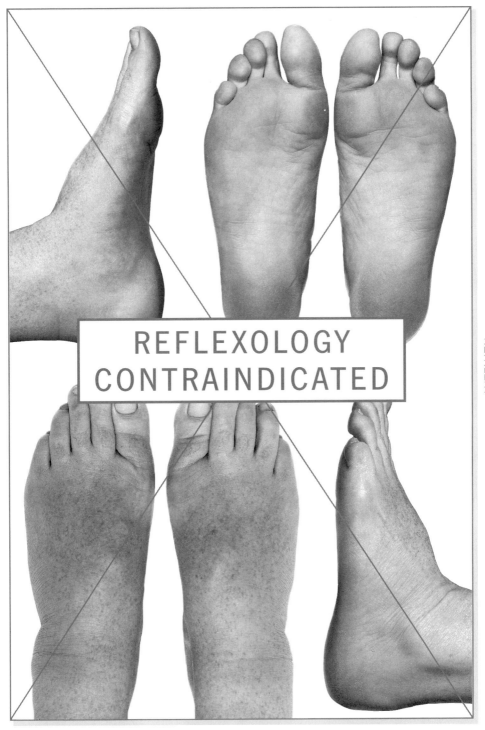

REFLEXOLOGY
CONTRAINDICATED

antenatal
rib pain

Constant dull localised aches in the rib area late in pregnancy are often due to the relaxation and widening of the rib cage. This is a normal process during pregnancy to allow more space for the growing baby. Breech presentation babies cause more rib pain than cephalic presentation babies (baby's bottom pressed against the ribs is harder than the head).

reflection zone	technique	intent
shoulder girdle	relaxation techniques: fish movement gentle 'flip flops'	to ease the tension
diaphragm	rotate onto thumb	to ease emotional stress
lungs	lung press	to re-establish balanced respirations
spine	gentle spinal twist spinal stretch	to increase mobility to give a little more abdominal space
solar plexus	bimanual thumb hold	to centre and calm

 Recommend that the client consults her obstetric caregiver to ensure that this chest pain is in fact rib pain. Reassure the client that this is normal and will be relieved when baby engages at about 38 weeks. Good posture will relieve discomfort.

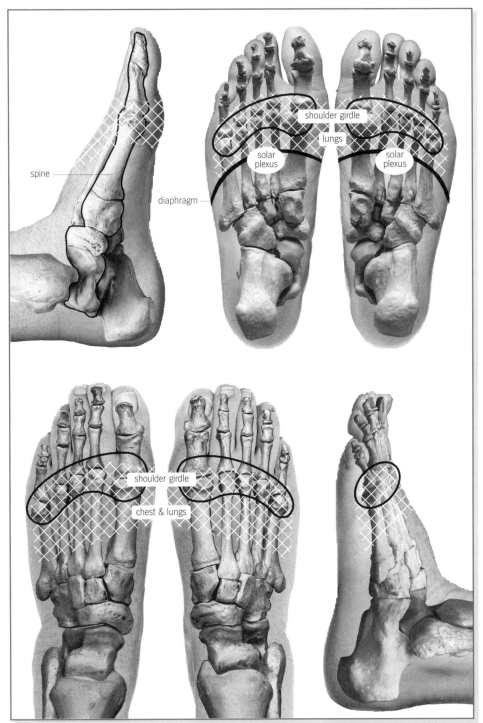

spine

shoulder girdle
lungs
solar plexus
solar plexus
diaphragm

shoulder girdle
chest & lungs

antenatal
rupture of membranes
spontaneous rupture of membranes

Spontaneous rupture of membranes is a sign of labour beginning. This "breaking of waters" can occur in a gush or a slow leak. Slow leaking amniotic fluid is sometimes difficult to distinguish from urine leakage - if unsure smell the fluid. Amniotic fluid has a distinctive sweet smell.

CONTACT THE OBSTETRIC CARE-GIVER

premature rupture of membranes

If spontaneous rupture of membranes occurs prematurely, immediate medical assistance must be sought. If baby is not born within 24–48 hours there is a risk of infection ascending through the vagina to the uterus. Admission to hospital will be for observation and rest. Hospitalisation will continue until the leak is sealed or the baby is born.

REFLEXOLOGY ONLY WITH OBSTETRIC CARE-GIVER'S PERMISSION

reflection zone	*technique*	*intent*
solar plexus	bimanual thumb hold	to ease anxiety
entire body	relaxation techniques	for general relaxation

Explain the situation to the client and/or reinforce doctor's explanation. Encourage discussion of possible management options with the obstetric care-givers.

108

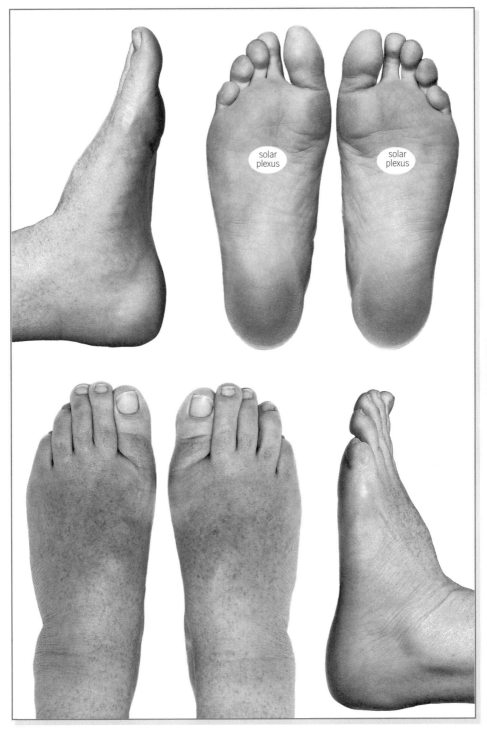

solar
plexus

solar
plexus

sciatica

Sharp pain shooting down the buttock and back of the leg is known as sciatica. Sciatica is caused by a pinching of the sciatic nerve as it exits the vertebral column in the lower back. It is often associated with movements such as climbing stairs or standing from a seated position. This pinching is more common during pregnancy due to an altered posture and the laxity of ligaments resulting from the pregnancy hormone relaxin.

reflection zone	technique	intent
greater sciatic notch	sedation grip	to release trapped energy
"chronic pelvic" zones	stroke/massage towards the ankle	to ease the tension
pelvic girdle	extremely gentle ankle boogie hip relaxation techniques	to relax the area
spine	gentle spinal twist	to increase energy flow
solar plexus	bimanual thumb hold	to relieve anxiety

 A warm pack eg towel or wheat pack placed over the painful area of the back is comforting. Gentle stretches are helpful to ease this condition.

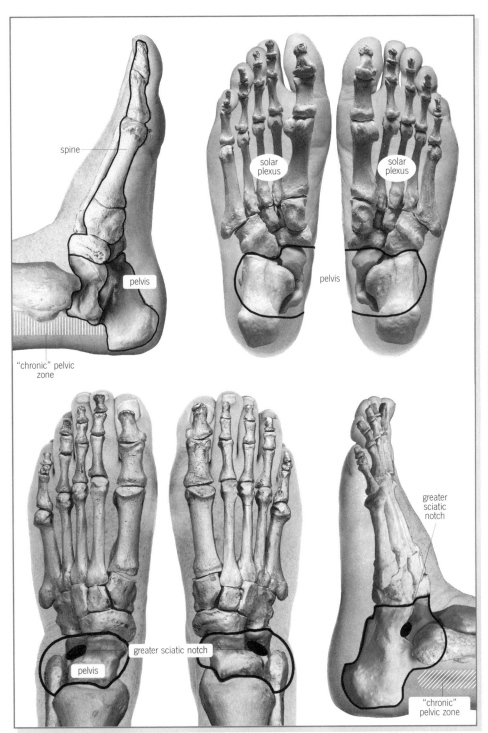

spine

pelvis

solar plexus

solar plexus

pelvis

"chronic" pelvic zone

greater sciatic notch

pelvis

greater sciatic notch

"chronic" pelvic zone

antenatal

separated symphysis
(pubic diastasis)

Separated symphysis is also known as pubic diastasis or pathological laxity of the symphysis pubis. Relaxation of the symphysis pubis joint is occasionally sufficient to cause separation of the pubic bones. This causes severe pain especially when walking. Medical treatment may include the prescription of pain killers, rest, pelvic support girdle or if close to the estimated delivery date, an induction of labour. Pain from a separated symphysis is likely to continue into the post-partum period.

reflection zone	technique	intent
symphysis pubis	sedation grip be sure to be accurate – bone only – DO NOT USE SEDATION GRIP ON INTERNAL PELVIC ZONES	for pain relief
solar plexus	thumb hold	to relieve anxiety

A pregnant client complaining of severe pain anywhere in the reproductive region must be advised to see her doctor. Once a diagnosis of separated symphysis has been made reflexology treatments may commence. Showing the client and/or her partner how to sedate the symptomatic zone on the feet can assist with pain management between sessions.

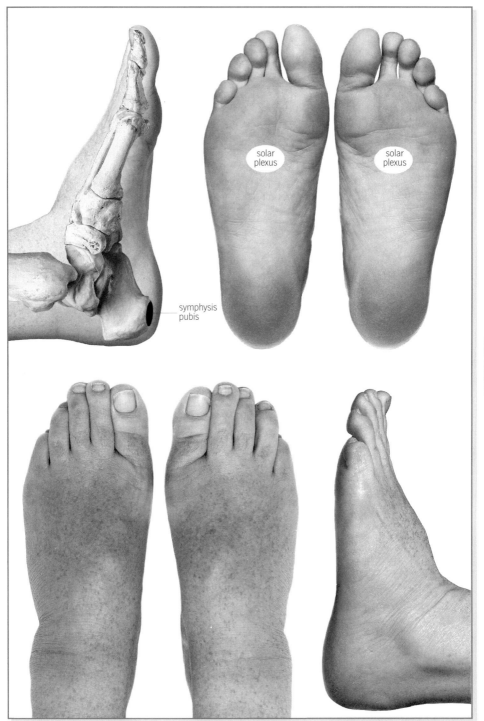

symphysis
pubis

solar
plexus

solar
plexus

antenatal
sleeplessness
(insomnia)

Nocturnal frequency of micturition (urination), excitement, nervousness, tension, anxiety, physical discomfort and an active baby can all cause loss of sleep and inability to fall asleep.

reflection zone	*technique*	*intent*
entire body	all relaxation techniques	to encourage restfulness and tranquillity
solar plexus	bimanual thumb hold	to settle and calm
chest and lung	fish movement lung press	to become aware of breathing
heart	sedate	to settle the spirit
head	all toes: rotations and stretches	to calm the mind
balance organ hypothalamus	linking technique	to balance body and mind

Encourage activities which treat any identifiable cause eg if the client has a busy mind suggest that she jots down whatever she is concentrating on then deal with it the next day. Relaxing music, a meditation tape, a warm bath, a cup of cocoa before bedtime are some suggestions which may encourage a good night's sleep. If possible a day time nap may balance the lack of sleep at night.

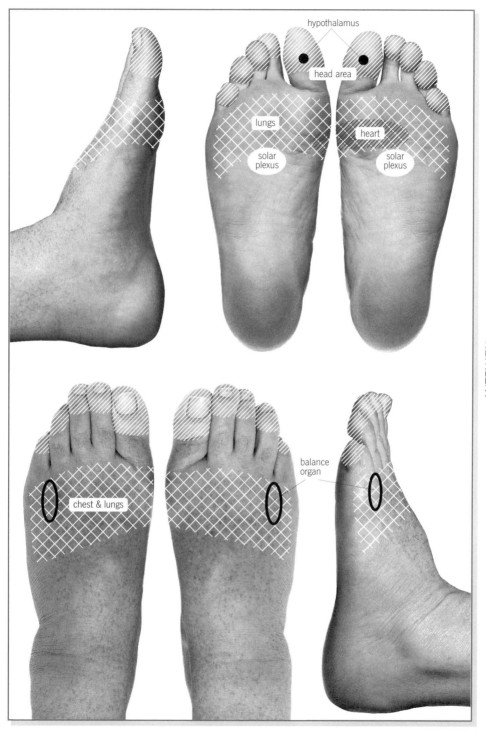

hypothalamus

head area

lungs

heart

solar
plexus

solar
plexus

chest & lungs

balance
organ

antenatal
stretch marks

Whenever the baby grows, the skin needs to expand to cover it. If the skin cannot stretch as quickly as the body part which it is covering, cells tear in the deeper epidermal layer. The result of this is the formation of stretch marks, which often appear as angry red or purple tracks through the skin. Rapid growth of the breasts, hips, thighs and abdomen are common during pregnancy and these are the most common sites for stretch marks to appear. Stretch marks cannot be prevented, however steady weight gain will minimise their occurrence and severity. Application of creams and oils has not been proved effective in preventing stretch marks.

reflection zone	*technique*	*intent*
lymphatic system	lymphatic drainage massage	to keep the skin glowing
liver	gentle stimulation	to remove toxins
entire body	relaxation techniques	to keep the body supple

If stretch marks have appeared reassure the client that they will fade to silvery lines during the following months. Remind her that natural oils eg olive, almond, macadamia will moisturise her outer skin layers just as effectively as expensive chemical-based cosmetic preparations.

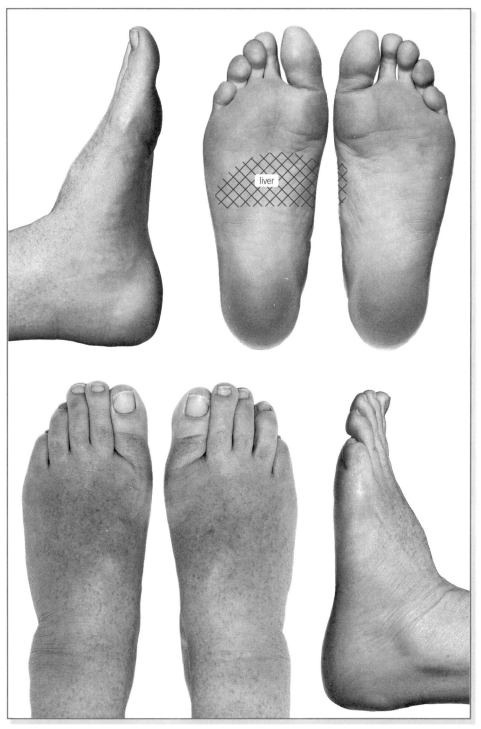

liver

antenatal
teeth & gums

Additional saliva is produced during pregnancy, making dental cavities more likely to occur. Oral hygiene is often neglected as the taste of toothpaste and brushing of rear molars may cause nausea and/or gagging when morning sickness is present. If not met with adequate nutrition, the baby's need for calcium will be supplied from the mother's teeth and bones. The old wives tale that a tooth is lost with each pregnancy comes from this empiric knowledge.

reflection zone	*technique*	*intent*
endocrine system	endocrine balance	to maintain hormonal balance
thyroid/parathyroid	gently stimulate	to maintain calcium balance

Encourage the client to use a small-headed soft bristled tooth brush with minimal amounts of toothpaste. Dental hygiene and the use of dental floss is important. Remind the client to visit the dentist regularly.

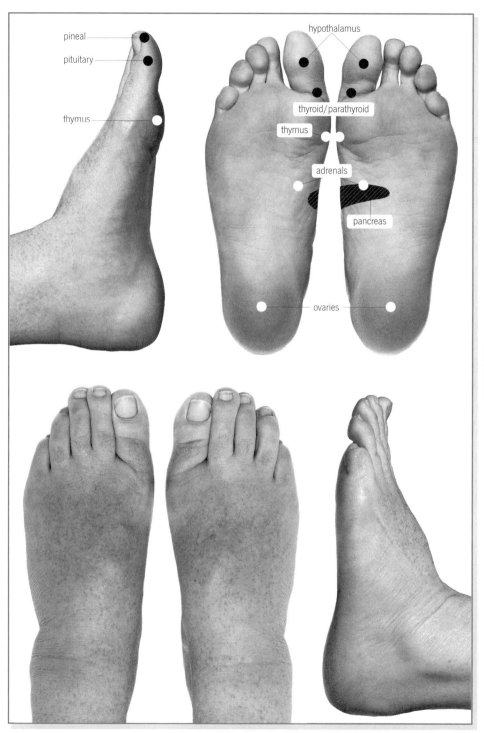

pineal

pituitary

thymus

hypothalamus

thyroid/parathyroid

thymus

adrenals

pancreas

ovaries

antenatal
twins or more

With two or more babies there are higher levels of pregnancy hormones and therefore greater discomforts and increased likelihood of the more common ailments of pregnancy. Carrying a twin pregnancy is heavier than a single pregnancy and may cause problems such as backache and varicose veins. Many women with multiple pregnancies are advised to rest in bed from about 24–34 weeks gestation. This encourages growth of the babies and reduces the risk of preterm labour.

reflection zone	technique	intent
entire foot	relaxation techniques	to keep the body in good state to allow for this huge experience
endocrine system	endocrine balance	to create balance
lymphatic system	lymphatic drainage massage	to assist the body remove extra quantity of waste

Remind the client that twins are twice as nice, not only double trouble. Encourage rest and good nutrition. Delivery options may be more limited with a multiple birth than a singleton. Discussion between Mother and the obstetric care-giver is important to clarify these options.

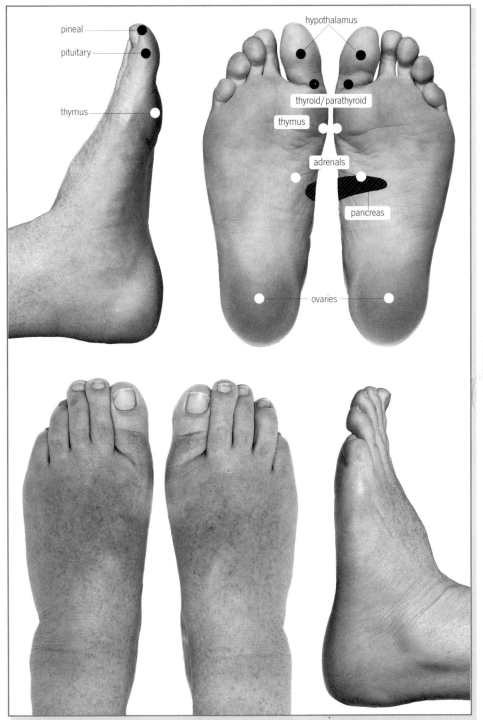

pineal

pituitary

thymus

hypothalamus

thyroid/parathyroid

thymus

adrenals

pancreas

ovaries

antenatal
urinary frequency

A combination of hormones and pressure on the bladder lead to frequency especially early and late in pregnancy. Always needing to know where the nearest toilet is located, needing to dash to the ladies in the middle of activities, and having interrupted nights sleep, is very tiresome. Urinary incontinence can also result, proving unpleasant and embarrassing. Pregnancy-induced frequency is not associated with irritation or burning sensations. These are signs of urinary tract infections (see page 124). Poor pelvic floor muscle tone and urinary tract infections are the most common cause of second trimester urinary frequency.

reflection zone	*technique*	*intent*
urine system	urinary system flush	to ensure balanced energy prevent irritation
pelvis	relaxation techniques: gentle ankle boogie ankle rotations	to relax the tension
"chronic" pelvic zones	massage gently	to prevent long term problems

 Reassure... urinary frequency will lessen (either with the second trimester or delivery, whichever is approaching). Suggest regular pelvic floor exercises as an increasing weakness of these muscles is likely during pregnancy leading to further frequency.

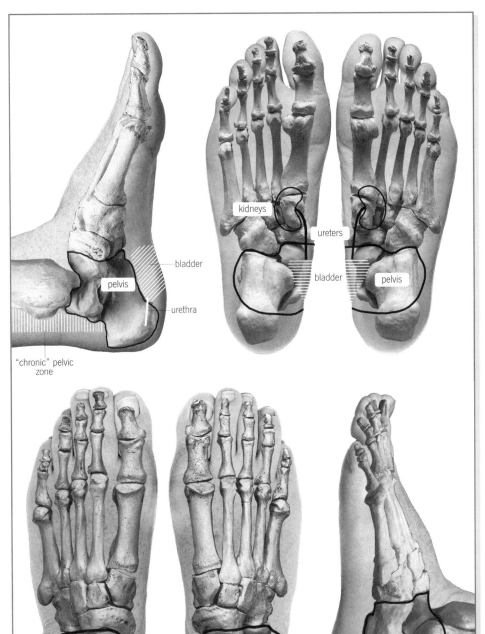

bladder

pelvis

urethra

"chronic" pelvic
zone

kidneys

ureters

bladder

pelvis

pelvis

pelvis

pelvis

"chronic"
pelvic zone

antenatal
urinary tract infections
(cystitis)

During the second half of pregnancy the growing uterus leans forward tilting and twisting to the right. This puts pressure on the ureters, especially the right ureter, allowing urine to be trapped. Consequential pooling of sedentary urine results in infection. The usual symptoms of a urinary tract infection (UTI) are pain/burning when passing urine and urinary frequency. UTIs in pregnancy maybe asymptomatic or present with a sudden onset of fever. UTI in pregnancy needs to be treated as the infection can lead to premature labour. Medical treatment includes rest, urinary alkalisers, antibiotics and possibly hospitalisation in case of premature birth.

reflection zone	*technique*	*intent*
bladder	sedate	to relieve discomfort
kidneys /ureters / bladder /urethra	bimanually urinary system flush	to promote excretion of urine
solar plexus	bimanually sedate	to relieve agitation
spleen	stimulate	to assist the immune system to ease worry
thymus	tapping	to assist the immune system
lower spine and hips	relaxation techniques	to allow the free flow of energy
lymphatic system	lymphatic drainage massage	to hasten the removal of toxins

 Advise the client to consult a doctor. Encourage an increased intake of fluids to flush the bacteria from the urinary tract. If antibiotics have been prescribed remind the client to complete the entire course. Discuss general hygiene. Tactfully remind her to wipe from clitoris to anus reducing the likelihood of bowel pathogens entering the vagina/urethra.

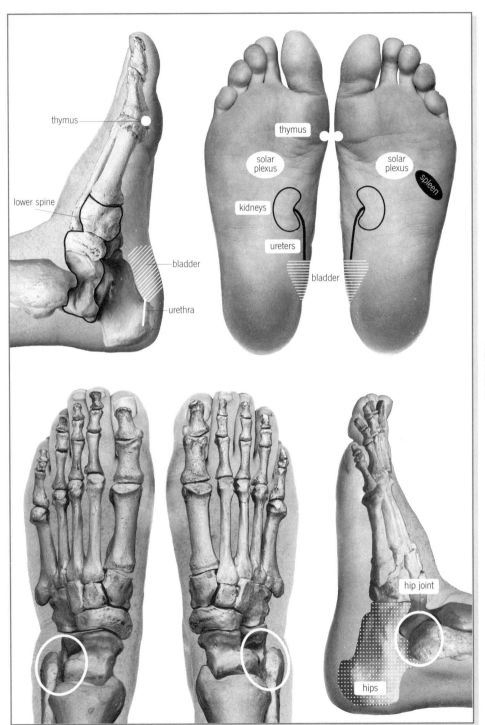

thymus

lower spine

bladder

urethra

thymus

solar plexus

solar plexus

spleen

kidneys

ureters

bladder

hip joint

hips

antenatal
vaginal discharge & thrush, (monilia)

It is quite normal for vaginal discharge to increase during pregnancy. Normal vaginal secretions are non-irritating, usually clear or clean white and should not have an offensive odour.

If the vaginal discharge becomes itchy, malodorous or changes colour this may indicate an infection such as an overgrowth of thrush/monilia. Monilia is normally found in small amounts in the vagina. Changes in the acidity of the vagina allows the monilia to multiply causing infection-like symptoms. Thrush is not uncommon during pregnancy due to the changed hormone levels, increased blood supply to the vagina and probability of raised blood sugar. A medical consultation is recommended for diagnosis. Medical treatment is likely to include an antifungal cream for the vulva and/or vagina. The woman's partner should be treated concurrently as cross infection and reinfection is possible, even if the partner is asymptomatic.

reflection zone	*technique*	*intent*
spleen	gently stimulate	to support the body's defence system
lymphatic system especially pelvic zones	lymphatic drainage massage	to promote cell health and nutrition and remove cell debris
endocrine system especially thymus	endocrine balance	to support the body's immune system

 reassure the client that thrush is not a sexually transmitted disease, although it can be passed on to sexual partners. Diagnosis of a thrush infection does not have the same connotation as diagnosis of sexually transmitted disease (STD).

126

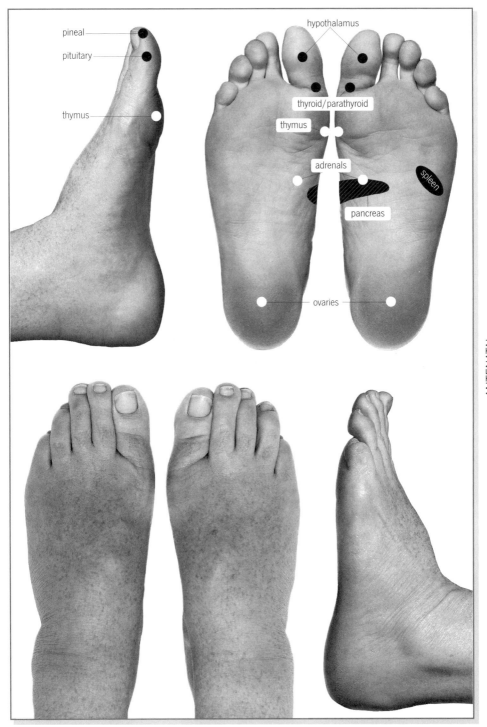

pineal

pituitary

thymus

hypothalamus

thyroid/parathyroid

thymus

adrenals

spleen

pancreas

ovaries

ANTENATAL

varicose veins

Varicose veins commonly occur on the vulva, anus (haemorrhoids), lower or upper leg. Softening of smooth muscle and peripheral resistance contribute to the increased risk of varicosities during pregnancy. The pregnancy itself may impede the venous return through the pelvis.

reflection zone	*technique*	*intent*
VULVA lymphatic system	lymphatic drainage massage	to improve the vitality of the system
ANUS see page 96 Piles (Haemorrhoids)		
LEGS "chronic" pelvic area	gently massage	to ease the tension
lymphatic system	lymphatic drainage massage	to improve the vitality of the body
uterus indirect ovary	linking technique	to balance yin/yang pelvic energy

Explain why variscosities have occurred or worsened. Remind the client to not restrict blood flow with tight clothing eg knee high stockings. Suggest support hose for leg veins or underwear with a firm crotch but loose leg elastic for vulval support. A medium thickness sanitary pad may provide additional vulval support. Discomfort may be relieved by varying activities, avoiding those that aggravate the variscosities and by resting with legs well supported and raised above the level of the pelvis.

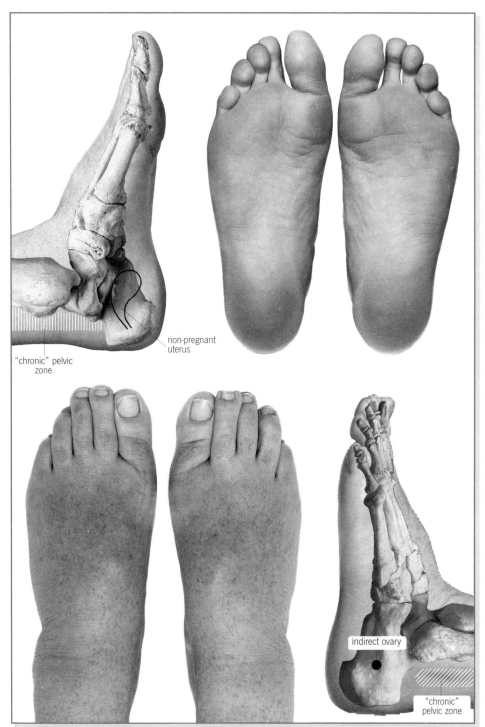

"chronic" pelvic zone

non-pregnant uterus

indirect ovary

"chronic" pelvic zone

antenatal
vomiting

An occasional episode of vomiting in pregnancy is unlikely to cause problems for mother or baby. If vomiting is persistent or severe, dehydration poses a health risk to mother and baby. Fevers and other symptoms associated with maternal illness can also be detrimental to baby. Vomiting episodes should be reported to the obstetric care-giver so that the health status of mother and baby can be monitored.

reflection zone	*technique*	*intent*
stomach	sedate	to calm and settle the stomach
solar plexus	bimanual hold	to ease anxiety
kidneys	bimanual hold	to balance the body's fluid and mineral levels
endocrine system	endocrine balance	to re-gain the body's hormone balance

 Encourage the client to drink plenty of clear fluids to replace those lost with vomiting. Rest is imperative for recuperation from illness.

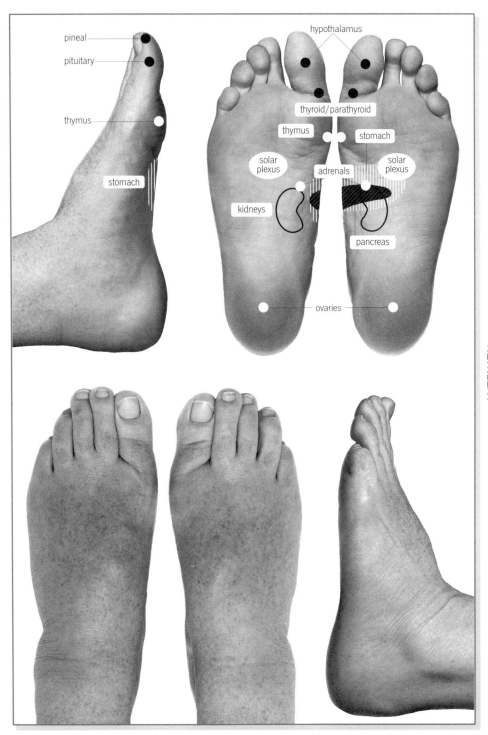

pineal

pituitary

thymus

stomach

hypothalamus

thyroid/parathyroid

thymus

stomach

solar
plexus

adrenals

solar
plexus

kidneys

pancreas

ovaries

postnatal care

The agony and ecstasy of labour can leave a woman feeling jubilant, exhausted, sore and sick, full of disbelief and wonder, with many other conflicting and confusing emotions.

The balancing, harmonising, and restoring qualities of reflexology therapy is superb at this time. Even if a woman has had a straight forward, uneventful labour, her entire system will appreciate balancing back to a non-pregnant state, and after all that hard work she deserves a reflexology session. If a woman has had a hard labour or traumatic experience the qualities of reflexology therapy can help enormously. A reflexology session is an excellent time to "debrief".

postnatal session

The first and third days after delivery are the optimum times to work. It is not always easy for a new "mum" to have time for reflexology. If possible in each session include:

• full reflexology session
• endocrine balance
• lymphatic drainage massage
• bimanual solar plexus balance
• reflexology therapy for the specific condition

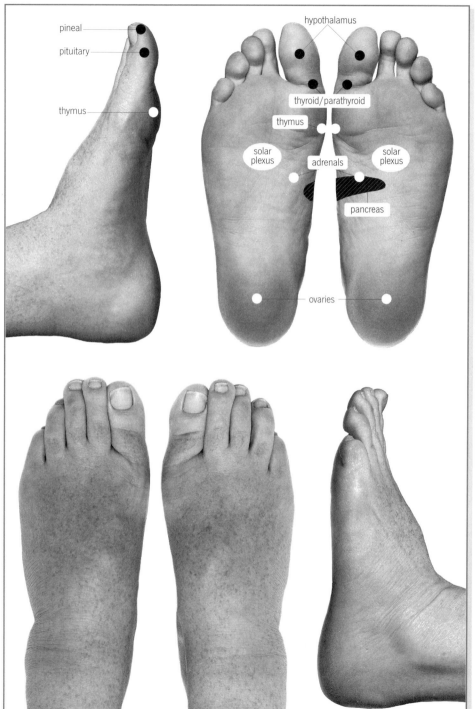

pineal

pituitary

thymus

hypothalamus

thyroid/parathyroid

thymus

solar plexus

adrenals

solar plexus

pancreas

ovaries

postnatal
aching joints

A strenuous active labour can cause muscles and joints to feel as though a marathon race has been run. After giving birth and for the duration of breast feeding, low oestrogen levels cause menopausal-like symptoms such as aching joints.

reflection zone	*technique*	*intent*
endocrine system	endocrine balance	to help the natural endocrine balance
entire body	all relaxation techniques	to relieve the aches

Reassure the client that this is a normal condition which will improve once menstruation returns. Suggest hot packs and gentle limbering up exercises for symptomatic relief.

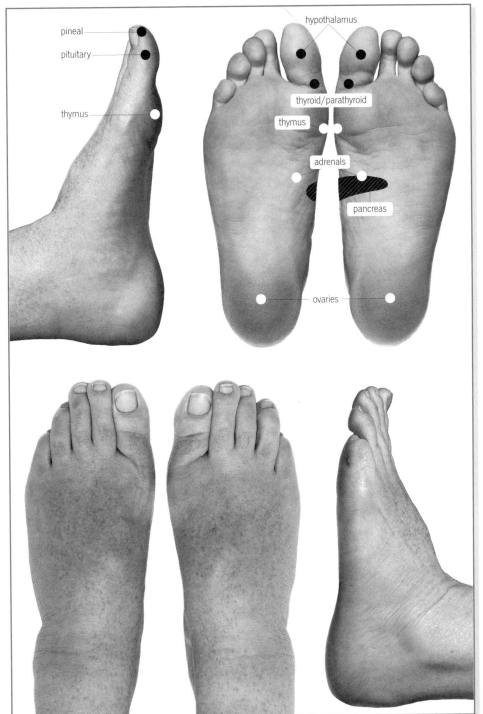

pineal

pituitary

thymus

hypothalamus

thyroid/parathyroid

thymus

adrenals

pancreas

ovaries

postnatal
after "caesarean"
caesarean section (C/S)

"Caesarean" (lower segment caesarean section [C/S]) deliveries are necessary for a number of reasons. They may be planned because of a non-urgent problem, or unplanned arising from an emergency situation. The most common reasons for C/S are that the mother's pelvic cavity is smaller than the baby's head and that the baby is too stressed to safely tolerate labour and/or vaginal delivery. Parents may easily adjust to the idea of a C/S or may grieve for the normal vaginal delivery which they could not have. The majority of C/S incisions are made horizontally (bikini line) and healing is excellent. Except in emergency situations, most mothers are given the option of a general anaesthetic (GA) or an epidural anaesthetic. Even with a "drip", urinary catheter or wound drain, women are encouraged to get out of bed the same day as the C/S to reduce the risk of DVT. By day three after C/S the mother is usually up and about and able to fully care for her baby. Pain relief medications are generally offered freely during the first 48 hours, it is recommended to take them before breast feeding and getting out of bed. The mother's oral intake will be restricted until she passes wind from the bowel. Abdominal wind pain can be very uncomfortable during this time. For at least six weeks after C/S it is recommended that the mother does not strain, lift, carry heavy weights or drive a car.

reflection zone	technique	intent
uterus	healing hold	to allow healing energy to flow
solar plexus	bimanual thumb hold	to calm and centre
spine	gentle spinal twist	to loosen stiffness
lungs/chest	fish movement metatarsal stretches lung press	to re-establish healthy breathing patterns especially after general anaesthetic
large intestines	thumb walk the direction of flow	to help move the 'wind'
splenic flexure	massage	a really good 'spot' to move 'wind'
lymphatic system	lymphatic drainage massage	to promote the removal of toxins
endocrine system	endocrine balance	to restore balance as soon as possible

Be understanding about the client's reduced ability to move, and encourage early mobilisation. Offer practical suggestions to reduce muscle strain eg bath the baby in the sink! Home visits could be a great idea.

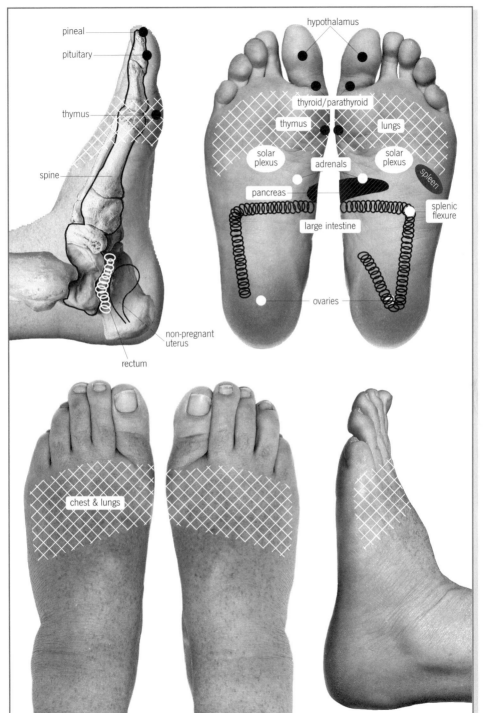

postnatal
after epidural

Epidural and spinal anaesthetics can provide total pain control from the diaphragm to the feet. Many women choose to use this anaesthetic during labour or for Caesarean Section (C/S) operation. After the birth the anaesthetic takes two to three hours to wear off. Back pain may result from an epidural or spinal anaesthetic and is thought to be due to bruising/inflammation of tissues around the insertion site and/or strain caused to the back muscles from awkward movements/postures while anaesthetised. Muscle pain occurs more often after labour than after a planned C/S with an epidural anaesthetic.

reflection zone	*technique*	*intent*
lumbar vertebrae	*sedation grip gently and with caution	to remove the energy blockage and reconnect the energy flow
spine	gentle spinal twist spine rubs	to relax the spine and promote re-establishment of energy
pelvis	gentle ankle boogie	to restore energy to the pelvis and hips
coccyx/head	linking technique	to rebalance the spine

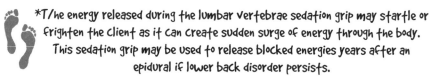

*T/he energy released during the lumbar vertebrae sedation grip may startle or frighten the client as it can create sudden surge of energy through the body. This sedation grip may be used to release blocked energies years after an epidural if lower back disorder persists.

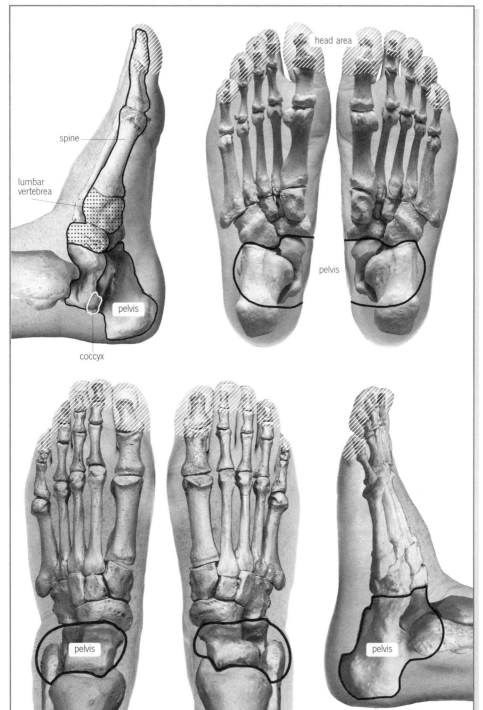

spine

lumbar
vertebrea

coccyx

pelvis

head area

pelvis

pelvis

pelvis

pelvis

postnatal
after forceps delivery

Forceps are used to assist the descent and/or rotation of the baby through the birth canal during the second stage of labour. The mother will feel bruised and sore, especially if an episiotomy has been performed. Baby may have facial bruising from the forceps and possibly trauma caused by a prolonged second stage of labour or foetal distress which may have necessitated the use of forceps.

reflection zone	*technique*	*intent*
internal pelvis	healing hold linking technique to hips and solar plexus	to promote healing energy and balance
internal aspect of the bones of the pelvis	gently sedate especially disordered zones	to ease the pain
perineum	gentle sedation	to promote healing
spine	spinal twist spinal rubs	to relax the tension
internal pelvis/hips	linking technique and link to solar plexus	to balance the energies
solar plexus	bimanual thumb hold	to restore calm

Help the client come to terms with the reason for the use of forceps. Give TLC+++ if she is separated from her baby due to admission to the special /intensive care baby nursery. Reflexology is supberb for sedating the disordered zones of the internal aspect of the bones of the pelvis.

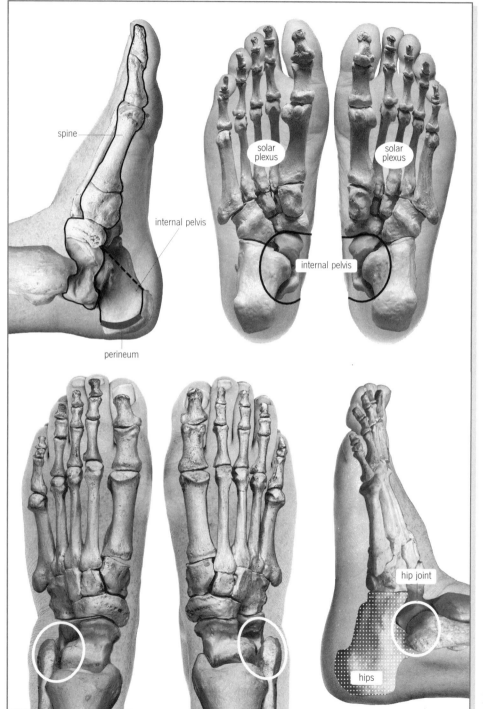

spine

internal pelvis

perineum

solar plexus

solar plexus

internal pelvis

hip joint

hips

postnatal
"after pains"

Nature has designed the uterus to continue contracting after the birth of the baby. This allows the placenta to separate from the uterine wall and reduces blood loss from the placental site. These contractions can continue for up to seven days after delivery. Many first time mothers are oblivious to these contractions, other new mothers will experience "cramping" pains similar to labour contractions or period pains, particularly at feeding time. Paracetamol tablets are often prescribed by the obstetric care-giver. These should be taken half an hour before breastfeeding for best results.

reflection zone	technique	intent
uterus	NO REFLEXOLOGY	uterus is meant to be contracting strongly leave well alone
solar plexus	bimanual thumb hold	to restore calm
hips	ankle boogie	to remove the tension
shoulder girdle	relaxation techniques: fish movement metatarsal stretching	to relax the rest of the body
spine	spinal twist spine stretch	to loosen tension in the spine

Explain to the client why these contractions are occuring. Knowing that they are normal and beneficial and of limited duration will help her tolerate the discomfort. Remind her of her relaxation strategies for labour - they will help while feeding the baby.

142

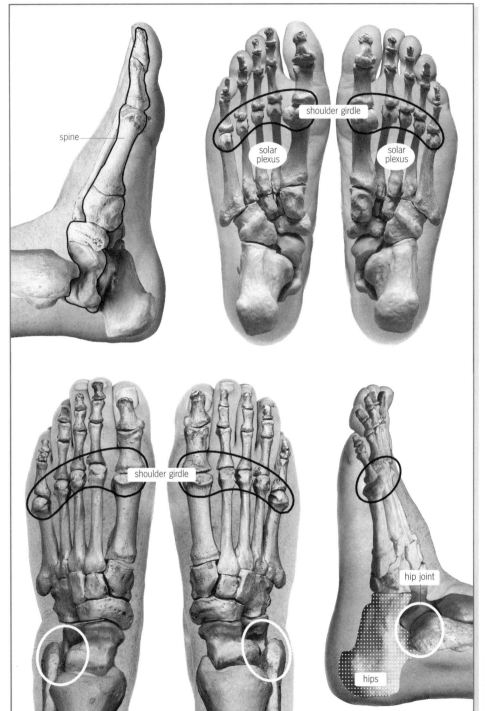

spine

shoulder girdle

solar
plexus

solar
plexus

shoulder girdle

hip joint

hips

postnatal
blood loss: vaginal
(lochia)

During the six weeks after delivery the vaginal discharge (lochia) should gradually lessen in amount, changing from a thick rich red/brown colour to a watery pink and then whitish discharge. Lochia should have an inoffensive smell (similar to menstrual period). Clots can be normal in the early days while the mother is lying down, as heavy blood loss pools and clots in the vagina. These are then passed out from the vagina as she stands up.

All clots including those dislodged from the vagina should be reported to the midwife/obstetric care-giver, as clots can be associated with retained fragments of placenta and membranes. An offensive odour indicates abnormal lochia and may be associated with the retained fragments. This usually indicates infection.

reflection zone	technique	intent
uterus	sedate or stimulate whichever is required to normalise the zone	to regain health and balance
pelvic lymphatics	gently stimulate	to assist clearing cell debris
solar plexus	bimanual thumb hold	to ease anxiety

Help the client to differentiate between normal and abnormal lochia. Encourage her to consult her obstetric care-giver if lochia is abnormal.

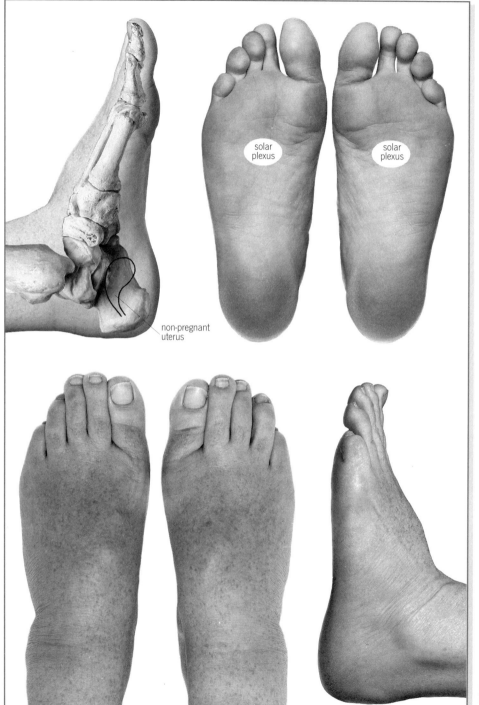

non-pregnant
uterus

solar
plexus

solar
plexus

postnatal
blood loss: vaginal
(secondary post partum haemorrhage)

A blood loss of 600mls or more is classified as a significant post partum haemorrhage (PPH). If such a heavy loss occurs suddenly at about 1-3 weeks after delivery this is described as a secondary PPH. A secondary PPH is usually caused by a uterine infection and requires immediate treatment.

A POST PARTUM HAEMORRHAGE IS AN OBSTETRIC EMERGENCY

REFLEXOLOGY CONTRAINDICATED

Help the client to differentiate between a secondary PPH and the return of her menstrual periods. These may occur within 4 weeks following delivery, unless the baby is fully breast fed. If antibiotics have been prescribed, encourage the client to complete the course.

146

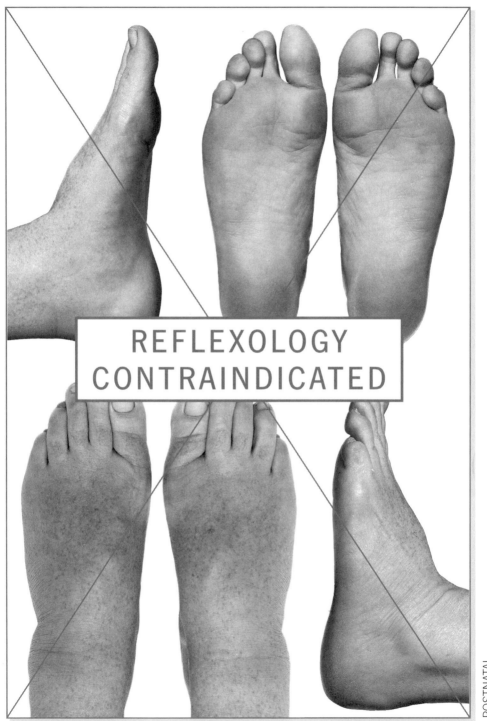

REFLEXOLOGY
CONTRAINDICATED

postnatal
breasts

Western societies tend to view breasts as fashion accessories and erogenous zones, therefore many young girls and women have had little or no opportunity to celebrate breasts as mammary glands. Instead of enjoying their development at menarche, knowing breast development to be a sign of fertility and woman-ness, many western women are displeased with their breasts, wanting them to be: bigger/smaller, softer/firmer, flatter/pertier, tanned, tempting, symmetrical etc, etc. Maternity time offers another chance for women to appreciate their breasts, seeing them in a new light. Not only do hormones change the physical structure and appearance of breasts, but also their function. Breasts now have a better chance of succeeding in their new role of sustaining and nurturing a baby. This is what they were designed for!

reflection zone	technique	intent
breast direct and indirect	thumb walk massage	to encourage and maintain normal function
axillary lymphatics	thumb walk	to maintain local lymphatic function
heart	gently stimulate	to acknowledge the love energy

 Remind the client that her breasts are wonderful – no matter what shape, size or colour. Help her adjust to her breast's new role with understanding and language which is positive and empowering. Remind her that no matter what her breasts role or appearance her baby will love her... and her breasts!

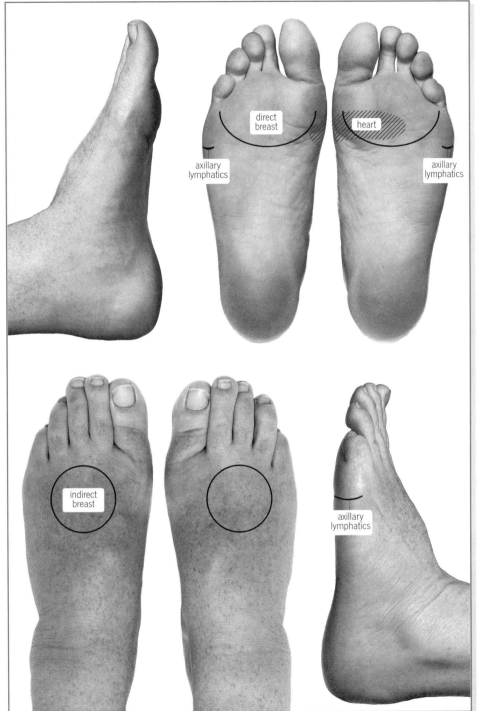

direct
breast

heart

axillary
lymphatics

axillary
lymphatics

indirect
breast

axillary
lymphatics

postnatal
breasts: engorgement

Nature initiates lactation whether or not there are plans to breast feed. During the first three or four days after giving birth lactation commences. Additional blood and lymphatic fluid is supplied to that area causing the breasts to enlarge and engorge. Medical treatment includes analgesia eg paracetamol. Short term use of cold, green cabbage leaves placed inside the bra give good relief.

reflection zone	technique	intent
direct breast	thumb walk massage	to encourage suppleness to relieve discomfort
axillary lymphatics	lymphatic drainage	to assist removal of excess fluid
solar plexus	bimanual thumb hold	to ease anxiety
direct breast and indirect breast	linking technique between both breast zones	to balance the energy

Encourage the client to continue to breast feed, after the initial discomfort breast feeding can be a great pleasure.

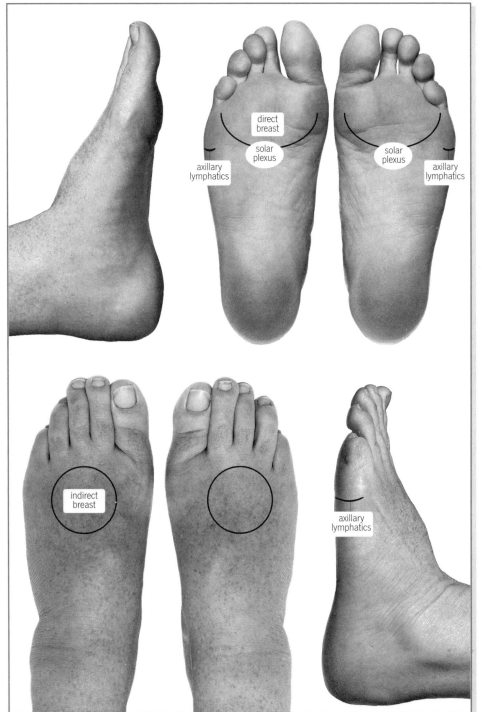

postnatal
breasts: mastisis

Mastitis, also known as milk fever, is caused by an inflammation of one or more milk ducts due to stagnation of the milk. Symptoms are usually sudden in onset and include fever and/or a red hot area over one or more lobes of the breast. Immediate treatment, ie draining the inflamed duct, is likely to lessen the severity of the illness. Baby is most effective at draining the breast - encourage baby to suckle at the effected breast. Medical treatment will include antibiotics, a supportive bra and massage of lumps. Mothers are also encouraged to fully drain one breast, alternating breasts, with each feed. Lecithin may be used as it emulsifies fats which contribute to clogged ducts. Lumps in the milk ducts which do not break down with sucking and/or massage may indicate a persistently blocked duct. These lumps may encapsulate forming a breast abscess. Breast abscesses require surgical drainage by a doctor.

reflection zone	*technique*	*intent*
breast direct and indirect	gently massage the total reflex zones in the direction the milk ducts flow	to ease the pain to loosen lumps and blockages
indirect breast	massage the centre of the disordered zone gently - it will be painful	to clear the blockage and hasten healing
axilliary lymphatics	lymphatic drainage massage with special attention to axillary lymphatics	to promote removal of cell debris and encourage cell health

 Encourage the client to continue breast feeding while being treated for mastitis. Encourage her to access breast feeding services eg Nursing Mothers Association, local lactation consultant, Tressilian Family Care Centre.

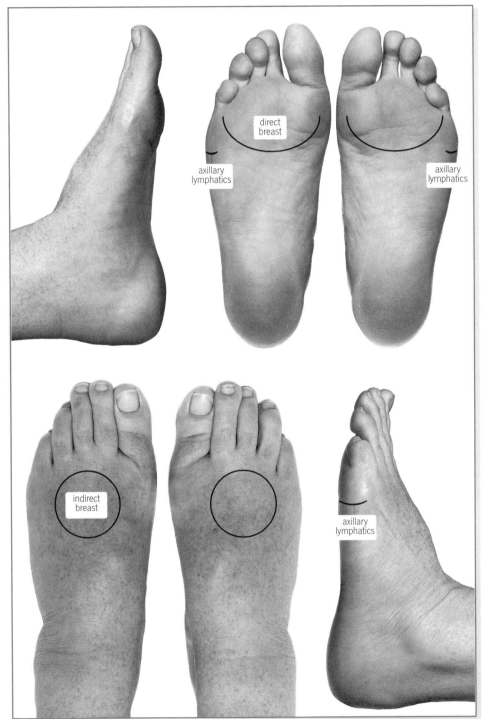

direct breast

axillary lymphatics

axillary lymphatics

indirect breast

axillary lymphatics

postnatal

constipation
after delivery

Immediately prior to labour the woman will naturally empty her bowels which may be diarrhoea-like. During labour the contents of the rectum will be expelled. After delivery several days may pass without the woman having her bowels open. If there has been perineal trauma there may be a great reluctance to defecate, and constipation will develop.

reflection zone	*technique*	*intent*
large intestine	stimulate	to increase energy to the area
	massage using the direction of flow	to reinstate the energy direction
anus	sedate	to ease pain and fear
spine	spinal twist spinal stretches	to relax the whole area especially the lower back
hips	ankle boogie ankle rotations	to relax the area

 It may take time to retrain the bowel after childbirth. Advise the client only to push gently when having her bowels open. Use aperients with caution as they may affect the breast fed baby.

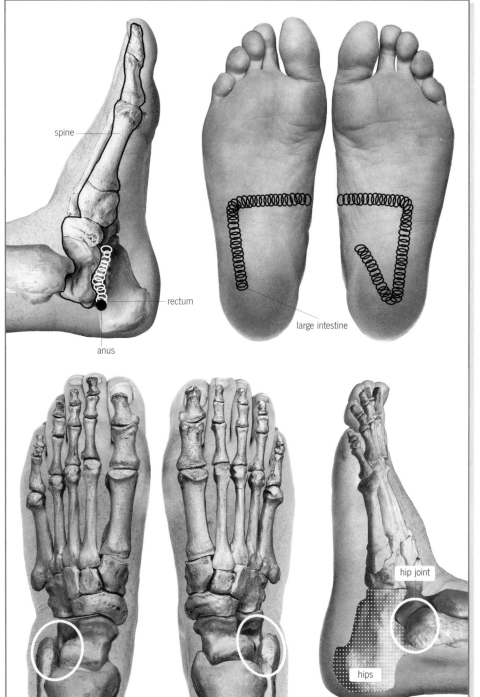

spine

rectum

anus

large intestine

hip joint

hips

postnatal
deep vein thrombosis

REFLEXOLOGY
CONTRAINDICATED

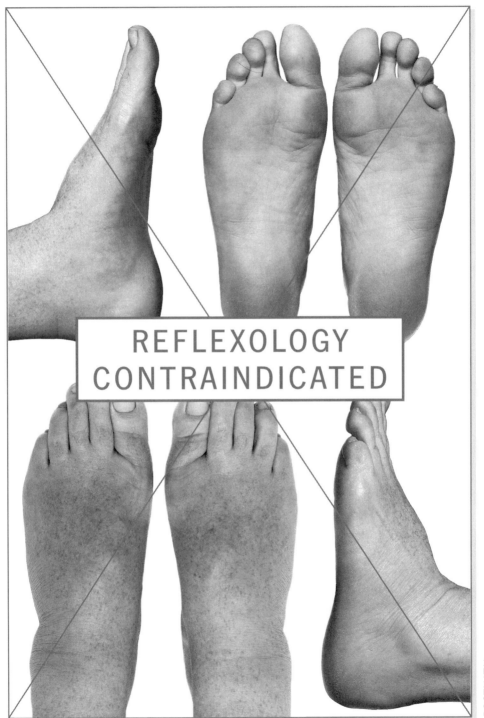

REFLEXOLOGY
CONTRAINDICATED

postnatal
exhaustion

The weeks and months following labour can be exhausting - a confusion of emotions both welcome and unwelcome, not to mention the physical strain a new baby inflicts on all family members. Recuperation from the birth is hindered by broken night time sleep patterns and the household toil of washing, feeding the family, receiving visitors and minimising sibling rivalry.

reflection zone	technique	intent
entire body	all relaxation techniques	to create a space for relaxation and recuperation
head and neck	Brazillian toe balance	to realign the body's energies

 Discuss work minimisation with the client, suggest that someone minds the baby or siblings while she rests. Reassure her that she can "let go" while receiving reflexology; if doing a home visit remind her that she can continue to relax at the end of the session while you "let yourself out". Be sensitive to her cues - she may be chatty to start with while she is "hyped up", when she is quiet allow her quietude.

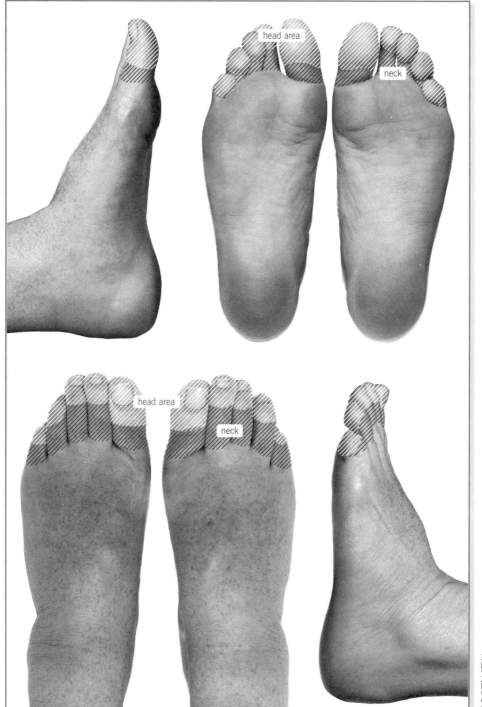

postnatal
lactation

During pregnancy some of the pregnancy hormones stimulate the breasts to produce colostrum. Colostrum is packed with nutrients but has little fluid volume; the baby is well hydrated in utero and therefore needs very little fluid during the first few days. The trigger for milk production is the lack of placental hormones; the mothers milk "comes in" on about the third day after delivery. Constant sucking by baby encourages an earlier start to lactation. For some races of people lactation does not normally start until five days after delivery. Pain, tension, stress, emotional upheaval, performance anxiety, maternal illness, traumatic labour, timed feedings and poor attachment to the breast can delay the lactation process and inhibit the let down reflex, making milk less available.

reflection zone	*technique*	*intent*
breast	stimulate	to increase the energy to the area
hypothalamus and pituitary	stimulate	to encourage the hormones of lactation
heart	gently stimulate	to help the love flow
chest	relaxation techniques: fish movement gentle flip flops	to relax the area

Remind the client to eat a healthy diet and drink plenty of fluids. If problems occur, remind her that help is available from her midwife, the local maternity hospital, community nurses and the Nursing Mothers Association

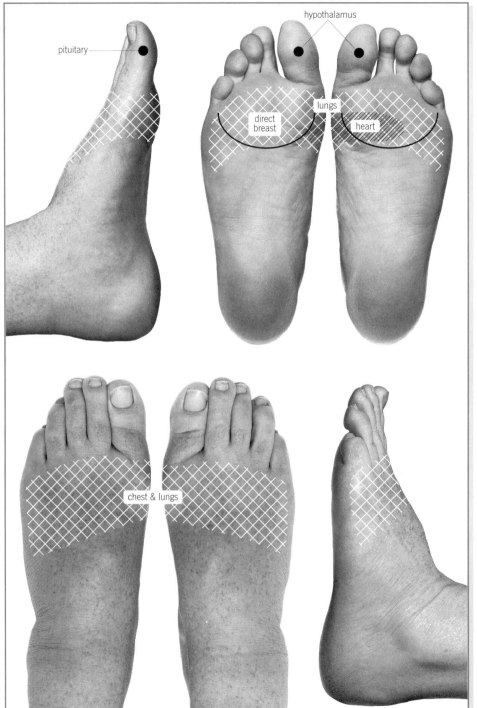

pituitary

hypothalamus

lungs

direct breast

heart

chest & lungs

postnatal
lactation
suppression

Lactation works on a supply and demand basis. Stimulation of the breast by baby's sucking produces the hormones to supply the amount of milk required by baby. The more the baby sucks, the more milk is made. If lactation is to be suppressed it is important to NOT STIMULATE the breasts. There are occasions when it is not possible to breast feed the baby, eg if the mother does not want to or is unable to. The reasons may be physical or emotional. The baby may not be able to feed due to immaturity, illness, death or adoption. Sometimes the baby will refuse to breast feed.

DO NOT TOUCH BREAST ZONES OR HYPOTHALAMUS AND PITUITARY ZONES

reflection zone	technique	intent
solar plexus	bimanual thumb hold	to lessen worry
lymphatic system	lymphatic drainage massage	to help the body remove excess fluid
kidney/ ureters/ bladder/ urethra	urinary system flush	to help the body excrete excess fluid

Support the client's choice to suppress lactation and/or give TLC +++ if the choice was not made by her. Be sympathetic. Women who have wanted to breast feed and are unable to, or who have enjoyed breast feeding but now need to wean the baby, will suffer some degree of loss and therefore grief when suppressing lactation. Remind the client that any breast stimulation will encourage lactation, therefore avoid hand expressing, friction from clothing, massage from the force of water in the shower, etc. Suggest a firm bra for support.
Ensure she is aware of symptoms of mastitis and the treatment of engorgement. Encourage her to contact Nursing Mother's Association for advice on weaning where appropriate.

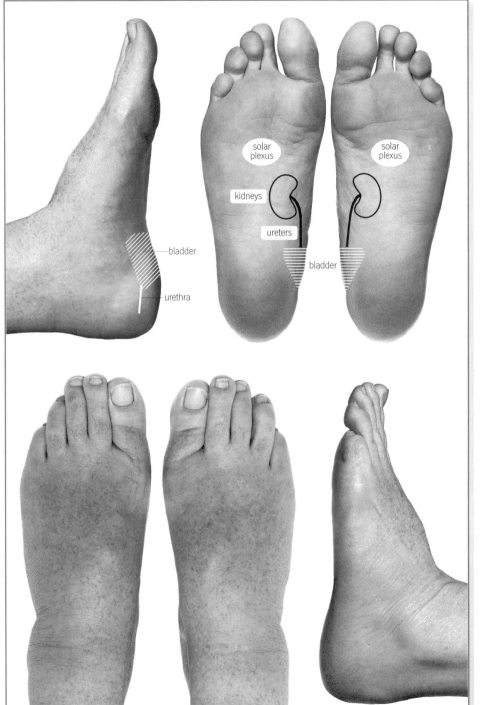

solar
plexus

solar
plexus

kidneys

ureters

bladder

bladder

urethra

postnatal
night sweats

It is quite common during the initial weeks of motherhood for a mother to wake up at night in a sweat. Many women have to change their night attire and bedding each night, sometimes numerous times, as these night sweats can be excessive. Night sweats can occur until hormone levels stabilise ie up to six weeks after delivery - but usually resolve much sooner. If persistent or if the mother is unwell a medical consultation is recommended as profuse sweating can also be associated with fever.

reflection zone	*technique*	*intent*
endocrine system	endocrine balance	to restore the body to a new state of balance

 Reassure the client that this condition will improve. A broken nights sleep is distressing, but additional laundry and extra disturbance at night can be devastating to a new mother. Help her differentiate between hormonal sweats and ill health.

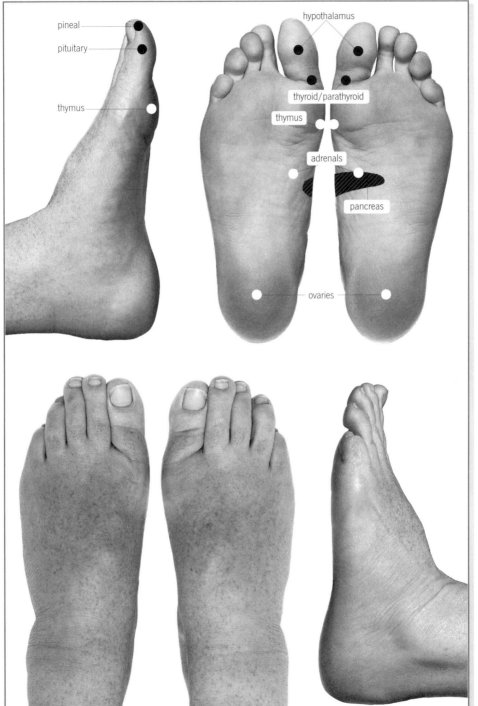

pineal

pituitary

thymus

hypothalamus

thyroid/parathyroid

thymus

adrenals

pancreas

ovaries

postnatal
nipple tenderness

Nipple care routines change frequently, often causing confusion for the mother with each new baby. Current trends recommend that hindmilk is the only substance used for routine nipple care when breast feeding. Commercial products eg. lotions and creams should be avoided as they dry the nipples and interfere with the mothers natural scent which is so important for bonding and baby learning tastes and smells. Ensuring that the baby latches on to the breast correctly prevents nipple trauma. Changing breast pads regularly helps prevent nipples from sitting in a sodden bra - the perfect environment for the growth of bacteria. Some nipple tenderness is normal in the postnatal period as nipples tend to be extra sensitive during pregnancy and after delivery but nipple soreness should not be assumed to be normal. Nipple soreness may be caused by a monilial infection, vasospasm or poor attachment while the baby is sucking. Correct diagnosis of conditions causing nipple pain is imperative as pain is often a causative factor for weaning baby.

reflection zone	technique	intent
nipple	sedation grip	to ease the pain
direct breast	sedate	to relieve the tension
chest and breast	relaxation and stroking	to encourage the love energy to flow

 The sedation grip may be used at each feed while nipples are very tender; begin the grip about half a minute to a minute before the feed, hold until mother is settled and baby is feeding. Nursing Mother's Association and lactation consultants attached to maternity units/health centres have access to the most recent research on breast and nipple care practices. They can be an invaluable source of advice and support to a new mother.

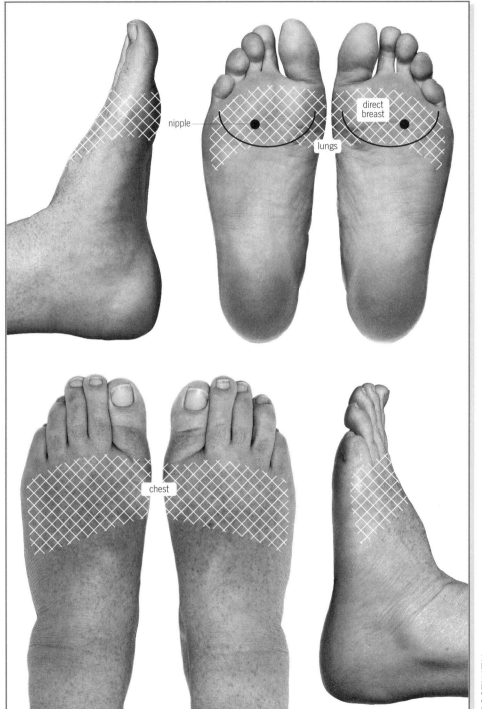

nipple

direct breast

lungs

chest

postnatal
perineal pain:
bruised perineum / painful episiotomy

The birthing process can be traumatic to the tissues of the vagina and perineum. During the second stage of labour contractions force the baby onto the pelvic floor muscles causing a certain amount of bruising and swelling. The vaginal opening is stretched thin, sometimes tearing to allow more space for the emerging baby. An episiotomy may have been performed to aid the birth. Stitches to repair a tear or episiotomy increase the discomfort associated with a bruised or swollen perineum. Perineal pain/discomfort is likely to increase during the first three or four days after the birth, gradually diminishing from then on. This area should be healed within about six weeks. After six weeks slight tenderness around the scarred area is quite normal with intimate physical contact. Vaginal dryness whilst breast feeding and tension if fearing pain will accentuate this tenderness.

reflection zone	technique	intent
perineum	sedate healing hold	to ease the pain to encourage tissue repair
pelvic lymphatics	stimulate	to promote cell regeneration and remove damaged cells
lymphatic system	lymphatic drainage massage	to promote health

 Suggest sitz baths and/or ice packs to reduce swelling. If the client complains of persistent discomfort or pain with intercourse, encourage her to see her doctor.

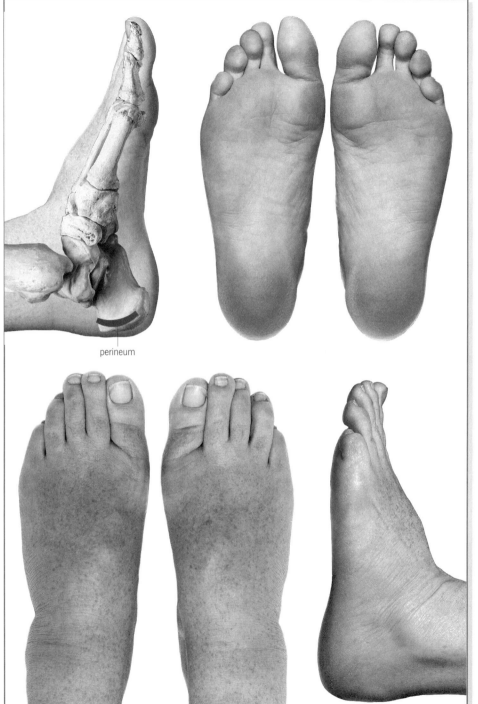

perineum

postnatal

piles
(haemorrhoids)

At delivery the anus is stretched as the baby's head pushes past. After delivery the anus closes again but sometimes some veins are trapped outside the body; these can become engorged and are very painful. Medical treatment is to use ice packs topically and prevent constipation. If there are perineal stitches creams cannot be used as these would make the stitches "soggy".

reflection zone	*technique*	*intent*
anus	sedation grip	for pain relief
hips/pelvis	ankle boogie ankle rotations	to relax the area
pelvic lymphatics	stimulate	to promote removal of cell debris

 Sedation grip may be used as a first aid measure whenever there is pain and before and after having bowels open.

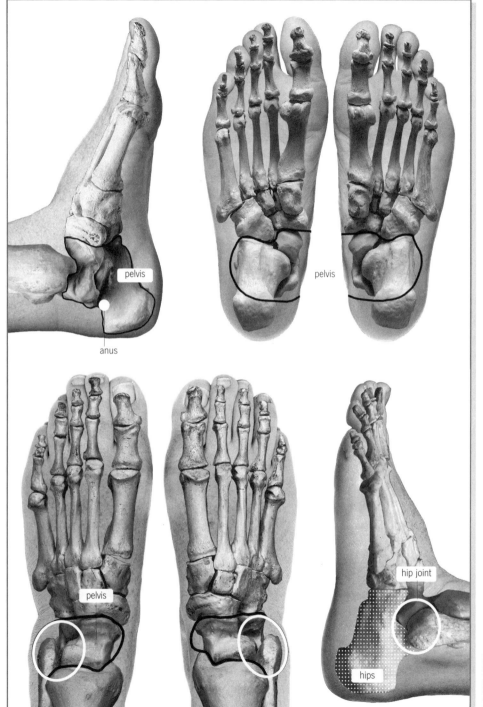

pelvis

anus

pelvis

pelvis

hip joint

hips

postnatal
post natal depression

Post natal depression (PND) should not be confused with "the blues" or puerperal psychosis, both of which occur very soon after the birth. PND is not usually diagnosed until the baby is over six weeks old. Prior to this depression is usually related to sleep deprivation. The cause of PND was thought to be from hormonal changes after the birth; this belief is now being questioned as both men and women suffer from PND. Some experts suggest that PND should be thought of as post traumatic stress ie the total change in lifestyle and the burden of parenthood is traumatic and this trauma leads to depression, as do other traumatic events. Whatever the cause, being depressed is a very real situation; sufferers cannot "just snap out of it". PND is not just "put on" for attention. Men and women with PND should seek professional help rather than trying to "put on a brave face" or struggle on unsupported. Medical management probably will include emotional support, counselling, a PND support group and possibly antidepressant medications. If the mother requires treatment in a psychiatric unit, mother and baby are not separated (except in the rarest of circumstances).

reflection zone	technique	intent
endocrine system	endocrine balance	to balance the whole being
solar plexus	bimanual thumb hold	to calm and centre
balance organ "sense of self"	linking technique	to help find the self
spine	spinal twist spinal runs and rubs	to promote energy flow
uterus indirect ovary solar plexus	linking technique	to balance the pelvic energy to the centre

Help the parents to differentiate between sleep deprivation and PND.
Encourage them to seek advice from their midwife, maternity hospital, early
childhood nurse, baby clinic sister, GP, obstetrician, Tresillian family care
centre, PND service, or local psychiatric hospital/mental health team.

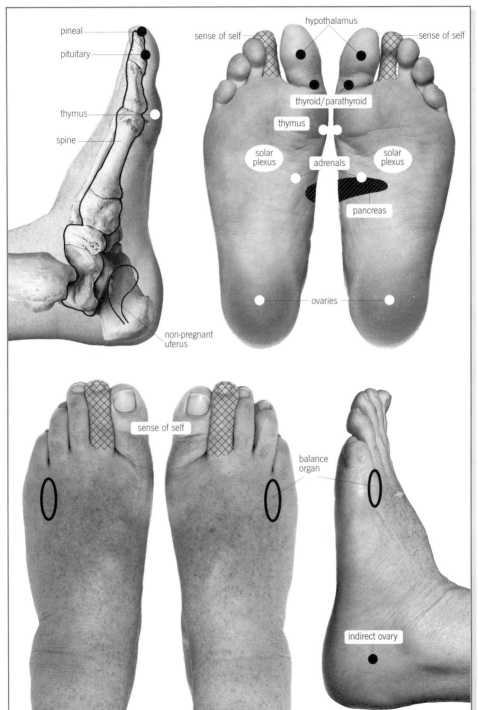

postnatal
sub involution of the uterus

After the delivery of the placenta and membranes, when the uterus is empty, continuing contractions ensure that the uterus involutes effectively, minimising the mother's blood loss. Within a week the uterus should be entirely in the pelvis and by 6 weeks after delivery reverted to its non-pregnant size. Infection, retained fragments of placenta and membranes, an over stretched or exhausted uterus can all lead to poor contractility of the uterine muscle and therefore poor involution. Laxity of the uterus immediately after delivery is signalled by haemorrhage.

reflection zone	*technique*	*intent*
uterus	firmly stimulate	to give the area energy to contract

 Before commencement be sure to warn the client that this technique can be quite painful.

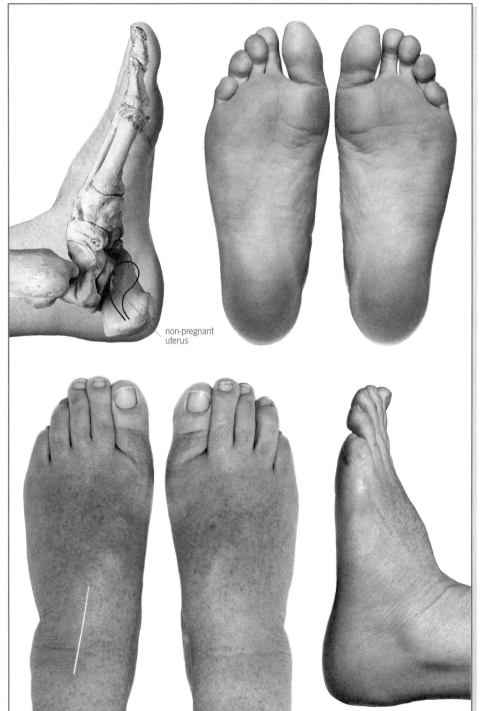

non-pregnant
uterus

postnatal
"third day blues"

On about day three after delivery the mother will probably become weepy. Often there is no obvious reason for the tears, although sore nipples, sleeplessness and the responsibility of motherhood may contribute to the emotional seesaw. The "blues" are due to hormonal changes after the birth and subside over 24-48 hours. This is a natural reaction and occurs after about 80% of births.

reflection zone	technique	intent
endocrine system	endocrine balance	to help balance the client's entire being.*
solar plexus	bimanual thumb hold	to settle the emotions
balance organ "sense of self"	linking technique	to help establish the new self
entire foot	all relaxation techniques	to help to experience the experience of early motherhood

*NB There are no placental hormones as there is no placenta after delivery!

 Weepy is wonderful! Encourage the client to experience the full impact; keep the tissues nearby.

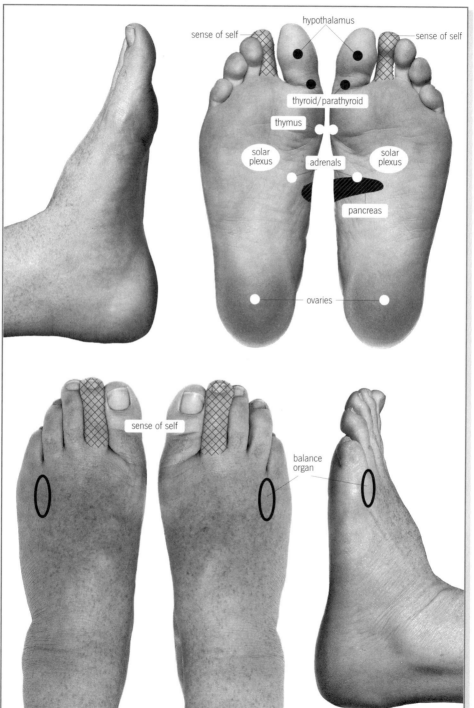

hypothalamus

sense of self

sense of self

thyroid/parathyroid

thymus

solar
plexus

adrenals

solar
plexus

pancreas

ovaries

sense of self

balance
organ

postnatal
urination: difficulty

As the baby descends through the birth canal, pressure is applied to the bladder and urethra. Occasionally the urethra becomes swollen and irritated due to this pressure, causing constriction or even blockage of the urethra. A fear of pain on micturition can make a client reluctant to pass urine.

failure to pass urine

Swelling of the urethra can cause urine to be retained in the bladder. The mother may receive an urge to pass urine but is unable to do so. Medical treatment usually involves urinary catheterisation to relieve pressure in the expanding bladder.

reflection zone	*technique*	*intent*
bladder	stimulate	to restore the tone
urethra	sedate	to ease the pain
urinary system	bimanual urinary system flush	to encourage balanced healthy energy flow
internal pelvis	sedate healing hold	to ease the tension
lower spine	sedate or stimulate as required	to balance the nerve supply to the area
hips	gentle ankle boogie ankle rotations	to relax the area

Remind the client of relaxation techniquesas passing urine may sting.
Reassure her that this situation does resolve with time but that treatment
may be necessary to prevent over-distension of the bladder.

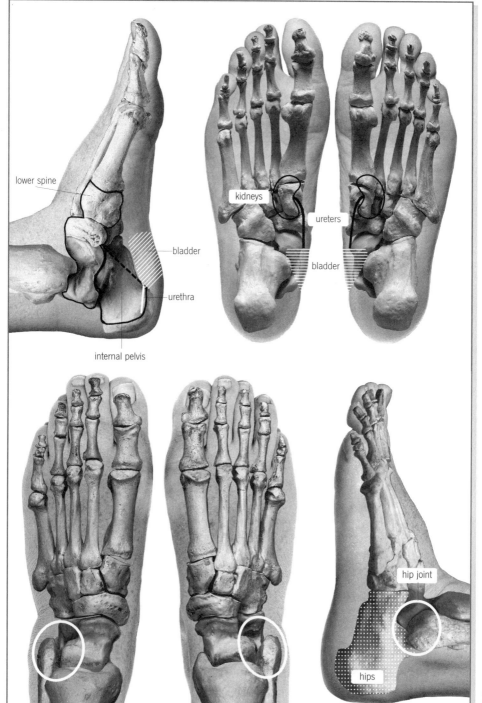

lower spine

kidneys

ureters

bladder

urethra

bladder

internal pelvis

hip joint

hips

postnatal
urination: painful
(dysuria)

Normally after delivery of the baby a large quantity of urine is passed by the mother.

Experiencing pain when passing urine is not uncommon for a few days after a vaginal delivery. Grazing, tears, or an episiotomy will sting with the passing of urine. Dysuria may occur after a urinary catheterisation due to irritation of the urethra. Although unpleasant it does not hinder the healing process.

reflection zone	technique	intent
bladder	stimulate	to regain the energy to function well
urethra	sedate	to ease pain
kidneys/ ureters/ bladder/ urethra	bimanual urinary system flush	to restore the integrity of the urinary system
internal pelvis	sedate healing hold	to ease the tension
hips	gentle ankle boogie ankle rotations	to relax the area

If it is acceptable to the client, suggest that she sits in a deep warm bath to pass urine.
Remind her to have a medical checkup if pain is ongoing and/or accompanied by frequency of micturition and/or fever.

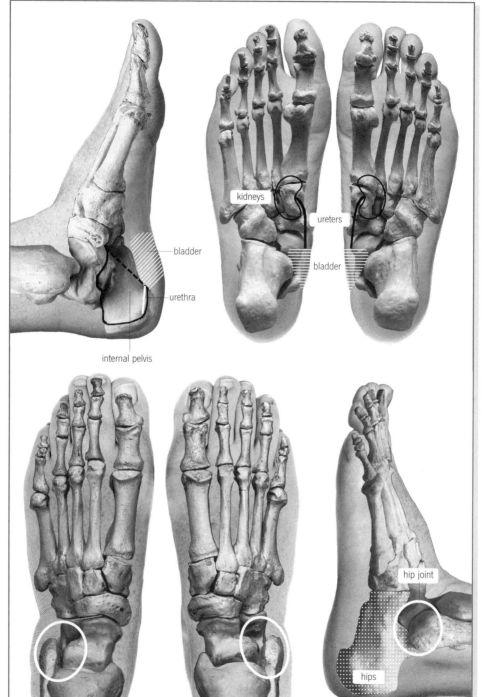

bladder

urethra

internal pelvis

kidneys

ureters

bladder

hip joint

hips

postnatal
varicose veins

Varicosities, or varicose veins, are surface veins with weakened walls, allowing a ballooning of the blood vessel. They may be asymptomatic but are likely to ache, be painful, look unsightly and may even hinder daily activities. Varicose veins commonly occur on the vulva, anus (haemorrhoids), lower and upper legs. Pregnancy tends to worsen existing varicosities and increases the risk of developing new ones. Most pregnancy induced varicosities improve during the post partum period but are unlikely to return to normal and continue to be problematic.

reflection zone	_technique_	_intent_
referral areas	thumb walk	to encourage healing
internal pelvis	*sedation grip	to clear the blocked energy
pelvic lymphatics	stimulate	to encourage pelvic health

*Sedation grip – to locate the exact zone gently palpate the internal pelvic zones; the area which is exquisitely tender is very probably the reflex to where the original energy blockage occurred. For client advice see antenatal varicose veins (p128).

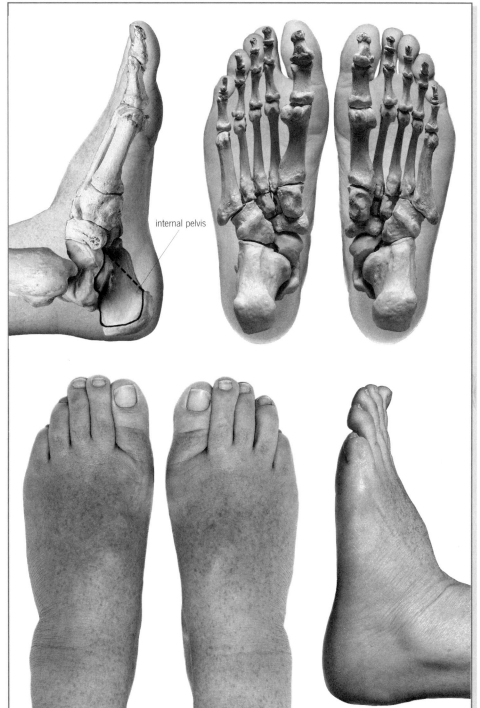

internal pelvis

glossary

maternity terms and abbreviations

after birth	the placenta and membranes ie the sack which enclosed the baby during pregnancy
abruptio placenta / placental abruption	separation of the placenta from the uterine wall
amniotic fluid	the watery fluid which surrounds the baby. It's functions include: temperature control, protection against external bumps, gives room for baby to move
antenatal / prenatal	before birth ie during pregnancy
anterior position	the baby is facing mother's spine with the back of his head to the front of her body
breech	pertaining to the baby's bottom
C/S	Caesarian Section; an abdominal operation to birth the baby
cephalic	pertaining to the baby's head
colostrum	a special substance produced in the breasts before lactation. It is rich in protein and antibodies and most beneficial to the baby
dysuria	painful urination
E.D.C.	Estimated Date of Confinement: 40 weeks from the Last Menstrual Period (L.M.P.)
E.D.D.	Estimated Date of Delivery: the same as E.D.C.
episiotomy	a cut made in the muscles of the perineum to allow more space for the baby to be born
first stage of labour	from the onset of labour to full dilation of the cervix

fetal/foetal	relating to the baby from the 12th week of pregnancy until delivery
forceps	instruments used by the obstetrician to extract the baby from the birth canal in the second stage of labour
full term	38 to 42 weeks of pregnancy
gestation	the period of time between conception and birth ie 38 weeks
hind milk	the higher fat content breast milk produced for the latter part of each feed
hypoglycaemia	low blood sugar
incontinence	leakage due to inefficient sphincter control - usually pertaining to urine unless faeces is stipulated
induction of labour	bringing on the labour prior to a spontaneous onset of labour
involution	shrinkage of the uterus after delivery
lochia	the discharge from the vagina after giving birth, containing the endometrial lining shed after delivery and blood loss from the placental site
micturition	passing urine, voiding
Montgomery's tubercles	pimple like bumps which appear on the areola in the first weeks of pregnancy
N.M.A N.M.A.A.	Nursing Mother's Association of Australia - an organisation established to help mothers breastfeed successfully. Groups with similar aims are: La Lèche League in the USA and The National Childbirth Trust in the UK
P.I.H.	Pregnancy Induced Hypertension ie high blood pressure caused by pregnancy
perineum	the area of the body between the vagina and anus
physiological	pertaining to a normal body function

glossary

maternity terms and abbreviations

placenta praevia	low lying placenta which encroaches on or covers the cervix
post dates	more than 42 weeks of pregnancy
postnatal	after the birth
post partum period	the time between delivery and six weeks post natal
posterior position	baby is facing mum's front, lying with his back to mum's back
pregnancy	the period of time between the last menstrual period (L.M.P.) and birth usually 40 weeks
presentation	the part of the baby which is in the lowest part of the uterus
preterm/premature	before 37 weeks of pregnancy
products of conception	a term used with miscarriage to describe the baby, placenta and membranes
puerperal	pertaining to the puerperium
puerperium	the period of time from the end of labour to complete involution of the uterus; pertaining to the six weeks after delivery
sebum	oily matter to lubricate the skin
second stage labour	from full dilation of the cervix to the baby's birth
sitz baths	warm shallow bath to soak and sooth the vulva, anus and perineum
spontaneus abortion	the official term for "miscarriage"
third stage labour	the period between the birth of the baby and delivery of the placenta and membranes

T.L.C.	tender loving care
trimester	one third of the duration of pregnancy ie three months/ thirteen weeks
Ventouse/ vacuum extractor	apparatus used by an obstetrician to extract the baby from the birth canal in the second stage of labour
vulva	female external genitalia

glossary

reflexology

ZONES

direct reflection zone	a zone or area on the foot which reflects a part of the being in a directly anatomically correct position
indirect reflection zone	a foot reflection zone which has an action on the named zone but is not in the correct anatomical position
coping point	noted in **The Foot Book** located on the indentation between second and third toes. Hold the coping reflexes on each foot simultaneously for one to five minutes. (Berkson, 1992, p98)
"chronic" pelvic zones	noted in **Better Health with Foot Reflexology** "on the inside of the leg halfway between the Achilles tendon and the ankle bone in the hollow starting four to six inches above the ankle bone" (Byers 1983, p156 & p191)
balance organ	noted in **The Rwo Shur Health Method**. "It is located at the end of the vestibular nerve in front of the internal ear. It controls the sense of balance. The reflex zone is located at both feet, at the top, in the hollow lines between the third and last toes." (Tay & Khaw, 1998, p98)
"sense of self"	observed by Valerie Barton, as energies reflecting a sense rather than a physical reflection. It is located on the second toe of each foot.

TECHNIQUES

bimanual thumb hold	place both thumbs on the same zones of each foot - apply gentle pressure - hold until the pulsating feels equal
brazilian toe balance	a balancing technique which uses the foot reflection zones of the head
endocrine balance	on both feet simultaneously bimanually hold each endocrine reflection zone in turn - link the energies to each other on each

	foot - then balance the energies across from one foot to the other
fish movement	created by the author to use during labour... hold one foot with fingers across the dorsal aspect of the phalange/metatarsal joints, thumb on the plantar aspect - support the same foot with the other hand - create a wave-like movement across the joints rolling one joint after the other
healing hold alternate term: calming hold	place solar plexus hand reflex zone over the foot reflection zone - remain still for several minutes
linking technique	created by Prue Hughes... "on one foot - use the middle finger of each hand - place them on the zones to be linked - hold until the pulsing feels equal. To link to solar plexus - retain the middle finger's hold and place both thumbs on solar plexus." (Hughes, 1994, p16)
lymphatic drainage massage	a routine which mimics a lymphatic drainage massage of the body onto the reflection zones of the feet
sedate alternate term: disperse	use thumbs or fingers... apply gentle pressure with an anticlockwise movement
sedation grip alternate term: trigger point	use thumb or finger... locate the epicentre of the disordered zone - press deeply into the zone - maintain the same pressure for a maximum of 2 minutes or until the acute pain is reduced
spinal rubs	use the lateral aspect of both hands - begin at the cervical vertebrae reflection zone, create a sawing movement at the same time move down the length of the spine reflection zone
spinal runs	bimanually use the tips of four fingers - very strongly run them up or down the spine refllection zones
stimulate alternate term: tonify	use thumbs or fingers... apply pressure with a clockwise movement increase the pressure and speed as tolerated
urinary system flush	on the foot reflection zones use middle fingers... bimanually apply fairly firm even pressure - moving from - kidneys - ureters - bladder - urethra - repeat three or four times

references

Berkson D. (1992) **The Foot Book** Harper Perennial, p98.

Byers D. (1983 seventh printing 1995) **Better Health with Foot Reflexology**. Ingham Publishing Inc., Fl. p156 and p191.

Hughes P. (1994) "The Technique of Linking with Reflexology" **Footprints** 3(4), 16-17.

Tay G and Khaw E H. (1988 3rd published 1991) **The Rwo Shur Health Method**. Gerdine Co (Goh Sim Ngan) p98.

information & addresses

FOR A LIST OF:
• reflexology therapists who work with maternity clients
• midwives who use reflexology therapy
send a stamped self addresses envelope to the address below

To be included on the practitioner's list send name, address, phone/fax and details of your qualifications, skills and practice to the address below.

FOR TRAINING IN:
• MATERNITY REFLEXOLOGY
Soul to Sole Reflexology provides a 16 hour course, Maternity Reflexology. To qualify for Certificate of Competency in Maternity Reflexology in addition to formal training, assignments and case studies are required.
Accredited with the Reflexology Association of Australia.

• REFLEXOLOGY FOR MIDWIVES
Soul to Sole Reflexology provides a 40 hour course, Reflexology for Midwives Award; Certificate of Reflexology for Midwives.
Accredited with the Professional Reflexologist's Association and the Reflexology Association of Australia.

afterword

Elsa and I are compiling the "big" book, "Maternity Reflexology". We plan to include:
• old wives tales and new wives tales about feet, fertility and birthing
• tips and treasures such as maternity reflexology observations, useful techniques and empiric knowledge
• case studies
We would love to include your thoughts and contributions, please send them to the address below

FOR ENQUIRIES, COMMENTS AND INFORMATION please contact:
Soul to Sole Reflexology
Susanne Enzer
14 Bourke Street
PYMBLE NSW 2073
Australia

TO ORDER COPIES OF
MATERNITY REFLEXOLOGY – A GUIDE FOR REFLEXOLOGISTS
PLEASE CONTACT

Soul to Sole Reflexology
Susanne Enzer
14 Bourke Street
PYMBLE NSW 2073
Australia